The Canterbury Preacher's Companion 2012

Some other books by Michael Counsell:

A Basic Bible Dictionary (Canterbury Press)

A Basic Christian Dictionary (Canterbury Press)

Every Pilgrim's Guide to the Journeys of the Apostles
(Canterbury Press)

Every Pilgrim's Guide to England's Holy Places
(Canterbury Press)

Every Pilgrim's Guide to Oberammergau and its Passion Play
(Canterbury Press) New edition 2008

*The Little Book of Heavenly Humour by Syd Little with
Chris Gidney and Michael Counsell* (Canterbury Press)

The Canterbury Preacher's Companion 2012

Sermons for Sundays, Holy Days,
Festivals and Special Occasions
Year B

Michael Counsell

CANTERBURY
PRESS
Norwich

© Canterbury Press 2011

First published in 2011 by the Canterbury Press Norwich
Editorial office
13–17 Long Lane
London, EC1A 9PN, UK

Canterbury Press is an imprint of Hymns Ancient &
Modern Ltd (a registered charity)
13A Hellesdon Park Road
Norwich NR6 5DR

www.scm-canterburypress.co.uk

Michael Counsell has asserted his right under the Copyright,
Designs and Patents Act, 1988, to be identified as the author
of this Work

British Library Cataloguing in Publication data

A catalogue record for this book is available
from the British Library

Scripture quotations are mainly drawn from the New Revised
Standard Version Bible © 1989 by the Division of Christian
Education of the National Council of Churches of
Christ in the USA

Readings are from *Common Worship: Services and Prayers
for the Chuch of England,* which is copyright © The
Archbishops' Council 2000: extracts and edited extracts are
used by permission.

Readings for days not covered by that book are from
Exciting Holiness, second edition 2003, edited by Brother
Tristram, copyright © European Province of the Society of
Saint Francis, 1997, 1999, 2003, published by Canterbury
Press, Norwich; see www.excitingholiness.org

978 1 84825 059 8

Typeset by Regent Typesetting, London
Printed in the UK by
CPI William Clowes Ltd, Beccles, NR34 7TL

LIST OF ADVERTISERS

Allen Organ cover
Cambridge University Press
Canterbury Press
Children's Society
Christian Aid
Church of England Pensions
   Board
Church House Bookshop
Church Times
English Clergy Association
HarperCollins
Heythrop
MHA

Peter Chalk
Prayer Book Society
Queen's Foundation
RAF Chaplaincy
SCM Press
Sing Praise
Sneaton Castle
Society of Catholic Priests
The Sign
Third Way
TMC
Towergate Russell-Plaice
Vanpoulles

All advertisements in this publication have been accepted in good faith and conform to the Advertising Standards Authority guidelines. Inclusion does not imply any commendation or approval by the Publishers who accept nom responsibility or liability fir goods or services provided.

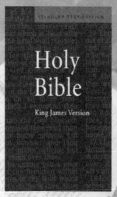
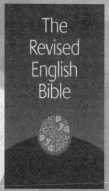

Contents

SUNDAYS

Unless otherwise stated, the readings and the verse numbers of the psalms are taken from *Common Worship: Services and Prayers for the Church of England* (Church House Publishing, 2000), with revisions, and are for Year B.

vi

3 hours
after the
bomb went off,
it hit him.

WHY THAT ROUTE?
WHY WAS IT THEIR VEHICLE THAT WAS HIT?
WHY WAS IT HIS MATE THAT DIED AND NOT HIM?
WHY ARE WE HERE? I didn't have all the answers.
                    But talking to him about it, one-to-one, helped.

        25th December 2007. Kandahar airbase.
        Padre Jonathan Chaffey. RAF Chaplain.

            After the Christmas Day service, I was with the groundcrew
            chatting over a mug of tea when the siren sounded.
            A rocket attack on the base.
            We huddled down behind a blast wall. Is that what they mean
            about getting close to your flock?

                The all clear came and we headed for the mess
                and Christmas dinner. I helped serve.
                Some wanted turkey, some vegetarian and others
                just a chat. And, of course a lot more questions.

                        Be part of the story.

ROYAL
AIR FORCE

Search online for RAF Chaplains

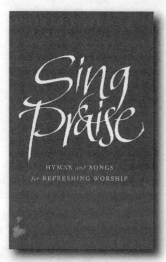

viii

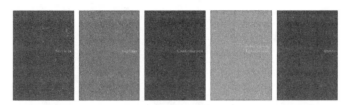

SERMONS FOR SAINTS' DAYS AND SPECIAL OCCASIONS

Readings are from *Common Worship,* or from *Exciting Holiness* by Brother Tristam SSF, second edition, Canterbury Press, 2003.

A Bible Designed For Anglicans

The New Revised Standard Version (NRSV) is the translation used in the Common Worship Lectionary, and beloved and trusted by clergy and laity.
This durable new hardback edition includes:

•

Prayer During the Day and Night Prayer from Common Worship

•

Daily Bible readings from the Additional Weekday Lectionary

•

Anglicized text

•

Readable typeface

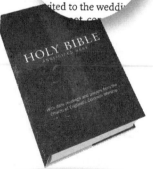

English Clergy Association
www.clergyassoc.co.uk

Patron: The Rt. Rev'd and Rt. Hon.
The Lord Bishop of London;

President:
Professor Sir Anthony Milnes Coates,
Bt., B.Sc., M.D., F.R.C.P.

The Association seeks to be a Church of England mutual resource for clergy, patrons and churchwardens requiring *information or insight*. We publish for Members, usually twice yearly, **Parson & Parish** – an independent, reflective eye on what is happening in the Church as an organisation, with editorial and comment, general articles, book reviews and letters to the Editor.

Men and women clergy and laity are equally welcome.
Our stance is to support the historic integrity of the Church.

Clerical and Lay Membership at £10 p.a. includes the magazine and the **A.G.M**. in London at St. Giles-in-the-Fields, on the second or third Monday in May, with speakers after a Service and Buffet lunch, who have recently included:
the Bishops of London and Rochester,
the Marquess of Salisbury,
the Rt. Hon. Dominic Grieve, Q.C., M.P., (Attorney-General),
Chancellor Dr. James Behrens, Dr. Brian Hanson,
Professor Norman Doe,
Mrs. Margaret Laird and Patrick, Lord Cormack.

Our charitable activity is to make **Holiday Grants to Clergy,** employing Donations to the Benefit Fund, Gifts, Legacies, Church Collections - all the more appreciated when interest rates are so low.
Registered Charity No. 258559

Benoporto-eca@yahoo.co.uk for Membership enquiries.
The Old School House, Norton Hawkfield, Bristol BS39 4HB
Chairman: The Rev'd John Masding, M.A., LL.M

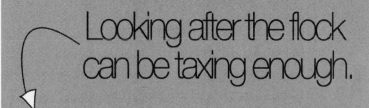

Spiritual Care
and people with dementia

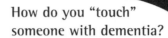

How do you "touch" someone with dementia?

How can you create a "magic moment" for them?

Help for family and friends, based on the experience of MHA's chaplains and dementia care staff is

Available Now!

Launched 67 years ago, MHA is a registered charity which aims to improve the quality of life for older people, inspired by Christian Concern

MHA cares for over 12,500 older people in a variety of settings throughout the UK by providing person centred care for both physical and spiritual well-being

Information on request:

- **Keeping in Touch** booklet – communicating with people living with dementia
- **Worship for people with dementia** guide
- **Spiritual Care and people with dementia** brochure
- **Methodist Homes Sunday** worship material
- **Request a presentation** about MHA at your church

Please call

0113 272 8482

A Methodist Charity for older people, of any faith or none

www.mha.org.uk

Methodist Homes is registered as a Charity No 1083995
Company Limited by Guaranteee no 4043124

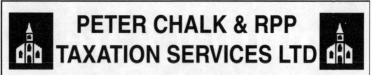

Preface

In one of P. G. Wodehouse's hilarious novels about Bertie Wooster and his infallible manservant, *The Inimitable Jeeves* – and that's the title of the book, too, by the way – Bertie and his young friends find themselves stranded in a country house, Twing Hall, far from the nearest race-course. It's the racing season, and the idle rich are desperate to place a few bets on the gee-gees. But of course there was no TV in those days, so they cannot keep in close touch with what's happening to their favourite horses. Reading the results in the next morning's newspapers somehow doesn't seem to have the same thrill to it. So the young men decide, instead, to place bets on the length of the sermons in the local village churches! Bertie Wooster's cousins Claude and Eustace, and six other friends, are being tutored for some examinations by the Revd Francis Heppenstall, vicar of Twing, and Bingo Little is tutoring the son of the Lord of the Manor, when they suddenly have this idea of betting on The Great Sermon Handicap, and invite Bertie Wooster to join them! Altogether there are ten village churches, and ten vicars, and whoever bets on the one who preaches the longest sermon will win their bet. A table of the odds on each of them has been drawn up.

The Revd Francis, the favourite, dropped half a dozen pages from his manuscript the previous Sunday, bringing a 45-minute sermon down to 20, and giving a misleading idea of his form. So Bertie persuaded him to preach again a very long sermon which he had delivered the previous year. Then he was discovered to have hay-fever, so they all bet on the second favourite, except for Jeeves, who discovered that Mr Heppenstall had sent the notes of his notoriously long sermon over to a neighbour, to preach it for him. Bingo protests that it's unfair for a vicar to preach another's sermon. Bertie replies, 'Clergymen do it all the time. They aren't expected always to make up the sermons they preach.'

I think that even in 1924, when P. G. Wodehouse wrote those words, they were a bit of an exaggeration. Today, when sermons are much shorter, most of the clergy preach from notes they have prepared themselves. But there is good precedent for borrowing a sermon from a book such as this, when time is short. There are also isolated lay preachers and readers who have little experience of preaching, and who may like to lift one of these sermons bodily from the book and read it from the pulpit. Better far, though, if time allows, is to base a sermon of your own on one of mine, either by preaching from notes you have made of my sermon, or by composing a completely new sermon based on my ideas, and using some of my illustrations.

But keep it short! Invariably my sermons are too long when I first draft them, and I have to work hard to shorten them so that they will hold the listener's attention. Each of these sermons is under 850 words, and should take about 12 minutes to preach if you put plenty of meaning and expression into the words. Remember, nobody is placing bets on your preaching longer than any of your neighbours!

Michael Counsell

How to Choose the Readings

Though we encourage Christians to read the Bible for themselves at home, for many their only contact with the Scriptures will be when they hear them read in church. Even those who are regular Bible readers will be grateful to hear a wide range of Scriptures expounded from the pulpit. This will present different problems according as your church is what we call 'liturgical' or 'non-liturgical'.

In a non-liturgical church the minister chooses the readings. This has the advantage that you can preach a series of connected sermons, or expound a whole book in the Scriptures over the course of several weeks. But the danger, if you are not careful, is that the readings may circle indefinitely around a little treadmill of the preacher's favourite passages, and large portions of the Scriptures will never be heard in church. It is my hope that preachers faced with this problem may look through this book and find ideas for sermon topics that might never have occurred to them otherwise.

Liturgical churches are those where the readings are already chosen for each Sunday. The advantage of this is that the minister is prompted to preach on most of the significant passages in the Bible over the course of a few years. The list of suggested readings is called a lectionary. Thirty-three per cent of the world's population are Christian, and 11 per cent of these are Eastern Orthodox, who have their own lectionary. Over 50 per cent of Christians are Roman Catholic, and they, together with most Anglicans, many Lutherans and Methodists, and some Presbyterians, Baptists and others, use what is called *The Revised Common Lectionary*. The yearly volumes of *The Canterbury Preacher's Companion* are based on the RCL, in the form used by the Church of England, which makes some changes in the names of the Sundays and Saints' Days, and adds to the RCL readings for a Principal Service sets of readings for a Second (and Third) Service as well. This book provides suggestions that may stimulate preachers using the RCL with new ideas for preaching on familiar texts.

The chief problem in liturgical churches is when a saint's day falls on an important Sunday. Then you must choose which set of readings will take precedence over the others. The simplest way to do this is to buy the lectionary booklets published by Church House Publishing, among others, or to look at the readings listed at the head of each of the sermons in this book, together with the calendar printed inside the front and back covers. The C of E allows preachers to depart from the set lectionary during 'ordinary time' if they wish, but even those who choose to do this will be able to get ideas from this book. Many preachers, however, will want to know the reasoning behind the choice of readings that is made here and in the lectionary booklets, and the principles on which they are based, to plan ahead, and to know how much flexibility exists. That is the purpose of this chapter.

For the Church of England, *The Christian Year: Calendar, Lectionary and Collects* was first authorized in 1997, and slightly modified when it was reprinted on pages 539–90 of *Common Worship: Services and Prayers for the Church of England*, with notes on several other pages. This was again amended in the General Synod reports numbered GS 1342A and B. My aim here is to explain all this varied information as clearly as possible in one place.

TABLES OF PRECEDENCE

There are four types of Red Letter Day: Principal Feasts; Other Principal Holy Days; Festivals; and Local Celebrations. Then there are Lesser Festivals and Commemorations, which are not observed on Sundays (but see below under Patronal Festival)

PRINCIPAL FEASTS, with the page numbers of the collect (modern language and traditional language) and the liturgical colours:

Christmas Day, pp. 381 & 454, Gold or White, 25 December

The Epiphany, pp. 383 & 456, Gold or White, 6 January or the Sunday between 2–8 January. (Where 6 January is a Sunday, 6 January is called The Epiphany and has the readings, collect and post-communion prayer for The Epiphany; 13 January is called the Baptism of Christ and has the readings etc. for The Baptism of Christ; 20 January is called Epiphany 3 and has the readings etc. for Epiphany 2; 27 January is called Epiphany 4 and has the readings etc. for Epiphany 3; 3 February is called Epiphany 5 and has the readings etc. for Epiphany 4. If 7 or 8 January is a Sunday, The Epiphany may be transferred to the Sunday. If so, The Baptism of Christ is transferred to Monday 8 or 9 January)

Candlemas, pp. 386 & 459, Gold or White, 2 February or the Sunday between 28 January and 3 February. If Candlemas falls on a Sunday the Candlemas readings replace the Sunday readings.

Annunciation, pp. 429 & 502, Gold or White, 25 March, (but if 25 March is a Sunday, The Annunciation is transferred to the following day, or if that is between Palm Sunday and Easter 2, transferred to the day following Easter 2)

Easter Day, pp. 400 & 472, Gold or White, see the table in *Common Worship*, p. 17

Ascension Day, pp. 404 & 477, Thursday after 6 Sunday of Easter, Gold or White

Pentecost, seven weeks after Easter, pp. 405 & 477, Red

Trinity Sunday, a week after Pentecost, pp. 406 & 478, Gold or White

All Saints' Day, pp. 402 & 494, Gold or White, 1 November (or the Sunday between 30 October and 5 November, in which case there is a secondary celebration on 1 November)

OTHER PRINCIPAL HOLY DAYS

Ash Wednesday, pp. 393 & 464, Violet or unbleached linen, six and a half weeks before Easter

Maundy Thursday, pp. 398 & 470, White, three days before Easter. The altars are stripped after the Maundy Thursday liturgy

Good Friday, pp. 398 & 471, two days before Easter. The altars are bare all day, except during the Good Friday liturgy when they are Red

FESTIVALS

The Naming and Circumcision of Jesus, pp. 427 & 499, White, 1 January. (When The Circumcision falls on Sunday and is transferred to Monday 2 January, then Sunday 1 January is called Christmas 2 but has the readings of Christmas 1; or The Circumcision may be observed on Sunday 8 January, in which case The Baptism of Christ is observed on 9 January)

The Baptism of Christ, pp. 383 & 456, Gold or White, Epiphany 1, or, when 6 January is a Sunday, on Epiphany 2

The Conversion of Paul, pp. 427 & 500, White, 25 January

Joseph of Nazareth, pp. 428 & 501, White, 19 March. (If 19 March falls between Palm Sunday and Easter 2, St Joseph's day is transferred to the Monday after Easter 2, or to the Tuesday if The Annunciation is on the Monday)

George, Martyr, Patron of England, pp. 427 & 503, Red, 23 April.

(If 23 April falls between Palm Sunday and Easter 2, St George's Day is transferred to the Monday after Easter 2)

Mark the Evangelist, pp. 431 & 504, Red, 25 April. (If 25 April falls between Palm Sunday and Easter 2, St Mark's Day is transferred to the Monday after Easter 2, or to the Tuesday if St George's Day is on the Monday)

Philip and James, Apostles, pp. 431 & 504, Red, 1 May

Matthias the Apostle, pp. 432 & 505, Red, 14 May

The Visit of the Blessed Virgin Mary to Elizabeth, pp. 432 & 505, White, 31 May

Barnabas the Apostle, pp. 433 & 506, Red, 11 June

The Birth of John the Baptist, pp. 434 & 507, White, 24 June

Peter and Paul, Apostles, pp. 435 & 508, Red, 29 June

Thomas the Apostle, pp. 436 & 509, Red, 3 July

Mary Magdalene, pp. 436 & 509, White, 22 July

James the Apostle, pp. 437 & 510, Red, 25 July

The Transfiguration of Our Lord, pp. 438 & 511, Gold or White, 6 August

The Blessed Virgin Mary, pp. 438 & 511, White, 15 August, or 8 September

Bartholomew the Apostle, pp. 439 & 512, Red, 24 August

Holy Cross Day, pp. 440 & 513, Red, 14 September

Matthew, Apostle and Evangelist, pp. 440 & 513, Red, 21 September

Michael and All Angels, pp. 441 & 514, White, 29 September

Luke the Evangelist, pp. 442 & 515, Red, 18 October

Simon and Jude, Apostles, pp. 442 & 515, Red, 28 October

Christ the King, pp. 426 & 498, Red or White, The Sunday next before Advent, never transferred

Andrew the Apostle, pp. 443 & 516, Red, 30 November

Stephen, Deacon, First Martyr, pp. 443 & 517, Red, 26 December

John, Apostle and Evangelist, pp. 444 & 518, White, 27 December

The Holy Innocents, pp. 445 & 519, Red, 28 December

Corpus Christi, pp. 407 & 479, White. (The Thursday following Trinity Sunday, replacing any other Festival, which must be transferred to the first available day)

Festivals falling on a Sunday are kept on that day or may be transferred to the Monday following, or the next suitable weekday; and may not be celebrated on Sundays in Advent, Lent or Eastertide. Festivals coinciding with a Principal Feast or Principal Holy Day are transferred to the next available day.

LOCAL CELEBRATIONS

The Patronal Festival, on the day of the saint(s) or title of the church, is kept as a Festival or Principal Feast. It may be transferred to the nearest Sunday, if that is not already a Principal Feast, the First Sunday in Advent, the Baptism of Christ, Lent 1, Lent 5 or Palm Sunday. Collects and readings for Lesser Festivals are in *Exciting Holiness* published by Canterbury Press, or *The Christian Year, Calendar, Lectionary and Collects*

Dedication Festival, pp. 441 & 520, readings in *Common Worship*, p. 587, White. (If the date when the church was dedicated is not known, the Festival may be observed on the first Sunday in October or the Last Sunday after Trinity, or any other locally chosen date that is not a Principal Feast or a Festival)

Harvest Festival, on any Sunday if not a Principal Feast or Festival, pp. 447 & 521, readings in *Common Worship*, p. 588

Saints and Martyrs of (our own country), White, 8 November, collects and readings in *Exciting Holiness*, p. 498, or *The Christian Year, Calendar, Lectionary and Collects*, pp. 109 & 211

St David, 1 March or the next available weekday, White, collects and readings in *Exciting Holiness*, p. 109, or *The Christian Year, Calendar, Lectionary and Collects*, pp. 109 & 167

St Patrick, 17 March or the next available weekday, White, collects and readings in *Exciting Holiness*, p. 123, or *The Christian Year, Calendar, Lectionary and Collects*, pp. 113 & 167

All Souls' Day, 2 November, collects and readings in *Exciting Holiness*, p. 481, or *The Christian Year, Calendar, Lectionary and Collects*, pp. 109 & 210

Remembrance Sunday is always the Sunday nearest to 11 November. The readings for the day may be used, or any of the readings for The Peace of the World (Collect, *Common Worship*, p. 105, readings in *The Christian Year, Calendar, Lectionary and Collects*, p. 116) or In Times of Trouble (Collects and readings in *The Christian Year, Calendar, Lectionary and Collects*, pp. 116 & 238). When Remembrance Sunday falls on 2 before Advent, the collect and post-communion for 3 before Advent may be used on Remembrance Sunday and those for 2 before Advent used on 3 before Advent. A service for Remembrance Sunday is published on www.ctbi.org/233

The Week of Prayer for Christian Unity lasts from 18 to 25 January, though other locally agreed dates may be used instead. Collects, *Common Worship*, pp. 104–5, readings in *The Christian Year, Calendar, Lectionary and Collects*, p. 116

LITURGICAL COLOURS

In addition to the above,

White is used from Christmas Day to Candlemas; Easter Day to Pentecost Eve; and for Marriages and Baptisms

Red is used on Palm Sunday until Good Friday (except Maundy Thursday Holy Communion); between All Saints' Day and the First Sunday of Advent; and for Baptisms, Confirmations and Ordinations

Purple or Violet is used in Advent; from Ash Wednesday until Palm Sunday Eve (unless unbleached linen is used); and for funerals. But Rose may be used for Advent 3 and Mothering Sunday (Lent 4)

Green is used from the day after Candlemas until Shrove Tuesday, and from the day after Pentecost until All Saints' Day Eve. It may be used between All Saints' Day and Advent 1 instead of red

Rose may be used on Advent 3 and Lent 4

LECTIONARY

Years A, B & C, see *Common Worship*, p. 530.

The readings for Propers 1, 2 and 3 are used on the Sundays between 4–10, 11–17 and 18–24 February respectively, if they are before the Second Sunday before Lent, with the collect and post-communion of the Sunday numbered before Lent.

The readings for Propers 4–25 are used as listed on pp. 564–74 of *Common Worship*, with the collect and post-communion of the Sunday numbered after Trinity.

From Easter Day to Pentecost, at the Principal Service, the reading from Acts must be used as either the first or the second reading.

On Monday, Tuesday and Wednesday of Holy Week, Maundy Thursday and Easter Eve, the Second Service is renamed Morning, and The Third Service is renamed Evening; on Good Friday the Second Service is renamed Evening, and The Third Service is renamed Morning, and the Genesis and Lamentations readings are transposed.

The number of verses used in some of the readings has been changed since *Common Worship* was first printed; the correct readings are given in *The Canterbury Preacher's Companion* volumes.

'A FALSE BALANCE IS AN ABOMINATION TO THE LORD, BUT AN ACCURATE WEIGHT IS HIS DELIGHT.' (Proverbs 11.1)

POVERTY

Photo: Christian Aid/Amanda Farrant

Tax dodging by multinational companies costs poor countries around US$160bn every year – more than one and a half times what they receive in aid.

Christian Aid is not afraid to challenge the 'false balances' and the structures that exploit the poor today. If we were to end international tax dodging, poor countries could collect the taxes they are due, strengthen their infrastructure and create healthy, educated workforces.

It is through large-scale changes that together we can achieve an end to poverty. Christian Aid is your agency, working alongside the churches in its mission to support the world's poor.

Visit our website for information on tax and other development issues and actions:

christianaid.org.uk

Christian Aid is the official development agency of 41 church denominations in the UK and Ireland.

UK registered charity no. 1105851 Company no. 5171525
Scot charity no. SC039150 NI charity no. XR94639 Company no. NI059154
ROI charity no. CHY 6998 Company no. 426928

YEAR B, the Year of Mark

(Year B begins on Advent Sunday in 2011, 2014, 2017, etc.)

ADVENT

The rhythm of the Christian year begins with Advent, the four Sundays leading up to Christmas. Advent means 'coming', so we think about Christ coming into the world at Christmas, coming into our lives every day, and coming to us at our death. To meet Jesus is a solemn event, especially if we have things on our conscience. So we use the season of Advent to confess our sins, and use the solemn colour of purple for the altar frontals and vestments in church (except that the Third Sunday in Advent may use rose-colour). The services are solemn: 'Glory to God in the highest' is usually omitted, and apart from carol services, we leave the Christmas music until Christmas. Candles are lit on an Advent wreath, one on the first Sunday, two on the second, and so on, leading up to five on Christmas Eve. A search of the internet will find suitable prayers to be said while the candles are lit.

First Sunday of Advent   27 November 2011
Principal Service   **Ready to Die**
Isa. 64.1–9 Rend the heavens; Ps. 80.1–8, 18–20 Repentance; 1 Cor. 1.3–9 Blameless on the Day of the Lord; Mark 13.24–37 Ready for the coming of the Son of Man

> *'Beware, keep alert; for you do not know when the time will come.' Mark 13.33*

Frightening

People reading the Scriptures aloud in church should give their all, in trying to bring out the meaning of the words. Yet after a dramatic reading of one of the apocalyptic passages from Isaiah, an elderly worshipper was visibly frightened. His friends told him the description of God's judgement was only picture-language, and was not to be taken literally. But the old man was sure that the passage applies to our own day. He knew that he couldn't realistically expect many more years on earth before he went to meet his maker. He was a good man, but he didn't fancy his chances of coming out unscathed if his own life was put under a microscope.

Context

His friends reassured him that it's important always to see Bible passages in the context of the age in which they were written. The later chapters of Isaiah were written in a period when the people were exiles in Babylon, and thought that God had lost interest in them. The prophet gave them renewed hope, by reminding them that even Babylon was under God's judgement, and wouldn't last for ever. God's judgement brings justice to the humble, and sets them free from their oppressors; so there is no need to be afraid.

Hospice

A chaplain in a hospice was trying to comfort a sick man, who had fought valiantly against his illness. At last he'd come to the conclusion that he was never going to leave the hospice alive. Now he was angry with the doctors, because, he said, 'they won't tell me when I'm going to die.' 'I don't expect they know,' answered the chaplain. Knowing the patient was a devout Roman Catholic, he went on: 'Does it really matter? We all have to die sometime, and for a Christian, death is no big deal.' The words just slipped out, and the chaplain bit his tongue, knowing that they sounded unsympathetic. But the patient took them to heart. 'I suppose that's right,' he mused. 'If you go to heaven when you die, what is there to be afraid of?' The chaplain realized he'd inadvertently helped the man to move one step onwards towards accepting our mortality, a journey that many people never even begin.

Mark 13

The thirteenth chapter of St Mark's Gospel is a collection of Jesus's warnings about the inevitability of death and judgement. People in Jerusalem were boasting about the grandeur of their Temple; he warned them that one day it would be destroyed. 'When?' they asked. Not yet, Jesus replied; first there'll be wars and natural disasters, and persecution of the Christians. The crisis will come when heathen idols are set up in the Temple precincts. Then Jesus talked about the coming of the Son of Man. These things will happen in the lifetime of the people he is talking to – so be ready, he warns them. What did he mean? The Temple was destroyed 40 years later, well within the lifetime of some of his hearers. But Jesus didn't literally appear in the clouds in their lifetime – he still hasn't, 2000 years later. It makes more sense if you realize that Jesus was talking about the *then* and the *now*, not the distant future. *Then,* their complacency was shattered by the destruction of the Temple – that was God's judgement on their arrogance. *Now,* Jesus comes to each one of us in a heavenly way when we die, and that could be any time. So we must all be ready to die whenever God calls us – don't leave your preparations too late. Make your peace with your neighbours, and with God, right now.

Memento mori

In days gone by, on elaborately sculpted tombs, they used to include a carving of a skull, or sometimes a complete skeleton, to remind passers-by that we must all die one day. They called these a '*Memento mori*', which means, 'Remember that you must die'. John Donne had the same idea when he wrote, 'Never send to know for whom the bell tolls; it tolls for thee.' This sounds gloomy to us, because death is the great unmentionable today. But where there's the Christian hope of heaven, then death truly is no big deal. We shouldn't be frightened; we should just quietly prepare our minds for the fact that one day we shall die, and pass to our eternal reward.

All-age worship

Make a large advent calendar, with the stable scene on the front, and windows showing items from the Nativity story.

3

A safe stronghold our God is still; All for Jesus; Come, thou long-expected Jesus; Hark, what a sound, and too divine for hearing.

First Sunday of Advent 27 November 2011
Second Service **Down with Religion!**

Ps. 25 Forgive me; Isa. 1.1–20 Social justice; Matt. 21.1–13 Triumphal entry

> *'Your new moons and your appointed festivals my soul hates.'*
> *Isaiah 1.14*

A humble king

Jesus rode into Jerusalem on a donkey. This was a symbol that he is a king, coming to take control of his kingdom. Those who saw him would immediately think of the prophecy from Zechariah: 'Lo, your king comes to you; triumphant and victorious is he, humble and riding on a donkey . . . and he shall command peace to the nations; his dominion shall be from sea to sea.' But there's also another passage in the first chapter of the first book of Kings when King David instructs that his son should ride into Jerusalem on a mule to be crowned as the king: 'Have my son Solomon ride on my own mule, and bring him down to Gihon. There let the priest Zadok and the prophet Nathan anoint him king over Israel . . . Let him enter and sit on my throne; he shall be king in my place; for I have appointed him to be ruler over Israel and over Judah.' So there's no doubt that Jesus saw his triumphal entry as his claim to the kingdom of God. That's why this passage is sometimes read not only on Palm Sunday, but at the beginning of Advent, when we prepare for the coming of Jesus, the Son of David, as our Saviour and King.

Blessed is the coming kingdom

The crowds in front of him were shouting, 'Hosanna to the Son of David. Blessed is the one who comes in the name of the Lord!' St Mark's Gospel adds the words, 'Blessed is the coming kingdom of our ancestor David!' Jesus was coming to judge his disobedient subjects. The Temple was built for worship, 'a house of prayer for all nations'. Jesus threw out the money changers and those who sold sacrificial animals and doves, for money changing isn't worship. Those who controlled the Temple were bringing judgement on themselves by losing sight of their priorities. So Jesus was joining with the prophets of the Old Testament in condemning the misuse of the holy place.

Down with the Temple!

The prophets loved the Temple, as Jesus did. But they prophesied its destruction nonetheless. Listen to what they said about it:

- Isaiah: 'Your new moons and your appointed festivals my soul hates; they have become a burden to me, I am weary of bearing them . . . even though you make many prayers, I will not listen; your hands are full of blood . . . cease to do evil, learn to do good; seek justice, rescue the oppressed, defend the orphan, plead for the widow.' 'My house shall be called a house of prayer for all peoples.' Yet 'When you come to appear before me, who asked this from your hand? Trample my courts no more; bringing offerings is futile; incense is an abomination to me.'
- Jeremiah: 'Has this house, which is called by my name, become a den of robbers in your sight? . . . therefore I will do to the house that is called by my name, in which you trust . . . just what I did to Shiloh.'
- Micah: 'Therefore I have hewn them by the prophets, I have killed them by the words of my mouth, and my judgment goes forth as the light . . . For I desire steadfast love and not sacrifice, the knowledge of God rather than burnt offerings.'

Down with religion!

Basically, the message of the prophets, and that of Jesus, was 'Down with religion!' That may astonish some people, but those who love God are far more critical of religion than those outside the Church, simply because so-called 'religion' is often an excuse for doing the opposite of what God commanded us. Micah again:

> 'With what shall I come before the LORD, and bow myself before God on high? Shall I come before him with burnt offerings? . . . what does the LORD require of you but to do justice, and to love kindness, and to walk humbly with your God?'

Pious practices and beautiful buildings sometimes become an idol, barring the way between the soul and God. Belief in God is a standpoint from which religious practices may be judged.

Beware

So beware! Some American missionaries pointed out that going to church doesn't necessarily make you a Christian, saying, 'Because the mouse is in the cookie jar, that doesn't make him a cookie!' Love God with all your heart and mind and soul and strength, and obey Jesus as your king. But watch out that the outward form of religion doesn't become, like the Temple of old, an excuse for indulging your prejudices, preening yourself for being better than your neighbours, or ignoring your duty to care for the needy. Being called 'religious' doesn't protect you when Jesus comes in judgement.

Suggested hymns

Creator of the starry height; Lo, he comes with clouds descending; O Lord, the clouds are gathering; Sleepers wake! (or other translations).

Second Sunday of Advent   4 December
Principal Service   Mark's Gospel
Isa. 40.1–11 Comfort my people; Ps. 85.1–2, 8–13 Salvation is at hand; 2 Peter 3.8–15a The Day of the Lord like a thief; Mark 1.1–8 John the Baptist, the voice in the wilderness

> 'The beginning of the good news of Jesus Christ, the Son of God.' Mark 1.1

The Gospel

St Mark describes the book he wrote as 'The beginning of the good news of Jesus Christ.' The word he wrote was *evangelion*, which is Greek for good news – it was used, for instance, when a messenger returned from the battle zone to say that there had been an important victory – and it gives us our word 'evangelism', which means spreading the good news. It had never been used as a book title before. It's the good news about Jesus. The story starts with

6

John the Baptist, and ends with the angel at the empty tomb. The beginning of the Gospel of Mark is a young man pointing into the distance and saying, 'Look, here comes your King!' It ends with a young man pointing into the distance, saying, 'Go, tell the world the good news about him.'

The kingdom of God

The central message of Mark's Gospel, which we shall be reading throughout the coming year, is that Jesus is our King. The kingdom of God doesn't mean a territory. It means the fact that Jesus is King; the *kingship* or rule of God. Jesus tells parables of the kingdom, to show how his kingship is spread: it's like a lamp, which mustn't be hidden under a basket, but put on a lamp-stand to give light to everyone. It's like a sower scattering the seed broadcast. It grows, like a mustard seed. It's like new wine, bubbling too vigorously for rigid minds to contain it. In other words, the good news of the kingdom is something that is entrusted to us on the understanding that we shall spread it to others.

Evangelism

As I just said, the process of spreading the gospel is called evangelism, or mission. This isn't a difficult activity to be done by a few specially trained experts. It's the job of each one of us – it's what we're here for. Jesus said, 'You did not choose me but I chose you. And I appointed you to go and bear fruit.' This means 'the fruit of good works'; it also means the harvest of new believers, those who come to believe that God loves them, because you told them so. The day after the crowds had shouted 'Blessed is the coming kingdom of our ancestor David' as Jesus rode into the Jerusalem, he found a fig tree with no fruit on it, and symbolically cursed it. This shows us that we have been given the good news of Christ's kingship so that we can spread that news to others. If we don't, we're no use to God or anyone else. A great preacher called Emil Brunner said that 'The church exists by mission as fire exists by burning!' In other words, if the fire isn't burning, it isn't a fire; if this church isn't spreading the gospel, it isn't a church.

Life

The message that Jesus is our king is good news, all through our lives. If you know that, your life takes on a new purpose and meaning. You're liberated from your past, because your sins are forgiven. You're no longer a prisoner of your bad habits, because Jesus will strengthen you to overcome. Evil won't tempt you, knowing that its attractions are worthless compared with the news that God loves you. You'll be triumphant against those who oppress you, knowing that God's on the side of goodness. Kingdom life is joyful, because God gives us strength to care for others. Telling people about God's love isn't trying to impose your will on them; it's a way of showing that you care. Evangelism has been compared to one starving beggar telling others where food is to be found.

Death

The message that Jesus is our king is good news, all through our lives, and past death, too. Only as he was dying on the cross was Jesus crowned as a king. Only in the light of his death can we understand the good news of his kingship. His crucifixion means even death can't defeat us. The media always portray death as a tragedy, because tragedies make news. But if death is the gateway into heaven, it's the best news you have ever heard. The beginning of the good news was John pointing to Jesus, saying, behold your king. The end is not yet, because the process continues as we share the news with others, that Jesus has conquered death, and eternal joy awaits us all on the other side.

All-age worship

Pin a label on your front saying 'Jesus loves me.' On your back pin one saying, 'Jesus loves you, too.' Or you could paint these words on a tee-shirt.

Suggested hymns

On Jordan's bank the Baptist's cry; The advent of our king; The kingdom of God is justice and joy; We have a gospel to proclaim.

Second Sunday of Advent   4 December
Second Service   **I Waited for the Lord**
Ps. 40 I waited for the Lord; 1 Kings 22.1–28 Conflict between
prophets; Rom. 15.4–13 Hope for Jews and Gentiles; *Gospel at
Holy Communion*: Matt. 11.2–11 Jesus praises John

> *'I waited patiently for the Lord; he inclined to me and heard my
> cry.' Psalm 40.1 (Common Worship)*

Unanswered prayer

Have you ever prayed desperately, asking for something you really
need, and nothing happened? You didn't get the healing, or the job,
or the partner you really wanted, and you began to ask yourself,
'What is all this that the Bible says about God answering prayer?'
But the Bible nowhere promises that God's answer to prayer will be
immediate. He may not be ready yet, and God's time is best. God
may know that *you're* not ready yet, and he'll give you what you
need when you can make best use of it. God always answers prayer,
but the answer may be '*yes*'; or '*no*, because what you've asked for
may not be what's best for you'; or '*wait*'.

Waiting

Advent is the season of waiting. We wait for Christmas, and sometimes it seems as though it will never come. Just think of all those
people in the Old Testament who waited for the coming of the
Messiah, and died without seeing his birth. Think of Simeon, the
old priest who blessed baby Jesus in the Temple, and Anna the
prophetess, who both spent all their lives waiting for God to show
mercy to his people, and recognized in this wee baby the answer
to their prayers. Who are we, then, if God's answer to our prayers
seems a long time coming? We must learn patience.

In our life

We wait for God to intervene in our own lives. God promised justice; why does he allow all the injustices in the world? God promised
guidance; why do we flounder for so long in a mire of doubt and
indecisiveness? God promised healing; so why do so many people
fall sick and die unhealed? To all these questions, God answers,
'Wait.' Wait patiently, and wait in hope. God will intervene, when

he's ready; it may not be in the way that you asked him to, and if you are not alert, you may not recognize God at work when he comes to you. But if you are ready for the 'God of surprises' to do the unexpected, and willing to co-operate with him when he calls you to, there's no limit to the good things you and God may be able to do together. Then, if what you specifically asked for doesn't actually come to pass in this life, but you have waited in faith, hope and love, God will come to you when you die, and reward your patience. Eternal life will be so wonderful, it will completely overshadow your temporary disappointments.

The end

In Advent we wait for 'the End', but people never stop arguing about what this means. Does it mean a second coming of Jesus to earth? Does it mean the disintegration of the physical universe, a sort of 'anti-Big Bang'? Or is it just a poetic image? Perhaps that doesn't concern us, as long as we're ready for anything. Jesus said, 'The end is not yet.' So don't be disappointed; there's plenty of work to be done in the meanwhile, in caring for the needy and spreading the good news of God's love.

Patience

There's a beautiful anthem for soprano duet and chorus, called 'I waited for the Lord'. It's taken from the last movement of Mendelssohn's second symphony, called *The Song of Praise*. The words are taken from Psalm 40, which begins, 'I waited patiently for the Lord; he inclined to me and heard my cry.' Here are some more quotes about patience: Ralph Waldo Emerson said, 'Patience and fortitude conquer all things.' Edward Bulwer-Lytton wrote, 'Patience is not passive; on the contrary it is active; it is concentrated strength.' From Jean-Jacques Rousseau we have: 'Patience is bitter, but its fruit is sweet.' Then there are three anonymous verses:

Patience is a virtue, possess it if you can;
seldom found in woman, never found in man.

Patience is a virtue, virtue is a grace,
both put together make a very pretty face.'

The last one is often parodied as,

Patience is a virtue, virtue is a grace,
Grace is a little girl who will not wash her face.

Come to my heart

Patience is a grace that only God can give. This Advent, will you wait patiently for the coming of Jesus, at Christmas, in moments of challenge, as you are dying and at the end? Will you welcome him when he comes at last in justice to right all worldly wrongs? Then sing in the words of the hymn: 'O come to my heart, Lord Jesus, there is room in my heart for thee.'

Suggested hymns

Hark the glad sound! The Saviour comes; Jesus shall reign where'er the sun; Thou didst leave thy throne; Thy kingdom come, O God.

Music to the duet may be downloaded free from http://choralwiki.net/wiki/images/sheet/mendelss/mend-hpo5.pdf

Third Sunday of Advent   11 December
Principal Service   Dying to the Old, Rising to the New
Isa. 61.1–4, 8–11 The year of the Lord's favour; Ps. 126 Salvation, *or Canticle*: Luke 1.46–55 Magnificat, Justice; 1 Thess. 5.16–24 Pray without ceasing; John 1.6–8, 19–28 Words of John the Baptist

> *'[John the Baptist] said, "I am the voice of one crying out in the wilderness, 'Make straight the way of the Lord,' as the prophet Isaiah said."' John 1.23*

John the Baptist

What a shock to the system! The scribes and Pharisees had every-thing stitched up. They were the leaders of God's Chosen People. They thought of God as tied down by a contract: they'd interpret God's laws, and make the people obey them. In return, God would look after his people – especially, of course, their leaders. If anyone who wasn't Jewish wanted to share in these blessings, they could join God's people by washing away the guilt of their pagan sins, and their false pagan beliefs – this washing was called the baptism of converts. Then a totally unauthorized prophet called John appeared in the wilderness, telling the people that *everyone* had to be baptized – Jews must ditch their traditions, and put themselves in the same position as a pagan convert. A clean start was needed, from everybody, even the scribes and Pharisees. That really upset the apple cart – talk of change always does.

Baptism

But that's what baptism means. Those who are baptized, or have their children christened, admit they have no claim on God. Nothing puts God in debt to us, or obliges him to save us: our nationality, our social status, the rituals we perform or the traditions we cling to. Of course, God is very anxious to save us, but what he needs from us isn't clinging to the past, but willingness to begin again from scratch, over and over again if necessary. Jesus continued this revolutionary approach to religion, taking over John's preaching about baptism and describing it as new birth. You can't put new wine in old bottles; you can't stitch a new patch onto an old garment, he said. Change is always required.

Change

I'm not advocating 'change for change's sake', the accusation hurled at anyone who proposes minor but unpopular alterations. Not all change is for the better, and as they say, 'If it ain't broke, don't fix it.' But some people, when they sing 'Change and decay in all around I see', imagine that the two words are synonymous. Yes, thank God we can always pray to 'thou who changest not', but we shouldn't resist every variation in our habits. When the late great Bishop Leonard Wilson appointed his chaplain to a conservative parish in Birmingham, the new incumbent apologized that he would 'have to make a few changes'. 'A few changes,' Leonard Wilson exploded; 'what they need is a bomb!' Of course nobody likes change. We're cosy in the familiar old rut. We're afraid of the discomfort that change might bring. So we water down the teaching of John and Jesus. We get baptized, but do very little about changing our selfish lifestyle. Follow the rules is all we want to do; jump through the right hoops, and God will be on our side. Change is as frightening as dying, we think – you can never be sure what's on the other side.

Dying

That, of course, is just the point. Change *is* like dying: dying to the old ways, dying to the past. But like dying, change leads to new life. Changing to a new way of living, a life modelled on that of Jesus, is like the sun breaking through the clouds. Old habits die hard, but once you have discarded them, you feel as though life has just begun. Like Jesus, you're unselfish in service to the poor and needy, you sacrifice your own comfort to bring comfort to others, and you share with others the joy of knowing that God loves you, not because you deserve it, but because that's how God is. And that makes you incredibly happy!

Rising

So dying to the old life means rising to the new. Resurrection isn't just something we wait for till we have died, it's something we enjoy *here and now* – a new quality of life, the life of the baptized. The Advent message of the coming of Christ is a joyful song, because the birth of Jesus leads us, through dying to the old ways, into joyful life, now and into eternity. Dying to the old means rising to the new. Changing to an unselfish way of living is uncomfortable; but when you realize what it leads to, it's worth it.

All-age worship

List what needs changing in the world, and ways that Christians could change them. Make posters for the outside of the church door, reading 'Jesus the same yesterday, today and for ever' and for the inside saying 'Behold, I make all things new'.

Suggested hymns

Hark, a thrilling voice is calling; Lo, from the desert homes; Lo, in the wilderness a voice; On Jordan's bank the Baptist's cry.

Third Sunday of Advent   11 December
Second Service   **Rejoice**
Ps. 68.1–19 A God of salvation; Mal. 3.1–4; 4 My messenger; Phil. 4.4–7 Rejoice in the Lord always; *Gospel at Holy Communion*: Matt. 14.1–12 Death of the Baptist

'Rejoice in the Lord always; again I will say, Rejoice.' *Philippians 4.4*

13

Have a nice day

'Rejoice in the Lord always.' Choristers know those words as the 'Bell Anthem' by Henry Purcell. They come in the closing chapter of St Paul's letter to the Philippians. Letters written in Greek still end with the word 'Rejoice!' Yet some readers might feel like answering, 'But I don't feel like rejoicing.' When you're having a tough time, being told to rejoice may sound as unsympathetic as 'Have a nice day!' To which grumpy people sometimes answer, 'Who are you to tell me what sort of day to have?' Many of our days are 'bad hair days'. If things go badly, we don't have much to rejoice about, either.

Philippians

Yet Paul's letter to the Christians in Philippi is full of joy. It was the first church that he founded in Greece, and was led by a business-woman called Lydia, who had been converted when she welcomed him into her household. There were no major splits in the congregation, like in Corinth. Yet little squabbles were hindering the spread of the gospel. Paul wrote, mentioning two women by name, 'I *beg* of you, Euodia and Syntyche [you-OWE-dear, SIN-ticky], that you would *agree* with each other . . .', and you can almost hear him adding underneath his breath, *'just for once!'* Visitors to that congregation would probably say, 'I'll not join a fellowship where those two are always arguing.' In the film *Secrets and Lies,* a character cries in frustration, 'Why is it that the people I love should hate each other?' Paul loved the Philippians, and instead of rebuking them, he told them to rejoice.

Reasons to rejoice

Despite their squabbling, Paul wrote: 'I thank my God every time I remember you.' They'd prayed for him while he was in prison. An Australian member of the Anglican congregation in Saigon was captured by the Vietcong in 1968; he was marched every night to a fresh camp in the jungle, starved and taunted for almost a year. When at last he was released, he told the church members that he used to say to himself the words of the communion service, which he knew by heart, every Sunday at the time when he knew his friends would be saying them and praying for him, and that kept him going. Paul rejoiced because the Philippians prayed for him, and believed the gospel, and so hoped for God's help in this life

14

and a joyful eternity in the world to come. So he quotes to them a hymn about Jesus who 'emptied himself . . . and became obedient to the point of death – even death on a cross . . . therefore God also highly exalted him'. Maybe this was the hymn that Paul and Silas sang at midnight in the prison at Philippi. Even in prison they found something to rejoice about.

Happiness

Joy is much greater than mere happiness. Happiness depends on chance: if there are no mishaps, and good hap comes your way by happenstance, then you may be happy. So happiness depends on what's happening to you – joy doesn't. You can be joyful even in the most awful circumstances, knowing that the good things God's promised us far outweigh any suffering in this life. To know that you are loved by another human being helps you through the bad days; to know you are loved by God turns even the worst days into days of joy.

Positive thinking

So Paul recommends the power of positive thinking:

Finally, beloved, whatever is true, whatever is honourable, whatever is just, whatever is pure, whatever is pleasing, whatever is commendable, if there is any excellence and if there is anything worthy of praise, think about these things.

For as Maria sang, in *The Sound of Music,* if you're thinking about your favourite things, there's no room for gloom.

Advent hope

Advent is a season of hope. We look forward to Christmas – not only the family gathering and the presents, but the remembrance that God loves us enough to come to earth for us and be born as a baby in a stable. In Advent, we also look forward in hope to the joys of heaven, when we shall live for ever in one great Christmas party with Jesus, and with those we love who have died. So we can sing with St Paul:

Rejoice in the Lord always; again I will say, Rejoice. Let your gentleness be known to everyone. The Lord is near. Do not worry about anything, but in everything by prayer and supplication with thanksgiving let your requests be made known to God. And the peace of God, which surpasses all understanding, will guard your hearts and your minds in Christ Jesus.

Suggested hymns

Come, thou long-expected Jesus; Hark, a herald voice is sounding; O come, O come Emmanuel; Rejoice! the Lord is king.

Fourth Sunday of Advent   18 December
Principal Service   **Expectation**
2 Sam. 7.1–11, 16 God promises King David peace; *Canticle*: Magnificat, *or* Ps. 89.1–4, 19–26 Covenant; Rom. 16.25–27 The mystery promised long ago; Luke 1.26–38 The Annunciation to Mary

> *'You will conceive in your womb and bear a son, and you will name him Jesus.' Luke 1.31*

Lady-in-waiting

An actress, welcoming children to an exhibition, and dressed as Queen Victoria, introduced her colleague as her 'lady-in-waiting'. 'Do you know what a lady-in-waiting is?' she asked. After a pause, one young hopeful suggested, 'Is it a woman who's going to have a baby?' The child wasn't far wrong; many people describe such a woman as an 'expectant mother'. And expectation is a term we use for waiting in hope.

Mary

The Virgin Mary hoped that she'd conceive a baby, after she got married to Joseph. Then the angel Gabriel appeared to her and told her that her hopes would be fulfilled, but earlier than she'd expected. The Holy Spirit overshadowed her, and she became pregnant, an expectant mother. She had hoped for a baby, and would have been quite satisfied with a perfectly ordinary child, but in fact, as the angel had told her, her baby was unique, the long-expected Messiah. God always gives us what we hope for, and sometimes more than we'd hoped for, but often his gifts fulfil our hopes, yet not in the way we expected.

The Messiah

The Jewish people had been hoping for a Messiah. They'd asked God for a king to defend them against their enemies. God gave them King Saul, who was a disaster; then King David, who was a mixed blessing; King Solomon, who was led into idolatry by his foreign wives; and then a whole succession of kings, who were, to say the least, a real disappointment. But they didn't lose hope. They still expected God to send them, one day, a perfect king who'd solve all their troubles. Of course, they expected this Messiah to be a great general, a military leader who would drive out the Roman army of occupation. And what did they get? A weak and helpless baby crying in a manger. I say it again: God always gives us what we hope for, and sometimes more than we had hoped for, but often his gifts fulfil our hopes, yet not in the way we expected.

Son of Man

Another title for the expected Messiah is 'Son of Man'. It was used in Daniel's vision to describe a completely human figure, the representative of God's Chosen People. Yet the Jews hoped their Messiah would be super human; they tried to force Jesus to take up arms against the Romans, but he wouldn't. Jesus, too, was a great disappointment to them, for he refused to behave as they expected him to. The only way the Son of God can save us is not by fighting for us, but by dying for us.

Christmas

So are you full of hope and expectation at Christmas? God's gift fulfils our hopes, and exceeds them. You won't be disappointed. But in what ways do you expect God to act? We wish each other a happy and peaceful Christmas. Ideally, in a perfect world, the whole family would be together at home, unwrapping the presents they've given each other. For many families that hope will be literally fulfilled. But for others the happiness will be limited by the absence of some faces round the table: people who are sick, or too far away, or who may, sadly, have died since last Christmas. Many people have to spend Christmas alone. But there is no perfect world – we usually have to be content with second best. Yet a second best Christmas is still something to rejoice about, if we recognize that God often gives us better gifts than we had ever dreamed of.

Solemn Advent

Advent, therefore, is a rather solemn season. The rejoicing is tempered by our awareness that the babe in the manger was born to die. Some of our loved ones fell ill, and we prayed for them to live, but still God took them. Yet, as Canon Scott-Holland wrote, 'death comes to us all', but the death of Jesus gave us the hope of immortality. So when our loved ones died, God gave them the gift of eternal life. That gift is immeasurably greater than any other. So amid the solemnity, we can still look forward in hope. Let's all be ladies and gentlemen in waiting, expectant with promise, but open for God to surprise us by giving, not what we asked for, but something much better. God always gives us what we hope for, and sometimes more than we had hoped for, but often his gifts fulfil our hopes, yet not in the way we expected.

All-age worship

Write Christmas cards 'To my perfect Daddy, from your perfect son' etc. Then add underneath 'Not yet, but I'm working on it.'

Suggested hymns

Come, thou long-expected Jesus; Long ago, prophets knew; The Lord will come and not be slow; Where is this stupendous stranger?

Fourth Sunday of Advent   18 December
Second Service   **Fulfilment**
Ps. 113 He makes her a joyous mother [131 My heart is not proud]; Zech. 2.10–13 I will dwell in your midst; Luke 1.39–55 Mary visits Elizabeth

> *'Blessed is she who believed that there would be a fulfilment of what was spoken to her by the Lord.' Luke 1.45*

Filled full

If you ask a witty person how they feel after eating a big meal, they'll reply, jokingly, 'I feel fulfilled!' The archangel Gabriel promised that Mary would have a baby. She soon felt the child moving inside her, and over the nine months it grew until it filled her whole womb full. So Mary was, in a sense, 'full-filled' as the baby grew within her. Her cousin Elizabeth said, 'Blessed is she who believed that there would be a fulfilment of what was spoken to her by the Lord.' Then, on that first Christmas day, the baby was born, and the promise that the angel gave to Mary was fulfilled. So, too, were all the promises that God had made in the Old Testament. So the birth of Jesus was in two ways a 'fulfilment'! Yes, I'm playing with words here, but sometimes a silly joke like that makes you think, and helps the ideas to stick in your mind.

Fulfilment

My dictionary says 'fulfil' means to complete; to accomplish; to carry into effect; to bring to consummation; to develop and realize the potential of (someone or something). So 'fulfilment' is the glorious moment when those things happen. We speak about the fulfilment of a prediction, a prophecy or a promise, when the thing that had been foretold comes true. Or the fulfilment of an ambition, when you achieve what you had hoped for.

Promising

Sometimes, if a promising child grows up to achieve striking success, people say they've fulfilled their early promise. If somebody's very busy, they'll protest, 'But I enjoy it. Better to wear out than to rust out. I find that filling every moment of the day with useful activity makes me feel fulfilled.' Jesus was a promising 12-year-old when he debated with the teachers of the Law in the Jerusalem Temple. Then, when he returned as an adult, he out-argued all his opponents. 'Do not think', he said, 'that I have come to abolish the law or the prophets; I have come not to abolish but to fulfil.' Jesus showed that he understood better than they did what their Scriptures were all about. They thought the laws were a list of narrow restrictions, and that the slightest transgression would be punished by an angry Deity. Jesus taught that the law is a set of pointers towards a fulfilling freedom. When we know that God loves us, love grows in our hearts, moving us to do loving things for our neighbours, to please our loving heavenly Father. St Paul went to the very heart of God's intentions, when he said that 'love is the fulfilling of the law.'

Old Testament promises

St Matthew's Gospel, in particular, repeatedly shows how the life of Jesus was a fulfilment of the promises that God made through his prophets in the Old Testament.

- At the massacre of the innocents, Matthew writes, 'Then was fulfilled what had been spoken through the prophet Jeremiah: "A voice was heard in Ramah . . . Rachel weeping for her children."'
- Jesus lived in Nazareth, 'so that what had been spoken through the prophets might be fulfilled, "He will be called a Nazorean."'
- He moved to 'Capernaum by the sea . . . so that what had been spoken through the prophet Isaiah might be fulfilled: ". . . Galilee of the Gentiles – the people who sat in darkness have seen a great light."'
- Jesus said that the Pharisees 'fulfilled the prophecy of Isaiah that says: "You will indeed listen, but never understand, and you will indeed look, but never perceive."'
- When Jesus was arrested, he said, 'all this has taken place, so that the scriptures of the prophets may be fulfilled.'
- When Judas Iscariot threw down the money he'd been paid to betray Jesus, 'Then was fulfilled what had been spoken through the prophet Jeremiah, "And they took the thirty pieces of silver . . . and they gave them for the potter's field."'

Christmas

The exact matches between what happened to Jesus and what the prophets foretold are certainly remarkable coincidences. But they are much more than that. They show that God is consistent, year by year, and century by century. Ever since the first human beings emerged, God has been working for their salvation. God, who created time, stands outside time, and knows in advance what's going to happen; so it's easy for God to reveal the future to his prophets. Those marvellous Old Testament readings in Advent show us that Christmas is the fulfilment of all that God had been planning. God's Son came to earth, sharing our vulnerability in order to win our love.

Suggested hymns

Long ago, prophets knew; O come, O come Emmanuel; People, look east; Tell out, my soul.

CHRISTMAS, EPIPHANY AND CANDLEMAS

Christmas is a season of joy, as we celebrate the coming of God into the world he created, in the shape of a child in a manger. It is the children's festival, and a time for family reunions; so we have family services, sharing the awe of the children when they see that Jesus became a child like them; and the whole family of God gather at God's table to share in the family meal of Christmas communion. The hangings and the vestments in church are in gold, if possible, on Christmas Day, and white on the Sundays from Christmas to Candlemas. January 6 is Epiphany, which means revealing to the whole world who Jesus is. The readings tell of times when the divinity of Christ was revealed. The wise men were the first non-Jews to recognize Jesus as 'King, and God, and Sacrifice'. He was revealed as Son of God by the voice from heaven at his Baptism. Nathanael exclaimed, 'Rabbi, you are the Son of God! You are the King of Israel!' The disciples saw his glory when he turned water into wine at the wedding in Cana. When baby Jesus was 40 days old he was presented to God in the Temple, and the aged priest, Simeon, hailed him as the one who would illuminate the nations. That is why the fortieth day after Christmas is called Candlemas. Yet Simeon foresaw that a sword of grief would pierce Mary's heart, so we turn, then, away from celebrating Christmas to preparing ourselves for Good Friday and Easter in the solemn season of Lent.

Christmas Day   25 December

Any of the following sets of readings may be used on the evening of Christmas Eve and on Christmas Day: Set III should be used at some service during the celebration.

Set I   **While Shepherds Watched**

Isa. 9.2–7 A child is born; Ps. 96 Tell of his salvation; Titus 2.11–14 Salvation has come; Luke 2.1–14 [15–20] The birth and the shepherds

> *'In that region there were shepherds living in the fields, keeping watch over their flock by night.' Luke 2.8*

Popular carol

'While shepherds watched their flocks by night' – see, I resisted the temptation to refer to the washing of socks. The reason for the popularity of this Christmas carol is that, for more than 80 years, it was the only carol 'permitted to be used in churches' – or at least, in Anglican ones. The words appeared in Tate and Brady's 1700 supplement to their *New Version of the Psalms of David.* Christians worried that heretical ideas might creep insidiously into Christian worship if people were allowed to sing any words that didn't come from the Bible. Worshippers were therefore restricted to singing the psalms, and several so-called 'Metrical Versions' appeared, attempting with greater or lesser success to cram the words into four-line verses, usually with eight syllables in lines 1 and 3, and six syllables in lines 2 and 4. In the Church of England, the metrical Psalter known as 'Tate and Brady' was the only version of the psalms in use: 'As pants the hart' and 'Through all the changing scenes of life' are psalm paraphrases from that book.

Tate

The only song based on the New Testament to find its way into this collection was 'While shepherds watched', from the second chapter of St Luke's Gospel. There's nothing to say who wrote it, but it's generally assumed to be by Nahum Tate. Born in 1652 in Dublin, he wrote a poem entitled *Panacea, a Poem upon Tea,* and a so-called 'improved version' of Shakespeare's plays, giving each of the tragedies a happy ending! He was not a great versifier – the fourth verse of 'While shepherds watched' requires you to breathe almost anywhere except at the ends of the lines – yet he was appointed Poet Laureate in 1692.

Music

The sixth edition of the *Supplement* to 'Tate and Brady' included no less than 75 tunes that could be sung to 'While shepherds watched'. Altogether more than 200 were composed. At least one choir has resolved to sing this carol to a different tune each Christmas – a project that will last for several lifetimes. There are some magnificent tunes among them. The one most commonly sung in the United States is based on an Italian aria from an opera by Handel. Many tunes were written to be sung unaccompanied in the new Methodist chapels, with repetition of words, and alternating voices, in the style familiar to us from 'Joy to the world', another of the melodies to which 'While shepherds watched' is sometimes sung. One of these 'fuguing tunes' is known to English people as a Yorkshire dialect song, 'On Ilkla Moor baht 'at'. Yet it was originally written, by a cobbler called Thomas Clark of Canterbury, for 'While shepherds watched', which it fits very well. Allegedly a Yorkshire choir went for a picnic on the moor at Ilkley, and noticed that one of the men singers was flirting with a soprano called Mary Jane. So they made up new words to the hymn tune to tease them, and sang it on the way home. The tune to which the carol is usually sung in England is one of the dullest, though it's based on an anthem by Christopher Tye. It was printed in the 1861 edition of *Hymns Ancient and Modern*, and soon ousted the more elaborate tunes that preceded it.

Shepherds

To sing this carol in the cave at the shepherds' fields outside Bethlehem until recently was to identify with the humble shepherds keeping their cold vigil there, who saw a vision of angels, first one and then millions, filling the sky, singing 'Glory to God' and 'peace on earth'. We can identify with the shepherds hurrying into the tiny village where King David had earlier been born, to find baby Jesus swathed in linen strips, called 'swaddling bands', and placed in the manger from which the animals ate their fodder. Before the kings came, the Son of God was welcomed to earth by working men, who recognized him as one of themselves, a plain and ordinary human being. Yet from that simple humanity, Jesus was able to transform the world, and bring us all hope for eternity. That surely is something to carol about!

All-age worship

Make toy sheep from cotton wool, shepherds from pipe-cleaners or plasticine®, and angels from paper and gauze.

Suggested carols

Angels from the realms of glory; Christians awake; What child is this?; While shepherds watched.

Christmas Day   25 December
Set II   A Wall around Bethlehem

Isa. 62.6–12 Prepare a way; Ps. 97 God comes to rescue his
people; Titus 3.4–7 Salvation by grace; Luke 2.[1–7] 8–20
Shepherds go to Bethlehem

> 'To you is born this day in the city of David a Saviour, who is the
> Messiah, the Lord.' Luke 2.11

A special place

Today we celebrate the birth of Jesus in Bethlehem – a very special
place to the Jewish people, because King David, the greatest of the
Kings of Israel, was born there in around 1000 BC. Before that,
Jacob's wife Rachel died on the way to Ephrath, also known as
Bethlehem. Then Ruth, a foreign woman, married Boaz in Beth-
lehem, and became the Granny of Jesse, who was King David's
Daddy. Samuel the prophet was sent by God to Bethlehem to anoint
David, the youngest son of Jesse, to be the next king. Subsequent
kings were known as the family line of David, or the family tree of
Jesse, but they were a real let down. The Jews hoped that one day
a perfect king would be born, of David's line and from the stump
of Jesse's tree, who would be called the Anointed, or the Messiah.
There were two places called Bethlehem in the Holy Land, so to
avoid confusion, this one was called Bethlehem Ephrata, and the
prophet Micah predicted the coming of the Messiah when he said,
'You, O Bethlehem of Ephrathah, who are one of the little clans
of Judah, from you shall come forth for me one who is to rule in
Israel.'

The birth of Jesus

Bethlehem was never more than a village, but it was so special to
the Jews that St Luke refers to Bethlehem as the City of David.
Israel was then an occupied country, full of Roman soldiers, and
the Roman Emperor commanded that a census should be taken.
Luke tells us that everybody had to be registered in the home town
of their family, and Joseph went 'to the city of David called Bethlehem, because he was descended from the house and family of
David'. There Jesus was born, and laid in a manger because there
was no room for them in the inn.

Shepherds

There were shepherds then living in Bethlehem. In the lambing season they spent all night with their flock in the fields outside the town. There they saw the angel, who told them, 'to you is born this day in the city of David a Saviour, who is the Messiah, the Lord.' Then the shepherds said to each other, 'Let's go to Bethlehem and see what's happened there.' For Christians, too, Bethlehem is a very special place.

Pilgrims

Unlike Jerusalem, Bethlehem wasn't important enough for the Romans to destroy it. St Jerome translated the Bible into Latin while living in a cave in Bethlehem, next to the cave-like stable where Jesus was born. The Empress Helena, mother of Constantine, the first Christian Emperor, made a pilgrimage to the Holy Land, and in AD 315 she had a magnificent church built over the cave. The foundations and floor of this can still be seen under the larger one built in the sixth century by Emperor Theodosius – the oldest complete church in the world – to receive the hordes of Christian pilgrims.

A wall round Bethlehem

Due to the accidents of history, most of the population of Bethlehem have been and are Arab Christians. The Israeli Government recently erected a 10-metre-high wall around the Arab areas, claiming it was to prevent suicide bombers. In 2004 the International Court of Justice ruled the wall illegal. If Mary and Joseph rode to Bethlehem this Christmas, they'd find that once again they are in occupied territory. Not only would there be no room for them in the inn, Jews are instructed not to enter a town where 'their enemies' live. The shepherds would be standing in a queue at a checkpoint seeking permission to visit their fields. Condemning this situation isn't anti-Semitic – many Jews, and many Israelis, strongly disapprove of the policies of the Government. A Christmas sermon is no place to discuss politics, but we can't turn a blind eye to the suffering of our Arab Christian brothers and sisters in Bethlehem.

Prayer

We *must* pray for all those involved. To make this very special town a centre of strife wounds the hearts of us all. Let's pray for Jews, Muslims and Christians to work together. For those who suffer, and those who leave the land of their birth because they can't face it any longer. For leaders on all sides to accept that violence will never achieve the ends they hope for, and hear the song the angels sing. We ask it in the name of Jesus, who was David's descendant and born in David's town. Amen.

All-age worship

Make Christmas cards saying 'Peace to all at Christmas'. A good artist could draw Joseph and Mary queuing to be admitted at a checkpoint.

Suggested carols

It came upon the midnight clear; O little town of Bethlehem; See, amid the winter's snow; See him, lying on a bed of straw.

Christmas Day   25 December
Set III   Carol Singing
Isa. 52.7–10 The messenger of peace; Ps. 98 God's victory; Heb. 1.1–4 [5–12] God speaks through a Son; John 1.1–14 The Word became flesh

> *'Sing to the Lord a new song, for he has done marvellous things.'*
> *Psalm 98.1 (Common Worship)*

Carolling

If you think it's only in Africa that people dance in church, you should know that all across Europe, Christians have been singing and dancing at Christmas time for at least a thousand years. The word 'carol' is thought to be the French name for a type of dance. In 1328 a German monk called Henry Suso had a vision in which he joined with angels in singing and dancing 'In dulci jubilo'. Carols were sung in many tongues; some, like that one, are called *macaronics*, a charming term for a plateful of languages all mixed up together. A brief history of the Christmas carol will help you to enjoy them even more.

Refrain

Typically, the early carols had a two-line refrain, or 'burden', which might be in Latin, after each four-line verse or 'stanza', which could be in the local language. The waits went round singing and begging: – 'if you haven't got a penny, a ha'penny will do' – and were sometimes accompanied by the mummers. 'Past three o'clock' is an example, probably sung in the seventeenth century by the London waits, but based on a much earlier cry of the watchmen as they patrolled the streets ready to stamp on troublemakers. But there were many variations. 'Lully, lullay' was used in the Coventry Mystery Plays.

Puritans

The Puritans made Christmas illegal, fearing it would lead to idolatry, so carols were not allowed to be sung in church. But they continued to be sung in pubs up until the early twentieth century. Each generation took the popular style of music of the day, and set Christian words to it. Popular ballads were sold as 'broadsheets' by hawkers in the eighteenth century; other carols such as 'While shepherds watched' resembled the metrical Psalms sung by the village choirs in church. As Dickens described it in *A Christmas Carol,* the waits used anonymous folksongs, best enjoyed when the lower orders came round on a frosty night and sang 'God rest you merry, gentlemen', outside the doors of the wealthy. 'Father Christmas', as Dickens describes him, was one of the morris-dancers. English Catholics of the 1740s gave us 'O come, all ye faithful'; the Methodists wrote many carols, beginning with Wesley's 'Hark! The herald-angels sing'. The great English hymns found in collections such as *Hymns Ancient and Modern* were a popular model for many new carols; think of Sullivan's 'It came upon the midnight clear', and Gauntlett's 'Once in royal David's city'. In the early twentieth century people like Cecil Sharp and Ralph Vaughan Williams went round the villages recording surviving examples of folk songs, which had probably never been written down before, such as 'The Holly and the Ivy'. They often set new Christian words to these: an example is 'O Little Town of Bethlehem' set to the tune called 'Forest Green'.

Modern compositions

When Vaughan Williams was asked to compile the *English Hymnal* and the *Oxford Book of Carols,* he introduced modern compositions, such as 'In the bleak mid-winter' by Gustav Holst, with words by Christina Rossetti. Modern carol books include French and German songs, like 'The Shepherds' Farewell' and 'Silent Night' – 'Deck the halls with boughs of holly' is Welsh, and 'We three kings' comes from America.

Nine lessons and carols

Meanwhile, carols weren't sung by English cathedral choirs until Eric Milner-White, the Dean, first of Truro Cathedral and then of King's College, Cambridge, developed in 1918 the Service of Nine Lessons and Carols out of the medieval morning services for a major festival, which did indeed have nine lessons. The thought-provoking selection of Old Testament prophecy and New Testament narrative that he chose became widespread, especially when the BBC began to broadcast the service on 'the wireless'. David Willcox and John Rutter published several volumes of *Carols for Choirs,* using tunes made popular at King's, and the college has regularly commissioned new compositions to widen the repertoire.

Community songs

There are fewer and fewer opportunities for people to sing together these days. But the Christmas carol can bring together Church and Chapel, Catholic and Protestant, and even those of no clearly defined faith, as one united human family. If even atheists find that something deep inside them resonates to the music of the carol singers, that must be a good thing. There's a wide range of Christmas music available now, from 'The Little Drummer-boy' to 'Mary's boy-child', and thank God that people are still willing to sing the old songs, with their reference to the birth of a Saviour, and find this an essential part of Christmas.

All-age worship

Dress up like carol singers in olden days.

Suggested carols

Choose your own from those listed above.

Christmas Day 25 December
Second Service **Sonship**

Morning Ps. 110 This day of your birth, 117 Steadfast love; Evening Ps. 8 Out of the mouths of babes; Isa. 65.17–25 A new creation; Phil. 2.5–11 Jesus emptied himself, *or* Luke 2.1–20 (*if it has not been used at the Principal Service of the day*)

> *'Though [Jesus] was in the form of God, [he] did not regard equality with God as something to be exploited.' Philippians 2.6*

> *'To you is born this day in the city of David a Saviour, who is the Messiah, the Lord.' Luke 2.11*

Crowds at Christmas

Many people come to church at Christmas who seldom come at any other time of year. And they are entirely welcome. They may not be very clear what they believe, or whether the Christmas story is literally true, but they have a feeling, which many would find it hard to put into words, that the story proclaims a truth that is deeper than historical accuracy. We have made a secular society which has no clear values, so that the emphasis in the modern Christmas is all on shopping. But there must be something else, people feel. In its pursuit of money and power, our society is not unlike the Roman Empire. The Jewish faith was almost the only movement that stood out against this. Yes, the scribes and Pharisees had reached a compromise with the powers that be, and the militant side of their religion was toned down, but many hoped for a Messiah, some day, who would call the Jews to arms against the Romans. Jesus, by opposing militancy, opposed the kingdoms of this world with God's kingdom of love – the mystical side of religion against the twin towers of money and power. Emphasis on the literal meaning of the Bible can easily turn into fundamentalist militancy. But the Christmas story, with its emphasis on the birth of a baby, shows us that the poor and vulnerable may have a truth that the rich and powerful are blind to – the truth of love.

A good story

The Christmas story is a really good read. That's why so many people come to church at this magical season. The birth of a baby is always a miracle, but the birth of a child who will change history is very special indeed. The laughter of children is captivating, and 'Love changes everything'; but discovering that the love, which this child went on to speak about and live, is at the centre of our existence – that's mind-blowing! Everyone can respond with wonder to the Christmas story, and many become more loving people as a result. Trying to put that meaning into words, and finding the right philosophical terms – that can come later. There's always room in the church for enquirers, and I hope there always will be.

Son of God

Some of these enquirers will say something like, 'I accept that Jesus was a good man, and he taught many wonderful things – but I can't accept that he was Son of God.' Many Christians sympathize with that position. We declare in the creeds that Jesus was the Son of God, but we're not quite sure what that means. We also believe in God the Father, yet we know that God is above and beyond the material world that God created, so God has no body and no gender. In the bad old patriarchal days, men had all the power, so it was natural to use masculine terms when talking about the all-powerful Creator – but inclusive language comes nearer to the reality.

Muslims

Christmas is a difficult time also for Muslims. They believe so strongly in the powerfulness of God, it's impossible for them to imagine Allah becoming incarnate. 'Allah has no sons,' they protest. Yet words can be very misleading, and a great deal is 'Lost in Translation'. When Christians talk about sonship, they don't mean a physical begetting. It's the father–son relationship that counts. We believe that the character of Jesus is like the character of God. Jesus is kind, so we know that God is kind. Jesus forgives those who are penitent, so God, too, must be merciful. Most startling of all, Jesus becomes vulnerable, and suffers for the sake of those he loves, so the character of God must be like that, too.

Sonship

So if you find it difficult to think of Jesus as the Son of God, that may be because you have got the wrong idea of sonship. Christians believe that Jesus was completely human. But we also believe that

30

the character of God can be fully revealed by a human personality. The events of the first Christmas are a beautiful story. But they also reveal a central fact of our existence: the reason and purpose of our lives here is love, for love is at the heart of the universe. Happy Christmas, everybody!

Suggested carols

A great and mighty wonder; Of the Father's love begotten; Thou didst leave thy throne; Unto us a son is born.

Second Sunday of Christmas 1 January 2012
(Naming and Circumcision of Jesus)
The Naming of Jesus can be observed on 1 January; or on 2 January, in which case 1 January is called Christmas 2 but the readings are those for Christmas 1, as follows; or on Sunday 8 January, in which case The Baptism of Christ is observed on 9 January.
Principal Service   **Covenant Service**
Isa. 61.10—62.3 Garments of salvation; Ps. 148 Young and old together; Gal. 4.4–7 God sent his Son, born of a woman; Luke 2.15–21 The shepherds visit Bethlehem

'You are observing special days.' Galatians 4.10

New Year's Day

St Paul was talking about days for worshipping heathen gods. But for centuries Christians have kept New Year's Day for asking God's blessing on the coming year. John Wesley compiled an annual Covenant Service, for use at this time in the Methodist Church. I've distributed some extracts; would you please stand to join in the parts in bold type?

Adoration

Let us adore the Father, the God of love. He created us; he continually preserves and sustains us; he has loved us with an everlasting love, and given us the light of the knowledge of his glory in the face of Jesus Christ.

31

You are God; we praise you; we acknowledge you to be the Lord.

Let us glory in the grace of our Lord Jesus Christ. Though he was rich, yet for our sakes he became poor; he was tempted in all points as we are, yet without sin; he went about doing good and preaching the gospel of the kingdom; he became obedient to death, death on the cross; he was dead and is alive for ever; he has opened the kingdom of heaven to all who trust in him; he sits at the right hand of God in the glory of the Father; he will come again to be our Judge.

You, Christ, are the King of Glory.

Let us rejoice in the fellowship of the Holy Spirit, the Lord, the Giver of life. By him we are born into the family of God, and made members of the body of Christ; his witness confirms us; his wisdom teaches us; his power enables us; he will do for us far more than we ask or think.

All praise to you, Holy Spirit.

Renewal of our Covenant

In the Old Covenant, God chose Israel to be his people and to obey his laws. Our Lord Jesus Christ, by his death and resurrection, has made a New Covenant with all who trust in him. We stand within this Covenant and we bear his name. On the one side, God promises in this Covenant to give us new life in Christ. On the other side, we are pledged to live no more for ourselves but for him. Today, therefore, we meet expressly, as generations before us have met, to renew the Covenant which bound them, and binds us, to God. Beloved in Christ, let us again claim for ourselves this Covenant which God has made with his people, and take the yoke of Christ upon us. To take his yoke upon us means that we are content that he appoints us our place and work, and that he himself be our regard. Christ has many services to be done; some are easy, some are difficult; some bring honour, others bring reproach; some are suitable to our natural inclinations and material interests, others are contrary to both. In some we may please Christ and please ourselves, in others we cannot please Christ except by denying ourselves. Yet the power to do all these things is given us in Christ, who strengthens us. Therefore let us make this Covenant of God our own. Let us give ourselves anew to him, trusting in his promises and relying on his grace.

32

The people sit or kneel.

Lord God, Holy Father, since you have called us through Christ to share in this gracious Covenant, we take upon ourselves with joy the yoke of obedience, and, for love of you, engage ourselves to seek and do your perfect will. We are no longer our own, but yours.

I am no longer my own, but yours. Put me to what you will, rank me with whom you will; put me to doing, put me to suffering; let me be employed for you or laid aside for you, exalted for you or brought low for you; let me be full, let me be empty; let me have all things, let me have nothing; I freely and wholeheartedly yield all things to your pleasure and disposal. And now, glorious and blessed God, Father, Son, and Holy Spirit, you are mine and I am yours. So be it. And the Covenant now made on earth, let it be ratified in heaven. Amen.

All-age worship

Write down your New Year's resolutions, and ask Jesus to help you keep them.

Suggested hymns

For your mercy and your grace; Great is thy faithfulness; Lord, for the years; Make me a channel of your peace.

Naming and Circumcision of Jesus 1 January 2012
Named as Our Saviour

Num. 6.22–27 Aaron's blessing; Ps. 8 From the mouths of babes; Gal. 4.4–7 Born under the Law; Luke 2.15–21 Naming and circumcision

> *'After eight days had passed, it was time to circumcise the child; and he was called Jesus, the name given by the angel before he was conceived in the womb.' Luke 2.21*

Names

People call their children by some pretty weird names these days. Which is a shame, because you've got to pity the child growing up with a peculiar name. They may be mocked by their classmates at school, and embarrassed about their name. Fortunately your name is whatever you choose to call yourself, and if you want to make your preference formal you can register a new name through a deed-poll.

Jesus

The name of Jesus is the Greek form of the Hebrew name 'Joshua'. Most Jews in those days spoke a dialect that we call Aramaic. The Aramaic form of Joshua was pronounced Yeh–SHOO–ah. The first part of the word 'Yeshua' means 'The Lord', as in 'Je-hovah'. The second part comes from a verb meaning 'to save'. In Joshua's day, his name probably expressed his parents' faith that the Lord would save them from their enemies. By Jesus's day, a more spiritual meaning was widespread, being a prayer that God would save his people from the guilt of sin and the fear of death. When the angel told Mary and Joseph to call their son 'Jesus', it was a statement of faith that God *does* save, and the incarnation of the Son of God in Bethlehem would usher in a new era of salvation. Jesus's name can be interpreted as meaning Saviour: Jesus is the one who saves us. Jesus said, 'Your sins are forgiven.' He saves us from the crippling sense of guilt that we carry around, based on all the selfish and thoughtless things we do every day. Jesus said, 'Anyone who hears my word and believes him who sent me has eternal life', so for believers, death is nothing to be afraid of. Since Jesus was born to be our Saviour, death has become the gateway to life eternal.

Named in the Gospels

Matthew's Gospel tells us that Joseph planned to divorce Mary when he discovered she was pregnant, but an angel appeared to him in a dream, telling him that 'the child conceived in her is from the Holy Spirit. She will bear a son, and you are to name him Jesus, for he will save his people from their sins.' Matthew explains at once that Jesus means Saviour, and that it is the guilt that makes us afraid of God that he will save us from – then Joseph gives the name to the baby. In Luke's Gospel, the angel appears to Mary, saying, 'You will conceive in your womb and bear a son, and you will name him Jesus. He will be great, and will be called the Son of the Most High, and the Lord God will give to him the throne of his ancestor David.' It's a very Jewish title here: Jesus is to sit on King

34

David's throne, and – to avoid taking the name of God in vain, the angel adds – will be son of 'the highest'. The baby was named when he was circumcised and admitted to the Jewish nation at one week old. Mark begins his book by stating that it's good news, because Jesus – the Saviour – is also the Christ – the Messiah, the anointed one – and the Son of God. St John calls him the Word of God, then says that the Law of Moses told us what not to do, but Jesus brought us the truth that love is at the heart of our obedience, and Jesus gave us the strength to love other people: 'the law indeed was given through Moses; grace and truth came through Jesus Christ.'

Named by the apostles

St Paul, writing mostly to non-Jews, prefers to use the Greek word 'Christ'. But he also says that because Jesus was crucified, 'Therefore God also highly exalted him and gave him the name that is above every name, so that at the name of Jesus every knee should bend, in heaven and on earth and under the earth, and every tongue should confess that Jesus Christ is Lord, to the glory of God the Father.' And St Peter said, 'There is salvation in no one else, for there is no other name under heaven given among mortals by which we must be saved.' This isn't to condemn the other faiths – but it's a fact that none of them claims to offer the salvation from sin and death that Jesus offers. That's why the name, Jesus, is so precious to us – for each of us, he is our personal Saviour.

Suggested hymns

At the name of Jesus; How sweet the name of Jesus sounds; Jesus, name above all names; O for a thousand tongues to sing.

The Baptism of Christ
(The First Sunday of Epiphany)   8 January
Principal Service   **A Fresh Start**
Gen. 1.1–5 The Spirit over the waters; Ps. 29 The voice of the Lord over the waters; Acts 19.1–7 Baptism and the Spirit; Mark 1.4–11 The baptism of Jesus

> *'John the baptizer appeared in the wilderness, proclaiming a baptism of repentance for the forgiveness of sins.' Mark 1.4*

35

Please forgive me

'Please forgive me,' we say. Often we thoughtlessly do things that hurt other people. With a gasp of horror at what we have done, we clasp the other person's hand, yelping, 'Please forgive me. I really didn't mean to upset you.' If we are lucky, the person we have harmed will put an arm around us saying, 'Of course I do. I knew you didn't mean any harm. But I'm glad you were honest enough to apologize.' Then you can make a fresh start, with mutual trust and understanding. The agonizing memory of the wrong we did fades out of the memory of each of us, and our friendship is stronger than it was before. But at other times we are so ashamed of what we have done we can't bring ourselves to own up. Then we may carry a burden of guilt for the rest of our life, which spoils not only that friendship but our ability to make new friends. Worst of all is when we like to think that we are perfect – to admit that we are anything less would be a painful wound to our pride. No feelings of guilt, then, but none of the finer feelings in life either – we are dead in heart and soul, just because we couldn't bring ourselves to say sorry.

Sorry, God

The Jewish people thought that God was their friend, and they were his chosen people. God told them, through his prophets, that he could only care for his people if they were united, and treated each other in an open and honest way. God gave them ten Commandments to outline what this meant. But their priests made it more complicated, by spelling out all the implications of this in a host of minor laws, until breaking even the least made them ashamed to look God in the face; and that was the end of a beautiful friendship. Yes, they could pay the priests to make sacrifices, and there was an annual day of atonement, but they felt as though they were wracked with remorse and ground down by guilt

The Baptist

So God sent John the Baptist, to help them to make a fresh start. St Mark says this was the beginning of the good news, when 'John the baptizer appeared in the wilderness, proclaiming a baptism of repentance for the forgiveness of sins.' Being baptized was a way for human beings to admit that they had grubby consciences, and needed to be washed clean. Then, when we have said sorry, baptism shows us that God forgives the past, and allows us a fresh start, as innocent as newborn babes.

Repentance

Repentance isn't the same as remorse. We Christians have a reputation for trying to turn the thumbscrews of remorse till everybody feels even guiltier than they did before. But God isn't interested in making people groan with guilt, he wants us to feel forgiven. Own up to what you have done, say sorry, then believe that God forgives you, thank God and forget about it. That's what the symbol of baptism means. The Greek word that we translate as 'repentance' is *metanoia,* which comes from *meta-,* meaning 'turning about', and *nous,* which means 'mind' or 'intelligence'. So 'the baptism of repentance' means making a fresh start with a changed attitude, depending not on our own goodness but on God's forgiveness.

Jesus

Jesus joined the family of the baptized – not that he had done anything wrong, but he wanted to identify with us in our total dependence on God's mercy. Then his message was the same as Cousin John's: 'The time is fulfilled, and the kingdom of God has come near; repent, and believe in the good news.' So Christianity is a religion of forgiveness and the fresh start. We must be willing to say sorry to our friends when we hurt them, and willing to forgive them when they apologize to us. Then we can pluck up courage to say sorry to God, absolutely certain that as soon as we have said those words, God will forgive us unreservedly. Then, in the knowledge that God has given us a clean slate, we can take the hardest step of all, which is to forgive ourselves. How can you go round feeling guilty when God regards you as pure as the water you were baptized in? Forget the past, and step confidently into the future, basking in the warm certainty of God's love.

All-age worship

Wear paper bracelets with 'I'm sorry – I forgive you –' written on them in a circle.

37

Suggested hymns

A little child the Saviour came; Baptized in water, sealed by the Spirit; On Jordan's bank the Baptist's cry; When Jesus came to Jordan to be baptized by John.

The Baptism of Christ   15 January
Second Service   **Be Still and Know**
Ps. 46 Our refuge [47 King of the nations]; Isa. 42.1–9 The servant a light to the nations; Eph. 2.1–10 From death to life; *Gospel at Holy Communion*: Matt. 3.13–17 Calling disciples

> *'Be still, and know that I am God! I will be exalted among the nations, I will be exalted in the earth.' Psalm 46.10 (Common Worship)*

Anthony Bloom

Metropolitan Anthony of Sourozh headed the Russian Church in exile in England, during the years when the Moscow Patriarchate was suspected of complicity with the Communist Party. Though he was a very down-to-earth man, to meet him was to become aware of a deep inner spirituality. He was still known as Bishop Anthony Bloom when he wrote a book called *School for Prayer*. In it, many readers discovered levels of prayer that can't be taught in a short sermon. He described an old lady coming to ask his advice. She had prayed regularly for 14 years, yet she had never sensed that God was present. Bishop Anthony advised her to sit in her room quietly and simply look around her. Some of the things she saw, he said, would remind her of things and people she wanted to pray about. But she needn't worry if her mind went completely blank. She returned to the bishop and reported what had happened when she took his advice. Gradually she'd become aware that the silence wasn't simply the absence of sound, but was 'filled with its own density. And,' she said, 'it began to pervade me. The silence around began to come and meet the silence in me . . . All of a sudden I perceived that the silence was a presence. At the heart of the silence there was Him.'

Contemplation

Many people, when they are praying, are tempted to talk too much. They worry about what words to use when they are speaking to God, and what it's OK to ask for. But prayer isn't a shopping list of things you want; God already knows what you really need, and knows which of the things you ask him for so desperately would actually do you more harm than good. The only reason for asking God for things is because it reminds us that we are completely dependent on his generous love. God gives them to you simply because he loves you – God's mighty arm will provide, you don't have to twist it into a half-nelson. That's why Jesus condemned 'vain repetitions': 'When you're praying,' he said, 'don't heap up empty phrases as the Gentiles do; for they think that they'll be heard because of their many words.' No, prayer as Jesus taught it is more like chatting with your Dad. No earthly father will be pleased if his children are always talking at him, and never let their Dad get a word in edgeways. God, too, wants you to allow time for listening to him. Sometimes some words from the Bible come to mind in the silence, and you're reminded of things God wants you to do for him. Sometimes, like the woman who asked the Bishop for advice, you may simply become aware of God's presence and love in the silence, and then you've nothing left to worry about. This is what's known as contemplative prayer; sitting in silence and contemplating God in the stillness.

'Be still, and know'

According to the book of Psalms, God tells us to slow down. 'Be still, and know that I am God! I will be exalted among the nations, I will be exalted in the earth.' This is advice for people who are worried about all the hostile nations which might attack them. So it could apply to people today who are worried about terrorism or recession: God is more powerful than all the hostile forces. But it can also apply to all of us who are caught up in the rush and bustle of everyday life. During the last war, a poster was displayed in many places which simply said, 'Keep calm and carry on.' Because if you're in a panic, you only make the problems worse. 'Be still, and know that I am God!'

Making spaces

We ought to make spaces for silence in our lives. We need times when we can shut out the din, or when we can go away to some quiet place to meditate. John Muir emigrated to the United States, and became the first great environmentalist. Over a century ago he argued for the importance of setting large areas of land aside as National Parks, and from this one man's efforts the movement spread to other countries around the world. John Muir wrote, 'Everybody needs beauty as well as bread, places to play in and pray in, where nature may heal and give strength to the body and soul.' End of quotation. In other words, we all need to be still and know that God is God.

Suggested hymns

Be still and know; Be still, for the presence of the Lord; Be still my soul; Dear Lord and Father of mankind.

Second Sunday of Epiphany   15 January
Principal Service   **Vision**
1 Sam. 3.1–10 [11–20] The child Samuel in the Temple; Ps. 139.1–5, 12–18 God knows us; Rev. 5.1–10 Worthy is the Lamb; John 1.43–51 'You are the Son of God'

> *'The word of the Lord was rare in those days; visions were not widespread.' 1 Samuel 3.1*

Vision

Artists must have a vision of what they are trying to create before they put brush to canvas. Young people will make little progress without a growing vision of what they hope to achieve in their life. No political party can win an election unless they present the electors with a vision of the world they wish to create. We all need people with vision to inspire us, otherwise we get nowhere; as the book of Proverbs puts it: 'Where there is no vision, the people perish.'

Samuel

So these words from the first book of Samuel show us a sad society, without purpose, and with no clear idea of why they were there: 'The word of the LORD was rare in those days; visions were not widespread.' God was speaking to them; but nobody listened to the divine voice. They wandered round like people lost in a fog, with nobody to point out the direction in which to travel. The only one who did hear God speaking to him was a small child, a servant to Eli the priest, carrying out menial tasks in the courts of the Jerusalem Temple – the last person you'd have expected God to use as his mouthpiece – an unlikely candidate to be the anointer and rebuker of kings! In fact, so unprecedented was what happened that night, that at first neither Samuel nor Eli realized what was going on. Twice Samuel reported to Eli saying, 'Did you call me?' 'Go back to bed,' snarled Eli. 'Don't wake me up again,' he growled at the little lad. Twice Samuel did as he was told. Then, the third time, Eli recognized that it must be God speaking. This time, Samuel answered the mysterious voice with the words, 'Speak, LORD, for your servant is listening.' Then God revealed what was going to happen to his nation and its leaders; it was a grim warning, because they had ignored God's words, and tried to run the country with no vision of what God had called them to do.

Today

Would you say of our nation today that the word of the LORD is rare in these days; visions are not widespread? I'm not talking about children hearing voices and people having spooky nightmares. I mean, does our country have a clear understanding of its place in the world, and the purpose of human life? Because, if not, 'Where there is no vision, the people perish.' Instead, we've fabricated a merely materialistic view of the world, where what makes people admired is what they have, not what they are. We've dismissed religion as a yesterday thing – an obsolete, pre-scientific delusion, an improbable superstition, which nobody with any brains could possibly believe. The voices warning us that there is a lot more to living than material existence are drowned out by the scoffing of the atheists. But if there is no God, there's no purpose to life other than to be as selfish as we can and clamber to the top on the shoulders of those less fortunate than ourselves. Beauty and compassion are of no value in a godless world. Those who put their family's need for love before their financial advancement are derided as misguided fools. The result? 'Where there is no vision, the people perish.' Or, at least, their spiritual life withers away and the soul of society dies from lack of nourishment.

Prophets

The boy Samuel grew into a great prophet. I do so hope that, before it's too late, the people of this nation today will listen to the voice of the prophets among us – those who point beyond the material to something more important and longer lasting. Those who remind us of the words of Jesus, that we shall not live by bread alone, but by every word that proceeds from the mouth of God. That God made us because he wanted creatures who would respond to his love, by loving him with all our heart and mind and soul and strength, and by loving our neighbour as ourselves. That's the real meaning of human life – in fact, the meaning of the universe. Would to God that the people of today would hear that word, God's word of love, and catch the vision of what the world could be if we forgot the kingdom of Mammon for a while, and worked as hard to build the kingdom of God.

All-age worship

Label a money-box and a Bible: 'Treasure on Earth' and 'Treasure in Heaven'.

Suggested hymns

Be thou my vision; Hushed was the Temple hymn; I, the Lord of sea and sky; O God of earth and altar.

Second Sunday of Epiphany   15 January
Second Service   The Wealth of Nations
Ps. 96 God will judge the peoples; Isa. 60.9–22 Nations shall bring their wealth; Heb. 6.17 – 7.10 Melchizedek; *Gospel at Holy Communion*: Matt. 8.5–13 Foreigners in the kingdom

> *'Nations shall bring you their wealth, with their kings led in procession.' Isaiah 60.11*

Adam Smith

Adam Smith was born in Kirkcaldy in Scotland in 1723. He became professor of logic at Glasgow University, and then professor of moral philosophy. The essence of morality, he wrote, is sympathy for others and an active conscience. In 1776 he moved to London, and was a friend of Doctor Johnson, Joshua Reynolds and David Garrick. The same year he wrote a book with a long title, usually known for short as *The Wealth of Nations*. It covered natural theology, ethics, politics and law. Examining the consequences of *laissez-faire* policies on a market economy, he saw the main ingredient of economic growth as the willing division of labour. Some call Adam Smith the inventor of capitalism, but he warned that it will only work if we behave in a moral way. He wrote, 'There is no art that one government sooner learns of another than that of draining money from the pockets of the people.'

Israel

There's a verse in the Old Testament that uses the words, 'The Wealth of Nations', which Adam Smith made the title of his book. According to Isaiah, God promised to the Israelites that 'Nations shall bring you their wealth, with their kings led in procession.' Maybe they thought of that in monetary terms, and believed that Jerusalem would become the richest city in the world. If so, they were sorely disappointed. The people of Israel today receive much financial help, especially from the United States, but it doesn't seem to bring peace and happiness. So perhaps we should be thinking, instead, of the wealth of nations being those spiritual gifts which different races bring into God's kingdom. Isaiah's words were fulfilled when the three kings rode in procession to Bethlehem, and presented their gifts of gold, frankincense and myrrh to the child Jesus. But it wasn't the financial value of those gifts which made the baby smile: the magi were foreigners, non-Jews, Gentiles. Their gifts were a symbol of the spiritual riches that all the nations of the world will bring into the kingdom of God.

Spiritual riches

Think how much poorer the world would be without the contributions that different cultures bring to our common life. Jesus founded the Christian faith within Judaism. He spoke in terms of Jewish traditions: the word of God in Scripture, the moral law, and God's covenant with his people. He taught that people from East and West would come and sit with Abraham in the kingdom of God. But the teaching of Jesus might soon have been forgotten, if it hadn't been for St Paul. Paul was also a Jew, but he grew up in the Roman Empire, with Greek as its common language and its thinking defined by the heritage of the Greek philosophers. Jews sometimes blame Paul as the founder of anti-Semitism, but on the contrary, his life's work was to turn an insignificant sect into a worldwide religion which all cultures could understand. He taught above all else that Christians of different traditions should tolerate each other, with Jewish Christians and Gentile Christians loving each other as sisters and brothers. Then, as the faith moved westwards, the influence of Roman law and Roman administrative methods began to be felt. Different cultures contributed more riches to the mix: to select but a few, we are all blessed by the gifts of French art, German music and British literature. The Americas brought their emphasis on individual freedom. Africans share their joy in dance and worship; the people of India bring a special gift for mysticism. The world would be poorer without the Muslim emphasis on absolute submission to God. Chinese bring their early scientific discoveries. And so it goes on, each new culture bringing onto the world stage its own gifts of language, music, art, government and thought.

Pride and tolerance

What a wonderful world we live in! We can each of us be proud of the contribution that our own region has made to world civilization. But we are terribly impoverished if we never move outside our own backyard to learn from and enjoy the wealth of other cultures. Although the words have been misapplied by some, a truly 'multicultural' world society is what we should all be gladly moving towards. Provided that we accept each other as of equal worth in the eyes of God, proud of our own traditions, tolerant of all and enjoying what makes others different. In this way will be fulfilled the words of Isaiah and Adam Smith about the Wealth of Nations, the symbolism of the magi, the promise of Jesus and the labours of St Paul.

Suggested hymns

As with gladness men of old; He's got the whole world in his hands; In Christ there is no East or West; The day thou gavest, Lord, is ended.

Third Sunday of Epiphany   22 January

See also 'Week of Prayer for Christian Unity', p. 295.
Principal Service   **A Love Feast**
Gen. 14.17–20 Melchizedek brought bread and wine; Ps. 128
God will bless your family; Rev. 19.6–10 The wedding feast of
the Lamb; John 2.1–11 A wedding at Cana

> *'Let us rejoice and exult and give him the glory, for the marriage of the Lamb has come, and his bride has made herself ready.' Revelation 19.7*

A love feast

Let's have a party! No, sit down; I don't mean with funny hats and dancing. I mean, let's think of this service as being like the best sort of party. In the early Church they used to have a shared meal, which they called by the Greek name for love, *agapē*. This love feast was a time when both sexes and all social classes could sit together for a shared meal, which was almost unheard of in the ancient world. It followed the example of Jesus, who was criticized for his frequent attendance at parties, but astonished people by his willingness to share table fellowship with Pharisees, tax-collectors and sinners – complete opposites gathered round the same table. They had to learn tolerance, and get along together if they wanted to be friends of Jesus, whether they liked it or not. Among his followers, the love feast became a preparation for the Holy Communion; in fact the local bishop might preside at the meal, and conclude by breaking bread and passing bread and wine round the meal table.

A wedding at Cana

Their thoughts must often have gone back to the wedding reception that Jesus attended at Cana of Galilee, where he turned water into wine. He was enjoying the party, and didn't want the couple's big day to be spoilt by running out of wine. But it had a deeper meaning, because it symbolized the shared love that would be the defining mark of the new Christian community. They would never run out of love; it would be like the new wine, bubbling up until it burst all the old containers and created a totally new kind of fellowship.

45

The wedding feast of the Lamb

In the book of Revelation, heaven is compared with a wedding reception. The voices of a great crowd are heard – like the sound of many waters, like rolling peals of thunder – and they cry out, 'Let us rejoice and exult and give him the glory, for the marriage of the Lamb has come, and his bride has made herself ready.' 'The wedding feast of the Lamb' is a strange mixed metaphor, but the phrase carries a wealth of meaning. It means that the people in heaven are having a great party. They're gathered round the table of Jesus, who's called 'the Lamb of God, who takes away the sin of the world'. The death of Jesus resembled the animal sacrifices of the Old Testament, bringing forgiveness of sins. But his was a once-and-for-all offering, and all we have to do is join the offering of our hearts and lives with his offering of himself to his father, then our redemption is certain.

Melchizedek

Then there's that strange story in the Old Testament, when Abraham came to the city of Salem, which would later be called Jerusalem. The king of Jerusalem at the time was called Melchizedek, which is Hebrew for 'King of Righteousness'. He threw a party to welcome Abraham. He brought out bread and wine; the commonest form of food and drink in the ancient world. But Jews will have thought of their ancestor Abraham as celebrating a Passover meal, more than six hundred years before the Israelites crossed the Red Sea. At the Passover they ate unleavened bread, shared a cup of wine, and sacrificed a lamb.

Worship

So all these thoughts come to mind when we worship together. Our meal of bread and wine commemorates the Passover, when God saved his people from the death of the first-born. It's like those shared meals that Jesus enjoyed, a superb party. It's a reminder of the wedding feast at Cana. It's a chance to offer our own lives afresh to our heavenly Father, for him to take control; and we offer them in union with the sacrifice of Jesus, the Lamb of God, on the cross. And it's a foretaste of heaven. What a wonderful party! Who could turn down an invitation to join in such a celebration, as often as we possibly can?

All-age worship

Have a mini party, with special food and drink. What do you like about parties? Does coming to church remind you of going to a party? Why?

Suggested hymns

At Cana's wedding, long ago; Crown him with many crowns; Let us break bread together, we are one; Songs of thankfulness and praise.

Third Sunday of Epiphany   22 January
Second Service   Pastoral Care

Ps. 33 All the inhabitants of the earth; Jer. 3.21—4.2 Nations blessed by him; Titus 2.1–8, 11–14 Pastoral care; *Gospel at Holy Communion*: Matt. 4.12–23 Ministry in Galilee

'Teach what is consistent with sound doctrine.' Titus 2.1

Titus

Titus was a Greek lad who became St Paul's helper. There was a row when Paul brought Titus into the Temple in Jerusalem. Had an uncircumcised Gentile wandered into the parts that were reserved only for Jews? Titus carried Paul's Second Letter to Corinth; he went to be a missionary in Dalmatia, in what's now Croatia. Later he went to the island of Crete to look after the Christians there. We know all this from mentions of him in the letters of St Paul.

Paul's letter

St Paul's letter to Titus contains advice to Christian pastors on caring for their flock. Titus is to be a bishop to the whole island, appointing elders to look after the congregations in each town. Elders and bishops are to be chosen from among those whose lives are blameless, not arrogant or quick-tempered; not in it for the money; and careful students of the Scriptures so that they can preach clear and helpful sermons. They must teach the older men in the congregation to be wise, loving and patient, sound in faith and love. The older women should be told to be reverent, not gossips or drunkards, and an example to the younger women. Younger women must be good at managing their family and home, and an example of good behaviour. Then Paul tells slaves to obey their masters – he had already written to Philemon telling him to treat his runaway slave as a Christian brother, and this would eventually lead to the abolition of slavery. But there was no sense in rushing things: if the slaves became rebellious, the state would clamp down on the young Christian Church. As always, Paul warns against those who cause divisions in the church.

Pastors

St Paul is advising Titus how to be a good Christian pastor. The word pastor, of course, means a shepherd. The Church's ministers are to be under-shepherds, caring for the flock of Christ the Good Shepherd, and following his example of self-sacrifice for the sake of those they serve. It's an enormous privilege to care for God's people as a minister, to share their joys and sorrows, to guide their spiritual growth and lead them towards heaven when they die. But the life of a pastor can also be intensely frustrating. If pastors get bogged down in paperwork, fundraising, and the care of buildings; if a few members of the congregation take out their personal grievances on their pastor; if the people ignore the pastor's guidance, and won't co-operate with the pastor's plans, then the pastor's life can be heartbreaking and soul-destroying.

Chrysostom

Another Greek, St John Chrysostom – his nickname means 'Goldenmouth' – some three hundred years later, wrote these words 'On the Priesthood':

The shepherd should be much better than his sheep, as a thinking man is better than dumb animals. A shepherd who allows sheep to die because of wolves, robbers, sickness, or some other accident, might perhaps be forgiven by the owner of the flock. But a priest who is entrusted with the shepherding of rational human beings, the flock of Christ, loses not his money but his own soul if the sheep perish. Besides, if an animal is sick, the illness is easily diagnosed and easily cured; for shepherds can force the sheep to be treated against their will. It is easy to tie them up for surgery or to cauterize a wound. But it is impossible to treat human beings

48

with the same authority as a shepherd has over the sheep. For Christians especially are not allowed to use violence in correcting the stumblings of the sinful. We have no legal authority to stop people sinning, and if we had, we shouldn't know how to use it – for God doesn't reward people who are forcibly prevented from doing wrong, but only those who make up their minds not to. So you have to be very tactful, so as to persuade sick souls to submit to the treatment the priests prescribe, and also thank the priests for curing them. I am afraid that if Jesus gave me his flock healthy and well fed, and I let it be injured because of my lack of experience, I should provoke the anger of God, who so loved his flock that he gave himself to save and redeem it

Caring for the carers

That's a terrifically high standard that John Chrysostom calls the clergy to aim at. It would be impossible without the grace of God. But it's made very much easier if the people accept some responsibility for caring for their pastor. Have you asked yourself what you could do to make your pastor feel encouraged and loved?

Suggested hymns

God of mercy, God of grace; O thou who camest from above; Pour out thy Spirit from on high; The Lord my pasture shall prepare.

Fourth Sunday of Epiphany   29 January
(or Candlemas; see p. 300)
Principal Service   Not Only by Christians
Deut. 18.15–20 God will raise up a prophet; Ps. 111 Salvation; Rev. 12.1–5a A woman in heaven; Mark 1.21–28 Demons recognize Christ

> *'He commands even the unclean spirits, and they obey him.' Mark 1.27*

Admiring Jesus

The great Indian leader, Mahatma Gandhi, always kept a copy of the Christian New Testament at his bedside, along with the Hindu

49

Bhagavad Gita. He wouldn't have called himself a Christian, but he admired Jesus of Nazareth – he thought the Sermon on the Mount was among the world's greatest moral teachings. Many other people are attracted by Jesus, without necessarily wanting to commit their lives to him. The goodness of Jesus is recognized by all sorts of people, shining through his words and deeds. Even bad people can see it. Some people avoid any contact with the Christian religion, because they know in their hearts what it means – if they let Jesus into their lives, they would have to change their ways, and give up their naughty behaviour. It's not only committed Christians who can recognize that Jesus is somebody special. But the words we choose to describe him will vary, depending on the language we speak and the ideas we trade in.

Words

You see, different languages, and different cultures within any one language group, talk in quite different ways. We each use different ideas, different images, and distinctive metaphors, to get our thoughts across to others. A phrase that means one thing to you may mean something completely different to me. You may completely misunderstand me, because you're not used to the phrases I use to express myself. If we go back into history, the problem's even worse. Today we use words that hadn't been invented then, based on theories that nobody had dreamt of yet. So the people of the past may have had the same feelings as we do, but they had to articulate them in words that would never occur to us. We may be brought up short by words that Henry the Eighth or Homer use, and draw completely wrong conclusions about what they were saying through the unfamiliarity of their imagery.

Demons

So you or I may say of a psychiatric patient, 'He's a schizophrenic, maybe even psychotic.' Well, some people would. But if you said that to St Mark, he'd have thought you were out of your mind yourself. What St Mark would have said was, the man was possessed by a demon. You and Mark would both be saying the same thing in your own way. Who's to judge whether one or other's words are more 'true'? In the first chapter of his Gospel, Mark describes what happened when Jesus was teaching in the synagogue in Capernaum. 'A man with an unclean spirit' (writes Mark) 'cried out, "What have you to do with *us*, Jesus of Nazareth? Have you come to destroy us? *I* know who you are: the Holy One of God.'" A strange choice of words, but who's going to reason with a madman? Should Jesus have said, 'I think you're suffering from a bipolar affective disorder, with traces of dual personality'? Not likely! He adopted the man's own terminology and shouted at the supposed evil spirit: 'Shut up – and come out of him!' St Mark tells us that 'the unclean spirit, convulsing him and crying with a loud voice, came out of him.' The people there were amazed – 'He commands even the unclean spirits,' they gasped, 'and they obey him!' It's not only committed Christians who can recognize that Jesus is somebody special – even demons can spot that.

The Holy One of God

What did those words mean that the madman used, describing Jesus as 'The Holy One of God'? I could list the times similar phrases occur in the Old Testament, but although it's obscured by the Hebrew way of speaking, we know in our hearts that it means Jesus is loving and kind, and reveals that God's the same. If we insist that, unless people call Jesus the 'Son of God', they are not really Christians, we're forgetting that those words mean different things in other languages than they did in the original Hebrew. Surely we must allow people a halfway house into the Christian faith, when they recognize that Jesus is somebody special, and tells us something profound about human life. Yet they must put this in their own words, which may not be the same as those of the creeds. Of course, the point of a halfway house is that you intend to move on from it when you've had time to think a little longer. Yet it's not only committed Christians who can recognize that Jesus shows us what God must be like.

All-age worship

Learn simple First Aid. Write on a bandage, sling or plaster, 'Jesus makes sick people better'.

Suggested hymns

Join all the glorious names; O for a thousand tongues to sing; There is a Redeemer; Thine arm, O Lord, in days of old.

Fourth Sunday of Epiphany 29 January
Second Service   **Think of the Visitors**

Ps. 34 Taste and see; 1 Sam. 3.1–20 The boy Samuel in the
Temple; 1 Cor. 14.12–20 Pray with the mind also; *Gospel at
Holy Communion*: Matt. 13.10–17 The purpose of parables

*'If you say a blessing with the spirit, how can anyone in the posi-
tion of an outsider say the "Amen" to your thanksgiving, since
the outsider does not know what you are saying?' 1 Corinthians
14.16*

Family hold back

In an Ian Hay film of 1911, important visitors have come to call,
and Mother's about to serve out the special pudding at dinner.
First she traces invisible letters in the air above the cream topping:
F H B. All the family members know that this stands for 'Family
Hold Back'. In other words, the fine food is in short supply, and
the host family must wait their turn and not ask for the best dishes
until the visitors have been served. Maybe the family would have
to make-do with second-best fodder, if the visitors had taken all
the superior offerings. In some families this has remained a catch-
phrase until today: Family Hold Back – think of the visitors first;
it's only common courtesy.

In church

It's only common courtesy to think of the visitors first in church,
too. St Paul had this problem in Corinth. Different factions in the
congregation wanted the worship to be in the manner they liked,
and blow all the rest. One particularly painful disagreement was
over 'speaking in tongues'. Then, as today in many charismatic
and Pentecostal churches, some people were so overcome by emo-
tion that they began to speak excitedly in syllables that belong to
no known language. They feel that God's Holy Spirit is speaking
through them. St Paul agreed – he'd had the experience himself,
and thanked God for it. Where it became divisive, though, was
when those who had the gift began speaking in tongues during
the service. They claimed that this proved that they possessed the
Holy Spirit, and that the rest didn't. Those who don't speak in
tongues, they claimed, aren't really Christians. So the congregation

in Corinth was split down the middle. St Paul tried to reconcile the factions, and show them that love for others is the greatest of God's gifts to us – nothing must get in the way of love. As part of his argument Paul wrote, 'think of the visitors'. He didn't actually write F H B, but that's what he meant. People who pray in tongues during worship seem to an outsider to utter meaningless babbling, comprehensible only to those who have the experience themselves. If you pray like this, asks the apostle, how can any visitor say the 'Amen' to your thanksgiving, since the outsider doesn't know what you're saying? Think of the visitors first, before you indulge your own preferences in worship.

In this church

We may not have exactly that problem in this church, but St Paul's words of wisdom apply in every church: think of the visitors first. If you invite your friend, who's had little experience of church services, to come to church with you, what will they think of it? Will they be inspired, or will they be baffled and confused? Will they enjoy it, or not? Will they say, 'What inspiring preaching', or will they think, 'I wish the preacher wouldn't go ranting on at me'? Will they think, 'I do enjoy these jolly new songs', or will they react against what they call 'happy-clappy worship'? Will they tell themselves that it's wonderfully dignified traditional ceremonial, or will the visitor write it off as fussy nonsense? I don't know – perhaps they'll love every minute of it. But it's something we should be thinking about. We all say sometimes, 'Why can't we do things in church always in the way I'm used to?' I'm not saying any of these things is wrong, but instead of thinking of ourselves always, we ought to consider first what other people like and find helpful.

Visitors first

And – Family Hold Back. Think of the visitors first. If you spot somebody you don't know, go up to them and say a friendly hello, without being pushy. Ask who they are, and invite them to come again if possible. Then, whatever part you play in the services, even if it's only sitting in the pews and saying 'Amen', try to do it in a way that will make the casual visitor feel welcome. Nobody can please everybody all the time, so no church can worship every Sunday in the way that you, personally, like. So don't demand your own way all the time. The first rule in worship is this: do your best, to the glory of God. Second rule: consider the casual visitor before anyone else. Third rule: always think of yourself and your own preferences last. Remember what those letters mean – *F – H – B!*

Suggested hymns

Be still and know; Dear Lord and Father of mankind; Seek ye first the kingdom of God; When I needed a neighbour.

Third Sunday before Lent (Proper 1) 5 February
Principal Service   **Always Available**

Isa. 40.21–31 God's greatness; Ps. 147.1–12, 21c God heals the broken-hearted; 1 Cor. 9.16–23 Evangelism and other faiths; Mark 1.29–39 Jesus heals and preaches

> *'That evening, at sundown, they brought to him all who were sick or possessed with demons. And the whole city was gathered around the door.' Mark 1.32–33*

Healings

Jesus went into Capernaum to teach. In the synagogue there was a crowd on the Sabbath day, eager to hear what the visiting preacher had to say. Jesus had come to share the good news of God's kingdom, and this was just the opportunity he needed. A madman, or as they described it, a man possessed by demons, came in and kicked up a fuss. A lesser man than Jesus would have demanded that the distraction be removed. But Jesus healed him, because, for him, healing and preaching went together. The power of God is stronger than any other power. Healing proves the truth of the preaching, and preaching explains the healing. Because Jesus was tired from his morning's work, his friend Simon Peter invited him to come home for a rest; but Peter's mother-in-law had a fever, and Jesus had to heal her first. Then, at sunset, when they were looking forward to a quiet meal together, Peter struggled into the house with bad news. 'I could hardly get here,' he said. 'The story of what you did this morning has got around. But nobody's allowed to carry anything on the Sabbath, because that's work. So they have all waited till Sabbath ends at sunset, and carried their sick relatives here for you to heal them! The whole street's blocked!' So poor Jesus abandoned his evening at home and went out into the street to cure everyone who asked for it. Healing in the synagogue, healing in the home, healing in the street, there was no end to it.

Always available

But Jesus was always available to those who needed him. He's always available to us, too. Here's a joke. A man came storming into the local medical practice, complaining that the doctors were never available. 'I've tried dozens of times to call the freephone number on your leaflet,' he grumbled, 'and I never get an answer.' 'Which number is that?' asked the puzzled doctor. '0800 1830,' replied the client. 'Actually, those are our opening hours,' said the doctor – '8 a.m. to 6.30 p.m. There's always one of us available between those times!' But Jesus is like that theatre which boasted during the war, 'We never closed.' He's always there when anybody needs him.

Time alone

Yet after that busy, busy day in Capernaum, he needed to recharge his batteries. So before dawn, he set off to have some 'me-time' away from the town. Which for Jesus meant time with his heavenly Father, for the Son of God was never alone. We can none of us keep going indefinitely without making regular times for prayer. Peter and his other friends came and found him, to warn him that other sick people were searching for him. So Jesus drew a deep breath, and outlined his plans for the next few months, or however long it took. He was going on tour, visiting every town in the Galilee region, preaching and healing, because the two things go together, and he wanted *everyone* to hear about the love of God.

Only when we feel like it

Jesus is always available – but people don't always call on him. You'll notice that church attendances always go up in times of trouble – war or recession – and down in times of prosperity. Many people forget to pray when life goes smoothly, then find they have forgotten how to, when they hit a bad patch. Somebody said that people look for religion to give them comfort in the casualty station, and forget that it's also there to give them strength in the front line of the battle against sin. The kingdom of God will never spread if we don't spread it by our loving words and deeds, and we can't do that unless we pray regularly, not just when we feel like it.

55

Always available

So, like Jesus, we must be always available to people who need us. Love never takes a holiday. Yes, it's exhausting to put yourself out for people whenever they call on you, and like Jesus we must find some 'me-time', spending some of it in conversation with God. Yet Jesus never separated teaching and action; soul and body; nor earth and heaven. Once we realize that God is always available to us, we must make ourselves always available to love other people, in word and in deed. The kingdom of God has no opening hours, because it's never closed.

All-age worship

Play at sales staff in God's supermarket. What would you sell, at what price? Put up a sign, 'Loving hearts available 24/7'.

Suggested hymns

At even, when the sun was set; Healing God, almighty Father; Restore, O Lord, the honour of your name; The Kingdom of God is justice and joy.

Third Sunday before Lent (Proper 1)   5 February
Second Service   **Slowly, Without Dragging**
Ps. 5 Lead me, Lord, in your righteousness; Num. 13.1–2, 27–33 The spies report; Phil. 2.12–28 Work out your own salvation; *Gospel at Holy Communion*: Luke 5.1–11 A miraculous catch of fish

> *'Lead me, O Lord, in your righteousness because of my enemies; make your way straight before me.' Psalm 5.8*

Curate's mistake

There is a beautiful anthem composed by Samuel Sebastian Wesley, setting words from the fifth Psalm: 'Lead me, Lord, lead me in thy righteousness'. Many choirs sing it from *The Church Anthem Book*, which in modern editions is a very clear score. But when Walford Davies first published it in 1934, he tried to squeeze the tonic-sol-fa notation in between the lines of music. This left very little room for the words and the tempo instructions, which could easily be confused. A newly ordained curate read out the words as they actually appeared above the first line of music: 'The choir will now sing the anthem: "Slowly, without dragging, Lead me, Lord"'!

Escape

It's a prayer that many of us wish to pray: 'Slowly, without dragging, lead me, Lord'! After a busy week, we come to church to escape from the hustle and bustle of the world outside. We need a time to relax and wind down, and the church provides it admirably. 'Jesu, lover of my soul,' we sing –

> let me to thy bosom fly,
> while the nearer waters roll,
> while the tempest still is high:
> hide me, O my Saviour, hide,
> till the storm of life is past;
> safe into the haven guide,
> O receive my soul at last –

words of Charles Wesley, which beautifully describe the escape from our daily troubles that religion supplies. God *can* lead us 'Slowly, without dragging'. But we must be careful that escape doesn't turn into escapism.

Escapism

The dictionary defines an escapist as 'someone who seeks to escape, especially from reality'. The reality of life is that the world's a tough place. We can withdraw from it for a while, but not for long. At some time we have to go out again and face its challenges. Each of us has to shoulder her or his responsibility, for our own small part in turning the hostile world into a better place. There's little enough that each of us can do on our own, but people of good will have pulled together and made some improvements down the centuries. If we dodge the tasks that God calls us to do in this process, we're helping evil to triumph.

Guidance and grace

Everyone can join in this struggle, including those of other religions or none. Where the Christian has the advantage is because we have recognized and accepted God's offer of guidance and grace. We are faced by many road junctions in life, and it's hard to know which way to choose. Thank God, if we read our Bibles and pray, the right path becomes clear. This guidance comes from God, and if we follow God's leading we shall receive grace to help us overcome the challenges in our way. God may not remove the obstacles, but he will show us a way round them, or give us the spiritual strength to climb over them. Living well takes grit and determination, and the ability to go on loving the unlovely – and the only place to find those virtues is in God's grace.

Slowly, without dragging

The first few words of the anthem, from Psalm 5, continue:

> Lead me, O Lord, in your righteousness because of my enemies; make your way straight before me . . . let all who take refuge in you rejoice; let them ever sing for joy. Spread your protection over them, so that those who love your name may exult in you. For you bless the righteous, O Lord; you cover them with favour as with a shield.

St Paul promises: 'No testing has overtaken you that is not common to everyone. God is faithful, and he will not let you be tested beyond your strength, but with the testing he will also provide the way out so that you may be able to endure it.' God will never *drag* us along the way he has planned for us; but he *will* guide us and support us. We may be surprised to find that we're capable of far more than we had assumed. We don't need the curate's prayer: 'Slowly, without dragging, lead me, Lord.' God will lead us at just the right pace, one which we can cope with, but slightly faster than we should have gone if he'd left us to amble along under our own steam.

Suggested hymns

Father, hear the prayer we offer; I, the Lord of sea and sky; Jesu, lover of my soul; Who would true valour see / He who would valiant be.

The Second Sunday before Lent 12 February
Principal Service **Seven Signs, Seven Claims**
Prov. 8.1, 22–31 Wisdom in creation; Ps. 104.26–37 Creation;
Col. 1.15–20 The head of the Church; John 1.1–14 The Word in
creation

> *'To all who received him, who believed in his name, he gave
> power to become children of God.' John 1.12*

The human race

In the beginning was the Word,
the Word that shared the heavenly throne.
That word was God; till he was heard
the Word and God were quite alone.

God spoke the Word, through whom all things _
began to be; no thing was formed _
apart from him; in him light springs _
to life, and by it we are warmed.

That's the beginning of a new rhyming translation of the beginning
of St John's Gospel. Some people think this 'Prologue', as we call
it, may have been a poem or a piece of poetic prose, whether by St
John or somebody earlier. It opens with the same words as Genesis,
the first book of the Bible: 'In the beginning'. Genesis describes
the origins of the human race – 'Adam' isn't really a proper name,
but it's the Hebrew word for 'humanity'. And that shows you that
Genesis isn't meant to be understood as history – it's more of a
picture of what human beings ought to be. Christians needn't quar-
rel with evolution, as a description of *how* things came to be as they
are now. What the Bible tells us is *why* it happened.

The new humanity

That light was life for humankind;
the beacon-Word shines in the night;
it strives with darkness in the mind,
and darkness cannot swallow light.

He formed the world with his own hand:
it would not recognize his name;

59

his chosen people, in his land,
would not accept him when he came.

St John, by quoting Genesis, lays out his manifesto: what he's going
to describe in his Gospel is nothing less than a new creation. The
new humanity will progress towards what God meant us to be. The
groundwork is already done, when God chose the Jews to be the
first to know him, and spread that knowledge to others, though
not all of them recognized this. So God decided to come to them
in person.

Incarnation

To those who welcomed true light's dawn
who marked his footsteps where he trod,
he gave the power to be born
as sons and daughters of our God.

The Word became a mortal man;
among us dwelt the one above,
God's only Son, such was his plan;
we saw his glory, truth and love.

So Jesus was the word of God, made flesh. The Gospel of John
tells his life-story – only in such a way that you see that it's meant
to be your life-story as well. Jesus *is* the new humanity, he *is* what
you and I are meant to be becoming. St John includes seven signs
and seven claims. Signs is the word John uses instead of miracles,
because they are pointers to who Jesus really was. They were the
wedding at Cana; healing a sick boy at Capernaum; the paralysed
man at the Pool of Bethesda; feeding the 5,000; walking on the
water; healing the man born blind; and the raising of Lazarus. If
these seven signs aren't enough to make you realize that Jesus is the
ideal human being, the Second Adam, he makes these seven claims,
using the Old Testament name of God, 'I AM': 'I am the Bread from
Heaven'; 'I am the Light of the World'; 'I am the Good Shepherd';
'I am the Gate for the Flock'; 'I am the Resurrection and the Life';
'I am the Way, the Truth and the Life'; 'I am the True Vine'. Jesus
is not only the ideal we're aiming for – he's also the way to achieve
it, through his love.

Grace

In this full love he let us share;
he poured upon the human race,
on those who love him, ev'rywhere,
love upon love, and grace on grace.

Genesis began in a garden, the Garden of Eden – John's Gospel ends in the Garden of the Resurrection, when Mary Magdalene saw what the ideal human being was meant to be, and was sent out to tell the world about it. John writes, 'These [words] are written so that you may come to believe that Jesus is the Messiah, the Son of God, and that through believing you may have life in his name.' The Gospel's written for *you*, so that through your faith in Jesus, and like him and with him, you may pass through birth, baptism, childhood, joy, suffering, death and resurrection to eternal life.

All-age worship

How many verses of the hymn above can you learn by heart?
(© Michael Counsell, can be copied under the terms of the CCLI licence (www.ccli.co.uk). Can be sung to 'Tallis's Canon' (Glory to thee, my God, this night).)

Suggested hymns

At the name of Jesus; Sing, my tongue, the glorious battle (tune Grafton); Thou didst leave thy throne and thy kingly crown; Word of God, come down on earth.

The Second Sunday before Lent   12 February
Second Service   **The Blueprint**
Ps. 65 Fecundity of nature; Gen. 2.4b–25 The Garden of Eden; Luke 8.22–35 Demons into pigs

> 'For the man there was not found a helper as his partner. So the Lord God caused a deep sleep to fall upon the man, and he slept; then he took one of his ribs and closed up its place with flesh. And the rib that the Lord God had taken from the man he made into a woman and brought her to the man. Then the man said, "This at last is bone of my bones and flesh of my flesh; this one shall be called Woman, for out of Man this one was taken." Therefore a

man leaves his father and his mother and clings to his wife, and they become one flesh.' Genesis 2.20–24

Paradise

Ah, Paradise! When have you ever said that? Some beautiful scenery? Your own garden? A drink with your friends? With your family after a delicious meal? Most people can point to moments in their own lives – all too rare, alas! – when everything in the garden was lovely. Not perfect, mind you – nothing in this life is ever completely perfect. But there are times when we seem to approach perfection. And in our struggles to live a good life, and to make the world a better place, we do seem to be making gradual progress – two steps forward and one step back, of course. But we can conceive what perfection would be like. Maybe we're gradually moving towards a time when we shall look at everything around us and say, 'Ah, paradise!'

The past

Was there ever a time when everything was perfect? There's no evidence for it, and the whole idea of progress implies that we should struggle towards an as yet unachieved goal. To inspire us in this struggle, we need someone to paint us a picture of what perfection would be like, so that we know in which direction to aim. Not the details, we would want our artist to use broad brushstrokes, undistracted by trivia. Or, because paintings are perishable, perhaps we'd rather have a writer to tell a story which sticks in the memory, a story about an ideal world, which we could try to copy in our own lives. We need a myth, in fact: a myth about paradise.

Genesis

Well, surprise, surprise! We've already got one: the story of paradise in the first book of the Bible, called Genesis. Don't get distracted by trivialities, like whether it's historically true. The important thing is that the story of the Garden of Eden shows us what the ideal world would be like. Then we can work on this imperfect world, trying to make it more like God wants it. The most obvious thing in the story is that human beings are in harmony with God. We can work on that by building a living prayer relationship with our heavenly Father – we can try to spread it around, by telling our friends and neighbours how good God has been to us. Then there's the world of nature. The first humans were told to till the garden, and look after the plants and animals. We need to put right a lot of mistakes that we've made in our care for the environment before we get anywhere near the earthly paradise.

Relationships

Our relationship with God, and our relationship with nature – what about our relationships with each other? In an ideal world, there would be no quarrelling and fighting, no oppression and inequality. John Ball, an English priest, was one of the leaders of the Peasants' Revolt in 1381. They demonstrated against society's divisions, with gentlemen and ladies getting richer and the peasants starving in poverty. John Ball was executed for his part in what would seem today to be a perfectly proper protest. On the eve of the revolt he preached a sermon, including this couplet:

> When Adam delved and Eve span,
> who was then the gentleman?

In a perfect world, there would be no class system, and all would share and share alike. That's how we're meant to be; so why aren't we doing more to bring it about?

Men and women

In the Garden of Eden story, before the serpent of sin intruded, the man and woman lived together in love and innocence. There's an anonymous quotation about that ideal relationship which goes like this:

> The woman came out of a man's rib.
> Not from his feet to be walked on;
> not from his head to be superior;
> but from the side to be equal;
> under the arm to be protected;
> and next to the heart to be loved.

So a perfect world would show harmony and respect in our relationship with God, with nature, and with each other. That's the ideal we're supposed to aim towards and work for. Then we could look around us and say, 'Ah paradise! Everything in the Garden's lovely!'

Suggested hymns

All creatures of our God and King; All things bright and beautiful; Morning has broken; Thou, whose almighty word.

Sunday next before Lent   19 February
Principal Service   **Glory**

2 Kings 2.1–12 Elisha sees Elijah's ascension in glory; Ps. 50.1–6 God speaks from heaven; 2 Cor. 4.3–6 The glory of God in the face of Jesus; Mark 9.2–9 The transfiguration

> *'For it is the God who said, "Let light shine out of darkness," who has shone in our hearts to give the light of the knowledge of the glory of God in the face of Jesus Christ.' 2 Corinthians 4.6*

Alice in Wonderland

St Paul wrote that we can see the glory of God in the face of Jesus Christ. What do we mean when we talk about 'glory'? Here's a conversation from *Alice in Wonderland:*

> 'There's glory for you.'
> 'I don't know what you mean by "glory",' Alice said.
> 'I meant, "There's a nice knock-down argument for you!"'
> 'But "glory" doesn't mean "a nice knock-down argument",' Alice objected.
> 'When I use a word,' Humpty-Dumpty said in a rather scornful tone, 'it means just what I choose it to mean – neither more nor less.'

I'm afraid many people use the words in the Bible in a similarly cavalier way, and it won't do. We must be precise in our use of language if we're to understand what the authors meant, and to understand anything at all about God.

Shekinah

So what does 'the Glory of God' actually mean? Glory is worthiness to be praised, honoured and respected. Glory is not the same as celebrity or fame. God's glory is seen in the wonders of nature. The glory of God was symbolized in the Old Testament as a brightly shining

64

cloud, the *shekinah,* guiding the Israelites on their 40-year tramp across the wilderness; a cloud hanging over the Tent of Meeting, and later over the Temple, to show them that God was there. God's love is like a high-voltage electric current – enormously powerful in doing good, but to be treated with respect and not mishandled.

God's glory in Christ

At the transfiguration, the disciples saw Jesus received into a cloud. This was a symbol of God's glory, present with them. God spoke from the cloud, as he did at Mount Sinai; God the Father said of Jesus, 'this is my Son'. In John 1.14 we read that 'The Word became flesh and lived among us, and *we have seen his glory*, the glory as of a father's only son, full of grace and truth.' The supreme example of God's love is when the Son of God willingly sacrifices himself for you and me: before his crucifixion Jesus said, 'Now the Son of Man has been glorified, and God has been glorified in him.'

Worship

The angels at Bethlehem sang, 'Glory be to God on high'. Once we realize how glorious God is, how beautiful God's creation and how deep God's love, then we can't help but praise him. We give glory to God, not because God's vain and likes to be flattered, but because it puts us in the right relationship with our heavenly Father. The purpose of worship is to remind us how completely dependent we are on God's feeding and God's forgiveness.

C. S. Lewis

St Paul wrote to the troublesome Christians in Corinth, 'And all of us, with unveiled faces, seeing the glory of the Lord as though reflected in a mirror, are being transformed into the same image from one degree of glory to another; for this comes from the Lord, the Spirit.' So human beings, too, are glorious. C. S. Lewis preached a sermon in St Mary's, Oxford, in 1942, to which he gave the title, 'The Weight of Glory'. He said:

> There are no ordinary people. You have never talked to a mere mortal. Nations, cultures, arts, civilizations – these are mortal, and their life is to ours as the life of a gnat. But it is immortals whom we joke with, work with, marry, snub, and exploit –

immortal horrors or everlasting splendours. Next to the Blessed Sacrament itself, your neighbour is the holiest object presented to your senses . . . When humans should have become as perfect in voluntary obedience as the inanimate creation is in its lifeless obedience, then they will put on its glory, or rather that greater glory of which Nature is only the first sketch.

So we get the idea that you can see glory in the face of your neighbours too, or at least the potential for glory. Just as we should worship and love God, so we should respect and love our neighbours, too. Because St Paul also tells us that we shall all enter into glory when we die: 'through [Jesus] we have obtained access to this grace in which we stand; and we boast in our hope of sharing the glory of God'. That's what 'glory' means.

All-age worship

Face painting. Write on the foreheads, 'I'm glorious'.

Suggested hymns

Father, we love you, we worship and adore you; Glory be to Jesus; Glory in the highest to the God of heaven!; God of grace and God of glory.

Sunday next before Lent   19 February
Second Service   Problems of Conscience
Ps. 2 He who sits in heaven [99 He spoke in the cloud]; 1 Kings 19.1–16 God speaks through silence; 2 Peter 1.16–21 We heard this voice; Gospel at Holy Communion: Mark 9.[2–8] 9–13 John the Baptist and Elijah

> 'First of all you must understand this, that no prophecy of scripture is a matter of one's own interpretation, because no prophecy ever came by human will, but men and women moved by the Holy Spirit spoke from God.' 2 Peter 1.19

The Nonjurors

James, the son of King Charles I of England, was received into the Roman Catholic Church in 1670. In 1685 he was crowned as James

VII of Scotland and James II of England and Ireland. Previously Catholics had been excluded from government jobs; King James changed that law by a 'Declaration of Liberty of Conscience'. He ordered the clergy to read this out in every church. William Sancroft, the Archbishop of Canterbury, saw this as an attempt to destroy the Church of England. He and seven other bishops refused to carry out the order and were imprisoned for a while in the Tower of London. When Prince William of Orange invaded, King James fled to France, and the Prince was crowned as King William III. Yet eight bishops, some four hundred priests and a few lay people refused to swear the oath of allegiance to William, arguing that they had already sworn an oath to James which they couldn't break, however much they disagreed with him. These 'Nonjurors', as they were called, meaning 'non-swearers', were sacked from their jobs, by act of parliament. They continued to worship privately, and illegally, proclaiming that oaths cannot be broken, and the church has its own laws overriding those of the state. They produced some fine devotional writers, but by the end of the eighteenth century they gradually died out as a separate movement.

Problems of conscience

What makes the story of the Nonjurors especially painful is that everybody, on both sides, wrestled with their consciences, and did what they sincerely believed to be right. Yet it brought them into conflict with each other, and with the law of the land. There are many problems of conscience like this; maybe there have been times in your own life when you were baffled to know what was the right thing to do. The Second Letter of Peter recommends consulting the Bible: 'We have the prophetic message . . . no prophecy of scripture is a matter of one's own interpretation, because . . . men and women moved by the Holy Spirit spoke from God.' So you read the Scripture, think about it, draw up a list of pros and cons, and pray. Then you make up your mind as best you can as to the right thing to do; and do it. If you suffer for doing what you believe to be right, that's part of the cost of Christian discipleship.

Thomas Ken

One of the most attractive of the Nonjurors was Bishop Ken. Thomas Ken taught at Winchester College, where he wrote a manual of devotion to show the boys how to pray, including the hymns

'Awake, my soul, and with the sun' and 'Glory to thee my God this night'. King Charles II made him Bishop of Bath and Wells, even though he refused to receive the royal mistress Nell Gwyn in his house. Although he was also critical of James II, he regarded him as the true king, and refused to take the oath of allegiance to William and Mary. He was deposed, and lived in retirement, mostly at Longleat House, refusing to return to his bishopric when it was offered back to him. In his will he wrote:

> I die in the Holy Catholic and Apostolic Faith, professed by the whole Church, before the disunion of East and West: more particularly I die in the communion of the Church of England, as it stands distinguished from all Papal and Puritan Innovations.

We might not feel comfortable with that wording today, but it reveals a man who had wrestled with his conscience.

Blessing

I'm going to end with Thomas Ken's Blessing:

> Blessing and honour, thanksgiving and praise
> more than we can utter, more than we can conceive,
> be unto thee, O most adorable Trinity, Father, Son, and Holy
>   Ghost,
> by all angels, all men, all creatures,
> for ever and ever. Amen and Amen.
> To God the Father, who first loved us,
> and made us accepted in the Beloved:
> To God the Son, who loved us,
> and washed us from our sins in His own blood:
> To God the Holy Ghost,
> who sheds the love of God abroad in our hearts,
> be all love and all glory for time and eternity. Amen.

Suggested hymns

Awake, my soul, and with the sun; Glory to thee, my God, this night; Glory to thee, who safe hast kept; Her virgin eyes saw God incarnate born.

LENT

In the first few centuries of the Christian Church, new converts were normally baptized at Easter time. In preparation for this they passed through a season of solemn preparation and instruction. The whole Christian community wanted to join with them in this, and so the forty days before Easter became what is called in English 'Lent'. Its name comes from an Old English word for 'Spring'; the forty days commemorate the forty days Jesus spent fasting in the wilderness, tempted by the Devil. It is calculated either by omitting the Sundays, when the Lenten discipline is relaxed, or by finishing on Palm Sunday. 'Giving up things for Lent' is a training in self-discipline, but it is not a bargain seeking a reward, and self-righteousness must be avoided. So our Lent discipline should include something positive: spending time in prayer and Bible reading, joining study groups and extra services, or doing something to help other people. Shrove Tuesday used to be a time to eat up all the rich food before fasting (pancake day or carnival) and have your sins forgiven, or be 'shriven'. Remembering that the Bible tells us to 'repent in dust and ashes', the first day of Lent is called Ash Wednesday and in some churches ashes are put on the foreheads of the worshippers in the shape of a cross. The altar frontal and vestments are purple, or unbleached linen to represent sackcloth. It is an opportunity to preach a series of sermons on the Ten Commandments, the Sermon on the Mount, or how we live as Christians.

Ash Wednesday   22 February
The Fellowship of Forgiven Felons

Joel 2.1–2, 12–17 Rend your hearts, or Isa. 58.1–12 Care for the needy; Ps. 51.1–18 Cleanse me from my sin; 2 Cor. 5.20b—6.10 Suffering of an apostle; Matt. 6.1–6, 16–21 Secret fasting, or John 8.1–11 Adultery and forgiveness

> 'We are treated as impostors, and yet are true . . . as dying, and see – we are alive.' 2 Corinthians 6.8–9

Welcome to the club

Welcome to the club! No, I mean it – each one of you here is a member of a very important club, and you should be proud of it. I wouldn't call it an exclusive club, though, because anyone can join it. All you have to do is pass the membership test. It's a very simple test, really. It must be, because we've all passed it! It's amazing that so many draw back, when they realize what it involves. You have to do something that nobody really likes doing, and that's to say sorry. Watch the news, and you'll see the amazing lengths people go to, to avoid saying that one little word – they'll wriggle and wriggle, to get out of having to say those two dreaded syllables, 'Sor-ree!'

Taking responsibility

Yet saying sorry will solve all our problems! But before we can say it, we have to do something even more difficult. That is, first you have to accept responsibility for everything you do. 'Aargh! You can't expect me to do that,' we wail. 'It wasn't my fault, officer, honestly. I didn't break it. It was an accident. The thing just came apart in my hands. Anyway, I wasn't even there at the time. It must have been somebody else!' Anything to avoid saying, 'Yes, I did it, I'm sorry.' So we blame everything we do on our upbringing or our circumstances. Wriggle, wriggle! It just won't wash, you know. You know, yourself, that whatever the extenuating circumstances, at some point you had a choice, you could have said no, and you took the wrong fork. But admitting it, and taking responsibility for what we've done – that's hard!

Sins

The Bible has a very short word for the unspoken things we know in our heart of hearts to be wrong. That word is 'sin'. 'Ah, now the preacher's calling me a sinner,' you think. 'Sinners are people who hurt other folk. I'm not like them at all.' But the Bible says that the sin is disobeying God, and God told us to love him with all our hearts, and to love our neighbours as much as we love ourselves. So everything that is unloving – even a little bit unkind – is a sin. We're all sinners. So admit it, and say sorry, to the people you've hurt, to yourself, and to God – it's as simple as that, yet everyone finds it so difficult.

Forgiveness

Next, we have to believe that God has forgiven us. God loves us, and made us to be his friends. If anything gets in the way of that friendship, God will get rid of it, just as soon as we allow him to. Then God promotes us to the highest dignity in the world: the splendour of sinners who have been forgiven. We've passed the test, we've been admitted to the club, and we should be proud of it. 'What club's that?' you ask. I was going to call it the Fellowship of Forgiven Sinners, but that doesn't alliterate. Everyone remembers a phrase where each word begins with the same letter. So I'm changing the name of our club to 'The Fellowship of Forgiven Felons'. Remember those unkind words you said this morning? The law doesn't define them as a felony, but to God, they're quite as serious as bodily harm or theft.

The Church

The other name for the Fellowship of Forgiven Felons is 'The Christian Church'. But that sounds a bit pompous. The great thing about our new name for it is that everybody is equal in the Church. Nobody boasts, 'I'm more important, 'cause God's forgiven *me* more sins than he's forgiven *you*, ya-dah-dee-ah-dah!' So we treat everybody in the Church with equal respect, and nobody can claim to be more important than others. In our club, people have different opinions, and sometimes heated disagreements, or even rows. But we can't expel anyone because we don't like them, nor can we split off into a holier-than-thou huddle. We have all passed the test by saying sorry, and our differences are far less important than what binds us together. There's no fundamental difference between one sort of forgiven felon and another, and we are all in the same club, like it or not.

Lent

Lent's a time for examining ourselves, taking responsibility for what we have done, saying sorry to God, and accepting his forgiveness. Thus we reaffirm our membership in the Church, the Fellowship of Forgiven Felons. If anyone's never done that, now's your chance – join the club!

Suggested hymns

O for a closer walk with God; O Jesus, I have promised; Thy hand, O God, has guided; To God be the glory.

First Sunday of Lent 26 February
Principal Service **Saved through Water**
Gen. 9.8–17 Noah's covenant; Ps. 25.1–9 God's grace and forgiveness; 1 Peter 3.18–22 Jesus speaks to Noah's generation; Mark 1.9–15 The baptism and temptation of Jesus

> *'Christ died for sins . . . in order to lead you to God . . . In his spiritual existence he went and preached to the . . . spirits of those who had not obeyed God, when he waited patiently during the days that Noah was building his boat. The few people in the boat – eight in all – were saved by the water.' 1 Peter 3.18–20 (Good News Bible)*

The Black Sea

The Black Sea fills the valley between Turkey and Russia, with several other nations on the shoreline. It's joined to the Mediterranean by the Bosphorus waterway. Recent surveys of the seabed showed what looks like the submerged coastline of a much smaller lake, with freshwater shellfish in the mud, and a channel suggesting a rapid flood of water out of, not into, the Bosphorus. Scientists have even found what might be the submerged foundations of houses. So a theory has been put forward, though by no means universally accepted, that when the glaciers melted at the end of the ice-age some 8,000 years ago, the waters in the Med. rose by about five feet. Then they broke down the land barrier where the Bosphorus is now, and sent a mass of salt water rushing into what had been a freshwater lake, drowning all the settlements on its shores and for many miles inland. If that really happened, it would be enough to preserve the folk memory of a great flood covering all the earth, which survives not only in the Hebrew story of Noah, but in the folklore of Mesopotamia, Greece, Rome and Persia. Particularly if a large population of *Homo sapiens*, having moved out of Africa and developed from hunter-gatherers into agriculturalists, had settled round the lake. The good news is that some may have survived, and fled into the Middle East and Europe, forming the origins of our modern civilization.

Noah

I don't know whether that theory's true, any more than I know whether the story of the flood in Genesis contains a core of literal truth. Either way, it reminds us that great good can come out of an appalling disaster. So St Peter, writing about baptism, was reminded of Noah. Jesus suffered on the cross, he said, and then went to the world of the dead, where he gave the disobedient people, who had been drowned in the flood, a second chance to be saved, just as Noah was saved by passing through the water. So we, too, can be saved, by passing through the waters of baptism. It's a complicated argument, but a clever analogy for those who know the Old Testament. And good came out of evil, with Noah given the opportunity to populate and cultivate new lands – which is exactly what those who survived the Black Sea flood may have done – and the suffering of Jesus resulting in our salvation through the waters of baptism – the baptism of Jesus in the River Jordan, and our own baptism in church.

Good out of evil

God can always bring good out of evil, if only we co-operate with him. There are many evil things happening today, from climate change to unemployment to famines and war. At the time, we're bowed down with the awfulness of them. But if we could take the long view, might we not see that terrible as these things are, God may be able to teach us something through the experience? Maybe he has plans for good things in the future, which he can only achieve if he has the co-operation of men and women who have been through the furnace of suffering. God doesn't want us to feel pain and grief, but if suffering comes, let's try and see what good he may be able to bring out of it.

Cross and resurrection

So, as we begin the season of Lent, leading up the contemplation of the agony of Jesus on the cross, remember that God sympathizes with our suffering, because he has been there himself, and he shares our burden with us. Then he rose again, and the resurrection couldn't have happened without the crucifixion. This was the only way he could bring us through death to eternal life. God will bear us up through the valley of the shadow, and bring us to the heavenly sunshine. We too can look at the bad things that happen to us, and instead of grumbling, try to find ways of bringing good out of evil.

All-age worship

Could someone bring a puppy and show how they wash it? The pet doesn't like it at the time, but it's happy when it's over. What do you dislike doing, though you know it's good for you?

Suggested hymns

As pants the hart; Forty days and forty nights; God moves in a mysterious way; O love that wilt not let me go.

First Sunday of Lent   26 February
Second Service   **Adam Lay Ybounden**
Ps. 119.17–32 The wonders of God's law; Gen. 2.15–17; 3.1–7 Adam's sin; Rom. 5.12–19 Adam and Christ, *or* Luke 13.31–35 Jesus grieves for Jerusalem

> 'The Lord God commanded the man, "You may freely eat of every tree of the garden; but of the tree of the knowledge of good and evil you shall not eat, for in the day that you eat of it you shall die."' Genesis 2.16–17

Carol

Here's an anonymous fifteenth-century poem. You'll have to listen very carefully, because it's in medieval English. Of course, if you've ever sung it to the tune by Peter Warlock you'll already know what it means. It goes like this:

> Adam lay ybounden,
> Bounden in a bond;
> Four thousand winter
> Thought he not too long.

And all was for an apple,
An apple that he took.
As clerkes finden –
Written in their book.

Ne had the apple taken been,
The apple taken been,
Ne had never our ladie
Abeen heav'ne queen.

Blessed be the time
That apple taken was,
Therefore we moun singen
Deo gracias!

Meaning

What does it mean? Adam is imagined bound by the chain of his
sins, like Marley's Ghost with a chain of money-boxes wrapped
round him in Charles Dickens's *A Christmas Carol*. Adam can't
enter heaven, as a result of his disobedience. When the poem was
written, they thought that the creation of the earth happened all
at once 4,000 years ago – now we know better. Adam's sin was
to take the fruit that God had told him not to eat. In English we
traditionally call it an apple, but the Bible simply calls it the fruit
of the tree of the knowledge of good and evil. In other words, the
newly evolved human race chose to seize power by disobeying God.
In the Middle Ages, a clerk was anyone who could read and write,
and since most of those were priests or monks, they were called
'Clerks in Holy Orders', and their book was the Bible.

Felix culpa

Next comes the controversial bit. 'Ne had the apple taken been'
means 'If Adam hadn't taken the forbidden fruit' . . . then the world
would have been a much worse place. Because if *Homo sapiens*
hadn't chosen to disobey God, Jesus would never have come to
earth to save us from the results of our sins. It's a paradox – God
would obviously have preferred us to be obedient. But when the
Son of God came to earth, he brought us many blessings. At the
traditional Easter Vigil the priest sings 'O *happy fault*, that merited
so great a Redeemer.' The logic's a bit doubtful, but there's no

75

doubt that God can bring good out of evil. Yet the poem would have us believe that the chief benefit that resulted was that Mary should be Queen of Heaven. Even the most devout catholic today would say that's coming it a bit strong; but honouring the Virgin was very important in the Middle Ages, and perhaps we should be tolerant of those who express the faith through different cultures in different periods.

Deo gracias

'Therefore we moun singen *Deo gracias!*' Which means, 'So we must sing, Thank you, God.' The old words are certainly very beautiful. But the word 'Adam' in Hebrew means 'everyman', the whole human race. This isn't a history of what happened 4,000 years ago. It's a parable of what's going on today, in your heart and mine. God's given us a choice: obey God or disobey. But we're also told that some actions have disastrous consequences, for ourselves or for others whom we might harm. Of course, it would be much better if we always obeyed God's commandments. But even if we don't – and nobody except Jesus ever has, completely – God can still bring good out of evil. God can teach us the value of civilization, so that people are restrained from harmful actions. And by leading us to repent of our sins, and accept God's forgiveness, Jesus can bring us to a much deeper gratitude and love for God than we should ever otherwise have felt. Lent is a time for penitence, for examining our good and bad actions, saying sorry, and learning never to do again those things that hurt the loving heart of God so deeply. But it can also be a time to thank God for forgiving us. Even out of our sins, terrible as they are, God can bring good, by teaching us to love our heavenly Father from the depths of our hearts. 'Therefore we moun singen *Deo gracias!*' 'So we must sing, Thank you, God.' *Amen!*

Suggested hymns

Forty days and forty nights; O for a closer walk with God; O love that wilt not let me go; The kingdom of God is justice and joy.

Second Sunday of Lent   4 March
Principal Service
To Gain the World but Lose One's Life
Gen. 17.1–7, 15–16 The covenant with Abraham; Ps. 22.23–31
Witnessing grace to all; Rom. 4.13–25 The covenant with
Abraham was through faith; Mark 8.31–38 Take up your cross

> '[Jesus said,] "What will it profit them to gain the whole world and forfeit their life?"' *Mark 8.36*

Self-sacrifice

Jesus warned his disciples that he was going to be killed. When Peter tried to stop him, Jesus insisted that his act of self-sacrifice was necessary, for all their sakes. Indeed, self-sacrifice is the basic principle of life for all his followers. We have to each take up our own cross, our willingly accepted suffering. We must voluntarily surrender our right to have our own way, living in comfort, ignoring the needs of others. We must exchange *our* plans and *our* self-will, for a life lived for the benefit of other people. We must each be 'a man [or woman] for others'. 'Those who want to save their life will lose it,' Jesus continued, 'and those who lose their life for my sake, and for the sake of the gospel, will save it.' For the martyrs this literally meant *dying*; but Jesus calls every Christian to *sacrificial living*.

Soul and life

'What good will it do anybody', asked Jesus, 'to gain the whole world at the cost of their life?' In another place, Jesus told a story about a rich fool, who heaped up riches, but they were no use to him because he died that very night, and left others to enjoy the money he'd worked so hard to accumulate. Perhaps you're puzzled because in one passage Jesus says that surrendering your life is a good thing to do, and in the other he warns that for some people dying is an unmitigated disaster. It may help to know that the word for 'life' in the original language of the New Testament was *'psyche'*, which the Authorized Version translates as 'soul'. What people call 'selling your soul to the Devil' does you no good in the long run, because what the Devil can give you doesn't last. But if we keep the spiritual side of us intact, the death of the body is almost insignificant, in the perspective of eternity.

77

Materialism

This warning is particularly relevant in a materialistic age. Many people only think in terms of making money, and finding material comfort – spiritual things like love, truth, beauty and self-sacrifice have gone out of the window. People still keep Sundays for religion, but the religion of so many people seems to be shopping, and they shop till they drop. The advertisers persuade people that, to keep up with the Joneses, they must buy things they don't need, and don't particularly want, out of money they haven't got. Rich fools! Those who only think of material things in fact lose out on everything that makes life worthwhile. Some atheist scientists would have you believe that the material world is all there is. How then do they explain the sensation of 'falling in love'? To describe the action of hormones doesn't begin to account for one of life's most enriching experiences. Albert Einstein was wiser. He wrote, 'For the scientist there is only "being", but no wishing, no valuing, no good, no evil; no goal.' By this he didn't mean that good and evil don't exist – only that they're spiritual values which science has no means of investigating. Science is incomplete without religion.

Suffering

A materialist sees no value in self-sacrifice – they can't explain altruism. Yet sacrifice is a basic principle of creation. Laurens van der Post described a mother ostrich deliberately pretending to be wounded and running in a crazy way towards a car full of humans, to distract them from attacking her chicks, which were being shooed away to safety by her mate. Every living thing has to sacrifice its life, eventually. The theory of evolution teaches that many random variations occur down the generations, and most of them are harmful, making the mutant unfit to survive. Millions have to die, therefore, to enable the species to progress to a higher level. That puts death into perspective. In fact, if we didn't have any death, the world would be overcrowded and there would be no room for new individuals to be born. Pain is essential, to warn us not to put our finger in the fire. So Jesus's attitude to suffering was the right one: we need to suffer and to die that others may live.

Lent

What are you willing to sacrifice for Jesus this Lent? Are you ready to live simply, that others may simply live? Sacrificial living is hard; but if we follow in the steps of Jesus to the cross, he will lead us on into the resurrection.

All-age worship

Make a diagram of a typical food-chain. How many animals and plants have to die that we may live?

Suggested hymns

New every morning is the love; Judge eternal, throned in splendour; Take up your cross, the Saviour said; Will you come and follow me?

Second Sunday of Lent   4 March
Second Service   **Monotheism**
Ps. 135 Their land a heritage for Israel; Gen. 12.1–9 Abram's call; Heb. 11.1–3, 8–16 Abraham's faith; *Gospel at Holy Communion*: John 8.51–59 Abraham rejoiced

> '[Abraham] moved on to the hill country on the east of Bethel, and pitched his tent, with Bethel on the west and Ai on the east; and there he built an altar to the LORD and invoked the name of the LORD.' Genesis 12.8

Abraham

Was Abraham a real person? Coming between the legendary Adam and Eve, and the mostly historical Moses, we can't be sure. He's typical of the period when the desert nomads began to settle into farming. Yet so many convincing stories are told about him that it's hard to believe there wasn't somebody like that once. The striking thing about Abraham was that, for the first time in the history of the human race, he believed in only one God.

Polytheism

It's easy not to notice what a radical innovation this was. It seems that early *Homo sapiens* believed from the start in the numinous. They were in awe of invisible powers. Seeing the desert wind, they worshipped the power that drove it. They were amazed at the view from a mountaintop. They depended on the moon to control the tides, and the sun to make the plants grow. Yet for nearly 200,000 years, they believed these were all different gods. Each plot of land had its own god, who had no power outside its national boundaries. So the forces of the universe were not under any single control. But with many gods, there were big problems. Each god had its own area of influence – you worshipped the god of war on Mondays but the god of love on Tuesdays, which left you free to decide which one suited you best. Belief in many gods is called polytheism, and the problem with it is that you can make gods in your own image. There's no single moral power to control your actions; you can bribe the 'godlets' with sacrifices to let you do exactly what you want. In fact you can ignore the idols when you leave their temples, because there's no reason to believe that they can see round corners. If you went into exile, you left your god behind. The only way to pray to a god outside his territory was to carry a sack filled with soil and kneel, literally, on the god's home ground. Polytheism doesn't work, because each god has so little power.

Monotheism

Yet Abraham had only one God, whom he worshipped when he lived in Iraq, and still worshipped when he arrived in the land of Israel. This one all-powerful God gave commands, and Abraham had to obey them wherever he was living; there's no hiding from an invisible God whose territory covers the whole earth. For the first time, religion developed a moral authority to rebuke behaviour that was wrong, and suggest unpopular actions which were beneficial. This was a great stride forward. Monotheism, meaning belief in one God, arose among Jews, and was the single most significant development in human thinking ever. For without a belief that the whole world is under a single authority, there could be no science. Without monotheism, there could be no morality, because there would be no outside reference point for deciding what was right and wrong.

The Abrahamic faiths

The Israelites kept returning to their idols, and it was a long struggle before monotheism was generally accepted. God intended them to spread what they had learnt of God to other nations, but they kept monotheism to themselves. It was left to the Christians to make monotheism a worldwide faith. In this way, Christianity can be thought of as an offshoot of the faith of Abraham. Without the Jewish belief in one God, we couldn't understood the teaching of Jesus that God is love. Jews allege that we believe in three gods, not one. The doctrine of the Trinity is our way of asserting that the God who is supreme, the God who has revealed in the life of Jesus, and the God in our hearts are really the same God. Christians argued a long time before getting this right, and Muhammad was born at a time when the Christians in Arabia misunderstood the doctrine of the Trinity – he, too, thought that Christians believe in three gods, a prejudice that still survives among the fiercely monotheistic Muslims.

Working together

It's a disaster that the three faiths descended from the faith of Abraham regard each other as rivals, not cousins. Instead of fighting, we should rejoice in what we have in common, learn from each other, and together teach the world the value of monotheism. Many problems could be solved if people would agree to believe in one supreme power, who loves us all, and expects us to behave to each other in a loving way.

Suggested hymns

How shall I sing that majesty?; Immortal, invisible, God only wise; Lord of all being, throned afar; The God of Abraham praise.

Third Sunday of Lent   11 March
Principal Service   **The Heavens are Telling**
Ex. 20.1–17 The first four commandments; Ps. 19 The heavens declare God's greatness; 1 Cor. 1.18–25 The cross is greater than human wisdom; John 2.13–22 Cleansing the Temple

'The heavens are telling the glory of God.' Psalm 19.1

Josef Haydn

In 1796 Josef Haydn started writing an oratorio loosely based on Milton's *Paradise Lost*. 'Loosely' is the operative word: Milton's elegant poetry was paraphrased by an anonymous English poet; Baron van Swieten translated this into German; and Haydn composed the music. Lastly, the Baron then translated the German back into English! The oratorio is called *The Creation*, and the best-known chorus begins with the words, 'The heavens are telling the glory of God', quoting Psalm 19. Though one conductor complained the choir was singing so loud that he renamed it, 'The tenors are yelling'! But the next line's pure gibberish: 'The wonder of his work displays the firmament' really should be 'The firmament displays the wonder of his work', but that wouldn't fit Haydn's music! Fortunately most listeners work out that this means the same as the first line: the beauty of the sky convinces us that God made it.

Is it true?

Is this really true? The beauty of a scarlet sunset, or the view of millions of distant stars through a telescope, arouses in many people a sense of awe and wonder. Religious people will respond, 'Wow! What a wonderful being our God must be, to create a world so vast and so appealing!' Poets down the ages, and indeed many scientists also, have echoed these words. I feel sorry for the atheist who retorts, 'Nonsense! It's all the result of random accidents. "Beauty is in the eye of the beholder" – it's *you* who create the glory of the heavens, in your brain, not some imaginary deity.' I pity materialists who think that beauty is purely imaginary; they seem to miss most of life's enjoyable experiences. But how do we answer this argument?

Multiverse or God?

Some scientists try to explain the origin of our universe by suggesting a 'multiverse' – a large number of universes alongside each other. One universe collided with another, causing the Big Bang. But this only takes the question further back – you still have to explain where all the earlier universes came from. In other words, it's even more improbable than belief in God. Many Christians, and top scientists also, believe that God made the universe: God was the cause of the Big Bang; then matter from the Big Bang condensed into galaxies, stars and planets. But why that should happen isn't a question that science, as such, can examine. There's no way of proving that God exists, and no way of proving that there is no God. Yet so many coincidences have to happen to make the world as it is, that it stretches our credibility to the limit to suggest that they were all accidental. A glimpse of the night sky shows that it's absurd to say that it all happened by accident. Believing that God caused it is much more straightforward than being an atheist. 'The heavens are telling the glory of God.'

Cause

But there's another aspect of this debate which is hardly ever discussed – what do we actually mean by cause and effect? Yes, it's obvious in events which you can repeat in the laboratory: the same effect is always brought about by the same cause. But time and space go together – where there's no space, there's no time, either. If space began with the Big Bang, that must have been the beginning of time, also. Now a cause always happens at a point in time before its effect is felt. So the Big Bang can't have had a cause in time; yet it's too much to believe that it was an accident. It must have had a cause outside time, in eternity: in other words, the universe must have had a cause, and nothing could have caused it except an eternal God. But if God made time, he knows what's going to happen in the future. So God knew from the very beginning that you would be here today. From God's point of view, to say that you chose to come, or that it happened by accident, or that God caused it, are only three ways of saying the same thing.

Complicated

Is this a bit complicated for you? Don't worry! All you need to remember is that it's not as simple being an atheist as some people make out! It's perfectly reasonable to look at the night sky and sing out, 'The heavens are telling the glory of God!'

All-age worship

Look at some pictures of distant stars and galaxies. Make up a prayer thanking God for making them (see http://hubblesite. org/gallery/).

Suggested hymns

Jesus is Lord! Creation's voice proclaims it; Lord of all being, throned afar; The heavens declare thy glory, Lord; The spacious firmament on high.

Third Sunday of Lent   11 March
Second Service   **No Testing**
Ps. 11 In the Lord I take refuge, 12 Help, Lord; Ex. 5.1—6.1
Bricks without straw; Phil. 3.4b–14 Pressing on for the prize *or*
Matt. 10.16–22 Coming persecutions

> '[Jesus said,] "They will hand you over to councils and flog you in their synagogues; and you will be dragged before governors and kings because of me, as a testimony to them and the Gentiles."'
> Matthew 10.17–18

Job descriptions

Before filling in the application form for a position in industry, you should always ask for the job description. What are you likely to be asked to do? Would you find the job interesting and satisfying? You'd be a fool to go into it without asking those questions. So what's the job description for being a Christian? Somebody once joked, 'The working conditions are lousy, but the retirement benefits are out of this world!' What did Jesus say? Jesus told his 12 key followers that he was sending them out like sheep among wolves. 'They will hand you over to councils,' he said, 'and flog you in their synagogues; and you will be dragged before governors and kings because of me, as a testimony to them and the Gentiles.' At that stage of their careers, the apostles can't have been very interested in what sort of an impression they made on foreigners. But Jesus left them in no doubt that the job description of a Christian involves suffering. Would you have applied for the job if you'd known that?

Suffering

You and I are unlikely to be flogged in synagogues, thank God. Yet Jesus foretold that long before the rise of Christian anti-Semitism, his disciples would suffer persecution from the Jewish authorities. Today, in India and elsewhere, Christians are attacked by members of other faiths, many losing their homes, and some even losing their lives under persecution. In this country, the worst we're likely to endure is mockery by our atheist neighbours. But we share with the whole human race the likelihood of suffering through disease, road accidents or financial loss. It's natural to grumble when pain and death come to us, or to those whom we love. But are we right to grumble, when Jesus told us quite clearly that suffering is to be our lot in this life? It's there in the job description.

God with us

Sometimes the burden of pain and grief seems too heavy for us to bear alone. We all have difficulties in our lives which test our faith and our endurance to the limit. But Jesus showed us that God knows what it is to suffer. God is beside us in our suffering, and shares the load, suffering with us. God won't allow us to bear a greater load of suffering than we're capable of. The Bible promises that, however great our burden, God will always give us enough strength to carry it without breaking down. St Paul wrote to the Christians in Corinth in these words:

> No testing has overtaken you that is not common to everyone. God is faithful, and he will not let you be tested beyond your strength, but with the testing he will also provide the way out so that you may be able to endure it.

The way out

The times when we suffer are testing times: our patience is tested to the limit. Job's wife advised him to 'curse God and die', and we're often tempted to do the same. God will, however, temper the wind to the shorn lamb; St Paul said that God won't let us be stretched beyond the breaking point, and will provide us with a 'way out'. Now that's good news. We urgently need to know where this 'way out' is situated. Well, God hasn't promised to end your suffering. As Mother Julian of Norwich put it, God 'said not: Thou shalt not be tempested, thou shalt not be travailed, thou shalt not be afflicted; but he said: Thou shalt not be overcome'. In other words, the way out of the problem of suffering is not through escapism, but by the grace of God, giving us the strength to endure.

Grace

Grace is such a lovely word. It means God's strength, graciously given to enable us to keep going, something we couldn't do on our own. Grace means God's love, which fills us with gratitude and confidence when we remember that God loves us, and flows through us, enabling us to love even our persecutors. Grace is God's forgiveness, so that, even when we slip up, and start to grumble, we know God's arms are open to welcome us back as soon as we turn to him. The job description of the Christian includes persecution, suffering and grief. But it also promises God's grace, empowering us to carry on without flagging until we reach our glorious goal in heaven.

Suggested hymns

Amazing grace; Be thou my guardian and my guide; Fight the good fight; Lord, for the years.

Fourth Sunday of Lent   18 March

(For Mothering Sunday, see the Second Service. If the Principal Service readings have been displaced by Mothering Sunday provisions, they may be used for the Second Service.) (Eve of St Joseph, see page 307.)

Principal Service   **The Goldilocks Enigma**

Num. 21.4–9 The bronze serpent; Ps. 107.1–3, 17–22 Thanks for healing; Eph. 2.1–10 Salvation by grace through faith, not by works; John 3.14–21 As Moses lifted the serpent, so must I be lifted

> '[Jesus said,] "Indeed, God did not send the Son into the world to condemn the world, but in order that the world might be saved through him."' John 3.17

The Goldilocks Enigma

The Goldilocks Enigma is a book by Paul Davies, a distinguished physicist. In the fairytale, Goldilocks found three bowls of porridge, one too hot, one too cold, and one just right. Paul Davies asks the question, why is the earth 'just right' for conscious life to emerge?

86

The primeval gases wouldn't have condensed into stars and planets if certain physical constants, such as the speed of light and the force of gravity, hadn't been 'just right' – otherwise it would have collapsed in again upon itself. Planet earth, if life was to form here, had to be a certain distance from the sun, and contain water, carbon, and an atmosphere of oxygen and nitrogen. A moon had to be formed, perhaps by a cosmic collision, giving rise to tides. Earth's temperature had to be within a narrow range, with the right amount of gravity to prevent the atmosphere escaping – and so on.

Evolution

Cells were formed which can reproduce themselves. They coalesced into complex organisms. Species developed features that enabled them to survive. Finally, one out of the millions of life forms developed consciousness, self-awareness and the power of choice. Each of these things could have happened by random chance. But the probability of just one of these variables being *just right* is so small, that it's billions to one that they should all have happened on one planet. Why was this unlikely combination of circumstances met? As Fred Hoyle said, 'it looks like a fix!' Unless, of course, some eternal being whom we call God either 'programmed' the matter that emerged in such a way that the development of intelligent life was inevitable, or else worked within and through the process of evolution. The simplest explanation is that God was behind the whole process, guiding the coincidences so that life should emerge. Taking the least likely explanation, random chance, in *every* case, is unscientific.

Why?

But why should God go to the trouble? Christians say that God is infinite love, and therefore God wanted people to love who would be able to return his love. So God willed *Homo sapiens* to evolve. Yet if the 4.5 billion years of the earth's existence were regarded as 24 hours, life would appear about 3.30 a.m., but human beings as we know them would first be seen when there were only about three seconds left! What's more, on this timescale, the human race looks likely to destroy itself very soon. Why should God go to so much trouble to make a universe in which sentient life was only present for such a minuscule portion of time? I suggest that *God's purpose in the formation of life on this planet was to have creatures who would learn that God loves them, and who would love God in return!*

God loves the world

The Bible says that God loves the world – not just a minority of religiously minded people. God wants every human being who is born on earth to live with him in eternity. Notice how many times the words 'the world' occur in Scripture:

> For God so loved *the world* that he gave his only Son, so that everyone who believes in him may not perish but may have eternal life.

> Indeed, God did not send the Son into the world to condemn the world, but in order that *the world* might be saved through him.

> [Jesus said,] 'I, when I am lifted up from the earth, will draw *all* people to myself.'

But to do this they have to learn that God loves them, and learn to love God in return. It's our job to tell them.

The answer to Goldilocks

If this is true, it explains the Goldilocks Enigma. If you can grasp it, this is a magnificent vision: that the universe is the school for souls, where we are trained to be ready for eternal life. God put us here so that we can share in his plan of filling heaven with every person who is born on earth, to live with God for all eternity.

All-age worship

Tell the story of Goldilocks and the Three Bears. List ways in which the earth is 'just right' for people to live on.

Suggested hymns

'Christ for the world' we sing; In the cross of Christ I glory; Lift high the cross; They shall come from the east.

A Service for Mothering Sunday

Introduction

Looking at those who sat round him, Jesus said, These are my mother and my brothers. Whoever does the will of God is my brother or sister or mother.

Mark 4.34–35

God our Father and Mother, you have given us this Mid-Lent Sunday as a time of refreshment in our self-discipline. Give us grace to use it as an opportunity to show our love to all mothers, as the servants and apprentices used to when they gathered wayside flowers to take home to their parents. Be with us in this service, and teach each of us to remember with love our own mother; Mary the Mother of Jesus; and your Church as mother of us all, through Jesus Christ our Lord. **Amen.**

Invitation to Confess

God says, When I called, no one answered, when I spoke, they did not listen; but they did what was evil in my sight, and chose what did not please me. For I know their works and their thoughts. So let us come and confess to God.

Isaiah 66.4,18

Confession

As parents are tender towards their children, so God is tender to those who trust: Lord, have mercy.
Lord, have mercy.
God will not always rebuke us, nor will God's displeasure last for ever: Christ, have mercy.
Christ, have mercy.
I have calmed and quieted my soul, my soul is like a child upon its mother's breast: Lord, have mercy.
Lord, have mercy.

Psalm 103.9, 13; Psalm 131.3

Absolution

God says, As a mother comforts her child, so will I myself comfort you. Your sins are forgiven: rest on God as on your mother's breast. **Amen.**

Isaiah 66.13

Collect

God of love, passionate and strong, tender and careful: watch over us and hold us all the days of our life; through Jesus Christ our Lord. **Amen.**

Statement of Faith

We believe in God who loves us
and wants us to love each other.
This is our God.
We believe in Jesus,
who cared about children and held them in his arms.
He wanted a world where everyone
could live together in peace.
This is Jesus Christ.
We believe in the Holy Spirit
who keeps working with us
until everything is good and true.
This is the Holy Spirit.
We can be the Church which reminds people of God
because we love each other.
This we believe.

Prepared by children for the World Council of
Churches Assembly

Passing the Peace

Peace be in your hearts and in your homes.
The peace of the Lord be always with you;
And also with you.
As the family of God, let us greet each other lovingly.

Offering Prayer

God of life, saviour of the poor, receive with this money gratitude for your goodness, penitence for our pride, and dedication to your service in Jesus Christ our Lord. **Amen.**

After Communion

O God, as truly as you are our father, so just as truly you are our mother. We thank you, God our Father, for your strength and goodness. We thank you, God our Mother, for the closeness of your caring. O God, we thank you for the great love you have for each one of us. **Amen.**

Mother Julian of Norwich

Blessing

May the eyes of Jesus look upon you; the lips of Jesus speak to you; the hands of Jesus bless you; the arms of Jesus enfold you; the feet of Jesus come to you; the heart of Jesus pour his love upon you; and the blessing of God almighty, Father, Son and Holy Spirit, be upon you all, evermore. **Amen.**

The Blessing of Flowers

O God, bless these flowers, bless us, and bless our mothers. May the flowers remind us how much our mothers have done for us; may they remind our mothers that we love them; and may they remind us all that God cares for us better than any mother ever could. **Amen.**

Fourth Sunday of Lent   18 March
A Mothering Sunday Talk
Responding to a Mother's Care
(This is the first set of readings for Mothering Sunday in *Common Worship*.)
Ex. 2.1–10 His mother hides Moses; Ps. 34.11–20 Advice to the young to be righteous; 2 Cor. 1.3–7 Helping others because God helps us; Luke 2.33–35 Simeon predicts Mary's suffering

'Blessed be the God and Father of our Lord Jesus Christ, the Father of mercies and the God of all consolation, who consoles us in all our affliction, so that we may be able to console those who are in any affliction with the consolation with which we ourselves are consoled by God.' 2 Corinthians 1.3–4

What are mothers for?

Happy Mothering Sunday! I have a question for you: What are mothers for? What's the purpose of them, why do we need them? You may think the answer's obvious, but it's worthwhile to ask the question, nonetheless. My answer would be something like this: we need mothers because they give birth to us, and feed us. They care for us throughout our childhood, and teach us how to do things. Their most important purpose is to teach us how to love, and how to receive love, a lesson that sets the pattern for the rest of our lives. Fathers, too, teach us how to love and be loved; but women are much better at that than men. Whoops! I'll just duck till the men here today stop throwing things at me! Here's a thought that might be even more controversial: mothers have a special role in teaching their daughters how to be women, and how to love men and be loved by them. Fathers can teach their sons how to be men, how to love women and be loved by them. Is that sexist? Of course in some families that's not possible, and other role-models have to be found. Caring for children can be, and should be, done by both parents; but today we're thinking especially of mothers, and the dads will have to wait till Father's Day for us to say 'thank you' to them.

Jesus and Mary

Jesus knew what mothers are for! Mary gave birth to him, and fed him. She cared for him throughout his childhood, and taught him how to do things. Her most important task was to teach Jesus how to love, and how to receive love, a lesson that set the pattern for the rest of his life. Today, as well as thanking our own mothers for all they do for us, we also thank God for making Jesus's mother Mary an example of motherhood. Jesus has always loved us with a god-like love, but human love was something he had to learn from Mary.

A mother's love

Before Jesus was born, people knew all about the importance of mothers. In the book of Isaiah, God says these words – I'm quoting from the King James Version – 'As one whom his mother comforteth, so will I comfort you; and ye shall be comforted in Jerusalem.' The modern versions of the Bible translate those words, 'As a mother comforts her child.' I'm sure that's accurate, and brings out the motherly side of God. But I like the old words, too, because they emphasize that none of us knows how to love until we have learnt it from our mothers. God also says in Isaiah, 'Can a woman forget her sucking child, that she should not have compassion on the son of her womb? yea, they may forget, yet will I not forget thee.' In other words, even the best of mothers can't be thinking of their children every minute of the day. God loves us like our mothers do, but his loving eyes are watching over us every single second of our lives. There's a hymn based on those words:

> Can a mother's tender care
> cease towards the child she bare?
> Yes, she may forgetful be,
> yet will I remember thee.

A little girl misheard those words, and asked if she could sing the hymn about 'the child she-bear'! Remember, it actually says, 'Can a mother's tender care cease toward the child . . . she . . . bear?' Thank you to all the mothers here, who are very, very seldom forgetful of your children!

All-age worship

Children may help prepare Mothering Sunday cards to distribute. Bunches of flowers may be blessed and the children come forward to collect them, then give them to their mothers, take them home, or place them on a grave.

Suggested hymns

God is our strength and refuge; Hark, my soul, it is the Lord; Jesus, good above all other; Lord of the home, your only Son.

Fifth Sunday of Lent   25 March

(Eve of The Annunciation, see page 309.)

Principal Service   **Janani Luwum**

Jer. 31.31–34 A new covenant; Ps. 51.1–13 Forgiveness, *or* Ps. 119.9–16 Law; Heb. 5.5–10 Jesus the priest; John 12.20–33 The death of the seed

> *'[Jesus said,] "Whoever serves me must follow me, and where I am, there will my servant be also."' John 12.26*

Persecution

James Hannington, one of the first missionaries to take the gospel to Uganda, was martyred in 1885; the next year a group of Christian boys who rejected the sexual advances of their chief were put to death. The British tried to keep the peace between several warring tribes, and Uganda became a British Protectorate in about 1900. In 1962 Uganda gained its independence within the British Commonwealth, with Milton Obote as Prime Minister. In 1966, Obote overthrew the President, but in 1971, he himself was overthrown by General Idi Amin, Chief of Staff of the Armed Forces. Amin immediately began arresting anybody he suspected of opposing him. All the 'Ugandan Asians', mostly small shopkeepers from India and Pakistan, were expelled, and 55,000 had to leave the country; many of them settled in Britain and contributed richly to the economy and the culture of the nation. Hundreds of soldiers were shot dead in their barracks. Many Christians were killed, among them Archbishop Janani Luwum.

Janani Luwum

Janani Luwum was born in Uganda in 1922. His father had converted to Christianity, but was a poor man, and couldn't afford to pay his son's school fees until Janani was ten years old. But the lad worked hard at school; went on to high school and then to a teacher-training college, becoming a teacher in a primary school. A Revival Movement was sweeping across East Africa at this time. Janani had a life-changing conversion experience, and from then on he worked to spread the revival. He studied to become a lay reader, and then went on to be ordained deacon and priest. He was selected for a one-year course in Christian leadership at St Augustine's

College, Canterbury, in England. Later he studied at the London College of Divinity, then returned to Uganda to become Principal of Buwalasi Theological College. He became Provincial Secretary, and then the Bishop of Northern Uganda. In 1974 Janani Luwum became Archbishop of the enormous Province of Uganda, Rwanda, Burundi and Boga-Zaire. John Sentamu, now the Archbishop of York, was his legal officer.

Tension between Church and state

Archbishop Luwum often had to visit the office of the secret police, the dreaded State Research Bureau, to plead for unjustly detained prisoners to be released. In 1976, Archbishop Luwum met with other religious leaders, to discuss the worsening situation. They asked for an interview with Idi Amin, but the dictator gave the Archbishop a telling-off. In 1977 a small army rebellion was put down, and Amin determined to stamp out every trace of opposition. Thousands of people were killed, including the entire population of Milton Obote's home village. In January 1978, one of Luwum's fellow bishops, Festo Kivengere, preached to an audience including many high government officials. He took as his title 'The Precious-ness of Life', denounced the bloodshed, and accused the govern-ment of abusing its God-given authority. Six days later there was a raid in the middle of the night on Archbishop Luwum's house; the soldiers claimed to be searching for hidden weapons.

Arrest and killing

The Archbishop and the other bishops sent a letter of protest about the killings and disappearances. President Amin accused the Archbishop of smuggling arms and treason, and arrested him and six other bishops. They weren't allowed to speak, and Amin's soldiers shouted 'Kill him now'. The Archbishop turned to his brother bishops and said: 'Don't be afraid. I can see God's hand in this.' They prayed together briefly, then Luwum and two other prisoners were put in a Land Rover, and never seen alive again. The government said they had died in a car crash. His body was sent to his native village, where the sealed coffin was opened and the bullet wounds were seen. Four and a half thousand people came to the funeral, when Luwum was buried next to James Hannington. Bishop Kivengere and the Archbishop's widow and orphans fled to Kenya.

A modern martyr

Jesus said, 'Whoever serves me must follow me, and where I am, there will my servant be also.' Jesus died on the cross of self-sacrifice for his people; and Luwum followed him to that altar. He became a modern martyr. Many who'd abandoned Christianity returned to the faith when they saw Archbishop Luwum's courage.

All-age worship

Print pictures of Archbishop Luwum and put them around the church or schoolroom: http://images.google.com/images?sourceid=navclient&rlz=1T4GGLR_enGB310GB310&q=janani%20luwum&um=1&ie=UTF-8&sa=N&hl=en&tab=wi

Suggested hymns

For all thy saints, O Lord; From heaven you came, helpless babe; Lo, round the throne, a glorious band; We are marching in the light of God (Siyahamba).

Fifth Sunday of Lent   25 March
Second Service   **You Are Accepted**
Ps. 34 God rescues the righteous; Ex. 7.8–24 Water turned to blood; Rom. 5.12–21 Adam and Christ; *Gospel at Holy Communion*: Luke 22.1–13 Preparing for Passover

> *'Law came in, with the result that the trespass multiplied; but where sin increased, grace abounded all the more.' Romans 5.20*

Paul Tillich

Paul Tillich was a professor at four German universities, one after the other, but was forced out of Germany in 1933 when Hitler came to power. Then he taught theology in New York, Harvard and Chicago. When he died in 1965 he'd become one of the most influential Protestant teachers in the world. He published a book of sermons called *The Shaking of the Foundations*. One of them, titled 'You are accepted', deeply influenced scores of people at the time, and its message is still important today. What follows is a summary in simple words of that sermon.

Sin

Two of the most important words for St Paul were words we find strange and hard to understand today: 'Sin' and 'Grace'. But we can rediscover their meaning in our own existence and experience of life. Sin doesn't mean an immoral act, and we should never speak about 'sins' in the plural. You can't divide people into 'sinners' and 'righteous'; just because you have avoided the more dramatic sins, you can't say that you are not a sinner. What sin consists of is separation – separation from others, separation from ourselves, and separation from God. We suffer because we're separated from these things with which we ought to be united. And it's our own fault.

Grace

Grace is the opposite of sin: it's the state of being reunited with our neighbours, with ourselves, and with God. Grace is the overcoming of our separation. Grace transforms fate into destiny; it transforms guilt into confidence. Grace totally overcomes sin. It comes when we, who had felt rejected, know that we are accepted. At a busy social event, have you never felt totally alone? Who hasn't? And when we're alone, we feel separated from every other human being. The walls of distance between people today have been knocked down by technical progress; but the walls of separation between classes, and between nations, are stronger than ever. The atrocities of the German Nazis, and the lynching of black people in the American South, may be nothing to do with us; but the millions dying of starvation around the world are a tragedy that we could have prevented. Sin abounds.

Separation from ourselves

We're not only separated from other people; we are separated from ourselves by selfishness and self-loathing. We don't love ourselves; so we can neither offer love to others nor receive love from them. As St Paul says, the power of sin, of separation, stops us doing the good that we'd like to do. Despair prevents us from escaping sin's mastery.

Acceptance

The apostle Paul, on the road to Damascus, felt this despair and estrangement from God. Yet grace overcame sin when he realized that God had accepted him. When God accepted him, Paul found he could accept himself and be reconciled with other people. Do you know, in your experience, what being struck by grace means? It's nothing to do with the words you assent to. It's the sudden realization that, although you thought your weakness and aimlessness make you quite unacceptable, God accepts you, just as you are. There's nothing you can do to earn God's acceptance – it's a free gift. Yet without it, we're separated from God and neighbour, and can't learn to love ourselves. It's as though a bright light shines into our darkness crying, 'You are accepted. You are accepted!' All you have to do is accept the fact that you're accepted! Then love changes everything!

Accepting others

Once you realize that God accepts you, you can begin to accept other people, just as they are, as your friends; even those who are hostile to you. This grace overcomes the separation between the sexes, between the generations, between the races, and even the disharmony between us and the natural world. We can learn to live happily with the world, and to live with ourselves. Peace enters our hearts; self-hatred and self-loathing disappear. When we learn that God has accepted us, then it's true to say that grace has come upon us, unasked-for, unsought, undeserved, solely through God's irresistible love.

Sin and grace

Sin and grace are strange words, but they are basic facts of our experience, and the ground of our being. They are the ground of everybody else's being, too. May God's grace abound within you, today and every day!

Suggested hymns

And can it be that I should gain?; Jesu, Lover of my soul; Morning glory, starlit sky; There's a wideness in God's mercy.

The full text of the sermon is at http://www.religion-online.org/showchapter.asp?title=378&C=84

HOLY WEEK

We call the week from Palm Sunday to Easter 'Holy Week', because we remember the events that happened in the last week of
Jesus' life on earth. On Palm Sunday we think of the children and
adults who waved palm branches as Jesus rode into Jerusalem as
the King on a donkey. In many churches palm crosses are held up
in the Procession of Palms, and taken home to be placed somewhere prominent. On Maundy Thursday we remember the Last
Supper which Jesus held in the Upper Room with his disciples:
the name comes from the 'new com-*mand*-ment' which Jesus
gave us, to love one another as he has loved us. At the end of the
Eucharist, commemorating the Last Supper, after the Washing of
Feet, in some churches the altars are stripped of their hangings to
remind us of Jesus stripped of his clothes by the mocking soldiers
who arrested him. Good Friday is a strange name to give to the
day when we remember the awful pain in which Jesus died on the
cross, but he showed there how God shares and understands our
pain, and promises that death will be followed by eternal life. So
we venerate the cross in commemoration of his willing sacrifice. A
series of sermons on the Passion, or on the seven words of Jesus
from the cross, can be preached throughout Holy week or during
a Good Friday service to mark the three hours that Jesus hung on
the cross.

Palm Sunday   1 April
Principal Service   Peter's Denial

Isa. 50.4–9a I gave my back to the smiters; Ps. 31.9–16
Assurance in suffering; Phil. 2.5–11 Jesus' obedience unto
death; Mark 14.1—15.47 The Last Supper to the burial, *or* Mark
15.1–39 [40–47] The trial to the death on the cross

> *'Peter remembered that Jesus had said to him, "Before the cock
> crows twice, you will deny me three times." And he broke down
> and wept.' Mark 14.72*

Jesus told the truth

When Jesus was on trial, the High Priest asked him, 'Are you the
Messiah, the Son of the Blessed One?' Jesus answered, 'I am!'

99

Remember that 'I am' was the name of God in the Old Testament. Jesus went on to describe himself as 'The Son of Man', the fully human but also divine figure described in the book of Daniel. So he was clearly claiming to be not only the human Messiah, but the divine Son of God. To Jews, this was blasphemy. Jesus could easily have refused to answer, or made a non-committal reply. But he had committed himself to speaking the truth; he did so, and thereby signed his own death warrant.

Peter told a lie

Jesus's friend Peter, a few yards away in the courtyard, was also put to the test. A servant girl asked him if he wasn't one of Jesus's followers. Admitting to being a disciple of a man who was on trial for his life, risked being condemned with him. So Peter told a lie. He saved his skin, but he lost something much more precious – his self-respect. How could Peter ever hold his head up again, having denied knowing his best friend? Jesus told the truth and it cost him his life; Peter told a lie, and it cost him his pride. At that moment the Lord turned and looked at Peter. Peter realized from the way his Master looked at him that Jesus had heard what he said. Those few careless words, Peter felt, had destroyed his right to call himself Jesus's friend. Peter broke down and cried bitter tears of shame.

Speaking up for Jesus

And you, have you ever felt like that? Do you know what it means to feel ashamed of yourself? Have you ever been put to the test, and avoided the challenge by words that seemed trivial at the time, but which you later realized were a betrayal of God's friendship? Many times in our lives we could have inserted a few words into a conversation that would have shown that we believe in Jesus; but we don't want to be thought a 'Holy Joe'. So we keep quiet, missing the chance to correct somebody's misunderstanding about God. Who knows, our simple acknowledgement that we believe might have made someone wonder about their own belief or lack of it, and started them off on a path leading to salvation. And if you and I don't feel a pang of shame when that happens, we certainly ought to. Oh yes, we all do it. Like Peter, we tell what we call 'little white lies', and shrug them off at the time as being trivial. Yet telling the truth matters, and like Jesus, we ought to be fully committed to telling the truth, the whole truth, and nothing but the truth, not just in court, but everywhere we go.

Jesus forgave Peter

Did Peter notice something else in his expression when Jesus turned to look at him? Did he realize that Jesus, knowing full well what Peter had done, was offering to forgive him? According to St Paul, Peter was one of the first people to whom Jesus appeared after his resurrection. Then, according to St John, the risen Christ walked with Peter by the shore of Lake Galilee and asked him, 'Peter, do you love me?' Not just once, but, because Peter had three times betrayed his Lord, Jesus gave him three chances to avow his love. Then Jesus told Peter, 'Go and feed my sheep.'

The wounded healer

To be a pastor, a guide and leader among the disciples, was a very responsible position. Far too responsible to give to a coward and a shameful liar. Yet somebody who's faced up to their own failures, confessed them and been forgiven, is the best person to be a shepherd. Somebody who thought themselves perfect wouldn't understand that we're all sinners. Peter was ideal, because he was a wounded healer. And you? Can you too learn from your failures? Sympathizing with others because you know you are no better than they are, can you show them that Jesus accepts failures and turns them into success stories? Then God bless you, because you're just the sort of follower that Jesus needs.

All-age worship

Tell Aesop's story of the boy who cried wolf. Under a picture of Jesus, write 'I will try to tell the truth.' Imagine that you are saying those words to him.

Suggested hymns

All glory, laud and honour; Forsaken once and thrice denied; Ride on, ride on in majesty; Thou art the Christ, O Lord.

Palm Sunday 1 April
Second Service **Fools for Christ**
Ps. 69.1–20 Save me, O God; Isa. 5.1–7 The Song of the
Vineyard; Mark 12.1–12 The parable of the wicked tenants

> *'I am the subject of gossip for those who sit in the gate, and the
> drunkards make songs about me.'* Psalm 69.12

All Fools' Day

Did anyone play a trick on you this morning? Yes, today, April 1st,
is All Fools' Day. The custom was probably introduced to Britain
from Germany in the seventeenth century. A favourite trick was to
send the apprentice to fetch a left-handed screwdriver, some hen's
teeth or pigeons' milk. In the nineteenth century, people were sent
to the Tower of London to watch the washing of the white lions. In
1957 BBC television showed film of Italians picking spaghetti from
trees. In 1986 *The Guardian* advertised a vacancy for a 'Rhubarb
Consultant to the West Midlands County Council'. An atheist took
the State of Florida to court for discrimination because, although
other religions each had their Holy Day, there was none for atheists. The judge quoted Psalm 14: 'The fool hath said in his heart,
There is no God' – so April 1st was obviously sacred to atheists
– and dismissed the case!

Christian humorists

Christians have often used jokes to prick the bubble of pomposity. Many of the parables of Jesus could be seen in this light. Can
you see yourself in the blind leading the blind, or the corrupt judge
refusing to give the poor widow justice until she made a thorough
nuisance of herself? Or in today's reading, the wicked tenants who
thought that because they couldn't see their landlord they had no
need to obey him?

Gossiping

In the early twentieth century there was an Italian priest of the Cap-
uchin order known as Padre Pio. He was a well-known spiritual
healer, and many flocked to him for advice. He spoke about gossiping, which has always been a problem – ruining other people's

reputation is a favourite pastime for those who are judgemental. The Psalmist moaned, 'I am the subject of gossip for those who sit in the gate, and the drunkards make songs about me.' A woman came to consult Padre Pio who admitted she was a bit of a gossip, but thought it didn't matter much. So the friar played a gentle joke on her. 'I want you to carry a feather pillow when you return home, and scatter its contents along the road as you go. Then come back to me for your next task.' When she returned, he told her to pick up all the feathers and put them back in the pillow case. 'I can't do that,' she spluttered. 'The wind has blown them everywhere by now.' 'Neither can you bring back all the hurtful lies you have told about other people,' continued the saint. 'Gossip spreads completely out of control. You fool! Much better not to say those things in the first place!'

Holy Fools

But Christians consider that the title of 'fool' can be a badge of pride. Some Christians in Corinth thought they were real clever-clogs. St Paul wrote to them, 'We are fools for the sake of Christ, but you are wise in Christ.' It's better to be naively trusting than to be proud of your superior intelligence. There's no proof of the truth of religion, other than the test of experience, but it's better to trust God and obey him than to be held back by doubts and uncertainties. You will be called a fool if you trust other people, and sometimes they will let you down. But you'll enjoy life more if you tell other people you trust them to do the right thing, than if you are a bitter sceptic. Sometimes, indeed, they may change their minds about cheating you, because you made them feel good about themselves. In Russia there was a movement of wandering holy men, calling themselves Holy Fools. They lived on charity in absolute poverty, uttering prophecies, and challenging the power of money over people's lives. They also challenged those in authority, up to and including the Tsars; rather as the court jester in medieval Europe was allowed to say critical things that nobody else could have got away with. There's also been a revival of clowning in Western Europe and America, using humour to challenge people's assumptions. After all, what Jesus did in Holy Week appears to some as utter foolishness.

Fools for Christ

So the message of April Fools' Day is not to be pompous, and never to gossip about others. Laugh when people play tricks on you, and tell jokes against yourself. Don't be afraid of going to ridiculous extremes in speaking and doing things for Jesus. Stop bothering about your reputation, and be prepared to make a fool of yourself by standing up for what's right. There's nothing to be ashamed of in being a 'fool for Christ'.

Suggested hymns

I cannot tell why he whom angels worship; In the cross of Christ I glory; My song is love unknown; When I survey the wondrous cross.

First Three Days in Holy Week   2–4 April
Death

(Following are the Monday readings, but this sermon may be used on any day this week.)
Isa. 42.1–9 The servant brings salvation; Ps. 36.5–11 Defend me against the wicked; Heb. 9.11–15 The sacrifice of the new covenant; John 12.1–11 Mary anoints Jesus for his death

> *'Jesus said, "Leave her alone. She bought it so that she might keep it for the day of my burial. You always have the poor with you, but you do not always have me."' John 12.7–8*

Talking about death

How shocked the people round the table must have been when Mary of Bethany poured the ointment on Jesus's feet! Yet they were even more appalled when he began to speak openly about his own death. They weren't as embarrassed in those days to talk about death as we are today, but for a young man to describe his own death as something that would happen soon and was to be welcomed, that was a step too far! Yet Jesus spoke of his death on the cross of shame as a triumph. He began to think about death when his cousin John the Baptist was slain by Herod, and realized that it might be his turn next. He started to speak about it at Caesarea Philippi when 'he began to teach them that the Son of Man must undergo great suffering, and be rejected by the elders, the chief priests, and the scribes, and be killed, and after three days rise again. He said all this quite openly.' We can learn from the life of Jesus how we should live; we can also learn from his death how to die.

Only for old people

Young people think it's only the very old who should be talking about death. Yet we all have to die sometime, and if you put off thinking about it, there's a risk of being caught unprepared. It isn't morbid to talk about death. Even the Greek philosopher Socrates, who was condemned to death four centuries before Jesus was, said that if death leads to nothingness there's nothing to be afraid of, and if death is the ante-room to a better life, we should welcome it.

Midlife to old age

As people grow older, they realize that it doesn't make sense to plan their life on earth too far ahead. What's often called the midlife crisis may actually be a real release from career and family worries, a chance to explore new directions, and to do what you always wanted to do when you were younger, now that you can afford it. Then you can begin to 'grow old gracefully', or disgracefully if you prefer, confident that nobody's going to blame you for enjoying the time that's left. You can begin to 'make peace with your Creator', by prayer and meditation learning to enjoy the presence of God, knowing that you'll have the honour of living with him through eternity.

Giving yourself away

This winding down is difficult, because we do so cling to our possessions. Yet there are no pockets in a shroud, and we have to learn to give everything away, or at least to plan who will have our things when we die. Last of all we have to learn to give ourselves away, not clinging selfishly to life, but handing it thankfully back to the God who gave it to us in the first place – ready to entrust ourselves into the darkness. Read again the Lord's Prayer, and see how suitable it is for someone setting off on their final journey – it says it all.

A hand to hold

To be loved unconditionally by another human being helps us to understand God's unconditional love. Lucky is the Christian who can have what Mother Teresa called 'a good death', peacefully at home, free from pain, with our family and friends gathered round us. Alas, it seldom works out quite like that, so we should be grateful if we have at least a hand to hold while we say farewell to the world. You can still show sympathy and concern for others, even on your deathbed. Better still, if we have come to know Jesus well enough to hold his hand as he leads us gently into the world to come.

Hymn

As the Puritan, Richard Baxter, wrote:

> Christ leads me through no darker rooms
> than he went through before;
> he that into God's kingdom comes
> must enter by this door . . .

> My knowledge of that life is small,
> the eye of faith is dim;
> but 'tis enough that Christ knows all
> and I shall be with him.

Suggested hymns

Go to dark Gethsemane; In the cross of Christ I glory; Lord, it belongs not to my care; Take up thy cross, the Saviour said.

Maundy Thursday   5 April
All-age Communion

(In some circumstances this could be used as a non-liturgical service.)

Ex. 12.1–4 [5–10] 11–14 The Passover; Ps. 116.1, 10–17 (or 116.9–17) The cup of salvation; 1 Cor. 11.23–26 The last supper; John 13.1–17, 31b–35 Foot-washing

'Do this in remembrance of me.' 1 Corinthians 11.24

What Jesus did

On Sundays, grown-ups eat bread and drink wine together in church. We do this because Jesus held a party with his friends, the evening before he died. At this Last Supper, Jesus did four things:

> he took bread and wine;
> he said thank you to God;
> he broke the bread; and
> he gave his friends the bread and wine.

Then he said, 'Do this in remembrance of me.' He wanted his friends to remember what he had said and done, and to remember that he is here with us.

What we do

So we do these same four things every Sunday. We eat bread and drink wine. Some churches use ordinary bread; others use little wafers, bread made without any yeast in it. That's because the Last Supper was at Passover time, when Jews remembered what a hurry they were in when Moses led them out of Egypt, and there wasn't even time to let the bread rise. This church has a policy about how old you need to be to eat the bread and drink the wine. [Tell them what it is.] For those who aren't ready to eat the bread and drink the wine, we invite them to come forward with their arms folded to receive a blessing, [and a small picture – don't eat it! – to remind them that Jesus is here, and with us wherever we go.] Usually the service is quite formal, using words from a book. For the sake of the young people here, I'll try to explain it now in quite simple words.

Take

We take the bread and wine, when it's brought forward while the collection is being taken. Bread and wine have to be bought with money, and money is earned by work. So we're actually giving our whole life to God.

Thank

Then we have some answers, which are very old, and may have been used by Jesus. You stand and I say:

The Lord is here; and you answer, 'His Spirit is with us.' Try it now:

The Lord is here;
His Spirit is with us.

To the next one you answer 'We lift them to the Lord':

Lift up your hearts;
We lift them to the Lord.

Then you answer 'It is right to give thanks and praise':

Let us give thanks to the Lord our God;
It is right to give thanks and praise.

We thank you, God, for making the world, and all the people in it;
for the life of Jesus, his death on the cross,
and his coming to life again.
We remember what he did at the Last Supper with his friends,
when he took bread and wine; said 'thank you' to God;
broke it and gave it to them, saying
'This is my body, given for you. Do this to remember me.
This is my blood, shed for you.
Do this, every time you drink it, to remember me.'
We thank you, God our Father, for everything that Jesus said and did,
and we thank you that he loves us.
Take us, Father God,
and use us to spread your love to all we meet.
Make us into one big happy family,
with each other, with those who died, and with you;
for you are alive, Father, Son and Holy Spirit,
one God, now and for ever. **Amen.**

We join these prayers in the words Jesus taught us,
the Lord's Prayer.

Broke

We break this bread, and eat it to make us one body in Christ.

Gave

We give the bread and wine saying:
The body of Christ.

108

Take and eat this to remember that Jesus is with us.
The blood of Christ.
Jesus loves you! May he bless you and guide you all through your life.

Ending

Thank you, Jesus, for giving us this service,
so that we can remember your love for us,
and so that we can learn to love each other better.
We remember that you're here with us,
and you'll stay with us wherever we go.
Help us to be kind to each other,
so that people will recognize that we are God's children. **Amen.**

May God bless you and guide you,
and fill you with his love, his joy and his peace;
and the blessing of God, Father, Son and Holy Spirit;
be on you and all for whom you have prayed,
this day and evermore. **Amen.**

Suggested hymns

An upper room did our Lord prepare; Bind us together, Lord; I am the Bread of Life; Let us break bread together.

Good Friday 6 April
God on Trial

Isa. 52.13—53.12 The suffering servant; Ps. 22 Why have you forsaken me?; Heb. 10.16–25 *or* Heb. 4.14–16; 5.7–9 Jesus the priest; John 18.1—19.42 The blood of the covenant

> *'My God, my God, why have you forsaken me? Why are you so far from helping me, from the words of my groaning?' Psalm 22.1*

Pain

Do you enjoy pain? Me neither! Some people do, however – doctors call them 'masochists' and consider it a symptom of mental illness. Obviously, people who like being in pain won't avoid painful situations, and that's not healthy. They probably won't live long, and they'll be a menace to themselves and to the people around them. Pain is a warning – it tells you something is challenging the body's self-defence mechanisms. It either triggers off some autoimmune system, which will produce antibodies to heal whatever is wrong, or it forces the brain to choose a strategy of fight or flight. In fact, when you look at it that way, pain is quite a good thing, because it's an essential mechanism for survival. But I still don't like it.

Darwin

Charles Darwin said that when a species of living things develops a new feature, it will only survive if this mutation is useful. If that's true, you could say that pain is one of evolution's finest developments: it prompts us to avoid and flee from perilous predicaments. From the scar tissue which develops when an animal or plant is wounded, to the screams of an animal caught in a trap, pain is a valuable warning that a life-threatening situation has arisen, and the creature must do something about it. Nature is 'red in tooth and claw', and pain is universal.

Suffering

We get upset if our pets are in pain, because we imagine that they suffer as we do. Certainly, the response of the higher animals to pain is almost human. What makes pain so terrible for humans, however, is that we can think about it, question its cause and complain about pain's unfairness. Can animals and plants do this? I don't know. To some extent, I suppose. 'Pathology' comes from two Greek words meaning the study of pain, and some philosophers talk scornfully of 'the pathetic fallacy'. This doesn't mean what you probably think it does; it's the assumption that inanimate objects and plants can suffer as we do. Where's all this leading to? Well, I wonder if the similarity between human pain and that of the animals means that we should accept our pain calmly as a useful evolutionary development. Whereas our developed ability to question it and rebel against it may mean that we're evolving a new ability to debate with our Creator? Mother Teresa, the saintly nun who helped poor folk who were dying on the streets in India, once said, 'When I die and meet God, he's going to have a lot of explaining to do!'

Good Friday

Good Friday teaches us to look at suffering in a new way. Jesus complained about pain when he cried from the cross, 'My God, my God, why have you forsaken me?' But he also accepted it, as we all have to, as a necessary part of human existence; and death as the beginning of eternal life. He even suggested that suffering, willingly borne for the sake of others, is creative, and an acceptable form of sacrifice.

Auschwitz

Recently, a story, widely accepted as true, was made into a play on television. The play, entitled *God on Trial*, movingly depicted a group of Jews waiting to go into the gas chambers at Auschwitz. As they argued, they remembered that, according to the Scriptures, God made a Covenant with his Chosen People. If they would obey his laws, he would defend them. Yet the Jews seem to have suffered beyond all other races. So they formed a court of law, and put God on trial for breach of contract. Unanimously they declared God guilty. Then, as they were called to go to their death, they all put on imaginary skullcaps and sang the Kaddish, a mourners' hymn of praise:

> May the great Name of God be exalted and sanctified, throughout the world, which he has created according to his will . . . May his great name be blessed, forever and ever . . . Blessed is he – above and beyond any blessings and hymns, praises and consolations which are uttered in the world; and say, Amen . . .

Jesus and suffering

Singing praise in the face of suffering and death – that's amazing! Obviously, to demand a world without suffering is asking the impossible. But why this person at that particular time? What Good Friday shows us, however, is that God is not aloof from all this; God stepped down from heaven and shared our suffering with us. We may never understand suffering, nor can we escape from it. But in all our pain, we must never stop praising God for his love in Christ Jesus.

Suggested hymns

I danced in the morning; In the cross of Christ I glory; It is a thing most wonderful; Were you there when they crucified my Lord?

EASTER

The forty days of Easter are a season of joyful celebration. We celebrate the resurrection of Jesus from the dead; we are filled with new life and hope. The altar frontals and vestments are white, or gold on Easter Day, and the Easter hymns resound with alleluias. If 'Glory to God in the highest' has been omitted in Lent, it is sung again for the first time at the Easter vigil. At the vigil, a new fire is lit, symbolizing the new life that began at the resurrection of Jesus; and the Easter candle, lit from it, symbolizes Christ the light of the world, and burns at all the services from Easter till Ascension Day, and at baptisms in the rest of the year. At Easter we may renew our baptism promises. By long tradition, we may make an Easter garden with a model of the empty tomb. Eastertide sermons expound our faith that Jesus is alive, and our hope for our own eternal future.

Easter Vigil   7–8 April
Daily Resurrection

(A minimum of three Old Testament readings should be chosen. The reading from Ex. 14 should always be used.)
Gen. 1.1—2.4a Creation, Ps. 136.1–9, 23–26; Gen. 7.1–5, 11–18, 8.6–18, 9.8–13 Noah, Ps. 46 Our refuge and strength; Gen. 22.1–18 Sacrifice of Isaac, Ps. 16 The path of life; Ex. 14.10–31, 15.20–21 The Exodus, *Canticle*: Ex. 15.1b–13, 17–18 The song of Moses; Isa. 55.1–11 Come to the waters, *Canticle*: Isa. 12.2–6 Great in your midst; Bar. 3.9–15, 32—4.4 God gives the light of wisdom, *or* Prov. 8.1–8, 19–21; 9.4b–6 Wisdom, Ps. 19 The heavens declare God's glory; Ezek. 36.24–28 I will sprinkle clean water on you, Ps. 42 and 43 Faith and hope; Ezek. 37.1–14 The valley of dry bones, Ps. 143 A prayer for deliverance; Zeph. 3.14–20 I will bring you home, Ps. 98 Salvation and Justice;

'We have been buried with [Christ] by baptism into death, so that, just as Christ was raised from the dead by the glory of the Father, so we too might walk in newness of life.' Romans 6.4

Resurrection

At some point, Jews came to believe in resurrection, but not as we think of it. They held that the Messiah would come, and then God would raise all the good Jews who had died, to walk again upon the earth. It was to be a purely material resuscitation. They hoped and hoped – but it never happened. When Jesus was raised from the dead, some of the disciples thought this is what had occurred. Yet, as the dead obviously weren't walking the earth again, they decided that resurrection would only happen when Jesus came again. Down the centuries, groups of believers have climbed mountains to await the imminent Second Coming. Most Christians, however, would say that they're looking in the wrong place.

Heaven

Should we, then, hope for a heavenly kingdom, and wait for resurrection when we die? Not in a physical body, but what St Paul calls a 'spiritual body'. This new understanding of resurrection changed the whole Christian attitude to death. We can enjoy life on earth until God calls us; we can endure its hardships, confident that earth's wrongs will be righted when we die. We have no need to fear death when it comes, because we expect a better life on the other side.

New Life

There's a danger, however, that this attitude is too other-worldly, too 'pie-in-the-sky'. As well as hoping for a heavenly resurrection, perhaps we should look for resurrection in the here and now also, as a new quality of life, a new way of living. St Paul wrote, 'We have been buried with [Christ] by baptism into death, so that, just as Christ was raised from the dead by the glory of the Father, so we too might walk in newness of life.' To walk in newness of life is something that happens here and now, when minds and hearts are open to see things in a new way. Resurrection is a daily experience, when we begin life over again, forgiven, renewed, and filled with the power of the living God.

A chaplain's story

A chaplain in a young offenders' institution told how he saw resurrection happening around him every day. Many of the lads had suffered a terrible up-bringing, and had never known what it was to be loved. Some were too deeply damaged to respond to love when they met it; some were too deeply influenced by their peers to want to change. Some of the staff had been so worn down by the life of the institution that they had forgotten how to love. Yet in a few cases, the chaplain was able to show the offenders that he cared for them and valued them as individuals. That he believed in them, and thought they could make a future for themselves if they wanted. Then a new light of self-respect shone in their eyes, and a determination to make a fresh start. They were, in effect, 'born again'. Isn't that what Jesus meant by resurrection, when he said 'Very truly, I tell you, whoever believes *has* eternal life . . . and this is eternal life, that [those who believe] may know . . . the only true God, and Jesus Christ whom [God has] sent.' Resurrection is not something we wait for in the far distant future; it's something we experience now – a new beginning, with our lives transformed because we know that God loves us.

Suggested hymns

Light's glittering morn bedecks the sky; Now is eternal life; Thine be the glory, risen, conquering Son; We have a gospel to proclaim.

Easter Day   8 April
Principal Service   **Flesh and Body**
Acts 10.34–43 Peter and other witnesses to the resurrection, *or* Isa. 25.6–9 Swallow up death; Ps. 118.1–2, 14–24 I shall not die but live; 1 Cor. 15.1–11 Resurrection appearances *or* Acts 10.34–43; John 20.1–18 Magdalene at the tomb, *or* Mark 16.1–8 The women see Jesus

> 'They put [Jesus] to death by hanging him on a tree; but God raised him on the third day and allowed him to appear, not to all

the people but to us who were chosen by God as witnesses, and who ate and drank with him after he rose from the dead.' Acts 10.39–41

Scientifically impossible

Jesus died on the cross; he was buried; and on the third day God raised him to life again, and he was seen by his disciples. That's what we say in the Creeds: we proclaim every Sunday that we believe in the resurrection of the body; and on Easter Sunday we celebrate the resurrection of Jesus. But any scientist will tell you that could never happen. Irreversible processes of decay begin in the brain within a few minutes of the heartbeat stopping, making life impossible. The usual Christian answer to this is to say that when the Son of God came to earth, that was a unique case. That's never happened before or since, so we can't test what occurred by repeated experiment. For God, all things are possible. On this basis, many top scientists are able to believe in the resurrection of Jesus. But what about you and me? Is it possible for *our* bodies to be raised?

Athens

A journalist, writing in an Athens newspaper, declared that the flesh of dead people couldn't return to life. But he picked the wrong word – he wrote about flesh when he should have chosen the word body instead. Flesh and body are two different words in Greek as they are in English, and they mean quite different things. Flesh is made up of protein molecules, which perish when their blood supply stops. St Paul described a war between the flesh and the Spirit, as though our physical nature holds our spiritual nature down. Writing to the Corinthians, Paul said that 'flesh and blood cannot inherit the kingdom of God'. Whereas in heaven, he wrote, we shall have a new sort of body – a 'spiritual body'.

The body

There are many sorts of body, from the stars in the sky, which we call heavenly bodies, to the body of water that separates Europe from America. What's special about our human body is that, through it, we can recognize each other, communicate and be creative. When we die, we can still do those things, but using a new sort of body. The resurrected body is not the same as the molecules of flesh and blood through which we express ourselves on earth. Unfortunately for the Athens journalist, the Greek Church does sometimes speak about 'the resurrection of the flesh' in its prayers; the Bible never does. Before his conversion, Paul the Pharisee believed there would be a physical resuscitation: dead flesh coming to life on the earth. When he had a vision of the risen Christ on the road to Damascus, however, he realized that when the dead are raised, their bodies will be much more wonderful than mere flesh.

Ghosts

It was when Paul came to Athens, however, that he realized that the details of this would have to be worked out. Enquiring Greeks scoffed at the idea of resurrection. Yet the Greeks believed that the soul is like a bird imprisoned inside a cage – when we die it escapes from the body to become a ghost. This idea wouldn't do either. The risen Christ wasn't a ghost; he was more alive than he had been before. We can't be sure what he caused his disciples to see, or to touch, at the resurrection; if it hadn't been something pretty positive they wouldn't have believed he was anything more than a disembodied spirit.

Reply

A Christian wrote a letter to the editor of the Athens newspaper, in reply to the journalist. Distinguish a little more clearly, he wrote, between the body and the flesh, and you'll find it's possible for Christians to have an enquiring mind. Yet we should be grateful to those who raise questions about the Christian faith, because it forces us all to think out our ideas more carefully. That will certainly make us grateful to God, who raised Jesus on the first Easter day, and has promised to raise us to live a much more glorious life with him when we die.

All-age worship

Collect pictures of things we use to be recognized by, to communicate, and to be creative. What does this tell us about our earthly bodies, and what we shall be like when we die?

Suggested hymns

Jesus Christ is risen today; Now the green blade rises; The day of resurrection; This is the day the Lord has made.

Easter Day   8 April
Second Service   **Happy Easter!**
Morning Ps. 114 The Exodus, 117 God's faithfulness endures for ever; Evening Ps. 105 The Exodus, *or* 66.1–11 God holds our souls in life; Ezek. 37.1–14 The valley of dry bones; Luke 24.13–35 The road to Emmaus

> *'Yes, and besides all this, it is now the third day since these things took place.' Luke 24.21*

Happy Easter

Happy Easter! On this day Jesus rose from the dead. Or at least, I think so. No, I'm in no doubt that he rose again, and lives for evermore. My uncertainty is about the date. The date of Easter has been a subject of furious controversy between Christians down the ages. Now the Easter celebrations are over, you might like a light-hearted look at this thorny question. Let's begin by saying that today is celebrated as Easter by most Christians, unless you happen to be Greek or Russian Orthodox, or an Old Calendarist. A what?! Well, I'll come to that later.

Jewish customs

Jesus was crucified on or around the Jewish Festival of Passover. The Last Supper was a Passover meal, usually celebrated on the evening that began the Day of Passover – Jewish days ran from sunset to sunset. St John's Gospel suggests that Jesus and his disciples anticipated this by 24 hours. It was the eve of the Sabbath, so this must have been a year when the Passover was on a Friday. Passover celebrated the Exodus, when the Israelites fled from Egypt, passed over the sea while fleeing from Egypt. The previous night, they ate unleavened bread; the angel of death passed over Jewish homes, leaving the first-born unharmed. In Aramaic, the language Jesus spoke, the word for Passover was *pascha*, which gives us our word paschal, as in 'the paschal candle'.

Other races

This celebration was combined with a Canaanite spring festival. Farming people celebrated the first green shoots of the growing crops. They fixed it by the spring equinox, when night and day are the same length. Then they observed the date of the next new moon, and declared that 14 days after that would be the full moon. Passover became the first full moon after the fourteenth day of the month Nisan. The moon rotates around the earth roughly every 28 days, and Jewish months were all 28 days long. Sometimes a thirteenth month was thrown in, because the earth rotates around the sun every 365 and a bit days – the solar calendar and the lunar calendar never precisely agree.

Julius Caesar

Julius Caesar tried to sort out this muddle by fixing 7 months of 31 days, 5 months of 30 days, and one of 28 days, and inventing the leap year every 4 years when February has 29. This is the Julian calendar, and it has nothing to do with the moon. Some Christians celebrated the resurrection of Jesus on the Jewish Passover, even if it wasn't a Sunday. Others celebrated Easter on the Sunday after Passover, and that eventually prevailed. This made Easter the first Sunday after the first full moon after the spring equinox. Yet when St Augustine brought Roman Christianity to England, he found that British Christians celebrated Easter on a different day – it took the Synod of Whitby to sort that out.

Pope Gregory

The Julian calendar wasn't quite accurate, and every 128 years it becomes one day out with the sun. So Pope Gregory XIII changed the arrangement for leap years, and docked 11 days from a year in the sixteenth century to set things right. There are reports of people rioting, demanding 'give us back our 11 days!' The Gregorian calendar was never accepted in the Eastern Orthodox Churches.

True story

An English Christian living in Greece was close friends with an Orthodox priest there. The Greeks can claim with some truth to be the original church founded by the apostles, and that the Western

118

churches have broken away. This makes the Pope the first 'protestant'! But they were visiting an island monastery together, when a Greek monk came in and tore the Orthodox priest off a strip. Later the Englishman asked the priest for a translation. He replied, 'Oh, he's an "Old Calendarist". He was telling me I'm not a true Christian, because I don't keep Easter on the same day as he does.' The irony of the situation was not lost on either of them.

Unity?

There have been attempts to fix the date of Easter in the World Council of Churches, the United Nations, and the parliaments of several nations. Many churches have agreed to this, but always with the proviso that every other church must agree first. And that will never happen! So happy Easter to you, whenever you celebrate it. Even if we can't agree the date, we're all agreed that Jesus rose again, and through him we shall live for ever in eternity – where, thank God, there are no calendars!

Suggested hymns

Abide with me; Hail thee, festival day (Easter); Jesus Christ is risen today; Most glorious Lord of life.

Second Sunday of Easter 15 April
Principal Service Butterflies

Ex. 14.10–31; 15.20–21 The Exodus (*if used, the reading from Acts must be used as the second reading*), *or* Acts 4.32–35 Witnessing to the resurrection; Ps. 133 Unity, life; 1 John 1.1—2.2 The word of life; John 20.19–31 Thomas's doubt and faith

> *'These [things] are written so that you may come to believe that Jesus is the Messiah, the Son of God, and that through believing you may have life in his name.' John 20.31*

Butterflies

What beautiful things butterflies are! They have wings coloured with every shade in the palette from bright lemon-yellow to iridescent purple, in patterns which Rubens or Rembrandt would have been proud to create. A dark woodland is transformed into a paradise by their brightness. They seem so fragile, yet they master the laws of aerodynamics. Their life seems idyllic, nothing to do but flutter by from flower to flower, sipping on nectar from dawn to dusk. They display their wonderful wings to attract an equally beautiful partner; they mate, lay eggs, ensure the survival of their species to the next generation, and then lay themselves down to rest. A short life but a happy one, or so it seems. Some moths are almost as brightly coloured; moths and butterflies form the order of *Lepidoptera,* which contains over 165,000 species, and the world's more beautiful for their fluttering. Modern scientists say that a single butterfly folding its wings in one place on earth can have consequences on the opposite side of the planet, such is the chain of cause and effect leading from such a tiny action. Yet what was the chain of cause and effect that brought these incredible creatures into being? Can we believe it was a series of random mutations in their genes, causing minor changes in the wing pattern of the next generation, some of which were suited to survive by their ability to attract mates and frighten predators, which alone tuned the earth into an art gallery? Anyone who can believe that such a wonderful thing happened purely by chance is more deluded than a rabid maniac!

Caterpillars

Butterflies emerge from a pupa, the shroud of a caterpillar. The caterpillars, some of which are nearly as beautiful as the butterflies they'll soon become, creep out of the tiny eggs laid by the butterfly. So the cycle of life continues. Have you seen the cartoon of two caterpillars sitting on a leaf, looking up at a frail butterfly fluttering overhead? One turns to the other, saying 'They'll never get me up in one of those!' If caterpillars could think and talk as we do, surely that's what they *would* say. Others could assure them that when they curl up and sleep, they'll wake up again to the delightful life of a butterfly, far better than their dull, leaf-bound caterpillar existence. But they have no evidence that this is true. Nobody can prove it to them. The only way they can believe it, is if they are willing to take it on faith, and behave accordingly.

Resurrection

Now you see why I'm talking about butterflies at Eastertide. Jesus said, 'in the resurrection they neither marry nor are given in marriage, but are like angels in heaven'. I don't think he meant that we shall have wings and trumpets like the angels in the paintings. Jesus wanted us to understand that after this life is ended, God will take us to another form of existence, which is unimaginably better than this world. We have no words to describe it. We have no evidence that it's so. Nobody can prove it to us. The only way we can believe this is if we're willing to take it on faith, and behave accordingly. Just like the caterpillar.

Why Jesus came

That's why Jesus came to earth, died on the cross, and rose again from the tomb. It was for you. So you should believe that you have a glorious future ahead of you in eternity, beyond your wildest imaginings. Of course, if you take the old-fashioned, literal interpretation of harps and haloes, you would be quite justified in saying, 'Nobody will ever get me up in one of those things!' But if you trust that Jesus would never mislead you, even though you can't fully understand his promises, you'll act on them. That means living a resurrected life here and now, in love and service to others, as Jesus did. And it means prayer, establishing a loving relationship with the risen Christ. The bond of love is one that the mere death of the body can never sever. Then you'll live in happiness with God and those you love for evermore. The Bible says, 'these [things] are written so that you may come to believe that Jesus is the . . . Son of God, and that through believing you may have life in his name'. That would be even better than being a beautiful butterfly.

All-age worship

Older children can read to the younger ones the story of 'The Very Hungry Caterpillar'.

Suggested hymns

Alleluia! O sons and daughters; If I were a butterfly; Light's glittering morn (Part 3); Love's redeeming work is done.

Second Sunday of Easter   15 April
Second Service   **Spreading the Word**
Ps. 143.1–11 Remember the days of old; Isa. 26.1–9, 19 Your dead shall live; Luke 24.1–12 The resurrection

> *'Returning from the tomb, they told all this to the eleven and to all the rest.' Luke 24.9*

We've all heard of Jesus

We've all heard of Jesus. In this country, almost everybody knows that Jesus lived some 2000 years ago, and most know that he taught people about love. But why do we know this? After all, many people have said wise things about love, but nobody even remembers their names today. Why is Jesus different? Around the same time, several other Jewish preachers led groups of disciples, proclaiming that the kingdom of God was coming. But nothing changed, the preachers were executed by the Romans, and the movements they started died out. Why didn't that happen to the movement that Jesus started? When he was crucified, his followers were shattered and hopeless. Something happened to change them. There was sufficient evidence to convince them that it wasn't all over, and to persuade them to tell other people about it. That something was the resurrection.

Resurrection

Some Jews expected there would be a resurrection, though not all. But what the Jews expected was a physical resuscitation: dead bodies of good Jews returning to inhabit an earthly kingdom of God when the Messiah destroyed their enemies. Jesus struggled to persuade his disciples to accept a new concept of what resurrection means. Yet the apostles couldn't absorb this paradigm shift. They still expected Jesus to lead a conquering army, and when he died, that was the end of all their hopes. Then a few women found that the tomb was empty, and the Bible says, 'Returning from the tomb, they told all this to the eleven and to all the rest.' Then they rushed round, telling the news to every shattered former follower of Jesus they could find. But Jewish women weren't even allowed to give evidence in the law courts. So nobody believed them.

Apostles

Then a few of the men reported actually seeing Jesus alive. When all eleven were gathered in the Upper Room, they *all* saw Jesus. What did it mean? Was this the end of the world? Had all the good Jews been resuscitated without anybody noticing? Had the dead body of Jesus returned to physical existence on earth? The evidence was there before their eyes, but they didn't know how to interpret it. Jesus wasn't a ghost – they could touch him; he ate food with them. Yet he appeared from nowhere, even in a locked room. The wounds he'd suffered on the cross hadn't affected his joyfulness. He was even more alive than before – his body more powerful than a merely physical one. You could almost say 'spiritual' – meaning empowered by the Holy Spirit – if the word 'spiritual' hadn't been spoilt by those who use it as a synonym for airy-fairy.

Spreading the word

The change in Jesus changed the apostles. They had seen the evidence, though they couldn't quite understand it. The first thing they wanted to do was tell other people – tell *all the rest*, in fact. It only got them into trouble; most of them became martyrs because of what they said. But that didn't stop them. They were so certain that Jesus is alive, they wanted the whole world to know. That's how the word spread, how the Christian Church grew, and continues to grow in most parts of the world. That's how you and I come to have heard of Jesus. The existence of the Church is the proof of the resurrection; if Jesus weren't alive, nobody would have heard of him. Atheists love to say there's no evidence for Christianity, but Christian belief is supported by the same sort of evidence as belief in evolution – observed facts with a reasonable explanation.

Babbling the gospel

When Jesus began to make disciples he told them, 'Go and proclaim the kingdom of God.' After he rose from the dead, he said to them, 'Go into all the world and proclaim the good news to the whole creation.' He gives the same command to you and me: 'Go and tell everyone.' That's because you and I are the best evidence of all for the resurrection. There's the evidence of the change that came in your life when you first realized that Jesus is alive; the growth of love and joy in your heart; the change in your attitude to death when you realized that God has promised you lasting life after you die. That's the evidence, and it mustn't stay hidden. The resurrection of Jesus, and of those who believe in him, is good news; too good to keep it to ourselves. We *must* tell our friends, and never stop babbling the gospel story until the whole world's been told!

Suggested hymns

Christ the Lord is risen again; God's Spirit is in my heart; One shall tell another, and he shall tell his friends; We have a gospel to proclaim.

Third Sunday of Easter 22 April
(Eve of St George, see page 312.)
Principal Service Children of God
Zeph. 3.14–20 The Lord is in your midst (*if used, the reading from Acts must be used as the second reading*), or Acts 3.12–19 Witnessing by caring; Ps. 4 Sleep in peace; 1 John 3.1–7 Adoption; Luke 24.36b–48 The upper room

> 'See what love the Father has given us, that we should be called children of God; and that is what we are.' 1 John 3.1

Tonsils

Out of the mouths of babes and sucklings can often come profound truths which put more sophisticated people to shame. A small boy was being comforted by his mother before an operation. He assured her that he wasn't afraid, because he knew that Jesus was there with him in the hospital. Impressed by this childish faith, his mother asked him how he knew that. He replied, 'Because two men in white came to my bedside, and one looked into my mouth and said to the other, "Jesus Christ, come and look at these tonsils!"'

Super heroes?

Aren't children wonderful? The Bible says, 'See what love the Father has given us, that we should be called children of God; and that is what we are.' St John was evidently dealing with some people who held that only those who have never sinned can be saved. John replies that every Christian is a child of God and is loved by God. You don't have to be a superhero to be a child of God. Most people imagine that if God's interested in them at all, it's only to give them commandments, forbid them to do things, and punish them when they do wrong. That sounds more like the way you treat slaves, not children.

Good news

To people like that, the news that we're God's children comes like a sunny day – the good news that we can revel in the marvel of God's love. It means we can talk to him as children chat with their father. It means that, although we're often like naughty children, the only punishment we have is to realize what pain we cause to our Father – then our sins are forgiven and forgotten. Good parents try to show their children a better way to behave, but also to show them that we still love them. God's children, too, are corrected, but still loved. On the cross, Jesus prayed, 'Father, forgive them, for they don't know what they are doing.' He prays for you and me, because we're still children in our understanding of the way he wants us to live.

Pictures

Children have to be spoken to in simple terms; so God in the Bible uses pictures and stories. Often these stories aren't meant to be taken literally, so long as we get to the truth behind them. In those 40 days between Easter and Ascension, Jesus was trying to teach us that there's life after death. So he appeared to them, obviously alive, but not in a normal body, behind closed doors. According to Luke, the risen Christ ate a piece of fish. To me, that's one of the hardest things in the Bible to understand – after we rise again we don't need food. But if the only way Jesus could make the disciples believe he was alive was to eat fish, very well then, he would eat fish!

Learning

Yet though we start off as simple children in our relationship with God, 'babes in Christ', God expects us to grow and develop. St Paul writes about all of us coming to 'the knowledge of the Son of God, to maturity, to the measure of the stature of Christ'. There's a lot of learning to do before we reach maturity. That's why we study the

Bible, and read Christian books, and listen closely to sermons, to help us develop into spiritually grown-up Christians.

Heaven

In particular, the idea of heaven is totally beyond our comprehension. So the Bible gives us pictures of a place above the clouds, with harps and white robes. But as the children of God grow to spiritual adulthood, we see that beyond the symbols lies the gift of eternal life, which is too wonderful for us to understand until we get there. We can no more understand the joy of heaven while we're on earth than a 5-year-old can understand the joy of driving a car – we have to extrapolate, and say it's like riding your tricycle only better. So God tells us that heaven's like all the most wonderful experiences we've ever had on earth rolled into one, only much, much better. Yet we can believe in what we can't understand. Just as children believe that one day they'll be adults, so we can believe that one day we'll be in heaven, mind-boggling as the thought is.

Limerick

I'll end with a limerick:

There once was an eager young priest
who lived almost entirely on yeast,
   for he said, 'It is plain
   we shall all rise again,
and I want to get started, at least.'

All-age worship

Discuss whether driving a car is more fun that riding a tricycle.

Suggested hymns

Alleluia, alleluia, give thanks to the risen Lord; Come, ye faithful, raise the anthem; Now the green blade riseth; The day of resurrection.

Third Sunday of Easter 22 April
Second Service **Above the Bright Blue Sky**

Ps. 142 Bring me out of prison; Deut. 7.7–13 Redeemed from slavery; Rev. 2.1–11 Letters to Ephesus and Smyrna; *Gospel at Holy Communion*: Luke 16.19–31 The rich man and Lazarus

> *'The poor man died and was carried away by the angels to be with Abraham.' Luke 16.22*

What to tell the children

What do you tell children when somebody they love has died? It's a problem, isn't it? We're none of us very good at putting our feelings into simple words which children could understand. Neither can we easily explain what we believe. I recommend you start at a very basic level:

'Good morning, darling. Dear Granny went to sleep last night, and when she woke up she was with Jesus.'

I wouldn't mention heaven at this stage, for reasons I'll come to later. Sooner or later you'll be asked, in response to this astonishing information, 'Can I go and talk to her?' 'No, darling,' you reply. 'She's been set free from that poor old body which was giving her so much pain. She doesn't need it any more. She's gone to be with Jesus.'

'Where's Jesus?' comes the insistent question.

'We know that, don't we? Jesus promised that he'd be with us always. And he's especially close to us when we pray.'

'Is Granny here with us, too?' 'Yes, dear. Isn't that nice?'

'Why can't I see her then?' (Children can be very persistent!)

'Well, she's sort of invisible,' you reply. The children probably know some story of an invisible man, or an invisible Hobbit, and when they ask you whether you mean Granny's like that, you must answer, 'Yes, something like that.' This is one of those times when you mustn't stop answering a child's questions until the child stops asking them. If you seem to be fobbing them off, they'll assume you regard them as too insignificant, and never trust you again on the subject of death. If you try your best, however, children can be remarkably tolerant of adult imperfections.

Funerals

Next comes the problem of the funeral. Every child is different, but I think they are probably the best judge of whether they should attend or not. You have already told them that Granny's finished with the old body; you can try suggesting that she's already been fitted for a lovely new body that never feels pain. Yet we loved her old body, because we used to cuddle up close to it, so we show our love for her by putting the old body in a beautiful box, and laying it to rest in the ground, or burning it to ashes and putting them in the ground. But here we must be very careful to avoid saying that Granny's under the ground. I think you should never take a child to a graveside to 'talk to Granny', because they'll be frightened that Granny's being crushed.

Acceptance

Children can be remarkably matter-of-fact. They usually recover from bereavement much quicker than adults do. 'Why was Auntie crying?' they ask. And if you answer, 'Because she misses being able to cuddle Granny,' they accept it and run off to play. To be honest, you may have to answer questions like, 'Is Granny still cross with me?' by saying something like, 'No dear, that was because of the pain she had, and Jesus has taken away everything that was wrong with her now' – meaning both physically or morally.

Above the bright blue sky

You notice I haven't spoken about heaven. That's because most children think of heaven as the sky, where the stars are. One day, they're going to discover that beyond the stars are more stars, and more stars beyond that, and there isn't a place for dead people up there. I may be wrong, but I think it's a shame to tell children stories that they will later discover to be untrue, because they'll wonder what other lies you told, and end by rejecting everything you said to them. Jesus didn't say dead people go to heaven; he said that Lazarus went to 'Abraham's bosom', using an old Jewish story for people who understood perfectly that stories are not meant to be taken literally. He said that in the resurrection, we are *like* the angels in heaven, but that we shall be free of all the restrictions of time and space. Children used to be taught a hymn that contained the words,

There's a home for little children
Above the bright blue sky,
Where Jesus reigns in glory,
A home of peace and joy.

Very sweet, but what will they say when they find out that there isn't? *Mission Praise* changes that to 'There's a place for all the children, where Jesus reigns in love'. Teaching children about death is very difficult, but we shouldn't make it harder by leaving others to clear up the mess we make.

Suggested hymns

A brighter dawn is breaking; Alleluia, alleluia, give thanks to the risen Lord; It is a thing most wonderful; There's a song for all the children.

Fourth Sunday of Easter 29 April
Principal Service **Trust and Obey**
Gen. 7.1–5, 11–18; 8.6–18; 9.8–13 Noah's flood (*if used, the reading from Acts must be used as the second reading*), *or* Acts 4.5–12 Peter's witness to resurrection; Ps. 23 The Lord is my shepherd; 1 John 3.16–24 Law, faith and love; John 10.11–18 The good shepherd

> *'We receive from [God] whatever we ask, because we obey his commandments and do what pleases him. And this is his commandment, that we should believe in the name of his Son Jesus Christ and love one another, just as he has commanded us. All who obey his commandments abide in him, and he abides in them. And by this we know that he abides in us, by the Spirit that he has given us.' 1 John 3.22–24*

Jewish atheists

In a newspaper article, a Jewish rabbi made the startling suggestion that it's perfectly possible to be a Jew and an atheist at the same time. Great crowds pack the synagogues on the Day of Atonement, the holiest day of the year. Yet the next Sabbath the synagogues are as empty, he said, as a church on the Sunday after Christmas!

Why don't the crowds keep coming? Paradoxically, he suggested, it may be because they don't believe in God. Yet they come on the holy days to show that they are Jewish. Does that sound shocking? Judaism is a religion based on obedience to God's commandments, wrote the rabbi. Being a good Jew, he said, doesn't necessarily mean believing in God, just doing what he says!

Dangers

I think there are obvious dangers in this. Being Jewish could become simply a matter of following certain meaningless rituals to preserve an already antiquated culture. But not if you look at the profoundly moral nature of the Old Testament Law. Nearly all the laws are concerned with human behaviour, so Judaism is often described as a religion of deed rather than creed. The nature of God has never been defined, so whether you believe in the distant power behind the universe or the intimate voice of conscience, and treat your neighbour lovingly, there's room for a range of belief or unbelief.

St John

It's important to listen to our Jewish friends, for the Good Shepherd foresaw one flock, Jews and Gentiles together. The good rabbi was probably exaggerating, to shock us into thinking things out for ourselves. Yet his emphasis on obedience ties in with what St John wrote in his first letter: 'We receive from [God] whatever we ask, because we obey his commandments and do what pleases him.' In other words, God answers our prayers because we obey him. This appears to contradict what St Paul says, that we're justified by our faith alone, not by good works. But it's a difference of emphasis, not of substance. Paul didn't want us to think we can earn our way into heaven by keeping the letter of the law, without any real love in our hearts for God or neighbour. We can never deserve salvation, it's always the free gift of a forgiving God. Yet, as St James wrote, nobody can claim to have faith unless it shows in their lives, making them more loving.

The Holy Spirit

What many Jews fail to appreciate, however, is the impossibility of obeying God without supernatural help. St Paul wailed about his Pharisee days, 'The good that I would, that I do not, and the

130

evil that I would not, that I do.' St John continues, 'This is [God's] commandment, that we should believe in the name of his Son Jesus Christ and love one another, just as he has commanded us . . . by this we know that he abides in us, by the Spirit that he has given us.' God commands us to love each other; we can only do this if we have the motive and the power. The Christian's motive springs from knowing that God first loved us – it's in order to show our gratitude for God's love that we channel his love to those around us. The power comes from God's Holy Spirit dwelling in our hearts. When God commands you to love somebody apparently unloveable, pray about it. Ask God to give you his grace. Then you'll surprise yourself by your ability to do things you previously thought were quite impossible.

Believing

You don't have to pass an examination, or explain the doctrine of the Trinity, to experience this. The rabbi is right, it doesn't ultimately matter precisely *what* you believe; but *who* you believe in is crucial. It's quite impossible to obey God's commands, unless your heart is filled with gratitude to God, and you trust God to give you the strength you need.

All-age worship

'When we walk with the Lord' was written following the testimony of a confirmation candidate. Learn the chorus by heart, and any verses you can.

Suggested hymns

I come with joy, a child of God; Love is his word, love is his way; O for a closer walk with God; When we walk with the Lord.

Fourth Sunday of Easter   29 April
Second Service   **On the Breadline**
Ps. 81.8–16 I would feed you; Ex. 16.4–15 Manna; Rev. 2.12–17 Letters to Pergamum and Thyatira; *Gospel at Holy Communion*: John 6.30–40 I am the bread

'I am the Lord your God, who brought you up from the land of Egypt; open your mouth wide and I shall fill it.' Psalm 81.10 (Common Worship)

Hunger

With increasing climate change goes spreading starvation. If the rains fail, and the crops die, a whole generation in parts of the Third World will go hungry. We talk light-heartedly about our longing for a decent meal. But real, gnawing hunger is something very few people in this country have ever experienced; so for most of us it's outside our ability to imagine. Try to imagine that you've eaten nothing but roots and grass for 24 hours, and it's months since you had a square meal. Imagine it's a couple of hour's walk to find water, which is not that fresh when you do find it. Your throat is like a barren desert, and the back of your stomach seems to stick to the front. You have no strength, and drag your feet wearily one in front of the other. Your children cry plaintively, until even that's too much effort for them, and you wonder which will be the first to die. *That's* hunger. Try to imagine it, because that's how half the world's population live, most of the time. On the breadline.

Nomads

Surprisingly, there's nothing new in this. What's new is the growth of population, due to improved medical care, and the long-term change in our earth's climate because of the thoughtless way we have polluted our environment. But ever since *Homo sapiens* came down from the trees, there have been good years and bad years. In the bad years, few children lived more than a year at most, while the frail and elderly collapsed by the side of the trail and were abandoned. High death rates were accepted as a normal pattern of life; perhaps it's the influence of Christianity that has led people today to see that there's anything wrong with this. Mothers have always grieved for the death of their babies. Few sympathized with them; that was just how things were. The patriarchs of the Old Testament were desert nomads; some of them were rich, by the standards of the day; but the shadow of drought always hung over them.

Manna

Against this background, think how powerful the story of the manna is! God has led his chosen people for nigh on 40 years through the howling wilderness, and now they are at the end of their tether. Are his promises of a land of their own going for nothing, because they'll all die before they get there? Then God tells Moses, 'Trust me', and they find little white things on the ground. When they gather it, they find it's delicious, and there's just enough. After all they had been through! If they didn't believe before in a God of love, who saves his people, they believed now.

Psalms

Later, in the Psalms, God says, 'I am the LORD your God, who brought you up from the land of Egypt; open your mouth wide and I shall fill it.' Only those who have endured grinding poverty and hunger can appreciate the generosity of this promise – open your mouth wide, not just a crack, and you'll be filled with all you want.

Jesus the bread

In the Gospel of John, Jesus tried to teach the crowds that spiritual starvation is even more serious than shortage of physical bread. '"Our ancestors ate the manna in the wilderness," they said, "as it is written, 'He gave them bread from heaven to eat.'" Then Jesus said to them, "Very truly, I tell you, it was not Moses who gave you the bread from heaven, but it is my Father who gives you the true bread from heaven. For the bread of God is that which comes down from heaven and gives life to the world." They said to him, "Sir, give us this bread always." Jesus said to them, "I am the bread of life. Whoever comes to me will never be hungry, and whoever believes in me will never be thirsty."' Jesus compares the Holy Communion to the manna. Yet he implies that a life without prayer is one without spiritual nourishment, as deprived as those who are starving in the Third World. Of course we must have compassion for those who suffer from physical starvation. But Jesus says to lack any spiritual dimension in your life is just as bad as having eaten nothing for a week. You're on the spiritual breadline. He's right, you know. Now there's a thought.

Suggested hymns

At the Lamb's high feast we sing; Bread of heaven, on thee we feed; Break thou the bread of life; Guide me, O thou great Redeemer.

Fifth Sunday of Easter   6 May
Principal Service   **The Ethiopian Eunuch**
Bar. 3.9–15, 32—4.4 Wisdom, *or* Gen. 22.1–18 Abraham willing to sacrifice Isaac (*if used, the reading from Acts must be used as the second reading*), *or* Acts 8.26–40 Baptism of an Ethiopian; Ps. 22.25–31 The poor shall eat; 1 John 4.7–21 Our love for one another, God's love for us; John 15.1–8 The true vine

> *'He commanded the chariot to stop, and both of them, Philip and the eunuch, went down into the water, and Philip baptized him. When they came up out of the water, the Spirit of the Lord snatched Philip away; the eunuch saw him no more, and went on his way rejoicing.' Acts 8.38–39*

Pinderponshe

The missionary was baptizing a baby and asked, 'Name this child.' The father stepped up and replied 'Pinderponshe'. The missionary was startled, but knew they had some strange names, so he began, 'Pinderponshe, I baptize you . . .' 'No, no,' protested the father. 'She name upon that piece of paper pinned upon she!'

Baptism of a Gentile

Baptism is when we give a baby a name, and welcome him or her into our family. More importantly, we welcome them into the family of the church. We see this in the story of the Ethiopian eunuch. He was reading the Scriptures as he rode along in his chariot, which shows he was interested in the Jewish faith. Could a black man be saved by the Jewish God, he wondered? Philip explained that Jesus died to save everyone. In baptism we're united with Christ; his Spirit gives us new life. The African asked, 'What's to stop me being baptized?' Judaism only admitted those who were physically perfect; eunuchs were disqualified by their castration. But Philip

134

was learning you don't have to be a Jew to become a Christian. So the African man was baptized, and welcomed into the Christian family.

Baptism in the Spirit

I don't understand the miracle that happened next, but obviously the Holy Spirit was at work. The Spirit is always at work in baptisms. At Pentecost, Peter said to the crowd, 'Be baptized . . . and you'll receive the gift of the Holy Spirit.' The fruit of the Spirit is love, and when we become baptized members of the Church, we receive power to love. The Spirit is God's love, flowing through our hearts into the world around. Some Christians talk as though being 'baptized in the Spirit' was an exotic emotional experience, quite separate from water baptism. Well, thank God if he gives you wonderful experiences. But the Bible says they are not essential – everyone has different spiritual gifts. The test of whether you have received the Spirit is whether you love other people. Love isn't gooey emotions, it's practical help offered to others. God's promised his Spirit to everyone who's baptized.

The vine

Imagine the picture Jesus gave us in the Gospel. Jesus said, 'I am the vine, you are the branches. Those who abide in me and I in them bear much fruit, because apart from me you can do nothing.' The life-giving juices flowing through the branches of the vine represent the Holy Spirit. The grapes are the practical deeds of love, which can only grow in our lives if we're joined onto the vine; in other words if we remain members of the Christian family.

Eucharistic Spirit

You *stay* joined to the vine by drinking the wine it yields: the wine of the Holy Communion. When you come to church and join in the family meal, the Lord's Supper, you are bonded closer to Jesus, so that he can give you the Spirit of love. 'I am the vine, you are the branches,' he said. 'Those who abide in me and I in them bear much fruit, because apart from me you can do nothing. Whoever does not abide in me is thrown away like a [withered] branch.' I've no doubt Jesus can find ways of giving the Spirit of love to those who hardly ever come to church, but why make things difficult for him, when he's provided the Eucharist as the normal means for topping up the love flowing through our veins?

The name of Christian

You became members of the Christian family when you were baptized and given your Christian name. On that day your fellow Christians could start calling you a Christian: you were given the name or title of Christian. You won't find the fact that you are a Christian written on a piece of paper 'pinned upon she', but it should show in your face. The fact that you're a Christian should be visible in the kindness and love you show to your neighbours; because that comes from the spirit of love, given to you at your baptism, and topped up when you receive the eucharistic Spirit each week at Mass.

All-age worship

Arrange a visit to a house or park where a vine is growing. Measure the length of the branches.

Suggested hymns

You are the vine, we are the branches; I hunger and I thirst; Love divine, all loves excelling; Love is his word, love is his way.

Fifth Sunday of Easter   6 May
Second Service   Problems and Opportunities
Ps. 96 A new song; Isa. 60.1–14 Arise, shine; Rev. 3.1–13
Letters to Sardis and Philadelphia; *Gospel at Holy Communion*:
Mark 16.9–16 Mary Magdalene

> *'Look, I have set before you an open door, which no one is able to shut.' Revelation 3.8*

A joke

The slogan in the hotel lobby during the religious conference was, 'There Are No Problems, Only Opportunities!' A clergyman came to the desk and said, 'I have a problem.' The manager pointed to the slogan, whereupon the clergyman corrected himself. 'I have an opportunity in my bedroom, and I don't think she wants to share it with me.'

Bishop Tom Butler

Bishop Tom Butler, the Bishop of Southwark, gave one of the 'Thought for the Day' talks on BBC Radio 4, which has often been quoted. It was in 2006, when the Archbishop of Canterbury was visiting the Pope, and many people were talking gloomily about problems that had arisen in relationships between Anglicans and Roman Catholics. Bishop Butler suggested that we learn to look at problems and see how they can be turned into opportunities. At the Reformation there were severe differences between Catholics and Protestants, over which people were willing to kill each other. Yet the Church of England saw itself as a part of the worldwide Catholic Church, which had learnt some of the lessons of Protestantism, without ever losing touch with its catholic roots. Gradually it tried to turn itself into a bridge-church, with a foot on each bank, trying to form a route for dialogue between the two sides. Whether or not you agree with this description, it's interesting to see how it worked out over subsequent centuries.

Vernacular liturgy

The first and most obvious example was the question of the language of church services. At the Reformation, the Catholic Mass was always in Latin. Most people in Europe thought that was the only way of preventing the church fragmenting into separate language groups. The Church of England discovered that when Christians worship in their own language, they can grow spiritually, because they can speak to God from the heart. Yet the structure of the old services was retained, in newly beautiful phrases. At the Second Vatican Council, Pope John XXIII felt that his church must address the problems of the modern world in the language that people understood. So he undertook a major reform of the church's structures and its liturgies. Roman Catholics suddenly discovered that the Anglican Church had shown them the way, by treating the problem of language as an opportunity for growth, from the very start.

Married priests

The second opportunity that Bishop Butler pointed to was that of married priests. For the first thousand years of the Church's history many Catholic priests were married. In the Eastern Orthodox Churches, parish priests *have* to be married. Yet gradually priestly celibacy became an invariable rule in the Roman Catholic Church. They argued that celibate priests were free of the distractions of family, didn't need to be paid much, and could be sent wherever they were needed at short notice, to devote themselves single-mindedly to the people under their care. From Archbishop Cranmer onwards, however, the C of E showed that the choice whether or not to marry could be left to each individual priest. Now the RC Church has accepted that married Anglican priests who become Catholics can continue to function as priests. This has been a step towards accepting that the celibacy of the clergy isn't a theological issue.

Women clergy

The ordination of women to the priesthood in the Anglican Communion was a long-drawn-out process, while care was taken to protect the needs of those who were opposed. But when it came, the church found that what had been thought of as a problem was in fact a blessing, and the distinctive gifts of women in the ministry brought a new depth and warmth to the spiritual lives of its members. Protestants had known this for years; can the bridge-church bring this blessing to the Catholic Church which has been so long opposed?

Gay clergy

Finally and most controversially, Bishop Tom addressed the problem of gay priests, which seems to be splitting the Anglican Communion with bitter disputes. Yet many in the priesthood who are celibate are quietly gay, and have been for years. They show a depth of compassion and care to their parishioners which may come out of their own suffering. Is it possible that in this area, too, the Church is discovering that the best way to deal with problems is to regard them as opportunities? The risen Christ said to the Church in Sardis, 'Look, I have set before you an open door, which no one is able to shut.' Are there any problems in your life that could be dealt with in this way?

Suggested hymns

God is love, and where true love is (Ubi caritas); Love is his word, love is his way; Once to every man and nation; Thy hand, O God, has guided.

Sixth Sunday of Easter (Rogation Sunday)   13 May
(Eve of St Matthias, see page 319.)
Principal Service   **Julian of Norwich**
Isa. 55.1–11 Come to the waters (*if used, the reading from Acts must be used as the second reading*), or Acts 10.44–48 Baptism of Gentiles; Ps. 98 In righteousness God shall judge; 1 John 5.1–6 Love and the commandments; John 15.9–17 The commandment to love

> *'By this we know that we love the children of God, when we love God and obey his commandments.' 1 John 5.2*

Julian of Norwich

For many years in the fifteenth century, Mother Julian lived walled into a chapel in one of the medieval churches in Norwich. Many people came to talk to her through its window, and she taught them about prayer. In a series of visions or 'Showings', Julian sees that the whole universe is no greater, compared to the greatness of God, than a hazelnut, yet God loves the creation with a mother's care. We should pray even when we don't feel like it, because it's God who is praying in us. Once you've heard Grace Warrack's old-fashioned translation, you can never forget its phrases – T. S. Eliot quoted several of them in his *Four Quartets*. Here are some extracts:

The hazelnut

1. God's love for the universe:

> Also in this he shewed me a little thing, the quantity of an hazel-nut, in the palm of my hand; and it was as round as a ball. I looked thereupon with the eye of my understanding, and thought: *What may this be?* And it was answered generally thus: *It is all that is made.* I marvelled how it might last, for methought it might suddenly have fallen to naught for littleness. And I was

139

answered in my understanding: *It lasteth, and ever shall last for that God loveth it.*

On prayer

2. About asking God for things in our prayers:

After this our Lord shewed concerning prayer. In which shewing I see two conditions in our Lord's signifying: one is rightfulness, another is sure trust. But yet oftentimes our trust is not full: for we are not sure that God heareth us, as we think because of our unworthiness . . . And all this brought our Lord suddenly to my mind, [who] said: *I am ground of thy beseeching: first it is my will that thou have it; and after, I make thee to will it; and after, I make thee to beseech it and thou beseechest it. How should it then be that thou shouldst not have thy beseeching? . . .* Full glad and merry is our Lord of our prayer; and he looketh thereafter and he willeth to have it . . .

Thou shalt not be overcome

3. God supports us in all dangers:

And this word: *Thou shalt not be overcome,* was said full clearly and full mightily, for assuredness and comfort against all tribulations that may come. He said not: *Thou shalt not be tempested, thou shalt not be travailed, thou shalt not be afflicted;* but he said: *Thou shalt not be overcome . . .* and *all shall be well . . .*

Love is his meaning

Fourth and last, God is love:

And from that time that it was shewed, I desired oftentimes to learn what was our Lord's meaning. And fifteen years after, and more, I was answered in ghostly understanding, saying thus: *Wouldst thou learn thy Lord's meaning in this thing? Learn it well. Love was his meaning. Who shewed it thee? Love. What shewed he thee? Love. Wherefore shewed it he? For Love. Hold thee therein and thou shalt learn as well as know more in the same . . .* Thus was I learned that Love was our Lord's meaning.

Love speaks to us

Maybe you found that old-fashioned English hard to follow. It's worth sticking with it, for once you grasp their meaning, the phrases stay in your memory for the rest of your life. For God is love, and, in everything that God says to us, 'Love is his meaning.' The universe is no bigger than a hazelnut in the eyes of God; yet it survives because God loves it. God wants us to pray, because he wants to give us what we ask for, if only we'll ask him for it. So God is the 'ground of our beseeching'. God didn't promise a life free from pain; but he did promise us the strength to survive: 'He said not: *Thou shalt not be tempested, thou shalt not be travailed, thou shalt not be afflicted*; but he said: *Thou shalt not be overcome* . . . and *all shall be well, and all shall be well, and all manner of thing shall be well*.' Words of God to you and me, written down by a holy Englishwoman in the fifteenth century.

All-age worship

Copy, in old-fashioned writing, one of the quotations, e.g.

All shall be well, and all shall be well.
and all manner of thing shall be well.

Suggested hymns

God is love, and where true love is, God himself is there; Jesus stand among us; Love of the Father, love of God the Son; Peace is flowing like a river

Sixth Sunday of Easter (Rogation Sunday) 13 May
Second Service **Growing Up**
Ps. 45 Royal wedding; S. of Sol. 4.16—5.2; 8.6–7 Many waters cannot quench love; Rev. 3.14–22 Letter to Laodicea; *Gospel at Holy Communion*: Luke 22.24–30 Greatness and service

> *'Set me as a seal upon your heart, as a seal upon your arm; for love is strong as death, passion fierce as the grave. Its flashes are flashes of fire, a raging flame. Many waters cannot quench love, neither can floods drown it. If one offered for love all the wealth of his house, it would be utterly scorned.' Song of Solomon 8.6–7*

Emotional illness

Psychologists tell us there's been a severe rise in emotional disturbances in recent years. It arises from the excessive expectations that people feel themselves bound to live up to. Fuelled by TV programmes like *Big Brother*, and pictures in fashion magazines, many people imagine that they will only be popular if they dress fashionably, and above all sexily. They fear rejection if they don't conform to the image of a desirable man or woman. So they starve themselves to make themselves slim, or overeat to make themselves sick, so that they can fit into the latest designs from clothing shops. They spend money they can scarcely afford, on clothes they don't really need, just to keep up with the latest trend. The most important thing in life for many people is to be alluring and desirable.

Children

Well, good luck to them, you say. It's a free country, and if that's the way they get their pleasures, who are we to stop them? Fair enough, when we're talking about adults. The sad thing, however, is that this is happening to children. The boys want to look like footballer superstars, because they want to be followed by the female fans and marry 'footballers' wives'. Little girls dress up sexy, because they think they'll be regarded as failures if they don't. The more obsessed they are with their appearance, the less well they do at their schoolwork. Sixty-three per cent of girls in a recent survey said they'd rather be a supermodel than a doctor or a teacher – a quarter thought that lap-dancing was a good profession. They are encouraged to have sexual emotions before they're emotionally mature; and the inevitable consequences are teenage pregnancies and abortions. Childhood could be the most precious part of their lives, and they are being encouraged to trade it in for a phoney adulthood which they're not yet ready for. Childhood has been sacrificed on the altar of desire. So our whole society has becoming hypersexualized. We have substituted true love with mere sex, lasting pleasure with transient happiness, and long-term commitment with serial relationships. We have lost far more than we've gained.

Freedom

The sad thing is that these terrible mistakes have been made in the name of freedom. People should be free to do what they like, they say, untrammelled by the restrictions of religious Puritanism. Ironically, we have thereby thrown away the freedoms that earlier generations fought for. The feminists struggled to have women, especially young women, regarded as people instead of things. Now all they want is to become objects of desire, rather than free subjects who can choose their own place in life with dignity. Victorian reformers fought to end the economic exploitation of child labour, only to have it replaced by their exploitation as consumers, and slavery to the world of fashion.

Desire in the Bible

The answer is not to impose a pious Puritanism. The Bible has a great deal to say in favour of sexual desire, mostly in the book we call the Song of Songs, or the Song of Solomon, the greatest love poem in the history of the world, where human love is used as an image of God's love for us, and our love for God. But always in the Bible, love leads to commitment, and the building of lasting relationships where children can be brought up in a secure environment. The Patriarchs were far from perfect, but they all aimed to become heads of families, surrounded by their children and their children's children, protecting each other from 'the slings and arrows of outrageous fortune'. Desire was celebrated, and then sublimated into the building of families and homes based on love, trust, kinship and responsibility.

Mature adults

Thank God then for Harry Potter, a role model for children, engaged in a thoroughly adult struggle against evil, but relying on the loyalty of his friends and the dependability of some, at least, among his teachers. Harry Potter matures in a healthy way, not by pretending to be an imitation adult, but by learning the lessons of childhood. By contrast, today's adults are encouraged to behave like irresponsible children, regressing to a sort of barbarism and throwing away the lessons that our ancestors learnt so painfully. Perhaps Harry Potter can teach children to enjoy their childhood, and can teach adults to grow up at last.

Suggested hymns

Child of the stable's secret birth; For the beauty of the earth; Love divine, all loves excelling; O love divine, how sweet thou art.

Ascension Day   17 May
Everywhere

Acts 1.1–11 The ascension (*must be used as either the first or second reading), or* Dan. 7.9–14 The Son of Man; Ps. 47 God has gone up, *or* Ps. 93 The Lord is king; Eph. 1.15–23 Christ is seated beside God; Luke 24.44–53 The ascension

> *'When [Jesus] had said this, as they were watching, he was lifted up, and a cloud took him out of their sight.' Acts 1.9*

Baby

There's a poem of quite appalling sentimentality by the nineteenth-century Scottish novelist George MacDonald. I'll be surprised if nobody wants to throw up by the time I've read it to you. The idea that babies come from somewhere above the clouds is about as dated as the story that the stork brings them. Yet there's a truth behind it all: children *are* the gift of God; and heaven isn't a place, it's a realm above space and time, which is with us everywhere. Are you sitting comfortably? Then I'll begin:

> Where did you come from, baby dear?
> Out of the everywhere into the here.
> Where did you get those eyes so blue?
> Out of the sky as I came through.
> What makes the light in them sparkle and spin?
> Some of the starry spikes left in.
> Where did you get the little tear?
> I found it waiting when I got here.
> What makes your forehead so smooth and high?
> A soft hand stroked it as I went by.
> What makes your cheek like a warm white rose?
> I saw something better than any one knows.
> Whence that three-cornered smile of bliss?
> Three angels gave me at once a kiss.
> Where did you get this pearly ear?

144

God spoke, and it came out to hear.
Where did you get those arms and hands?
Love made itself into bonds and bands.
Feet, whence did you come, you darling things?
From the same box as the cherubs' wings.
How did they all just come to be you?
God thought about me, and so I grew.
But how did you come to us, you dear?
God thought about you, and so I am here.

Yuck!

Ascension

So the baby came 'out of the everywhere, into the here', it says. From a world untrammelled by space and time, into our world where you can only be in one place at any one moment. If we reverse that process, it gives us an idea of what Jesus did at the ascension. Immediately after he'd risen from the dead, Jesus had many new powers, yet he was located in one spot. To talk to him you had to go to that place, and wait at the back of the queue. So Jesus changed into a higher state of existence, giving unrestricted access to him for everybody, anywhere, at any time. So you might say, he came 'out of the here, into the everywhere'.

Luke and Matthew

St Matthew brings this out very clearly when he ends his Gospel with these words of Jesus: 'remember, I am with you always, to the end of the age'. St Luke begins the Acts of the Apostles with a more spiritual version, implying that the ascension was more of a vision than a physical event:

> [Jesus said] 'You will receive power when the Holy Spirit has come upon you; and you will be my witnesses in Jerusalem, in all Judea and Samaria, and to the ends of the earth.' When he had said this, as they were watching, he was lifted up, and a cloud took him out of their sight.

Invisible presence

According to Acts, the invisible presence of Jesus, with us wherever we go, is mediated to us by the Holy Spirit. A long time ago in Canada, the only way to cross a broad river was over a narrow plank bridge with no handrails. A young girl was asked by her father whether she dared to cross it, and she replied that she had a good head for heights. But half way across she looked down and lost her nerve. She could neither go forward nor back. Her father came up behind her and placed his hand on her shoulder. 'Trust me, I'm with you,' he said, and although she couldn't see him, she gained the confidence to carry on safely to the other side. We can't see Jesus, but since the ascension, Jesus is with us, his hand on our shoulder.

Trust him

Will you trust him, the risen and ascended Christ? Jesus had a moment of doubt himself, on the cross, when he thought his heavenly Father had forsaken him. But although he couldn't see God, he continued to pray to him. Will you do the same, talking to your invisible Saviour wherever you go – invisible precisely because he's ascended 'out of the here into the everywhere'?

Suggested hymns

Christ triumphant, ever reigning; Crown him with many crowns; Hail the day that sees him rise; Jesus is Lord! Creation's voice proclaims it.

Seventh Sunday of Easter   20 May
(Sunday after Ascension Day)
Principal Service   Otherworldly? No!
Acts 1.15–17, 21–26 Choosing Matthias (*must be used as either the first or second reading*), or Ezek. 36.24–28 I will put my Spirit in you; Ps. 1 Righteousness; 1 John 5.9–13 Faith and life; John 17.6–19 Sanctified in truth

> *'I am not asking you to take them out of the world, but I ask you to protect them from the evil one.' John 17.15*

Otherworldly?

Sometimes, Christians are criticized as being so heavenly minded they're no earthly use! You could never accuse Jesus of being otherworldly – he was completely down to earth. That was the whole point of his birth in Bethlehem – 'he came down to earth from heaven'. He didn't seek to escape from the world; instead he tried to transform the world into a better place. If that's what Jesus was like, that's how his followers should be, too. You and I often find this rotten old world a terrible place to live in, but we mustn't run away from it; rather, we must enter wholeheartedly into earthly life, in order to change it.

Ascension

When Jesus ascended into heaven, this was to warn us that we should no longer expect to see him on earth. But he's still here with us. As Tennyson said, 'Speak to him, thou, for he hears, and spirit with Spirit can meet – Closer is he than breathing, and nearer than hands and feet.' Yet Christ's actual work has been handed over to us to do. That's why it's so important that we should be down to earth. No otherworldliness for us Christians, or we can't do the work that Jesus has called us to, in transforming this world into a better place.

No escape

But people have always been tempted by the path of escape. Every so often, some ancient text is rediscovered, which presents a different picture of Jesus from that in the New Testament. Then a lot of people go overboard in recommending the alternative view. Recently there's been a fuss about a document called *The Gospel of Judas*. This is an Ethiopian translation of a Greek book dating back to some time in the second century AD. It portrays a laughing Jesus, but not laughing with humour and with joy, but with sardonic sarcasm at the ridiculousness of the world. People who trouble about changing the world are wasting their time, the book suggests – the world's a big mistake, and we need to get away from it, mentally, as quickly as we can. Judas Iscariot's job was to help Jesus to die, so that he could escape, and show us the way to distance ourselves from earthly concerns.

Absurd

Most Christians will reply that it's not the world that's absurd, but this understanding of it – and it's not as uncommon as you might think. It's one of the heresies condemned by the Christian writer Irenaus in around AD 180, and many books presenting this sort of view were discovered at Nag Hamadi in Egypt in the 1940s. They're not interested in what Jesus did for us by his death and resurrection. All they care about is some supposed secret teachings which Jesus gave to his disciples, and which are passed on to the privileged few in these documents. Their concern is not love, but knowledge. They take their name from the Greek word for knowledge, and are called Gnostics. That's G N O S T I C S, with a silent G at the beginning, and rhyming with joss-sticks. They believe that this world was not created by the Supreme Being, but by some inferior, malicious god with a small g. The ruler of the universe is too exalted for mere humans to speak to, they say – we have to approach him through a string of intermediaries.

Jesus

Jesus asked his Father to give us not a way of escape, but the power to transform the world. 'I am not asking you to take them out of the world,' he prayed, 'but I ask you to protect them.' You see, the evil in the world doesn't come from some malign under-god, but from human hearts, yours and mine included. No amount of 'knowledge falsely so called' can save us from the sin within us. Only love can do that – God's love and ours. You might think the way-out ideas of the Gnostic heretics should be tolerated as an alternative approach to Christianity. But in fact they are extremely dangerous, because they encourage escapism. They distract us from spreading the good news of God's love shown in the death, resurrection and ascension of Jesus, and the power of the Holy Spirit available to all of us, to strengthen us in the task of redeeming the world for God.

All-age worship

Make paper crowns for people to wear, reading 'Changing the world for Jesus, King of kings'.

Suggested hymns

Alleluia, sing to Jesus; Christ triumphant, ever reigning; Crown him with many crowns; See, the conqueror mounts in triumph.

Seventh Sunday of Easter   20 May
Second Service   **The Nazareth Manifesto**
Ps. 147.1–12 God's care; Isa. 61.1–11 The Spirit is upon me;
Luke 4.14–21 Rejected at Nazareth

> *'The Spirit of the Lord is upon me, because he has anointed me to bring good news to the poor. He has sent me to proclaim release to the captives and recovery of sight to the blind, to let the oppressed go free, to proclaim the year of the Lord's favour.'*
> *Luke 4.18–19*

Manifestos

The word 'manifesto' comes from the Italian, and means a public statement of principles, making manifest your future policies. It's usually a political party's electoral platform, but there are many other types of manifesto as well. The most famous was the Communist Manifesto, by Karl Marx and Friedrich Engels in 1848. You don't hear the term so much nowadays. Perhaps that's because so many political parties have made long lists of promises, before the election, of the wonderful things they were going to do if they were elected – and then totally ignored them when they came to power!

The Nazareth Manifesto

Has it ever occurred to you that Jesus issued a manifesto when he began his campaign to build the kingdom of God on earth, as it is in heaven? It was a short summary of what he hoped to achieve, easily memorized, and with the advantage that it comes from the Old Testament, so many of his Jewish hearers could repeat it by heart. But he put a completely new meaning on the familiar words, and many people didn't like it. I call it the Nazareth Manifesto, and it was spelt out in today's reading from St Luke's Gospel.

Context

First, let's put it into context. Jesus was brought up in Joseph's carpentry shop in Nazareth. When he was nearly 30, he went off to join his cousin John's religious reform movement by the River Jordan. He proclaimed a baptism of repentance for the remission of sins. He called a group of followers to join them, and settled in Simon Peter's house in the fishing port of Capernaum, on the shore of Lake Galilee. Then he paid a return visit to his home town, the first since he left to join John the Baptist's revival. He was invited to speak in the synagogue there, and read these verses from Isaiah, his programme for what he was going to do from now on:

> The Spirit of the Lord is upon me, because he has anointed me to bring good news to the poor. He has sent me to proclaim release to the captives and recovery of sight to the blind, to let the oppressed go free, to proclaim the year of the Lord's favour.

Opposition

There was a puzzled pause; Jesus rolled up the scroll, and said, 'Today this scripture has been fulfilled in your hearing.' The people of his home town were so angry at a mere carpenter making these claims, that they tried to throw him down the steep hillside. Why? I think it was because these promises were no longer a pious hope for a distant future, but a political manifesto for what Jesus wanted his followers to achieve here and now. He meant it both literally and spiritually. Physically, Jesus intended to become a compassionate healer; many of his followers today seek medical training, or co-operate with those who have, to bring about bodily healing by the power of prayer. The liberation of slaves took nineteen hundred years, but it began when Galilean serfs were converted, and their masters had to treat them as brothers. The under-class and social outcasts were treated as God's precious children. And so on.

Spiritual

Yet even more radical was the spiritual interpretation of these verses. Those who were blind to what God was up to, had their eyes opened to the importance of equality; bidding farewell to the status quo; and welcoming the changes that Jesus was bringing. Those imprisoned by moral rules were liberated to follow the law of love. Christians find themselves engaged in a never-ending search for tolerance between races and nations, different understandings of the faith, and different lifestyles. The first Christians were called those who are 'turning the world upside down' – no wonder they were unpopular! The Nazareth Manifesto wasn't just a programme for Jesus. It was, and still is, a manifesto for the Church: a call to a radical change in attitudes; a new relationship with our heavenly Father; a bloodless revolution in the way the world is run. And you and I are part of the process, God help us!

The Spirit of the Lord is upon me, because he has anointed me to bring good news to the poor. He has sent me to proclaim release to the captives and recovery of sight to the blind, to let the oppressed go free, to proclaim the year of the Lord's favour.

Suggested hymns

God's Spirit is within my heart; Oh Lord, all the world belongs to you; The kingdom of God is justice and joy; Will you come and follow me?

Day of Pentecost (Whit Sunday)   27 May
Principal Service   The Go-Between God
Acts 2.1–21 The day of Pentecost (must be used as either the first or second reading), or Ezek. 37.1–14 The valley of dry bones; Ps. 104.26–36, 37b The Spirit in creation; Rom. 8.22–27 The Spirit's prayer; John 15.26–27; 16.4b–15 The Advocate will lead you to truth

'When the Spirit of truth comes, he will guide you into all the truth; for he will not speak on his own, but will speak whatever he hears.' John 16.13

The go-between

When the Government of Northern Ireland collapsed in 1972, Frank Steele, working for the SIS, was sent by the British Government to investigate. He contacted the leaders of the Provisional IRA and suggested they come to London to meet the Northern Ireland Secretary. The meeting never took place, but this was the first ever contact between the Republicans and the British Government. Steele's work was continued by another SIS agent, Michael Oatley, who contacted a Derry businessman, Brendan Duffy. Duffy was a strong Republican, but a pacifist – he set up a meeting for Oatley with Martin McGuiness. Officially the British Government refused to negotiate with terrorists. But through these mediators, it persuaded the IRA that they'd never achieve their goal of a united Ireland, but if they laid down their arms, the British would withdraw their troops. Twenty years and hundreds of needless deaths later, the work of these intermediaries resulted in peace. The go-betweens didn't try to negotiate, but they believed that enemies must always talk to each other.

The go-between God

A go-between can often bridge the gap between people who are at loggerheads, whether between nations, classes, businesses, neighbours or members of a family. In 1972, the same year as the mediators were beginning to contact the IRA, John Taylor, the General Secretary of the Church Missionary Society, wrote a book about the Holy Spirit called *The Go-Between God*. The Holy Spirit, he said, isn't a difficult theological theory. The Holy Spirit is the intermediary, helping to bring about peace talks between God and the Christian, between one Christian and another Christian, and between Christians and unbelievers. The Holy Spirit facilitates communication between God and the world.

Anonymous

Now the go-betweens who set up the talks in Ireland were deliberately anonymous. Their names didn't come out until after the peace agreement was signed. That was because they didn't want to draw attention to themselves. Their aim was to point the listener beyond themselves to the person they were representing. In the same way, God doesn't want us to think about the Holy Spirit, but to think about God our heavenly Father, for whom the Holy Spirit speaks. Don't worry if the theology seems difficult – look beyond the Spirit to God's message of love. The Holy Spirit is only the go-between.

Mission

The Spirit, wrote John Taylor, enables God to speak to the world through his Christian people – through you and me. Don't worry; the Spirit will put the words into your mouth. You, the Christian, are the go-between between God and the world, the channel through whom God speaks his message of love. The Creator Spirit is involved in the creation of the world, the creation of the Church, and every creative thing we do. The life of the Church is like the birth of a child. Conception was when Jesus, in love, called his disciples, and the idea of a world movement of love was conceived in their hearts. Gestation is the power of the Spirit helping the Church to grow. Labour is the revelation of God's love; birth is the Spirit working through Jesus; and the child's first breath is God's Spirit breathed into us and dwelling within.

Lifestyle

Part Two of John Taylor's book *The Go-Between God* concerns the lifestyle of the growing Church, shown in our desire to share the good news. Children, as they grow, explore things for themselves, and the Church is still exploring new expressions of faith and new ways of behaving. The Spirit is involved in our meetings with other people, helping us to understand each other. This includes our meetings with people of other denominations and other faiths. The Spirit is involved in our playing, as we enjoy new ways of worship and new styles of music. The go-between God is there in our loving – not only in the family, but in our care for the needy and the relationships between nations.

Anonymity

But just as the go-betweens in Ireland remained anonymous, so the Church points away from itself to the God who inspires our mission. We hardly talk about ourselves at all, nor about God – we simply get on with loving others and leave them to ask why we do it. What I've just said is a drastic oversimplification of a book which is full of profound insights. Today's a day to celebrate God's gift to us of his Spirit. Let's use it to point away from ourselves to the love of God, for whom we act as a go-between.

All-age worship

Children make paper crowns of flames.

Suggested hymns

Fear not, rejoice and be glad; Gracious Spirit, Holy Ghost; O thou who camest from above; Spirit of holiness.

Day of Pentecost (Whit Sunday)   27 May
Second Service   **One Shall Tell Another**
Morning Ps. 145 One shall tell another; Evening Ps. 139.1–11 [13–18, 23–24] God is present in death; Ezek. 36.22–28 I will put my spirit within you; Acts 2.22–38 You will receive the Spirit; *Gospel at Holy Communion*: John 20.19–23 He breathed on them

> *'One generation shall praise your works to another, and declare your mighty acts.' Psalm 145.4 (Common Worship);* or:

> *'Peter said to them, ". . . you will receive the gift of the Holy Spirit. For the promise is for you, for your children, and for all who are far away, everyone whom the Lord our God calls to him."' Acts 2.38–39*

Chinese whispers

In the 1914 war, a commanding officer sent a message to the next army group: 'Send reinforcements, we're going to advance.' It was passed from one soldier to another down the trenches, and, to the puzzlement of those who received it, the message finished up as 'Send three and fourpence, we're going to a dance'! Have you played the game of Chinese whispers? You sit in a circle, but far enough apart not to be able to hear the person next to your immediate neighbour. The leader whispers to the person next to them a slightly unexpected message, and they have to whisper it to the next one and so on. If anyone mishears what their neighbour's whispering, you can get some quite absurd distortions in the message by the time it completes the circle! The point of the game, I suppose, is to stress the need for clarity when you pass on a message.

The Holy Spirit

At Pentecost, we remember how Jesus gave his disciples the gift of the Holy Spirit, to help them to pass on the message of God's love to others. The Spirit gives us clarity and confidence, as we share with others his message – the good news of God's power to save us through the death of Christ on the cross. This morning's Psalm read, 'One generation shall praise your works to another, and declare your mighty acts'; and in the Acts of the Apostles, Peter said to the crowd, '. . . you will receive the gift of the Holy Spirit. For the promise is for you, for your children, and for all who are far away, everyone whom the Lord our God calls to him.' Being a Christian is like taking part in a worldwide game of Chinese whispers, where you have to pass on to everybody you meet, as accurately as you can, the message of God's love.

Graham Kendrick

Based on that Psalm I just quoted, 'One shall tell another, and he shall tell his friends' is the first line of a song written in 1981 by Graham Kendrick. Graham was one of the key figures in the development of new hymns in modern hymnbooks, and in the 1980s he led the worship at many of the 'Spring Harvest' gatherings for families. 'The Servant King' and 'Shine, Jesus, shine' by Graham Kendrick are familiar even among congregations that usually sing traditional church music. The theme of *One shall tell another* is the spreading of the gospel through personal conversations, what some people have called 'gossiping the gospel'. The repeated refrain is the invitation to 'Come on in and taste the new wine.' The kingdom of God is represented as a family party to which everyone is invited, and the invitation is passed on by word of mouth from one individual to another.

Pentecost

So Pentecost, the birthday of the Church, is about the colossal growth of the Christian community around the world, especially today in Africa, America and China, through the power of the Holy Spirit bubbling up like new wine. But it's also about you and me. Don't worry that you can't see clear signs of church growth in your neighbourhood; they may well be there beneath the surface. But they'll only blossom if you, too, play your part in gossiping the gospel – if you'll drop into casual conversation your own experience of the love of God. When your friends protest, 'Don't go all religious on me,' answer, 'There's nothing killjoy or solemn about God's love; the Bible says it's like new wine.' There's nothing off-putting about an invitation to share a glass of Beaujolais Nouveau! Don't worry about the way the conversation turns after that – the Spirit will give you the words to say. Sometimes you'll get it wrong, talking about morals rather than about love, like the soldiers saying 'going to a dance' when they should have said 'going to advance'! No matter, even if your friends decide to drop the subject, the Spirit will make sure they've already heard what they need to. Years later, maybe, they'll remember that you loved them enough to share the good news. Like Chinese whispers, the word will get around somehow, if you're willing to let the Spirit speak through you.

Suggested hymns

I vow to thee, my country; One shall tell another; The Spirit lives to set us free; There's a Spirit in the air.

Trinity Sunday   3 June
Principal Service   **Baptizing in the Name of the Trinity**
Isa. 6.1–8 Holy, holy, holy; Ps. 29 God's greatness; Rom. 8.12–17 The Spirit makes us heirs of God, with Christ; John 3.1–17 Born of the Spirit

> 'Holy, holy, holy is the Lord of hosts; the whole earth is full of his glory.' Isaiah 6.1–3

Football chants

Every football team has its own football chant – a set of words that the supporters shout out repeatedly and with gusto. Sometimes the words are nonsense, but no matter – they give a sense of solidarity among the supporters, and passionate purpose to the players. Suppose the team chant of the Much-Binding-in-the-Marsh Rangers goes like this: 'Hop hop hop, Rangers are top, the rest are all slop, sweep them out with a mop.' Thought-provoking, isn't it? Let's ask one of the supporters – you, sir, you've just been yelling the Much-Binding team chant; do you understand it? Yes, of course you do, you've been chanting it ever since you were a nipper. What does it mean, then? Take your time, there's no hurry. Oh, I see, it means you're a Rangers supporter. Anything else? No, no, that's a good enough reason for chanting it. Thank you for your intelligent answers.

Holy, holy, holy

You see what I mean? The literal meaning of the words doesn't matter, it's the togetherness that counts, when we all say them together. And our common admiration for the team we support. Some passages in the Bible make about as much sense as a football chant. Take this one, from the prophet Isaiah:

> In the year that King Uzziah died, I saw the Lord sitting on a throne, high and lofty; and the hem of his robe filled the temple. Seraphs were in attendance above him; each had six wings: with two they covered their faces, and with two they covered their feet, and with two they flew. And one called to another and said: 'Holy, holy, holy is the LORD of hosts; the whole earth is full of his glory.'

Books try to explain the meaning of the words, yet still we boggle. Nevertheless, many people say it's one of the most beautiful passages in the Bible. What they really mean is that it claims that the Lord God is the tops, we're his supporters, and we'll stick by him come what may!

Trinity

Christians like those verses, because they use the word 'holy' three times. This is Trinity Sunday, meaning 'three-ness'; today we affirm that we know God as our Creator and loving heavenly Father; we recognize the character of God in the words and life of Jesus; and the Spirit of love is working in our hearts. The Father's God; the Son's God; the Spirit's God; yet there are not three Gods but one. Do you understand that? No, neither does anybody else; it's a mystery: true, but incomprehensible. God is bigger than we are; how could our puny little minds even begin to understand God? The doctrine of the Trinity is the Christian's team chant.

157

Baptism in the name of the Trinity

According to Matthew's Gospel, Jesus said, 'Go therefore and make disciples of all nations, baptizing them in the name of the Father and of the Son and of the Holy Spirit.' When St Matthew wrote, some people were denying the very basis of what Jesus taught. Some said the true God is too remote for us to know anything about him, and the universe was created by another, wicked god. Some taught that Jesus was a mere man, and knew no more about God than we do. No, said others: Jesus couldn't really have been human, he was a spirit floating around six inches above the ground. And so on. The Church invented a definition, which was the doctrine of the Trinity: three persons in one God, and they enshrined it in the team chant, called the Creed, meaning 'I believe'. You don't have to understand the Creed; but you mustn't disagree with it, if you call yourself a Christian.

Why baptize?

If someone is baptized using the words, 'in the name of the Father and the Son and the Holy Spirit', their baptism should be recognized by all Christians – there's no need to be re-baptized if you change churches. So why do we bring babies to be christened? The official answer is that they're signed-up as members of the Church, the family of God, and start on their journey towards heaven. Yet I doubt whether many parents and godparents could explain those words. What's important is that they're our team chant. From baptism onwards the baby supports the same team as you and I, the team of God who is love, Jesus who conquered death, and the Spirit who fills our hearts with love. As babies grow up, parents, godparents, and friends in the congregation try and show them how to put that love into practice, as fellow supporters of Team Trinity.

All-age worship

Make paper bracelets, writing on them 'Member of God's Family'.

Suggested hymns

Bright the vision that delighted; Holy, holy, holy is the Lord; Holy, holy, holy, Lord God almighty; There is a Redeemer.

Trinity Sunday 3 June

(For Corpus Christi, the Thursday after Trinity Sunday, see page 324.)

Second Service   **Holier than Thou**

Morning Ps. 33.1–12 All earth's inhabitants; Evening Ps. 104.1–10 God's greatness; Ezek. 1.4–10, 22–28a A vision of God; Rev. 4.1–11 Holy, holy, holy; *Gospel at Holy Communion*: Mark 1.1–13 The Father sends the Spirit on the Son

> *'Day and night without ceasing they sing, "Holy, holy, holy, the Lord God the Almighty, who was and is and is to come."' Revelation 4.8*

Sanctimonious

Mark Twain described a repellent character whose religion had made him thoroughly unattractive. He was, according to the American humorist, 'a solemn, unsmiling, sanctimonious old iceberg that looked like he was waiting for a vacancy in the Trinity'. This could serve as a definition for the word 'sanctimonious'. A sanctimonious person is offensively self-righteous and hypocritically pious. Jesus condemned the Pharisees for their teaching that we can only please God by obeying every nit-picking little regulation in the Law of Moses. They implied that they alone were righteous, and lumped all the rest together as 'sinners'. Yet Jesus said to them, 'Truly I tell you, the tax-collectors and the prostitutes are going into the kingdom of God ahead of you.' He'd no time for the smug, sanctimonious, Pharisaical attitude, which has always been a temptation for religious people.

Holier than thou

A phrase that's often flung at sanctimonious people is: 'I don't like your holier-than-thou attitude.' This is the answer rightly given to anyone who feigns piety or righteousness, who pretends that they've a superior record of moral behaviour to that of those around them, or a cosy relationship with the Deity, private, exclusive and privileged. As soon as Christians start comparing themselves favourably with other people, they are vulnerable to the accusation of humbug, and that they're being holier than thou. Yet you may be surprised to know that the first person to use that phrase was God himself.

In the book of the prophet Isaiah, God launches a stinging rebuke to his people. God wanted them to know and love him, but they were so full of themselves that they ignored God altogether. Instead they took a superior attitude to everyone else. God describes them as those 'Which say, Stand by thyself, come not near to me; for I am holier than thou.' So it's not only atheists who dislike the holier-than-thou attitude – God hates it too.

Avoid it

So you and I must avoid that trap at all costs. Any trace of smugness and superiority will undo any good that our words about the love of God may have done; we shall be dismissed as hypocrites. Jesus was more interested in our humble attitude than he was in our superior moral achievements. The most important piece of moral instruction he gave in the Sermon on the Mount was 'Judge not, that ye be not judged.' Christians, as a whole, are not very good at following that instruction – judgementalism seems to be a core part of many people's understanding of religion.

Be holy

What makes it difficult for Christians to avoid the temptation to the holier-than-thou attitude, the HTTA, is that God definitely calls us to be holy. In many places God says, 'I am the LORD your God: ye shall therefore . . . be holy; for I am holy,' or words like that. So perhaps we need to look at what God means by holiness, which is very different from what the Pharisees meant. Holiness is the character of God – in the book of Revelation the angels in heaven sing day and night without ceasing: 'Holy, holy, holy, the Lord God the Almighty, who was and is and is to come.' Christians have seen in the threefold holiness of God in this verse, as in Isaiah's vision from which the words are quoted, a premonition of the doctrine of the Trinity which we celebrate today: God as Father, Son and Holy Spirit. The holiness of God is what makes it dangerous to approach him, like a high-voltage electric cable. Yet Isaiah was the first to see that it was not just God's power, but his moral purity, which makes it terrifying for 'people of unclean lips' to come near him. We have said so many unloving things with our mouths, that it's awesome to come into contact with God who is pure love. God's holiness is his love, and it rubs off onto us when we pray. But nobody with love in their hearts could possibly adopt a judgemental, 'holier-than-thou attitude' towards other people. Instead, if we want to be friends of God, we must count others better than ourselves. Even criticizing others for being sanctimonious is an unloving thing to do.

Cartoon

To end on a lighter note: a cartoon showed two soldiers watching their chaplain laughing and drinking with others at the bar. One says to the other, 'What I can't stand about our Padre is his *un-holier-than-thou* attitude.' You can't win!

Suggested hymns

Come down, O Love divine; Immortal, invisible, God only wise; My God, how wonderful thou art; Stand up and bless the Lord.

ORDINARY TIME

Sundays after Trinity are referred to as 'Ordinary Time' – what the poet John Meade Falkner calls 'The passionless Sundays after Trinity, neither feast day nor fast.' Other seasons are preparing for or responding to Christmas and Easter; this is just a season of steady growth, which is why the church hangings and vestments are green, the colour of growing things. See the chapter in this book on 'How to Choose the Readings' for why the Collect and Post-communion Prayer depend on the number of Sundays after Trinity Sunday, the date of which varies with the movement of Easter, but the Bible readings are 'Proper', or appropriate, to a particular range of dates. At the Principal Service, there are two alternative series of Old Testament readings and Psalms, which the minister may choose between. The 'Continuous' series follow the chapters of an Old Testament book in sequence Sunday after Sunday. The 'Related' series are chosen to illuminate the set New Testament reading and Gospel. If a saint's day falls on the Sunday, the minister may choose to use the readings for the saint instead of those for the Sunday. In these cases, this book provides a sermon on the saint's day readings in place of the Second Service.

First Sunday after Trinity (Proper 5) 10 June

(Eve of St Barnabas, see page 326.)

Principal Service **Adam and Eve**

(*Continuous*): 1 Sam. 8.4–11 [12–15] 16–20 [11.14–15] King
Saul anointed; Ps. 138 God's greatness; *or* (*Related*): Gen.
3.8–15 God in the Garden of Eden; Ps. 130 Hope for salvation;
2 Cor. 4.13—5.1 Grace, suffering and resurrection; Mark
3.20–35 Family, Obedience

> *'The man named his wife Eve, because she was the mother of all
> living.'* Genesis 3.20

Fantasy

I wonder why it is that fantasy literature is so popular these days.
People want to read books or watch films that tell a good story
about amazing people or creatures caught up in the struggle
between good and evil in some weird and wonderful universe, as
unlike the real world we live in as possible. I'll leave you to think of
recent examples in the best-seller lists and among the most-watched
movies. I think their popularity must be because in the fantasy
world you are not distracted by the need to be accurate about your
facts. Instead you can concentrate on the tensions people are under,
and the choices they have to make. Then you can identify with the
characters, and draw parallels with your own life. Sometimes you
don't even realize you're doing this, but you certainly can't do it
when you're reading a list of facts.

Bores

That's why facts are so boring. Try reading an encyclopaedia from
cover to cover! If you can't avoid it, listen to the local bore. Bores
recite a series of events that happened to them, without any light and
shade, or attempt to understand the reasons why people behaved as
they did. Their recital of brute facts can drive you up the wall. Like
the speaking clock, the bore gives you no hope of hearing anything
novel or thought-provoking ever again. What they need is a touch
of fantasy. This doesn't mean that they should invent events in their
lives which never really happened; they probably do that already.
They need to recognize that universal truths, with relevance to people in every age, can only be drawn out of fictional stories.

Myth

That's why nobody reads old science books, which are sure to be out of date by now. But people love to read the fictional myths of former civilizations, because you can learn from them about unchanging human nature. The old stories tell you how heroes behave, and how easy it is to betray your highest principles. They help you to understand your family and friends – you may even begin to understand yourself. A community's myths are useful from generation to generation; yesterday's science will be irrelevant tomorrow.

Misreading

It's sad when somebody takes a book of fiction and reads it as though it was fact. It's like reading the most wonderful poetry in the flat voice we use for the telephone directory. Anyone who reads the legends of the Greek gods and goddesses as though they were accurate accounts of historical events misses the whole point. It's truly tragic when Christians take the poetic fictions in the Bible as though they were scientific fact. Don't misunderstand me – there are many accounts of historical events in the Bible, though they're often told in such a way as to point to the moral truths they reveal. But other stories, with little or no basis in historical fact, aren't worthless – by the skilful use of fiction, they draw our attention to profound truths.

Adam and Eve

Most Christians believe that the story of Adam and Eve in the book of Genesis is one such. There must have been a point at which a pair of anthropoid apes became sufficiently human in their behaviour to be called *Homo sapiens*. But any attempt to imagine what their lives were like is bound to be fictional. 'Would you Adam and Eve it?' is Cockney rhyming slang for 'Would you believe it?' But in the case of the Garden of Eden story, the question ought really to be, in which sense do you believe it, the scientific sense or the mythological meaning? If it were science it would be a terrible bore. But if you read it as fiction, it tells you a lot about human nature, and what happens when we disobey God's commands. We all want to know more about evil than is good for us. God warns us against immorality, because he knows that dabbling in it will only harm us.

163

Yet the fact that it's forbidden tempts us to rebellion, and then we lose the paradise of close friendship with God. Most of our pain and suffering is our own fault, caused by our self-will. Yet Jesus forgives us and redeems us. You won't find that in any scientific textbook, but it's there in the story of the Garden of Eden. Fancy that. Would you Adam and Eve it?

All-age worship

Make up a story about someone who suffered because of their curiosity.

Suggested hymns

All hail the power of Jesus' name; Join all the glorious names; Praise to the holiest in the height; Walking in a garden.

First Sunday after Trinity (Proper 5) 10 June
Second Service **Conscience**
Ps. 37.1–11 [12–17] Trust in the Lord; Jer. 6.16–21 Ask for the ancient paths; Rom. 9.1–13 God and Israel; *Gospel at Holy Communion*: Luke 7.11–17 The widow's son at Nain

> *'I am speaking the truth in Christ – I am not lying; my conscience confirms it by the Holy Spirit.' Romans 9.1*

Scientific discovery

A report in the scientific magazine *Neuron* announced a remarkable new discovery – or so they claimed. Swiss scientists had inflicted on some volunteers a so-called 'game' that relied on mutual trust. Scientists can scan our heads in such a way that the parts of the brain where there's electrical activity – what you and I call 'thinking' – turn a different colour on the monitor screen. In this case, specific parts of the prefrontal cortex light up when we resist the temptation to do something that would get us punished if we were caught. And there you have it. A tiny area of the human brain gets very agitated when it wants to do something that it knows is wrong. Of course, we've known this for ages – we call it 'conscience'. The scientists added that psychopaths – people who do criminal or immoral acts without appearing to care about right and wrong – seem to have brain damage in this area. The British newspaper reporting this headlined it 'Prefrontal police', describing it humorously as an 'internal ASBO'. It's nice when scientists confirm that what we have always believed has a scientific basis, and isn't mere imagination. Most humans feel uncomfortable when they are about to do something that will make their friends feel let down. An interesting sidelight was added at the end of the item in the newspaper – something we've always suspected, but haven't dared to put into words. Apparently in teenagers, this part of the brain which houses the conscience, and the awareness of right and wrong, *isn't yet fully grown*! So we can't blame the teens when they do wrong without realizing how serious it is; we must just pray that they develop an adult conscience before it's too late.

Conscience and the Christian

There's much here that Christians need to pay attention to. The word conscience, in the New Testament, always describes this feeling of unease when you are about to do something you already know to be wrong; or else in phrases such as 'having a clear conscience'. St Paul declares that he could never tell a lie without suffering from terrible qualms: 'I am speaking the truth in Christ – I am not lying; my conscience confirms it by the Holy Spirit . . .' What the Bible *never* says is that your conscience tells you what you should and shouldn't do. You *can* find out which choice to make when you're on the horns of a dilemma; it's called 'the guidance of the Holy Spirit'. But it doesn't come easily, through some sort of internal hunch – if you've an unshakeable conviction that you ought to do this and not do that, without needing to puzzle over it, you're probably wrong.

Educating the conscience

That's why Christians say that conscience must always be educated. We have to read the Bible to see what moral guidance it gives; submit that to a rigorous examination to be sure we have understood it the way other Christians do; talk it over with our friends and pastors; make a list of pros and cons; and pray about it long and hard. Only then can we say that we should always avoid the path of evil, because our conscience warns us not to go that way. Perhaps 'educating my conscience' is what the scientists call the growth of the prefrontal cortex. If you have no conscience, you're a psychopath – and a menace.

Morality

Some philosophers tell you there's no difference between right and wrong, and morality is a delusion, imposed upon us by those who want to control us for their own benefit. Some neo-Darwinists say that every choice should be made on the sole basis of what will help us to survive. Yet, moral societies have survived, and lawless ones have perished. This feeling that I'm doing wrong when I hurt or harm someone else is widespread and inexplicable, unless the prefrontal cortex really is a built-in ASBO. Altruism – willingness to suffer for the sake of others – is admired, yet there's no logical basis for it unless there's a real difference between right and wrong.

Christian teaching

It's better, then, to return to the teaching of Jesus. What helps us to survive, on earth and in eternity, is having a clear sense of what God wants us to do. Love God with all your heart, and love your neighbour imaginatively, understanding how you yourself would like to be treated if you were in their place. Your prefrontal cortex may tell you what you *shouldn't* do: only God can tell you how you *should* behave.

Suggested hymns

An army of ordinary people; Lord of the Church, we pray for our renewing; O for a closer walk with God; O Lord of heaven and earth and sea.

Second Sunday after Trinity (Proper 6)   17 June
Principal Service   **Humour in Parables**
(*Continuous*): 1 Sam. 15.34—16.13 David anointed king; Ps. 20 Give victory to the king; *or* (*Related*): Ezek. 17.22–24 God's call; Ps. 92.1–4, 12–15 Righteousness; 2 Cor. 5.6–10 [11–13] 14–17 Faith, life and death; Mark 4.26–34 Parables of the kingdom

> 'With many such parables [Jesus] spoke the word to them, as they were able to hear it; he did not speak to them except in

parables, but he explained everything in private to his disciples.'
Mark 4.33–34

Stories

Jesus was a great storyteller. What wonderful stories they were! The crowds gathered to hear him, because he kept them entertained. They had never heard such stories before – stories of sheep and shepherds; naughty sons and forgiving fathers; passers-by refusing to help the victim of a mugging – it seemed like an endless stream of verbal picture painting. Jesus, it hardly needs to be said, knew what he was doing. People will listen to a rattling good yarn, who would quickly be bored by a lecture. None of us likes other people telling us what to do; we want to make up our own minds how to behave. Yet the stories of Jesus allow you to do just that – he describes an event in everyday life, and asks you to decide what you would do in that situation. Then, when similar problems arise in your relationship with God or with your neighbour, you'll deal with them in the same way.

Parables

The Gospels don't call the tales that Jesus told just stories; they use a special word: 'Parables'. What do you think it means? Something to do with tossing something beyond or throwing it beside another object. It's a type of tale that carries your thinking beyond the literal meaning of the words to a deeper, symbolic level. Yet it's quite painless: the listeners are challenged to answer a simple question, such as 'What man among you, having a hundred sheep, and losing one, wouldn't go after it?' – a question any fool can answer – and then they discover a profound truth about how God comes looking for us, and regards nobody as beyond hope. Anybody who enjoys soap operas on the television, knows you can discuss them for hours: 'Oo, she shouldn't have done that, what she ought to have done is this; nobody in their right senses would behave like that; mind you, in his circumstances, I'd have done the same; she really ought to have forgiven him, if she'd thought about it.' And so we chatter on. Such is the power of fiction. Parables have been called 'earthly stories with a heavenly meaning'.

Humour

Jesus used every means at his disposal to challenge his listeners. Any storyteller knows that the best way to keep people's attention is by humour. Shakespeare interspersed his moments of high drama with scenes of comic relief; nobody can stay on a solemn, tragic level for long without coming down to earth for a breather. Jesus, too, was very down to earth, and his parables are full of humour. The trouble is, we hear them read in church in a solemn tone of voice, or we read them from a black-covered book in a Bible study group, and we imagine we're not supposed to laugh. So we miss the whole point of the story. Jesus told the one about one blind man taking another by the hand to show him the way, and them both falling into the ditch, not because he found anything amusing in visual impairment. He wanted us to laugh, and then in the pause that follows the laughter, to start feeling uncomfortable as we slowly realize that we ourselves are just as ridiculous, whenever we give other people moral advice, though we're no better at obeying God than they are – the blind leading the blind.

Examples

Finally, let's take a quick look at the parables in today's reading.

A man sowed good seed in the earth, and his enemy sowed weeds among them. Would he be such a fool as to dig them up before they were ripe? The listeners laugh at the idea of such idiocy. Then why do you ask God to remove the wicked people in the world, when there's good and bad in each of us?

Do you despise a seed because it's tiny? Seeds can push over paving-stones, and mighty oaks from tiny acorns grow! A wry smile appears on our faces. So why do we despair because only a minority in Western Europe go to church? In Africa and Asia the number of Christians is growing faster than they can build new churches to hold them.

So your smiles and laughter change your attitudes. Who can say that God hasn't got a sense of humour?

All-age worship

Collect funny pictures of animals, birds and fish. Display them under the heading, 'God's jokes'.

Suggested hymns

I danced in the morning; If I were a butterfly; Tell me the stories of Jesus; There's a home for all the children.

Second Sunday after Trinity (Proper 6)   17 June
Second Service   **The Quarrelsome Jug**

Ps. 39 Let me know my end; Jer. 7.1–16 Morality, not nationalism; Rom. 9.14–26 God and his people; *Gospel at Holy Communion*: Luke 7.36—8.3 Jesus and women

> *'Who indeed are you, a human being, to argue with God? Will what is moulded say to the one who moulds it, "Why have you made me like this?" Has the potter no right over the clay, to make out of the same lump one object for special use and another for ordinary use?' Romans 9.20–21*

Funny story

Do you know the story of the quarrelsome jug? It's quite a funny story, and it's there in the Bible, among the writings of St Paul. There, you didn't think gloomy old Paul was capable of cracking a joke, did you? Yet on this occasion he did. Like the best humour, it forms a well-aimed dart to burst the bubble of pompous self-satisfaction.

Chosen people

Paul was a Jew. Yet he was called by God to proclaim the gospel to non-Jews, mostly Greeks and Romans, whom the Jews despised. God signed a contract with us Jews, they said, making us his Chosen People. When God judges the world, Jews are the only ones whom God will declare 'Not Guilty', or 'righteous'. We Jews will be all alone in the kingdom of God, when Messiah comes. All this foreign rubbish will be burnt on the garbage tip of hell. It's sad, when you consider how badly Jews have suffered from racism themselves down the ages, to hear of them in St Paul's time mouthing this racial prejudice themselves. But there's a lot more racism in many people's attitudes than they'll own up to, even today.

169

The Potter

So Paul quoted to his fellow Jews some words that had already been used by the prophet Jeremiah: 'I went down to the potter's house, and there he was working at his wheel. The vessel he was making of clay was spoiled in the potter's hand, and he reworked it into another vessel, as seemed good to him.' Have you ever watched a potter spinning clay on a wheel? The horizontal wheel spins round. The potter throws a lump of soft clay onto the wheel, and presses it until it forms the shape he wants, of vase, dish or jug. It's skilled work; if the potter presses too hard in one place, the whole thing may be ruined. But the potter starts again, changing the design so that it will work better with the raw material. Jeremiah had already used this picture to show the Chosen People that they couldn't rely on God's favour if they refused to do what God wanted them to. God can rework his plan to make a different sort of Chosen People out of those who do obey him, just like the potter with the jug. Which was exactly what St Paul was saying: God's new plan is for a Christian church, made up of Jews who believe in Jesus, but also members of all the other races in the world as well.

The quarrelsome jug

What Paul added to Jeremiah's parable, however, was the whimsical idea of the quarrelsome jug which argues with the potter. Imagine, he says, a misshape jumping up from the discard pile and saying, 'Oy! You there, Mr Potter, what do you mean by throwing me over here? Just because I'm ugly, you can't treat me like that!' But the idea is ridiculous. Even if they could speak, jugs have no right to argue with their maker. Neither do those Jews who reject Jesus, says Paul the Jew, have any right to complain because God chooses filthy foreigners to take their place in his plans. Ouch! Pop goes their pompous racial prejudice!

You and I

But you and I, who aren't Jews, can't sit back and laugh at this joke at their expense. The moral is clear: having the right parents doesn't ensure a 'not guilty' verdict. Just because you call yourself a Christian, and have done so all your life, that won't save you, if you ignore everything God calls you to do. OK, no one is perfect, and God has promised to forgive our errors and backslidings. But you have to want to serve him the best you can.

Arguing with God

Who are we, mere human beings, to argue with our maker? We fall ill, or things go wrong at work or in our relationships, and we're just like the quarrelsome jug. 'Oy,' we say, 'Mr God! What have I done to deserve this?' And if you listen carefully, you might hear a word in your ear, replying, 'I never promised you a rose garden, my child. Some people have to suffer in this life, and I pay you Christians the compliment of assuming that you are best able to bear it without losing your faith. But who do you think you are, arguing with God?' Do you sometimes need God to talk to you like that? Me too.

Suggested hymns

God is working his purpose out; God moves in a mysterious way; Majesty; There's a quiet understanding.

Third Sunday after Trinity (Proper 7) 24 June
(Birth of St John the Baptist)
Principal Service **Stilling the Storm**
(*Continuous*): 1 Sam. 17.[1a, 4–11, 19–23] 32–49 David and Goliath; Ps. 9.9–20 God lifts me from death, *or* 1 Sam. 17.57—18.5, 10–16 David and Jonathan; Ps. 133 Unity; *or* (*Related*): Job 38.1–11 God's greatness in creation; Ps. 107.1–3, 23–32 Protection from the storm; 2 Cor. 6.1–13 The suffering of the apostles; Mark 4.35–41 Stilling the storm

> *'Who then is this, that even the wind and the sea obey him?'* Mark 4.41

Storm on the lake

Imagine the scene. The disciples and Jesus set out for a quiet sail on Lake Galilee. The still waters reflect the mountains of the Golan Heights in the background. It's so calm that Jesus, resting on the seat in the stern, falls asleep with his head on a pillow. The disciples were still puzzling over who Jesus really was. Was he a prophet, the new Elijah? Was he a military saviour like Moses and Joshua, sent by God to deliver his people from the occupying Roman army? Or was he more than that? Who did Jesus see himself as? Suddenly, the weather changed. A howling gale screamed down from the Golan, and the boat rocked amid waves as high as a house, it seemed. Picture their predicament. The waves came sloshing and slopping over the gunwales, and swilled around in the keel. If the water rose any higher the boat would sink and they would have to swim for their lives. Some try to steer into the wind, others furl the sails – most of them try desperately to bail out the water. Peter grabs Jesus by the shoulders and roughly shakes him awake. They're all shouting at once, 'Jesus! Master! We're going to die – don't you even care?' Jesus stands up in the rocking boat and yells out, 'Shut up and be quiet!' Yet he wasn't shouting at the disciples, but at the tempest. And as suddenly as it had started, the storm died down, and there was perfect silence.

Rough patches

Do you have rough patches in your life? Who doesn't? Times when everything goes pear shaped, when it never rains but it pours. Maybe it's trivial, like when the soufflé goes flat, or perhaps its serious, like a painful illness for yourself or someone you love. 'Oh my God,' you say, and it's something between a swear and a prayer. 'Jesus, why don't you do something?' At the time it seems as though nobody's listening. But looking back, you can see that things did change when you prayed. Perhaps the cookery went better the next day; maybe the illness led into a slow recovery. Even if the person you prayed for died, God helped you to see death in a different light – not a disaster, but the blessing of eternal life. In your agony, Jesus said to you, 'Peace, be still. Where's all your faith gone?' Perhaps only during the rough patches do we begin to see who Jesus really is: a prophet, a saviour, yes; but even more.

The Psalms

The disciples, being Jews, knew the book of Psalms by heart. It was their hymnbook; they learnt them at their mother's knee. In Psalm 107 they sang,

> Some went down to the sea in ships,
>   doing business on the mighty waters;
> they saw the deeds of the LORD,
>   his wondrous works in the deep.

For he commanded and raised the stormy wind,
   which lifted up the waves of the sea.
They mounted up to heaven, they went down to the depths;
   their courage melted away in their calamity;
they reeled and staggered like drunkards,
   and were at their wits' end.
Then they cried to the LORD in their trouble,
   and he brought them out from their distress;
he made the storm be still,
   and the waves of the sea were hushed.

Nobody but God

Who can still the storm, according to the Psalms? God can, and only God; nobody but God can bring calm to the waves of the sea, and the rough patches in our lives. So who is Jesus? Our friend, who helps us out of the sea of troubles in which we're being tossed. Jesus wants us to chat to him, like two bosom pals, trusting him to be there when we need him. But our friend is more than just that. Jesus is the Son of God, come to save the human race and lead us to heaven. He wanted the disciples in the boat to realize this. At moments of stress he murmurs to you, too, 'Calm down, calm down! Where's your faith slipped away to?' So when you hear yourself saying, 'Oh my God', turn your swear into a prayer to Jesus!

All-age worship

Select a prayer-stone, to clutch when you're frightened. Write on it, 'Jesus says, calm down'.

Suggested hymns

I, the Lord of sea and sky; Jesu, lover of my soul; Lord, when the storms of life arise; O, the deep, deep love of Jesus.

The Birth of St John the Baptist 24 June
I Must Decrease

Isa. 40.1–11 A voice in the wilderness; Ps. 85.7–13 Salvation
is at hand; Acts 13.14b–26 A baptism of repentance, *or* Gal.
3.23–29 The law our schoolmaster; Luke 1.57–66, 80 Birth of
the Baptist

> *'Fear came over all their neighbours, and all these things were
> talked about throughout the entire hill country of Judaea. All who
> heard them pondered them and said, "What then will this child
> become?" For, indeed, the hand of the Lord was with him.' Luke
> 1.65–66*

A back seat

Once you find yourself with a fan club of your own, it's an awful
temptation to start hogging the limelight and driving everybody else
into the background. There aren't many people who willingly step
aside, and take a back seat, so as to allow somebody else to shine
in their place. John the Baptist was one of those rare and humble
people who did just that.

Cousins

John and Jesus were cousins. Or to be more accurate, second
cousins, probably. The Angel Gabriel said to Mary, 'Your relative
Elizabeth . . . has also conceived a son; and this is the sixth month
for her.' The Bible isn't particularly precise about their relationship,
but assuming Mary and Elizabeth were first cousins, that would
make their sons second cousins. John the Baptist, however, was
born six months before Jesus, which would entitle him to claim
precedence as the older of the two.

Preparing the way

John began his work for the Lord first. The people gathered to listen as he preached by the River Jordan. It was not enough to have
been born one of the Chosen People, he said. His fellow Jews must
make their own decision to obey God, and seal it by the ceremony
that non-Jews were made to perform when they converted: a public
washing away of their personal wrongdoings, a baptism of repent-

ance for the remission of sins. John chose a phrase from Isaiah to describe what he was doing: preparing the way of the Lord. Everyone thought that this was code for making the people ready for the coming of the Messiah, who would lead them into battle against the Romans, and inaugurate the kingdom of God on earth.

Anonymous

There was a figure standing anonymous and unrecognized in the crowd who gathered to listen to John: John's cousin. John said, 'Among you stands one whom you do not know, the one who is coming after me; I am not worthy to untie the thong of his sandal.' 'I am not the Messiah,' said John, 'but I have been sent ahead of him. He who has the bride is the bridegroom. The friend of the bridegroom, who stands and hears him, rejoices greatly at the bridegroom's voice. For this reason my joy has been fulfilled. He must increase, but I must decrease.' Such astonishing humility! It's almost unknown for a distinguished public figure, at the pinnacle of his career, voluntarily to step down, making room for another. But that's what John did. 'He must increase, but I must decrease.'

'Not unto us'

How good are you at stepping down? Of course, before you can step down, you have to step up and accept God's challenge to do whatever it is he's calling you to. God's got a job tailor-made for each one of us – it may be serving on the local council, or arranging the church flowers. Quite likely, if you do your best, that may bring you the respect and even admiration of your family, neighbours and colleagues. You can rejoice in the satisfaction of knowing that you worked hard, and did a good job, to the best of your ability. But don't seek personal glory. After winning the Battle of Agincourt, Henry V and his troops marched home singing Psalm 115, 'Not to us, O LORD, not to us, but to your name give glory.' Would that we could all be as humble.

Successors

You must always be willing to carry on with the task until the job's thoroughly finished. But at an early stage, everyone needs to keep an eye open for someone who could succeed them, beginning to train them to take over. The moment of the handover is crucial – your successor must be ready for the challenge, yet not be kept hanging around for dead men's shoes. Then you need to be willing, like John the Baptist, to step back graciously, saying, 'He (or she) must increase, and I must decrease.' Even if your other achievements are forgotten, you'll be remembered, by God at least and probably by a few people on earth, as the one who knew when you had done enough, with the humility to surrender the prestigious position to someone else when the time had come.

Suggested hymns

How lovely on the mountains; Lo, in the wilderness a voice; On Jordan's bank the Baptist's cry; The great forerunner of the morn.

Fourth Sunday after Trinity (Proper 8)   1 July
Principal Service   **Faith and Healing**
(*Continuous*): 2 Sam. 1.1, 17–27 David's lament over Saul and Jonathan; Ps. 130 Out of the depths; *or* (*Related*): Wisd. 1.13–15; 2.23–24 Made for life not death, *or* Lam. 3.22–33; *Canticle*: Lam. 3.22–33 New every morning, *or* Ps. 30 Healing and life; 2 Cor. 8.7–15 Giving to the needy; Mark 5.21–43 Healing Jairus' daughter, a sick woman's faith

'*Your faith has made you well.*' *Mark 5.34*

Bargaining with God

A man had a bad back, and one Sunday he decided to make a bargain with God. 'Listen here, God,' he said, very rudely, 'I'm in pain, and if you make me better by next Sunday I'll put £30 in the church collection.' Next Sunday, feeling no better, he said to God, 'If you heal my back by next Sunday I'll put £300 in the collection.' The following Sunday he felt a lot worse, so he promised that if God would cure his back by the Sunday after, he'd donate £3000 to the church. During the next few days, the pain completely vanished. The following Sunday the man said, 'God, you can forget our bargain. The pain just got better by itself!'

Inbuilt powers

God does heal people. He's doing it all the time. Often we just don't notice, or put it down to coincidence. But God has many different ways of healing us. God has caused our bodies to develop powers of resistance. Evolution tells us *how* this happens, but it doesn't tell us *why*. When we encounter a new virus, for instance, many people develop antibodies, which fight against and overcome the threat. Those who survive pass on the antibodies to their children, and so on. Over time, many diseases have been defeated by what we choose to call 'the body's inbuilt power of healing itself'. Many people believe this isn't just chance, but that God caused us to have powers of self-healing.

Inspired doctors

The second way God heals us is by inspiring doctors and researchers to find new ways of curing disease. God can inspire anyone, believer or unbeliever, but I expect he finds it easier when the believing researcher prays and asks God for the answer. Our faith makes it easier for God.

Believing patients

So does a patient who has faith in God. Peace of mind and relaxation helps the medicines and the body's own powers to work better; worry and tension hinders them. A patient who prays, and then leaves the result to God, is more likely to recover than one who's terrified of suffering and death, lacking the power to endure them calmly.

Believing prayer

Fourthly, there's the power of believing prayer by the patient's family and friends. Sharing their faith with the sick person causes the patient to relax and trust in God. The relatives can surround the patient with love, and knowing that you are loved has an amazing healing effect. God can heal, and God wants to heal. But sometimes God needs people to work through.

Your faith has healed you

In those four ways God is busy healing people today: by built-in powers of self-healing; by inspiring the medical profession; bringing peace of mind to the sufferer; and using the prayers of others. Is this a miracle? Yes, in every case, yes. The definition of a miracle is something that makes you admire God. You can praise God for working in each of these ways. Medicine isn't a precise science, and your doctor can only give you an opinion of the probability of recovery. We can't claim a healing is a miracle because the doctors hadn't expected it. In today's Gospel reading there's a sort of healing sandwich – one miracle in the middle of another. Jesus healed Jairus's daughter, telling the relatives to trust him. On his way, he healed the woman with a gynaecological problem, saying to her, 'Your faith has healed you.'

Answers

Just as God has different ways of healing, so he has different ways of answering prayer. Prayer is always answered, but sometimes the answer is 'yes'; sometimes 'no'; sometimes 'wait'; and sometimes God says, 'I've got a better idea.' If someone's prayers for healing are not answered in the way they had hoped for, it's wickedly cruel to blame it on their lack of faith; Jesus said faith like a grain of mustard seed is enough. Yet sometimes he decides that the person you prayed for needs the peace of heaven more than to go on suffering. Always pray in faith. But you can't bargain with God.

All-age worship

Make a list of sick people. As each name is read out, all say, 'Lord, heal [this person] in the way you know is best.'

Suggested hymns

At even, ere the sun was set; Healing God, almighty Father; O for a thousand tongues to sing; Peter and John went to pray.

Fourth Sunday after Trinity (Proper 8)   1 July
Second Service   **Fools**
Ps. [52 Tyrants] 53 Fools; Jer. 11.1–14 Breaking God's covenant;
Rom. 13.1–10 State authority; *Gospel at Holy Communion*:
Luke 9.51–62 Tolerance and sacrifice

*'The fool has said in his heart, "There is no God."' Psalm 53.1
(Common Worship)*

Oppressors

The author of Psalm 53 was much troubled. People in authority
were abusing their power, in order to grow rich at the expense of
the weak and defenceless. The author of this poem dared to criticize
them, trying to point out that the Lord God disapproves of such
oppressive behaviour. He wrote:

> They are corrupt, they commit abominable acts;
> there is no one who does good.
> God looks down from heaven on humankind to see if there are
>   any who are wise, who seek after God.
> They have all fallen away, they are all alike perverse;
> there is no one who does good, no, not one.
> Have they no knowledge, those evildoers, who eat up my people
>   as they eat bread, and do not call upon God?

Atheists

He might just as well have saved his breath. These wicked people
only laughed at him. 'Don't talk religion at me,' they said. 'You
claim that your God disapproves of what I'm doing. God – who's
he? There is no God.' Sometimes it can be quite convenient to be
an atheist. Because, if there isn't a God, there's nobody to question
your behaviour. Then you can do just as you please, with no fear
that you'll ever have to answer for your actions. I'm not saying
that all atheists are like that. Some are well-meaning people who
just can't see a logical reason for faith in God. But the powerful
people who were troubling the psalmist weren't being logical. They
were just using their lack of faith as an excuse for being as selfish
as they wished. So the psalm writer called them 'fools'; he wrote:
'Fools say in their hearts, "There is no God."' I can understand his

exasperation. But I don't think he was wise to express himself like that: as soon as you lose your temper, you've lost the argument.

Troubled

Are you troubled by atheists? Many people are. Christians have spent many generations learning to tolerate those of different opinions from us. We don't always succeed in being tolerant, but that's the aim. But atheists don't even try. Far from respecting the opinion of religious people, many of them seem to be on a crusade to impose their beliefs on us, and a campaign to convert the simple faithful to their materialistic gospel of 'Only Matter matters.' What makes it difficult is that they are right in saying that nobody can prove the existence of God; but then, nobody can prove that God doesn't exist, either. It's good if religious people can join in courteous, rational discussion with our atheist friends, with the limited aim of showing them that truth isn't limited to what we can see and measure. Love and beauty are beyond the reach of the scientist, yet nobody can live a fulfilled life without them.

Loving

But we must always be loving. Some accuse us of trying to ram religion down their throats, yet frankly, I wouldn't know how to begin doing that. But being rude, or using cheap threats of hell-fire and damnation gets you nowhere. The only thing that will make another person see the truth of our religion is if we show such love in our lives that they begin to ask where we get it from. Oh, and 'religion' is a bad word to use, because people associate it with the power of the Church and the misdeeds of so-called religious people. And faith must be distinguished from credulity: there's nothing unreasonable about trusting someone who loves you.

Pity

Actually, I feel deeply sorry for the atheists, and there's no harm in telling them so. My prayer relationship with God gives me so much joy; to know that God loves me fills my life with hope; and God's promises provide such meaning and purpose for my life, that I feel sad that everybody can't enjoy those things as I do. Atheists remind me of a lonely person who pushes away the warm affection of somebody who's deeply in love with them. The only reason we want to share our faith with them is because it would bring them so much happiness.

God is everywhere

Finally, I feel sorry for atheists because they're looking in the wrong place. God is everywhere, but you won't find God by looking through a microscope. There is one experiment that can prove to you that God exists, however, but it's very costly. It involves letting God take charge of your life, and asking God to make you a more loving person. If that prayer is answered, then it would be very foolish to say in your heart, 'There is no God.'

Suggested hymns

God moves in a mysterious way; God is working his purpose out; I the Lord of sea and sky; O God of earth and altar.

Fifth Sunday after Trinity (Proper 9)   8 July
Principal Service   **Rejected by his Family**
(*Continuous*): 2 Sam. 5.1–5, 9–10 David's victory; Ps. 48 God's protection of the city; *or* (*Related*): Ezek. 2.1–5 Speak the word; Ps. 123 Hope for God's grace; 2 Cor. 12.2–10 God's grace is sufficient; Mark 6.1–13 Jesus rejected

> 'Prophets are not without honour, except in their hometown, and among their own kin, and in their own house.' *Mark 6.4*

Back home

Jesus went back home – something we all long to do when we have been away. But sometimes hidden tensions, buried while we were apart, rise to the surface when we meet again. Mothers are said to treat their grown offspring as though they were little children still. Maybe that's because, as we grew up, they saw the faults we've kept hidden from others. But it makes their grown-up children furious! Other relationships show similar strains. Parents often find it hard to let go, wanting to control their children long after they have flown the nest. They demand respect, forgetting that respect has to be earned. Rebelling against everything your parents stand for is a necessary part of growing up. Yet it's something we should grow out of when we leave our teens. Sadly, some people never do. Then, when one of their parents dies, they realize it's too late to make their parents their friends. There are, in fact, many happy families, where a family reunion is a joy for everyone. That's because not everybody gives in to the temptation to take out their rage at the world on their family. But that temptation is there for us all; we need to be aware of it, and make up our minds to resist it. Creating happy families is hard work.

Nazareth

Jesus found this when he went home to Nazareth. It should have been a happy reunion with his family and neighbours. He spoke in the synagogue, and impressed them by his wisdom and his healings. But the villagers couldn't accept that he was more than a local lad who had struck lucky. 'He's just our local carpenter,' they sneered. His neighbours found any claims that he was more than that deeply offensive. They knew his family well; Joseph seems to have been dead by now, but his mother Mary lived as one of them, with Jesus's brothers James, Joseph, Judas and Simon. He also had some sisters, though they're not named. One of his brothers became his loyal supporter after Jesus rose again, but during his earthly ministry they were opposed to him – a typical family set-up! Jesus was amazed at their unbelief. Sadly he said, 'Prophets are not without honour, except in their hometown, and among their own kin, and in their own house.' Meaning, your own family and neighbours never treat you with the same respect that strangers show.

Reconciliation

But it's no use getting angry with them. Where there's a breakdown in family relationships, or between neighbours, we have to labour at the task of reconciliation. Jesus had no time for that in Nazareth, he had other fish to fry, but it would be wrong for you and me to simply write off our relations. Our task is to apologize for the things that have offended them, explaining that we didn't mean to hurt them. We must assure them that we ourselves bear no grudges – though without bringing up again the things that have upset us.

Sharing good news

For we each have a unique opportunity to share the love of Jesus with our own families. It's the most difficult form of evangelism, because every unkind word and selfish action makes it harder for our relations to believe we know what we're talking about when we speak of love. But if you tell those close to you what a change it's made to you, to know that Jesus loves and forgives you, and how you would like to share that joy and happiness with them, then, with patience, you may succeed. The apostle Andrew brought his brother Simon Peter to Christ. After Jesus rose again, the first task Jesus gave to Mary Magdalene was to 'Go and tell my brothers.' In the case of James, it seems to have worked – eventually.

All in love

Yet everything must be done with love. People say, 'You choose your friends, you can't choose your relations.' That's why our family is so important for us. It's easy to love people when we can choose whether or not we like them. With the family, we've no choice – we're stuck with them, and we must learn to love them, whether we like them or not. Jesus told us to love all our neighbours, even our enemies; and the best training ground for Christian love is to practise on our awful relations.

All-age worship

Draw your family tree, with photographs if you can. Add phrases such as 'My Granny taught me . . .'

Suggested hymns

Abide with me; Blest be the tie that binds; Father, I place into your hands; Make me a channel of your peace.

Fifth Sunday after Trinity (Proper 9)   8 July
Second Service   **A Bad Name**

Ps. [63 My soul clings to you] 64 Protection from enemies; Jer. 20.1–11a Jeremiah's prayer; Rom. 14.1–17 Do not judge others; *Gospel at Holy Communion*: Luke 10.1–11, 16–20 Mission of the seventy

> *'Whenever I speak, I must cry out, I must shout, "Violence and destruction!"' Jeremiah 20.7–9*

What's in a name?

We're proud of our personal name, because it distinguishes us from anybody else. We'll defend our good name if anybody criticizes us, and the worst harm you can do to anybody is to give them a bad name. A small group of people have given their name to a common object, or a characteristic, or a scientific term. Mostly this is something to proud of, but not always. Thus Monsieur Bougainville can be proud to have given his name to the bright purple leaves of the bougainvillea, and Herr Fuchs must be pleased that his name is used for the bright red fuchsia flower. Herr Zeppelin is remembered whenever we speak of the airship he invented, and Monsieur Guillotine is associated with the gruesome machine that goes by his name. The fictional Ebenezer Scrooge gave his name to everyone who's mean, greedy and grasping. You can probably think of many more examples.

Jeremiah

Our Old Testament reading today came from the book of the prophet Jeremiah. His name's forever associated with doom and gloom. 'Will you stop being so pessimistic?' we say to our friends. 'You're a real Jeremiah. Why can't you look on the bright side for once?' That's a little unfair, because Jeremiah wasn't naturally a gloomy person. But God had given him a warning to deliver to the people of Judah, which made him very unpopular. He hated having to deliver such a grim message, and begged God to give him something more cheerful to proclaim. But at that point in their history, there wasn't much that was optimistic that could be said.

Jeremiah's prayer

Poor Jeremiah felt that he had no choice in the matter – God was forcing him to deliver a message that he'd no wish to utter. He complained at the unfairness of this: 'O LORD,' he prayed, 'you have overpowered me, and you have prevailed. I have become a laughingstock all day long; everyone mocks me. For whenever I speak, I must cry out, I must shout, "Violence and destruction!"' It was no use him turning his back and ignoring God – he felt compelled to speak. 'For the word of the LORD has become for me a reproach and derision all day long,' he wailed. 'If I say, "I will not mention him, or speak any more in his name", then within me there is something like a burning fire shut up in my bones; I am weary with holding it in, and I cannot.'

Jewish history

Let's put this in its historical context. King David united the 12 tribes of Israel into a single nation, and under his son Solomon they were still united. But following Solomon's death, two rival kings divided the nation, the two tribes in the south forming the nation of Judah, and the other ten tribes formed the nation of Israel in the north. Neither kingdom was strong enough to stand on its own, and they were trapped between two superpowers, one in Egypt and the other in Mesopotamia. The northern kingdom was defeated by Assyria, and many of them were scattered. Then Assyria was replaced by the Babylonians, who now threatened Judah. Jeremiah warned them that if they were self-willed and rebellious, Babylon would destroy them. Only if they obeyed the Lord could God save them. The people ignored the prophet; the majority were exiled to Babylon for 70 years, but a few, including Jeremiah, escaped to Egypt; Jerusalem was destroyed. With a prophecy like that to deliver, no wander Jeremiah was gloomy.

Today

Many commentators today have an equally grim prediction to deliver. It may be the inevitability of climate change, with fertile land flooded or turned to desert. Then there's the growth of population, with millions on our doorstep clamouring to be fed. Some warn us of the overfishing of the oceans, others of the extinction of rare species. With the possibility of pandemics and the threat of terrorism to consider, many people warn us that time is short. There's a slim chance of salvation if we become less selfish, more generous and considerate. Sadly, few people respond to a Jeremiad of gloom; a change in human nature is the only thing that will save us, and religion is the only force that can achieve that. But with the flight from religion, in Western Europe at least, something pretty drastic will need to happen before people will turn back to God in sufficient numbers. I'm sorry, but Jeremiah's call to repentance is the only message that will meet the needs of the day.

Suggested hymns

A safe stronghold our God is still; Lord of the Church, we pray for our renewing; O God of earth and altar; O Lord, the clouds are gathering.

Sixth Sunday after Trinity (Proper 10) 15 July
Principal Service **Salome**
(*Continuous*): 2 Sam. 6.1–5, 12b–19 The ark comes to the city; Ps. 24 Lift up your heads; *or* (*Related*): Amos 7.7–15 The plumbline: judgement on the city; Ps. 85.8–13 Peace, faith and works; Eph. 1.3–14 Called to adoption; Mark 6.14–29 Herod beheads the Baptist

> 'When his daughter . . . came in and danced, she pleased Herod and his guests; and the king said to the girl, "Ask me for whatever you wish, and I will give it" . . . she requested, "I want you to give me at once the head of John the Baptist on a platter."' Mark 6.22–25

A story from the bazaar

John the Baptist was put to death by King Herod Antipas. His story is told in two historical documents: Josephus's *Antiquities*, and the New Testament. The version we have in the Gospels has all the characteristics of a popular tale, told over and over in the bazaars of the Middle East, and improved with each telling. It's a gruesome touch to report that Herodias's daughter asked for the head to be brought to her '*on a dish*'. The old translations use the word 'charger' instead, which gave rise to a famous joke attributed to W. S. Gilbert. He saw the Master of St John's College riding through Cambridge on a horse, and said: 'Behold, the head of St John on a charger!'

Josephus

The Jewish historian Josephus gives a slightly different version of the death of the Baptist. He wrote:

> Aretas, the king of Arabia, and Herod Antipas quarrelled because Herod, having married Aretas's daughter, took another wife. It happened when he was staying in Rome with his half-brother, also called Herod, that he fell in love with Herodias, the latter's wife. Herodias was the daughter of another half-brother called Aristobulus. It was agreed that she could marry him, provided he divorced Aretas's daughter . . . The latter found out about it and went to . . . the fortress of Macherus, on the border with her father's territory, so that she could tell her father secretly about what had happened . . . So Aretas and Herod . . . raised armies and prepared for war. When their generals met in battle, Herod's army was totally destroyed . . . Some of the Jews thought that the destruction of Herod's army was a punishment from God, because Herod Antipas had killed John, who was called 'the Baptist'. John was a good man, and told the Jews to be virtuous in their behaviour towards each other and in reverence for God. So John urged them to come to baptism; because washing with water would . . . not only bring remission of a few sins, but the purification of the body, provided that the soul had been thoroughly purified beforehand by good behaviour. So great were the crowds who came to John, being greatly moved by hearing his words, that Herod Antipas was afraid that John's influence over the people might be able to raise a rebellion if he wanted, for the crowds seemed ready to do anything he told them to. Antipas thought it best, by putting John to death, to stop him causing trouble . . . So Antipas made John a prisoner in the fortress of Macherus, and he was put to death there.

Salome

Josephus agrees with the four Gospels that the whole family of the Herods were an evil lot. The dancer was the daughter of Queen Herodias, and was called Salome. Oscar Wilde wrote a play about her, which was made into an opera by Richard Strauss. Despite the sensational 'Dance of the Seven Veils', it's a profound analysis of the conflict between sensuality and religion. Salome's anger against John arises because he's the only man she's quite unable to seduce. So John the Baptist stands out as the prophet who was unwilling to compromise on his moral principles. His courage in withstanding Herod led to his death.

Challenge

Every sermon should end with a challenge: what are you going to do about it. But I'm going to leave that part to you, because I don't know what moral challenges will face you in the coming weeks, in the world, in your neighbourhood, your work or your family. But I'm sure there will be times when God calls you to stand up for the truth, and for right against wrong, like John the Baptist did. I hope you won't die for it, but you will certainly be unpopular for being the whistle-blower. You'll be told you are meddling in politics, like John and Amos were. But to do nothing is also a political act. Be certain, however, that God will support you and your family, whatever happens, and reward you for your courage.

All-age worship

Tell the story of a public figure recently who stood up for what was right.

Suggested hymns

I the Lord of sea and sky; I want to walk with Jesus Christ; God has spoken by his prophets; On Jordan's bank the Baptist's cry.

Sixth Sunday after Trinity (Proper 10)   15 July
Second Service   What God has Done
Ps. 66 What God has done; Job 4.1; 5.6–27 Whom God reproves *or* Ecclus. (Sirach) 4.11–31 Wisdom's teaching; Rom. 15.14–29 The apostle to the Gentiles; *Gospel at Holy Communion*: Luke 10.25–37 The Good Samaritan

'Come and see what God has done: he is awesome in his deeds.' Psalm 66.5 (NRSV)

What's God been up to?

A well-known preacher used to settle down after lunch on Sundays, open the newspaper and say, 'Now let's see what God's been up to this week!' It takes a lot of faith to recognize that God has been active in the things we read about in the news, or see on the television newscasts. That's because bad news sells newspapers, so they concentrate on stories of fighting, natural disasters, and corruption. God doesn't cause those things to happen. But if you read the stories carefully, you'll find that individuals are mentioned who have been selflessly serving their neighbours, resisting evil and trying to bring peace. Who can doubt that God is, in fact, inspiring and strengthening these people? To realize that, changes the whole perspective of human history. What had seemed like a random series of accidents and the effects of human malevolence, suddenly turns into an ongoing story of liberation and salvation. You can turn to the history books, too, and say, 'Now let's see what God's been up to!'

Biblical precedents

There's nothing new in this way of reading history and contemporary events. The Bible is full of it. Most people, if their country or tribe wins a battle, will congratulate themselves, saying, 'Didn't we do well?' Instead, the prophets taught them to be more humble, attributing their success to God's assistance. Psalm 66 calls on the people to thank God for their victories:

> Come and see what God has done:
> he is awesome in his deeds.

Exodus

In particular, the Israelites were reminded again and again about the Exodus from Egypt. When they escaped from slavery in Egypt, they recognized that God had saved them, chosen them, and covenanted with them for continuing protection:

> He turned the sea into dry land;
> they passed through the river on foot.
> There we rejoiced in him,
> who rules by his might forever,
> whose eyes keep watch on the nations.

Punishment

They were encouraged to see God's hand in their disasters also, punishing them for not keeping their side of the bargain. As parents discipline their children, to teach them the importance of obedience and the difference between right and wrong, so God allows us to suffer for a while, so that we may repent and turn back to him:

> For you, O God, have tested us;
> you have tried us as silver is tried.
> You brought us into the net;
> you laid burdens on our backs;
> you let people ride over our heads;
> we went through fire and through water;
> yet you have brought us out to a spacious place.

God in history

So can we actually see what God has been up to when we read the history of the world? Yes we can, but it takes insight to sort the golden thread of God's purpose out of the dark chaos that surrounds it. Our caveman ancestors grabbed what they wanted and killed those who disagreed with them; but by the time of the ancient Greeks, people realized that if we're to live together in society, there must be a form of democracy. The Roman Empire prevented crime by means of Roman law, and yet tyrants arose who dominated their subjects through fear. In the centuries of feudalism, all the land belonged to a few rich families, and the rest had to work for them or they'd starve. So if you look at the world today, with all its faults, you can clearly see that over the long run some progress has been made. I believe the writings of the Holy Scriptures had a real influence on people's attitudes and morals.

Science

Or think of our physical well-being. May not it have been due to God, who inspired the scientists to search for remedies for our illnesses, and new sources of nourishment? You have only to look at the way your grandparents lived, to see that life is much more comfortable for us today than it was for them. It would be conceited to pat ourselves on the back over these improvements; much better to say with the psalmist, 'Come and see what God has done: he is awesome in his deeds.'

Human malice

The trouble is, that there's so much wrong with the world today, that we miss the gold among the dross. Yet we should attribute the bad news to human malice and selfishness. Ninety-nine per cent of the time that's true; only in a few cases can it be blamed on unavoidable accident. So take a new look at history; open your newspaper, exclaiming, 'Now let's see what God's been up to this week!'

Suggested hymns

Father, hear the prayer we offer; God is working his purpose out; God works in a mysterious way; There's a wideness (Souls of men).

Seventh Sunday after Trinity (Proper 11)   22 July
(St Mary Magdalene)
Principal Service   The Lord's My Shepherd
(*Continuous*): 2 Sam. 7.1–14a King David not to build the Temple; Ps. 89.20–37 Covenant with King David; *or* (*Related*): Jer. 23.1–6 Promise of a righteous king and shepherd; Ps. 23 The Lord is my shepherd; Eph. 2.11–22 Unity and forgiveness; Mark 6.30–34, 53–56 Sheep without a shepherd (*for this sermon, the reading should be* Mark 6.30–44, 53–56)

> '[Jesus] said to them, "Come away to a deserted place all by yourselves and rest a while." For many were coming and going, and they had no leisure even to eat.' Mark 6.31

A shepherd he

In Gilbert and Sullivan's operetta *Iolanthe*, the soloist and chorus echo each other like this: 'A shepherd I.' 'A shepherd he.' 'Of arca-die.' 'Of arca-dee.' Not great poetry, but it gently mocks the romantic picture of the pastoral idyll of shepherds and shepherdesses in Arcadia. Marie Antoinette and her friends used to dress up as shepherdesses, and I'm sure they knew nothing of the hardships that real shepherds endure. In the part of the Peloponnese in Greece that is called Arcadia, you can still meet modern-day shepherds leading their flocks across the hillside in search of good pasturage. Theirs is a tough life: they can't leave their sheep for a minute, such is their need for nourishing grazing.

The good shepherd

The Bible is full of references to shepherds feeding their flocks. Jeremiah calls the national leaders 'bad shepherds', because they neglect their people's needs; and God promises that he himself will be a shepherd to the nation. In Psalm 23, everybody's favourite Psalm, David the shepherd king sings of the Lord as his shepherd. We echo his words, proclaiming that God will lead us to green pastures, and will spread out a banquet before us in the face of our enemies. Isaiah says the Lord God will feed his flock like a shepherd, and in St John's Gospel, Jesus says that he is the Good Shepherd. Calling God a shepherd is a striking metaphor, showing how he cares for those he loves, and meets their deepest needs.

Our needs

Our most basic need of all is our need for food and drink. Have you ever been on the brink of starvation? Probably not. Yet in some countries, there's an annual risk that, if your crops fail or your flocks and herds die, you and your family will die of hunger before the year's out. The inhabitants of these lands take very literally the promise that God will feed his people, like a shepherd feeds his sheep. They realize their utter dependence on God's love.

Feeding the crowds

So when Jesus fed the hungry crowds in the dry lands around Galilee, the people will immediately have thought about God as the great feeder. Each of the Gospels tells at least one such story, and usually two. It's been suggested that the feeding of the four thousand represents Jesus as the leader of the Jewish Church and the five thousand show him as the one who meets the needs of the non-Jewish Christians. It brings home to the many Christians who live in abject poverty that God will bring them food. How does God do that today? Very often God relies on you and me to feed the hungry for him, through aid or fair trading structures. Yet often we do the opposite, by climate change killing off the crops and grassland, by protective tariffs and subsidized selling preventing farmers in other countries getting a fair price for their products.

Spiritual food

But there's more to these feeding stories than just physical nourishment. They remind us that God meets our spiritual needs, too. Almost as basic as our need for food and drink is our need for love. And God meets that hunger, often, as in the case of physical food, by using other Christians to bring us the love we so much need. By prayer and Bible reading we come close to God and our souls are fed. By regular worship with other Christians, we're inspired and encouraged for our work in God's service. And in Holy Communion, under the symbols of bread and wine, God feeds us by the visible reminders that Jesus was the Good Shepherd who laid down his life for his sheep. Though our resources as a congregation may be limited, down as low as five loaves and a few fish, we can always get an overdraft from the Bank of God's Love; then we shall be able to feed thousands by offering them our service, our care, and the Good News of God's Love.

All-age worship

Role-play the feeding in the wilderness, using real bread and a tin of sardines.

Suggested hymns

Bread of heaven, on thee we feed; Break thou the bread of life; Lead me, O thou great Redeemer; The Lord's my Shepherd.

St Mary Magdalene   22 July
Do Not Touch Me

S. of Sol. 3.1–4 Seeking and finding; Ps. 42.1–10 As deer long for water; 2 Cor. 5.14–17 A new creation; John 20.1–2, 11–18 Go and tell

> *'Jesus said to [Mary], "Do not hold on to me, because I have not yet ascended to the Father. But go to my brothers and say to them, 'I am ascending to my Father and your Father, to my God and your God.'"' John 20.17*

Mimosa

'Touch-me-not' is the popular name for several species of plants. There's a mimosa that grows in the tropics, also known as 'The Sensitive Plant', because the leaves immediately fold up when you touch them. I once read a little verse that runs like this:

Mimosa, my sensitive plant,
why do you shrink at a touch?
Fearing that things are what they aren't,
frightened of feeling too much.
And yet there are those who assert,
and I think they rightly discern,
that unless you're prepared to be hurt,
to be loved you never will learn.

Balsam

There's also a species of balsam known as 'touch-me-not', because it ejects its ripe seeds at a light touch. The Latin name of the genus is *Impatiens,* and the species is called *noli me tangere,* a phrase taken from the Latin Vulgate translation of the Bible. These were the words that the risen Christ spoke to Mary Magdalene in the Garden, 'do not touch me', though a better translation would be 'stop clinging to me'. In the medieval plainsong, *noli-me-tangere* was set to a splendid flourish in the Easter story, and the Latin words also became the title for any painting showing Jesus and Mary Magdalene together.

Tactile

Mary Magdalene may have been what we call a very 'tactile' person. 'Tactile' comes from the same root as *tangere,* and means 'concerning the sense of touch'. Sculptors have to be tactile, highly aware of the texture of their materials, and how they feel when you take them in your hands. Blind people have to discover the nature of their surroundings by feeling them. And when Mary Magdalene found herself face to face with the man she loved, and thought she had lost, her first instinct was to reach out and touch him. This habit can be seen as good and bad. Those who are very uptight, restrained and withdrawn hate it when others touch them. They may spring back in alarm; they may even cry 'take your paws off me!' We must sympathize with those who don't even like shaking hands in church during the 'passing of the Peace'. But they're missing a lot of what makes life worthwhile. We all have feelings of friendship and love which we can't put into speech, when an arm placed gently round the shoulders can say more than a thousand words. Those who are 'frightened of feeling too much' are emotionally malnourished, suffering from 'cuddle starvation'. They often don't realize how much the people around them like them, which deprives them of a proper sense of self-worth.

Thomas

Jesus told Mary Magdalene not to touch him. I don't think this was because he was like the mimosa, the 'sensitive plant which shrinks at a touch'. During his lifetime I expect he, too, was quite tactile – certainly the paintings of the Virgin and Child suggest this. But now that he'd died and risen, things were different. He said to Thomas, 'Put your finger here and see my hands. Reach out your hand and put it in my side.' But that was to convince Thomas that Jesus wasn't a ghost. Mary Magdalene already knew that Jesus was real. Now she had to progress still further, learning to love Jesus without being able to touch him. When Jesus had ascended into heaven, she would have to be our teacher, showing us all how to form a relationship with our Saviour which doesn't depend on being able to touch him, or even to see and hear him.

Sacraments

Yet knowing how we long to touch him, Jesus has given us a wonderful solution to our yearning. At the Last Supper, Jesus picked up the bread, saying 'This is my body – take it in your hands, kiss it with your mouth, until I become a part of you.' That's why we call the Holy Communion a 'sacrament', which the Book of Common Prayer defines as 'an outward and visible sign of an inward and spiritual grace'. We can't *see* the love that Jesus has for us, we can't hug him or cuddle him. But he's given us the bread and wine instead, a tactile reminder that he's still invisibly with us. '*Noli me tangere*', he said to Mary Magdalene, so that she could learn that there's a better way of showing him our love. To you and me, Jesus says, 'You can't touch my flesh. Let the bread serve instead, until we meet at last face to face in heaven.'

Suggested hymns

Bread of heaven, on thee we feed; Open our eyes, Lord; Sweet Sacrament divine; Walking in the garden.

Eighth Sunday after Trinity (Proper 12)   29 July
Principal Service   **The Wesley Brothers**
(*Continuous*): 2 Sam. 11.1–15 David and Bathsheba; Ps. 14
Repentance and the needy; *or* (*Related*): 2 Kings 4.42–44 Elisha
feeds a crowd; Ps. 145.10–19 Prayer and providence; Eph.
3.14–21 Prayer and providence; John 6.1–21 Feeding the five
thousand

> 'When he looked up and saw a large crowd coming toward him,
> Jesus said to Philip, "Where are we to buy bread for these people
> to eat?"' John 6.5

The Wesley family

The Reverend Samuel Wesley, who was born in 1662, was the
Rector of Epworth in Lincolnshire, and the ancestor of a remarkable dynasty. His wife Susanna bore him 19 children, of whom
John, born 1703, was the fifteenth and Charles, born 1707, the
eighteenth. Samuel's political opinions were disliked by his parishioners, and once they burnt down the Rectory. Little John Wesley
was rescued from the blaze when his family passed him out through
an open window. Remembering this, he felt that God must have
some special purpose for him because he was 'a brand plucked from
the burning'.

John Wesley

A group of friends who gathered round John Wesley in Oxford
were so methodical in their practice of daily prayer and holiness
of life that they were derisively nicknamed 'Methodists'. John was
ordained in the Church of England, and went as a missionary to the
American state of Georgia, preaching to the British people who'd
settled there, but were without clergy. Preaching against slavery
and gin didn't make him popular, and two years later he returned
to England. Some Moravians persuaded him that he still lacked the
faith that is necessary for salvation, and he was attending a meeting

in Albemarle Street, London, and reading Luther's Commentary on Romans, when he felt his heart 'strangely warmed'.

An evangelist

John Wesley felt like Jesus did when he fed the 5,000 hungry people. St John reports that Jesus said to Philip, 'Where are we to buy bread for these people to eat?' St Mark tells us, 'He had compassion for them, because they were like sheep without a shepherd; and he began to teach them many things.' Wesley knew the British people were hungry for spiritual teaching, and felt called to evangelize. The churches were closed to him, so he became an open-air preacher, travelling an average of 8,000 miles each year on horseback, preaching the gospel. In many places the established church had far too few clergy, and Wesley was sowing the seed of the word, in effect, in virgin soil. Methodism met with an overwhelming welcome, and to this day the Methodists are the strongest denomination in some parts of England. He arranged annual conferences for lay preachers. The congregations were organized into class meetings for instruction, yet continued to receive communion in their parish churches. The British Government refused to appoint bishops for America, so Wesley took it upon himself to ordain ministers there, although he was not a bishop. He struck a balance between love for God and love for our neighbour, and taught the importance of preaching, frequent Holy Communion, extempore prayer, perfection and assurance.

Charles Wesley

Charles Wesley went with his brother John to Georgia from 1735 to 1736, where he served as secretary to the Governor. Like John, he was influenced by the Moravians on his return to London, and converted on Whitsunday 1738. Charles then spent 17 years as a travelling preacher, before settling at the City Road Chapel in London. He wrote over 5,500 hymns, so important in evangelism and in teaching Christians to pray. They include 'Jesu, lover of my soul'; 'Love divine, all loves excelling'; 'Lo! he comes with clouds descending'; and 'Hark, how all the welkin rings' – later changed to 'Hark, the herald angels sing'. He remained loyal to the Church of England and was irritated by John's ordinations. His son Samuel Wesley, and Samuel's son Samuel Sebastian Wesley, were both distinguished church musicians and composers.

The Methodist Church

Despite the narrowness and inflexibility of some parts of the Church of England in the eighteenth century, which forced the Wesleys to work outside its structures, they remained members until their death, and encouraged their followers in 'occasional conformity'. It was only after their death that Methodism formed a separate denomination. Considering that the Wesleys didn't want this, and that the two churches are so close in many ways, we must continue to pray earnestly for their eventual reunion. Yet progress has been painfully slow, and while all Christians must be honest about the bigotry of their ancestors, there's no excuse for perpetuating old resentments. We must pray, as Jesus did, 'that they may all be one'.

All-age worship

Learn some of the great Wesleyan hymns. What do they teach us?

Suggested hymns

And can it be that I should gain?; Jesu, lover of my soul; Love divine, all loves excelling; Lo! he comes with clouds descending.

Eighth Sunday after Trinity (Proper 12)   29 July
Second Service   God's Forgettery
Ps. 74 National defeat; Job 19.1–27a My Redeemer lives, *or* Ecclus. (Sirach) 38.24–34 Labour; Heb. 8 Mediator of a better Covenant; *Gospel at Holy Communion*: Luke 11.1–13 Prayer

> 'For I will be merciful toward their iniquities, and I will remember their sins no more.' Hebrews 8.12

Forgettery

> 'The horror of that moment,' the [White] King went on, 'I shall *never* forget.'
> 'You will, though,' the Queen said, 'if you don't make a memorandum of it.'

In that quotation from *Through the Looking Glass* by Lewis Carroll, the White Queen put her finger on a universal problem. There are so many things we ought to remember, but which slip right out of our minds. In fact, someone unknown once invented a name for our ability to forget – it's facetiously called a 'forgettery'.

Selective amnesia

But in some circumstances, a powerful forgettery can be a very useful tool. It's like 'diplomatic deafness'. Diplomats, representing their own government in a foreign land, overhear many things that they're not supposed to hear. They'll store them away for their own information, but they know it would be more diplomatic to pretend, in public at least, that they haven't heard them. The term 'diplomatic deafness' has been coined to define this stratagem. Many other people, as well as diplomats, are struck by this sickness from time to time! And there's a similar trick known as 'selective amnesia'. There are many things that we remember perfectly well, but it's more tactful to pretend that we don't. Then we can bring our powerful forgettery into play, by not mentioning things in the past which would cause embarrassment to those we're talking to. The past is past, and there's no sense in dredging up mistakes our friends have made. It serves no purpose, and spoils our relationship in the present.

God's forgettery

Thank God, God's very good at selective amnesia. Sadly, there are many bad things that each of us has done in the past, which we would rather forget about. If we say we're sorry, God gladly offers us his complete forgiveness. He's perfectly willing to play the game of selective amnesia. Our forgiven sins are placed in God's ample forgettery – he forgives and pretends to forget. Of course, nobody can completely forget the past. But if you decide to make the effort to ignore things that have been forgiven, they no longer play an important part in your thinking. In the New Testament Letter to the Hebrews, the author is talking about the bargain that God struck with the Jews on Mount Sinai, that they would obey the commandments and he would protect them. Then the writer goes on to discuss the new contract that was signed in the blood of Jesus. The terms are that we will love our neighbour, and God will forgive our sins. God says, 'I will be merciful toward their iniquities, and I will remember their sins no more.' God is willing to forgive and forget. A woman asked a wise old monk how he could be sure God had forgiven him. He told her to ask God in her prayers what sins the monk had confessed the previous day. Next day he asked what God had replied. 'God said he couldn't remember,' she answered. 'He said he'd forgotten all about them already!'

Our side

But don't forget there are two sides to this bargain. God forgives us; our job is to love God in return, and love our neighbour for his sake. There are some people who go round crippled with remorse. They can never forget the terrible mistakes they have made in the past. Because of this, they remain enslaved to the past, and can never get on with the task of loving in the present. Whenever Jesus met someone like this, he said to them, 'Your sins are forgiven.' He didn't actually say, 'Of course they are, you silly ass, how could you possibly doubt it?' But I expect he thought it! If God can forget our past misdemeanours, the least we can do is to forget them also. The only thing we must remember is that we have the colossal privilege of being forgiven sinners. And when other people hurt us, we mustn't bear a grudge. We must offer them what God gives us: complete forgiveness and a clean slate. If they show the slightest sign of being willing to accept this, and to forgive the harm we in turn have done to them, then we must play the game of 'selective amnesia'. If we're to be God's children, we need a forgettery as big as God's.

Suggested hymns

Father of heaven, whose love profound; God forgave my sin in Jesus' name; Great is thy faithfulness, O God my Father; I will sing the wondrous story.

Ninth Sunday after Trinity (Proper 13)   5 August
(Eve of The Transfiguration, see page 336.)
Principal Service   **Nourishment**
(*Continuous*): 2 Sam. 11.26—12.13a The parable of the one ewe lamb; Ps. 51.1–13 Forgiveness; or (*Related*): Ex. 16.2–4, 9–15 The manna; Ps. 78.23–29 The manna; Eph. 4.1–16 Gifts of the Spirit, unity of the Church; John 6.24–35 I am the bread of life

'Jesus said to them, "I am the bread of life. Whoever comes to me will never be hungry, and whoever believes in me will never be thirsty."' John 6.35

Regular meals

Are you getting regular meals? Or do you just grab a bite now and then, and fit in a snack when you have a moment? Most of us are careless about our eating habits. That's OK occasionally; but nutritionists tell us that if we never have a regular eating pattern, we shall pay for it with digestive problems. Moreover, family life breaks down if we don't regularly eat together. For a balanced diet you need protein, carbohydrate, fibre and vitamins.

Bread of life

Jesus said, 'I am the bread of life. Whoever comes to me will never be hungry, and whoever believes in me will never be thirsty.' Just as our bodies need bread, otherwise we shall die, so our souls need nourishment by Jesus. Without him, we're spiritually dead. In which case, we need to be as regular in our contacts with Jesus as we ought to be in our physical eating patterns. We feed on Jesus by prayer, Bible reading, weekly worship, and by life in the Spirit. Prayer is the *protein* in our spiritual nourishment. Bible reading is the fibre – the *bulk* if you like. Church is the *carbohydrate*. The life-giving Spirit corresponds to the vitamins. I'm sure you can remember that: Prayer for Protein; Bible for Bulk; Church for Carbohydrate, and the life-giving Spirit for vitamins. You need regular doses of each for a healthy spiritual diet.

Prayer for Protein

Prayer is for Protein – the body-building part of our diet developing strong bones and muscles. Regular habits of prayer make us spiritually strong, to resist temptation and struggle against what's wrong in the world. Do you sometimes feel too weak to cope with the problems that face you? If you have these symptoms, Doctor Jesus's prescription is regular doses of prayer. If you miss your prayer-time one day, God doesn't mind, but you'll suffer. Your prayers aren't meant to make God feel good; they are for your sake, to help you keep in touch with him. You don't need to memorize special words to pray – just chat to God like you talk to your friends. The more regular your prayer habits become, the stronger you'll feel.

Bible for Bulk

Prayer for Protein, Bible for Bulk. Without regular supplies of fibre, your digestive system becomes clogged up. Again, a fixed time for Bible reading each day helps. The Bible isn't always easy to understand, and you need help in drawing the spiritual meaning out of the text. This can be from Daily Bible Notes, or a basic Bible dictionary, or a simple commentary. Or, like prayer, we can learn from each other by doing it together.

Church for Carbohydrate

Church worship is like the carbohydrate – it gives us regular supplies of energy. We all have Sundays when we're working, or not feeling well, or visiting relatives. Then we have to offer up a quick prayer and send God our apologies for absence. Apart from that, we need regular doses of worship Sunday by Sunday. In worship, we encourage each other, like soldiers singing together to keep their spirits up on the way to battle. We get to know God better. We learn to pray, and to understand the Bible, and the sermon gives us hints on what to do about it. But you must come to church determined to look for nourishment – looking for one simple phrase that you can memorize, and repeat to yourself during the week. That will give you energy to keep going.

Spirit-life for Vitamins

Finally, the Spirit is the life-giver; living a life of love in the power of the Spirit is as essential to our spiritual health as the vitamins are to the health of the body. Jesus said, 'I am the bread of life.' Are you getting regular spiritual meals? Prayer for Protein; Bible for Bulk; Church for Carbohydrate, and the life-giving Spirit for vitamins? We need them all, and we need them regularly. Someone was once asked, 'Why do you go to hear sermons when you don't remember what they were about?' He replied, 'Sermons are like meals – I don't remember the menu, but without them I'd be dead.'

All-age worship

Read a Bible verse. Each make up a prayer about it. Then say these prayers together. Sing, 'Read your Bible, pray every day, if you'd follow me.'

Suggested hymns

Glorious things of thee are spoken; I am the bread of life; Jesus, stand among us at the meeting of our lives; Prayer is the soul's sincere desire.

Ninth Sunday after Trinity (Proper 13)   5 August
Second Service   Faith

Ps. 88 The pit of despair; Job 28 Where is wisdom found?, *or* Ecclus. (Sirach) 42.15–25 The works of the Lord; Heb. 11.17–31 Heroes of faith; *Gospel at Holy Communion*: Luke 12.13–21 The rich fool

> *'By faith the walls of Jericho fell after they had been encircled for seven days.'* Hebrews 11.30

Walls of Jericho

Those of you familiar with Walls™ ice-cream will appreciate the old joke that asks: 'When was the first time ice-cream was mentioned in the Bible?' The answer, of course, is, 'In the passage about Walls of Jericho!' Jericho – the name means 'city of palms'. It's the oldest still inhabited town in the world. It's also the lowest, at 1,300 feet below sea-level, standing in the Jordan Valley about ten miles from the north end of the Dead Sea. Archaeological diggings have revealed many layers of habitation. According to the Bible, the wall collapsed when Joshua's troops walked round blowing trumpets, but unfortunately it's not been possible to identify these walls in the excavations. Here Elisha purified the water in the spring; Jesus healed the blind, and dined with the tax-collector Zacchaeus; here he located the parable of the good Samaritan. The Letter to the Hebrews lists the Jericho story among its examples of faith: 'By faith the walls of Jericho fell after they had been encircled for seven days.' How true! If Joshua and his companions hadn't believed God's promises they would have soon given up the apparently pointless processions round the city walls.

Examples of faith

Several other examples of faith in God are given in Hebrews:

- Abel, who sacrificed to God – 'he died, but through his faith he still speaks'.
- Enoch who 'pleased God', which you can't do without believing that God exists.
- Noah, who believed that there would be a flood.
- Abraham, who set out for a Promised Land he'd never seen.
- Isaac and Jacob, who promised future blessings for their children and grandchildren.
- Joseph, who promised the Exodus.
- Moses, 'who chose ill-treatment with the people of God rather than to enjoy the fleeting pleasures of sin'.
- The Israelites who passed through the Red Sea.
- Rahab the prostitute who welcomed the Hebrew spies in Jericho.

None of these, says the author, would have been able to achieve what they did, if they hadn't first trusted God to keep his promises. Hebrews defines faith like this: 'Faith is the assurance of things hoped for, the conviction of things not seen'; or in modern words: 'Faith is the firm belief that we shall receive the things we hope for, the certainty that things we can't see really do exist.'

Proof

Don't we all sometimes wish we could prove that God exists? That we could produce a 'good knock-down argument' that would prove to the doubters that there *is* a life beyond death? But of course we can't, because God doesn't work that way. If there *was* a logical proof that God exists, then we would be *forced* to believe in him, and God doesn't want forced love, only love that is freely given. Faith isn't contrary to reason: we must weigh up the evidence. But when you look at this vast and beautiful universe, it seems much more probable that God is the cause lying behind it, than that it all happened by chance. Not certain, but probable. Then you have to choose to step out in faith. We can't prove that the bus is going to the destination on the front, we just have to trust the driver. A man can't prove that the pretty young woman he proposes marriage to is going to turn into a loving wife, he just has to have faith in her – and vice versa for the young woman accepting the proposal. But pity the person who takes no actions in life until they have complete proof that what they are doing is right. You just have to take risks, sometimes: God can use our mistakes, and bring good out of them, but God can't help us if we dither.

Trusting Dad

A child was stuck up a tree after dark and couldn't get down. His dad found him, and stood underneath the tree, saying, 'If you can't climb down, just jump; I'm here, trust me, I'll catch you.' The child couldn't be sure his father would catch him; but Dad had promised, and the child trusted him.

Trusting God

'We live by faith, not by sight,' said St Paul. Your eyes will show you that the world is a wonderful place; but only faith will show you that God loves you. Pray for faith, then trust God and make the 'leap of faith' by believing in him. Trust him that he will do what we ask, and step out in faith to serve God and your neighbour.

Suggested hymns

In the Lord I'll be ever thankful (Taizé); Lead, kindly light; Oft in danger, oft in woe; When we walk with the Lord.

Tenth Sunday after Trinity (Proper 14) 12 August
Principal Service Stealing

(*Continuous*): 2 Sam. 18.5–9, 15, 31–33 David's grief over Absalom's death; Ps. 130 Grief and forgiveness; or (*Related*): 1 Kings 19.4–8 God gives Elijah food; Ps. 34.1–8 Prayer and providence; Eph. 4.25—5.2 Live in love; John 6.35, 41–51 I am the bread of life

> 'Thieves must give up stealing; rather let them labour and work honestly with their own hands, so as to have something to share with the needy.' Ephesians 4.28

Ephesus

Ephesus was a huge city, and the remains today are one of the most impressive archaeological sites in the world. The Temple of Artemis there was bigger than St Paul's Cathedral in London, though now only one pillar remains. The apostle Paul established a Christian community there, but when Demetrius the silversmith heard that Paul was preaching against the worship of idols, he started a riot, because his trade in silver models of the Temple would collapse. Paul wanted to speak to the rioters, but his followers persuaded him to escape till things calmed down. The crowd surged into the vast theatre, the remains of which are still amazing today. It seats 24,000 people, and theatres in Roman cities had to provide a seat for every free man. Women were not admitted, nor were slaves, and it's reckoned that there were eight slaves for every free couple, because the Roman Empire was built on slave labour. So the population of Ephesus was probably approaching a quarter of a million, the fourth largest city in the Empire. But, as in all great cities, there were some pretty dodgy characters.

Ephesians

In prison in Rome, St Paul wrote a letter to his friends in Ephesus, with instructions for them to read it to the whole congregation, or congregations there when they met for worship, whom he calls 'the saints in Ephesus'. You may think that's an odd name for them, when you read the sort of things they got up to. For, after a profound analysis of how his thinking had developed throughout his long ministry, Paul finishes with a few words of practical advice. Listen to the list, and picture to yourself a congregation where these warnings were necessary: he tells slave-owners to stop threatening their slaves, and slaves to obey their owners; children to obey their parents, and parents not to provoke their children; wives to respect their husbands and husbands to sacrifice their own wishes in the interests of their wives. He warns them not to get drunk; he warns against casual sex and obscene language. Paul forbids bitterness and wrath, anger, wrangling, slander, malice, evil talk and lying. *Therefore all these things must have been going on among the congregation in Ephesus.* Most surprising of all, he warns them, 'Thieves must give up stealing; rather let them labour and work honestly with their own hands, so as to have something to share with the needy.'

Love, not criticism

So, among the Christians in Ephesus, you would find even burglars, shoplifters and muggers. The Ephesian Christians must have started by showing these people that God loves them, despite their dishonesty; and therefore they were tolerated, loved and accepted in the Christian congregation. *Only then* did they start trying to get them to reform. This must have required great maturity and self-control among the church members, for even one critical remark about their neighbours' behaviour would have scared them away for good, beyond any hope of improvement. Love converts people, not criticism. Even in our own country today, you'll find lads who grow up in an area where hardly anyone is employed, and where their parents have survived by thieving. They get among a bad crowd, who tease them into doing the same as everyone else. They feel remorse, particularly when they're caught and sent to prison. But the only thing that will make them change their ways is to show them that you love them.

Theft

Yet we can't just go on stealing. It's forbidden by the eighth commandment, 'thou shalt not steal'. Where society recognizes the right to own personal property, the state has to make regulations against taking what belongs to another. Yet we're all thieves, to some extent. For the opposite of stealing is honesty and generosity; transparent accounting; fairness towards employees; responsibility towards employers; generosity towards the needy; fairness in world trade; avoiding exploitation of developing nations; stewardship of the environment and stewardship towards one's church. None of us would score 100 per cent in a test for honesty on that definition. Paul's challenging words apply to me, too: 'Thieves must give up stealing; rather let them labour and work honestly with their own hands, so as to have something to share with the needy.'

All-age worship

Make pipe-cleaner models of the congregation at Ephesus seated round a rich man's table.

Suggested hymns

A new commandment I give unto you; God forgave my sin; I want to walk with Jesus Christ; Seek ye first the kingdom of God.

Tenth Sunday after Trinity (Proper 14) 12 August
Second Service **A Cloud of Witnesses**

Ps. 91 Angels guard you; Job 39.1—40.4 God answers Job; *or* Ecclus. (Sirach) 43.13–33 Nature; Heb. 12.1–17 A cloud of witnesses; *Gospel at Holy Communion*: Luke 12.32–40 Be prepared

> *'Since we are surrounded by so great a cloud of witnesses, let us also lay aside every weight and the sin that clings so closely, and let us run with perseverance the race that is set before us, looking to Jesus the pioneer and perfecter of our faith, who . . . has taken his seat at the right hand of the throne of God.' Hebrews 12.1–2*

The arena

What sport do you watch? Is it football? Cricket? Baseball? Athletics? Or none of the above? Even if you're not a great sports fan, you can imagine the excitement when there's a huge crowd of spectators cheering the players on. In the days when the New Testament was written, one of the favourite sports was athletics. The Greek cities competed to put on the most spectacular games. In a stadium, like the one where the chariot race was held in the film of *Ben Hur,* which seated thousands of spectators, the foot-races went round and round. In Corinth, the finishing line for the foot races was in the middle of the main town square, so that the whole population could gather to cheer on the winners. What a buzz that must have given to the athletes, knowing that a crowd of thousands was cheering them on, wanting them to win.

The cloud of witnesses

That's the image used in the Epistle to the Hebrews: a cloud of witnesses. You think you are struggling alone as you try to live a Christian life? No, says the author, there's a crowd watching you, cheering you on. You can't see them, but they can see you. This invisible audience is made up of the souls of earlier generations of

Christians, who are with God in eternity, but are fully aware of what's going on here on earth. They want you to succeed; they cheer you every time you resist a temptation, they roar their approval whenever you make the effort to help somebody else.

Hebrews

Nobody is quite sure who wrote Hebrews; older translations suggested it was by St Paul, but there's nothing in the text to suggest that. Perhaps it was Paul's friend Apollos, who was a Jew from Alexandria, the great port city in Egypt. There was a great university in Alexandria, with many Jews who could write in Greek and argue in the style of the Greek philosophers, and this is the style that Hebrews is written in. Many of the Jews of the Dispersion, those who lived outside the Holy Land in different parts of the Roman Empire, spoke Greek more fluently than their native Hebrew. It was to scattered groups of Jews who'd become Christians that this letter was written. They must have thought they were too few to be of any importance. Not at all, writes the author; you're making history; don't give up, because the eyes of Christians past, present and future are on you.

Athletes

The letter uses details of the life of the athlete in its analogy with the Christian life. First, the runners have to be fit; they must lose weight, giving them a powerful, fast physique. For the Christian, it's not the physical pounds or kilograms we have to lose, but 'the sin that clings so closely'. Unrepented sin, selfish habits that we're unwilling to give up, secret bitterness in our heart, they all hold us back in running the Christian race. Then, says the writer, 'let us run with perseverance the race that is set before us'. When you get half way through a race, it's no use turning round and looking behind you, to see what you've accomplished already. You've got to keep going till you reach the finishing line. It's no use starting with a fine example of Christian living in your teens and twenties, and then slacking off when you reach the age when you stop counting your birthdays. You've got to go on being a keen and enthusiastic Christian to the very last. Because there's someone waiting at the finishing line, ready to clap you on the back and give you the prize. It's Jesus, of course, who has run the race before us, and has now taken his seat at the right hand of the throne of God. If that isn't motive enough to help you keep on going to the end of the race, I don't know what is! Cheer up, stand up straight, put a grin on your face, and love God and your neighbour with all your might until the race is over.

Suggested hymns

Fight the good fight; Give us the wings of faith to rise; One more step along the road I go; Ye holy angels bright.

Eleventh Sunday after Trinity (Proper 15)
19 August
Principal Service   **Redeeming the Time**
(*Continuous*): 1 Kings 2.10–12; 3.3–14 Solomon's dream;
Ps. 111 The beginning of wisdom; or (*Related*): Prov. 9.1–6
Wisdom's call; Ps. 34.9–14 Providence and peace; Eph. 5.15–20
Wisdom; John 6.51–58 Eat and live

> 'Be careful then how you live, not as unwise people but as wise, making the most of the time, because the days are evil. So do not be foolish, but understand what the will of the Lord is.' Ephesians 5.15–17

Wisdom and knowledge

What is the wise way to spend your time? St Paul advised the Ephesians to acquire wisdom, writing: 'Be careful then how you live, not as unwise people but as wise ... Don't be foolish, but understand what the will of the Lord is.' Wisdom isn't cleverness, or knowledge. A doctor wrote in the newspaper about doing a test which won't change anything, but makes the patient feel someone is listening to them. He wrote: 'When asked to perform a test on a patient, I'm wise enough to know that it's pointless but I do it anyway. Knowledge alone – for example, learning that tomatoes are fruits not vegetables – is not enough. Wisdom is deciding not to serve them with custard.' Wisdom, he suggests, is practical common sense. St Paul goes further, and says wisdom is understanding what God wants us to do, and doing it. Ah, but ... if only God would tell us clearly what that is!

Memo from God

If you receive emails, you'll probably at some time have found in your in-box a message entitled 'Memo from God'. It's a bit corny, but it's wise advice. I imagine that this is what God would write to us, if we asked to be taught wisdom. Listen:

Memo from God

I am God. Today I will be handling all your problems. Please remember that I don't need your help. If life brings you a situation that you can't handle, don't try to resolve it. Just put it in the SFGTD (something for God to do) box. It will be addressed in my time, not yours. Once the matter's placed in the box, don't hold unto it.

If you find yourself stuck in traffic, don't despair. There are people in this world for whom driving is an unheard of privilege.

If you have a bad day at work, think of the man who's been out of work for years.

If you despair over a relationship gone bad, think of the person who's never known what it's like to love and be loved in return.

If you grieve the passing of another weekend, think of the woman in dire straits, working twelve hours a day, seven days a week to feed her children.

If your car breaks down, leaving you miles away from help, think of the paraplegic who'd love the opportunity to take that walk.

If you notice a new grey hair in the mirror, think of the cancer patient undergoing chemotherapy, who wishes she had any hair at all.

If you find yourself at a loss, and wondering what life is all about, asking, 'what am I here for?' – be thankful. There are those who didn't live long enough to get the chance.

If you find yourself the victim of other people's bitterness, ignorance, smallness or insecurities, remember, things could be worse. You could be them!

Redeeming the time

That's the end of the imaginary Memo from God. I like it! St Paul tells us to get wisdom, understanding what God's will is for us, describing it as 'redeeming the time'. That's the old translation; modern ones avoid the word 'redeeming' because it's difficult. But redeeming something simply means buying it back. Suppose you take your watch to the pawn shop because you're short of cash, then, when your money comes in on payday, you go and redeem your watch, setting it free, so to speak. In Bible times, slaves could be redeemed by buying back their freedom. God has lent each of us a certain amount of time, so we're all 'living on borrowed time'. We should be grateful for the time God lends us, however long or short our lives are. Time is meant to be our servant, but often we're so busy that we become the slaves of time. We need the wisdom to redeem our time from the rat race, to set free our days and hours from the busy, busy demands we make of them, and enjoy the moments that God gives us. There are 60 minutes in every hour, and we can do one of four things with them: wasting time; saving time; killing time; or using our time thankfully to serve God. I know which is the wisest.

All-age worship

Older children can teach younger children how to tell the time. Make a big calendar, with the heading 'The Days God's Lent Me'.

Suggested hymns

Blessed assurance, Jesus is mine; Immortal, invisible, God only wise; O for a closer walk with God; O God, our help in ages past.

Eleventh Sunday after Trinity (Proper 15)
19 August
Second Service **Jesus the Outcast**
Ps. [92 Giving thanks] 100 All the earth; Ex. 2.23—3.10 The burning bush; Heb. 13.1–15 Outside the gate; *Gospel at Holy Communion*: Luke 12.49–56 Divisions

> *'For the bodies of those animals whose blood is brought into the sanctuary by the high priest as a sacrifice for sin are burned outside the camp. Therefore Jesus also suffered outside the city gate in order to sanctify the people by his own blood. Let us then go to him outside the camp and bear the abuse he endured.' Hebrews 13.11–13*

Respectable?

Are Christians supposed to be respectable? At first glance the answer's obvious. We're not supposed to have any notorious bad habits, or if we do, we should be working on them like alcoholics work on their addiction. That doesn't mean that only sinless people can become Christians – we've all sinned at some time. But we're all forgiven sinners: we've acknowledged our sins, repented, accepted God's forgiveness, and asked his help to avoid temptation and overcome it in the future. So we certainly wouldn't be welcome in the society of those who consider they've never done anything wrong. But that's not the sort of company we want to keep, anyway. Jesus mixed with the outcast and despised, and so should we. Some would say this isn't respectable, and would be shocked to hear me say it. But look at the evidence.

Mixing with sinners

Jesus was a carpenter – respectable artisan, you might say – and his first disciples were fishermen, small businessmen with their capital invested in their boats. But then he met a tax-collector; accepted his invitation to dinner; and made him one of his inner circle. Nowadays I know some very respectable people who work for the Department of Revenue and Customs, but in Jesus's time the tax-collectors were notorious. They bought the right to collect taxes in a particular district, and then charged as much as they dared. They cheated and swindled their fellow countrymen, in order to raise money to pay the wages of a hated occupying army. No respectable person would be seen in their company, but Jesus enjoyed himself at their parties. Then there were the prostitutes. Few people choose to follow the oldest profession, then or now; most are forced into it by poverty. Jesus mixed with prostitutes, and allowed one or two to make emotional scenes, washing his feet with their tears and so on. Mary Magdalene may or may not have been a prostitute – the Bible says Jesus cast seven devils out of her, which probably means he healed her from a severe mental breakdown. Then she became one of his closest friends and messengers. There were others, too, who committed no spectacular sin, but just found keeping up with all the regulations of the Jewish Law too much to manage in the modern world. They too were lumped together by the respectable people under the heading of 'sinners'. Jesus became notorious for spending all his time eating and drinking with disreputable 'tax-collectors and sinners' – the dregs, the outcasts of society.

Jesus the outcast

Then Jesus himself became an outcast. He was condemned for blasphemy, and the respectable folk brayed for his death. It wasn't a nice death; crucifixion was a brutal and bloody affair, and was always done outside the city walls, so that the respectable areas shouldn't be polluted. The author of the Letter to the Hebrews reminds his Jewish readers that this is where lepers and other unclean people were banished to, 'outside the camp', even in the days before they built city walls. Blasphemers and adulterers were stoned to death outside the camp; so was a man who had been seen collecting firewood on the Sabbath day. So Jesus, in death as in life, was identified with the outcast and the pariahs, the social lepers, the disreputable, the reprobates and the untouchables.

A sin offering

Then the Letter to the Hebrews makes a startling comparison. 'Outside the camp', according to the Old Testament, was also where the sacrifice of the sin offering had to be made, as though the sins of the people inside were forgiven when they were transferred to the poor innocent 'outsider', be it slaughtered beast or human scapegoat! We can offer the crucifixion of Jesus on Calvary to God as a sign of our repentance; he is the sin offering whose death brings us forgiveness. It's a powerful metaphor.

Disreputable

So should Christians be respectable? Surely not, if we're followers of Jesus the outcast! Still today we make the poor wretches who form the dregs of society our scapegoats, blaming them for the social ills that have been brought about by our own selfishness. The least we can do in reparation is to mix with the outcasts as Jesus did, show them that they are loved, and that they can tread with us the road to forgiveness and recovery. But if you follow that path, goodbye to respectability!

Suggested hymns

Amazing grace; And can it be?; Just as I am; To God be the glory.

Twelfth Sunday after Trinity (Proper 16)

26 August

Principal Service   **Materialism or the Spirit?**

(*Continuous*): 1 Kings 8.[1, 6, 10–11] 22–30, 41–43 Solomon prays; Ps. 84 How lovely is your Temple; *or* (*Related*): Joshua 24.1–2a, 14–18 Choose the Lord; Ps. 34.15–22 The Lord's salvation; Eph. 6.10–20 The armour of God; John 6.56–69 Spirit and life

> '[Jesus said,] "It is the spirit that gives life; the flesh is useless. The words that I have spoken to you are spirit and life."' John 6.63

Flesh and spirit

Jesus had got embroiled in an argument. He told his fellow Jews that he is the bread of life. His flesh was given as a willing sacrifice on the cross. If they would make this sacrificial approach their own, they would receive his life within themselves. So he used the symbol of eating bread, which gives us strength, saying that whoever eats his flesh and drinks his blood will have eternal life. The opposition erupted. 'Does he want us to be cannibals? How can we eat his flesh?' So Jesus explained a very important principle. When you read the Bible: if you have a problem with the literal meaning of the words, that's because God's pointing you beyond the material level, to see their spiritual and symbolic meaning instead.

Sacraments

When he talked about bread and wine, Jesus was obviously already planning the Last Supper. He would take bread and wine, saying, 'this is my body, this is my blood', and telling his disciples to eat and drink them. To take these words literally would be horrific: the charge of cannibalism has often been levelled at Christians. The bread and wine are obviously meant to be symbols. But not 'empty symbols' – say those words to an artist and they'll laugh at you, because artists know that symbols are enormously powerful things. The whole direction of people's lives has been changed by the use of symbolism. So the Church calls the bread and wine a 'sacrament'. The Book of Common Prayer defines a sacrament as 'an outward and visible sign of an inward and spiritual grace'. It's like a kiss: the physical action does nothing, but give it the added value of a symbol, and it actually conveys love. The love's invisible; the kiss makes it visible. So, the Catechism continues, a sacrament is 'given unto us ... by Christ himself, as a means whereby we receive [God's life-changing grace]'. Bread and wine in Communion are a symbol, but they're an *effective* symbol; they actually make us better people. This isn't magic; it depends on us accepting God's grace by faith, going beyond the material to the spiritual meaning. Or as Jesus put it, 'It is the spirit that gives life; the flesh is useless.'

Materialism

That means that a merely materialistic approach to life is barren. Materialistic Communism got nowhere, because it didn't give people the spiritual motive to work for the benefit of others. Scientific materialism is useless without the spiritual understanding of why we're here and how we should live.

Interpretation

Christians who stay merely on the material level are also losing out. If you waste time worrying whether a whale could swallow Jonah, you're missing the point of the story – which is to warn us against keeping our religion to ourselves, and encourage us to share it with people of different backgrounds. From the first, Christians distinguished four layers of meaning in the Bible:

The *literal* meaning, describing what happened.
The *allegorical* meaning, telling us what to believe.
The *moral* meaning, telling us what to do.
The *spiritual* meaning, pointing our way to heaven.

We need all four to reach a full understanding of what the Bible is saying. That doesn't mean we can avoid our responsibilities by being 'so heavenly minded that we're no earthly use'! The gospel has practical, material consequences. But Jesus said: 'It is the spirit that gives life; the flesh is useless. The words that I have spoken to you are spirit and life.'

All-age worship

Draw symbols of the seven sacraments: Holy Communion, Baptism, Confirmation, Ordination, Marriage, Forgiveness and Healing. Add other powerful symbols like a kiss.

216

Suggested hymns

Broken for me; Here, O my Lord, I see thee face to face; Sweet feast of love divine; We come as guests invited.

Twelfth Sunday after Trinity (Proper 16)
26 August
Second Service   The Latest Decalogue
Ps. 116 Recovery from illness; Ex. 4.27—5.1 Aaron speaks for Moses; Heb. 13.16–21 Do good; *Gospel at Holy Communion*: Luke 13.10–17 Healing on the Sabbath

> *'[Jesus said,] "You hypocrites! Does not each of you on the sab-bath untie his ox or his donkey from the manger, and lead it away to give it water? And ought not this woman, a daughter of Abra-ham whom Satan bound for eighteen long years, be set free from this bondage on the sabbath day?"' Luke 13.15–16*

Commandments

The great Commandments in the Bible are to love God and love your neighbour, in all situations. All the other Commandments are attempts to apply those Commandments to particular circum-stances. Yet a slavish attempt to apply every one of the Command-ments to situations to which they're not relevant frequently leads to very unloving behaviour. Jesus received a good old telling off from his religious neighbours, for healing a sick woman on the Sabbath day. Healing was work, they said, forbidden on Saturdays by the Ten Commandments. Jesus turned on his accusers with some very strong language. They thought they were very moral people, but he called them hypocrites. He told a little parable about setting domestic animals free from their bonds on the Sabbath, comparing this to setting the woman free from her sickness. Anyone can twist the Ten Commandments to their own advantage, he suggested, but nothing overrides the law of love.

'The Latest Decalogue'

In the early nineteenth century, Arthur Hugh Clough wrote a satiri-cal poem about this. I'll split it up, to let every few lines sink in, and then read it in full at the end. He called it 'The Latest Decalogue':

217

Thou shalt have one God only; who
Would be at the expense of two?

The poet suggests that many Christians obey the first Commandment for merely economic reasons.

No graven images may be
Worshipp'd, except the currency:

British coins have an image of the Queen on one side, and many people make money their main aim in life, their idol.

Swear not at all; for, for thy curse
Thine enemy is none the worse:

Swearing is to be avoided, people think, not because it's wrong, but because it's ineffective.

At church on Sunday to attend
Will serve to keep the world thy friend:

Worldly motives again, worshipping so as to be admired.

Honour thy parents; that is, all
From whom advancement may befall:

Many Christians have widened the scope of the Commandment to include all those in authority over us, who should be respected and obeyed for God's sake. Here, however, they're only flattered because that could lead to promotion.

Thou shalt not kill; but need'st not strive,
Officiously, to keep alive:

This is the most challenging satire of all, because we all ignore the fate of the under-class and the Third World, casually allowing them to die of poverty, without realizing that by our neglect we're guilty of murder, just as much as the man who sticks a knife into somebody.

Do not adultery commit;
Advantage rarely comes of it:

No comment!

Thou shalt not steal; an empty feat,
When it's so lucrative to cheat:

By our dishonesty in business, or on our tax return or social security claim, our greed makes somebody else poorer – maybe it's the other taxpayers who suffer, but it amounts to stealing just the same.

Bear not false witness; let the lie
Have time on its own wings to fly:

Gossiping about others is as bad as lying in the law court.

Thou shalt not covet; but tradition
Approves all forms of competition.

Greed and envy are against God's will, whatever form they take.

The sum of all is, thou shalt love,
If anybody, God above:
At any rate shalt never labour,
More than thyself, to love thy neighbour.

Complete

Now as I read it again, ask yourself if you're ever guilty of twisting God's Commandments to your own advantage, like the Jews did with the law of the Sabbath:

Thou shalt have one God only; who
Would be at the expense of two?
No graven images may be
Worshipp'd, except the currency:

Swear not at all; for, for thy curse
Thine enemy is none the worse:
At church on Sunday to attend
Will serve to keep the world thy friend:

Honour thy parents; that is, all
From whom advancement may befall:
Thou shalt not kill; but need'st not strive,
Officiously, to keep alive:

Do not adultery commit;
Advantage rarely comes of it:
Thou shalt not steal; an empty feat,
When it's so lucrative to cheat:

Bear not false witness; let the lie
Have time on its own wings to fly:
Thou shalt not covet; but tradition
Approves all forms of competition.

The sum of all is, thou shalt love,
If anybody, God above:
At any rate shalt never labour,
More than thyself, to love thy neighbour.

Suggested hymns

Awake, my soul, and with the sun; Come, let us sing of a wonderful love; Lord, thy word abideth; Take my life, and let it be.

Thirteenth Sunday after Trinity (Proper 17)
2 September
Principal Service   **Danger Signs and Direction Signs**
(*Continuous*): S. of Sol. 2.8–13 Love in springtime; Ps. 45.1–2, 6–9 The king's wedding; *or* (*Related*): Deut. 4.1–2, 6–9 Teach your family obedience to law; Ps. 15 The Temple; James 1.17–27 Doers of the word; Mark 7.1–8, 14–15, 21–23 Inner cleanness

> '[Jesus said,] "You abandon the commandment of God and hold to human tradition."' Mark 7.8

Roadsigns

A clergyman in a hurry was stuck in a traffic jam. He decided the only way to get past was to drive to the right of the 'Keep Left' sign, in the other lane, which seemed to be clear. Of course he met a police car. They pulled him over, and he said, 'Officer, please let me carry on; if you don't, I shall be late for a funeral.' 'If you drive like that, sir,' replied the constable, 'you'll be early for your own funeral!' 'You've been waiting all your life to say that, haven't you?' said the clergyman. 'Yes,' answered the policeman with a cheeky grin – 'off you go, and don't do it again!' Travelling along the highway, you will see many road signs. Some are danger signs, and some are direction signs. God has provided many signposts to help us along the journey of life. Some are God's danger signs, warning us of hazards ahead if we keep on going as we are; other signs from God are direction signs, pointing out which way we should be travelling. In either case, we ignore them at our peril.

Law

Danger markers on the road are signs like 'No Through Road'; 'Beware of falling rocks'; 'No overtaking'; 'Do not exceed the speed limit'; and so on. There's nothing to stop you driving fast over the speed bumps you were warned about; but as you hit your head on the roof of the car, you'll wish you had slowed down. The signs are there to stop you hurting yourself. The Commandments are God's danger signs. If you steal, kill, lie, or are unfaithful to your partner, you'll suffer the consequences, and live to regret what you have done. It's not that a cruel God has thought up a lot of rules and regulations to make life difficult, or takes any pleasure in punishing those who break them. God wants to help us, and in his kindness gives us warnings when we look like hurting ourselves, physically, mentally or spiritually. Before God gave the laws of the Old Testament, the only chance of justice was if you could persuade an arbitrary ruler or an unpredictable judge to side with you in the conflict with your enemy. God gave the Ten Commandments to bring some order to an unjust legal system. God is like a wise parent, setting the boundaries of acceptable behaviour to help his unruly children.

Conflict

The difficulty comes when we start applying the commandments to particular situations. Then it becomes complicated. If a killer asks you where his intended victim is hiding, a lie may be necessary to protect the innocent. A parent may be forced to steal to feed their starving family. If two commandments seem to be in conflict, how do you decide which should override the other? The Israelites tried to solve this dilemma by making more and more detailed laws to cover every situation. It's said that there are 613 commandments in the Old Testament. Jesus found this situation intolerable; hygiene is an admirable way of avoiding infection, but when the Jews refused to eat with those who didn't bother with their ritual way of washing, Jesus said, 'You abandon the commandment of God and hold to human tradition.' The foundation of all law, he told us, is the law of love.

Love

Love is like the direction signs you find at a road junction: 'If you want to get to wherever, turn left here.' You won't get into danger if you ignore the direction signs, and you won't be punished if you disobey them. But it's wise to observe them, even so. And God gives us the law of love to help us to travel the right road, living at peace with our neighbours, and in harmony with our Creator, until we reach our happy destination in heaven. Love doesn't contradict law; laws are still needed to warn you of the dangers; but love goes beyond law. Through the grace of God, love helps us to make choices in situations that the law can't possibly cover. A good policeman knows when to be flexible in the application of the statutes. A good Christian knows that it's more important to behave in a loving way than to follow every pernickety detail of the laws of the Bible.

All-age worship

Study relevant parts of the Highway Code. Try to write a Code for Christians on the Highway of Life.

Suggested hymns

Amazing grace; O for a heart to praise my God; O thou who camest from above; Take my life, and let it be.

Thirteenth Sunday after Trinity (Proper 17)
2 September
Second Service   **Meditation**
Ps. 119.1–16 I will meditate; Ex. 12.21–27 Passover; Matt. 4.23—5.20 Sermon on the Mount

> *'I will meditate on your precepts, and contemplate your ways.'*
> *Psalm 119.15*

How to read the Bible?

How should we read the Bible? Suppose you hear a passage from the Bible read in church, and you're not one of those who switch off their brains as soon as someone gets up to read. But it's a bit obscure. So you go home and look it up in the Bible which you keep for propping up the table leg . . . er, I mean, which you keep beside your bed. If you've got a reasonably modern translation – although the words may not be as beautiful as the Authorized Version, but the meaning's much clearer – you think, 'Hey, this is exciting. I'd like to read more.' You can read St Mark's Gospel, for instance, right the way through in just over an hour, and it helps you, sometimes, to get everything in perspective. What's more important, though, is to take a few minutes *every day,* when you wake up or before you go to sleep or during your lunch hour, and read through just one short section or paragraph. Then think about them for a few minutes. In a year or two of daily Bible reading, you'll be quite proficient at hearing what God is saying to you through the Scriptures, and you'll wonder how you ever managed without it.

Where to start?

Where do we start? Some people misguidedly start with the first book of the Old Testament or the first book of the New Testament. Not many sections into Genesis or Matthew, you find yourself floundering in 'Abraham begat Jacob, and Jacob begat Judas and his brethren', and so on. We call them the 'who-begats'! They are important, showing that the Bible sees Jesus as the fulfilment of the past. But like many other passages, they're quite unsuitable for daily reading. Much better to get one of the little booklets of daily Bible reading notes, from the Bible Reading Fellowship or the Scripture Union. These suggest a few verses to read each day, then have a few words of comment and suggestions to start you thinking.

Meditation

After a few years of this, you may want to take it a bit further, perhaps when you're on holiday. Now's the time to learn the art of meditation. Not Transcendental Meditation or Buddhist meditation, but the meditation that Christians have been doing for two thousand years, which brings you closer to Jesus. It's the art of thinking about God. The problem is, most of us aren't much good at logical thought. Usually, we jump to and fro from one idea to another, and come to a decision that is really a hunch derived from intuition. So thinking about God isn't very easy, and you won't be very good at it when you start out. But it's worth the effort to learn, because eventually you'll have a much clearer idea of who Jesus is, and you'll be able to talk to him as your friend.

Methods

When you have had some practice at meditation, you can look at the 'Ignatian method' or the 'Salesian method'. But let's start with something very simple, which needs no books except a Bible. The word ACTS, spelt A C T S, is often used as an outline for prayer; let's see how it can be a framework for reading the Bible. The letters stand for Adoration, Confession, Thanksgiving, and Supplication; or simpler still, Adore, Confess, Thank you, and Supplies (asking for spiritual supplies, for yourself and other people). So take your chosen passage of Scripture, read it, and ask yourself, what does this tell me to adore God for? Then tell him, in your own stumbling words, how wonderful he is and how much you love him. Next, confess: does the Bible passage remind you of ways in which you have fallen short of the highest standards of love in your own life? Tell God you are sorry and receive his forgiveness. Next, thank God for any of the blessings that are mentioned in this paragraph of Scripture – there's always something. Finally, ask for your bodily needs, food and shelter, and also, for instance, for the grace of patience and deeper love. Then pray for the same things for your family, and the hungry people of the third world. Finally, end with a quiet period of relaxed silence.

Contemplation

Psalm 119 says, 'I will meditate on your precepts, and contemplate your ways.' That's what we've been learning to do today. Contemplation is the quiet period at the end. It deserves a sermon to itself. Good luck as you progress in the art of meditation and contemplation, and God bless you.

Suggested hymns

Dear Lord and Father of mankind; Lord, I have made thy word my choice; My God, how wonderful thou art; O Christ, the Word incarnate.

Fourteenth Sunday after Trinity (Proper 18)

9 September

Principal Service   **Does He Take Sugar?**

(*Continuous*): Prov. 22.1–2, 8–9, 22–23 The needy; Ps. 125 God rewards the righteous; or (*Related*): Isa. 35.4–7a Water in the desert; Ps. 146 Healing and salvation; James 2.1–10 [11–13] 14–17 Rich and poor; Mark 7.24–37 Crumbs from the table, healing the deaf

> *'Now the woman was a Gentile, of Syrophoenician origin. She begged him to cast the demon out of her daughter.' Mark 7.26*

Does he take sugar?

There was a series on BBC radio a while ago about disability, with the title, *Does he take sugar?* The phrase was taken from an incident when a man who was being pushed by his carer in a wheelchair, but was otherwise in possession of all his faculties, was introduced to somebody who had not met him before. The stranger offered him a cup of tea. But she looked over the head of the man in the wheelchair at the carer, and asked, 'Does he take sugar?' She could perfectly well have asked the man in the chair, who wasn't deaf, could speak clearly, and was very intelligent. But somehow, because he was in a wheelchair, she forgot he was a real person, and started talking about him in the third person. This was the epitome of exclusion: we must learn to welcome people with any illness or disability as full members of society, and as worthy of dignity and respect as anyone else.

The Syro-Phoenician woman

Jesus met a mother and daughter who were suffering from social exclusion. On one of his rare excursions outside the land of Israel, he visited the region around Tyre and Sidon. He wanted to get away to somewhere where nobody knew him, so that he could think calmly about his mission. But this mother and child sought him out. The little girl was sick – the Gospel says she had a demon, which may have been literally true, or maybe it was the language they used then for what we would call mental illness. For whatever mistaken reasons, some people try to avoid meeting sick children, and anyone who's mentally disturbed. There's no mention of the child's father, so perhaps the mother was a widow, or even a single parent. There was no sexual equality in those days, and everyone accepted that women were second-class citizens. But the real reason why this family was excluded was because they were foreigners. St Mark describes them as from the part of the Roman Province of Syria where the Phoenician people lived, or had lived in the past. Phoenicians were the boat people, the first travellers to make their way round the Mediterranean by sea. Some settled near Tyre; others near Carthage in North Africa; and some in Malta, where the language today is thought by some to be based on the ancient Phoenician tongue. They were migrants, and hated by the local people just as the Romany people are in some places today. Yet this woman had heard that Jesus was a healer, and she found where he was living and begged him to heal her daughter.

A test

Jesus knew that it would take him a whole lifetime to persuade his fellow Jews that he was their Messiah. If he started accepting appeals to help foreigners, it would be more than one man could manage. He said to her, 'Let the children be fed first, for it is not fair to take the children's food and throw it to the dogs.' The Jews referred to non-Jews as 'Gentile dogs', but Jesus wasn't being rude – he used the word for 'puppy dogs' – but he was testing her. The woman persisted, and made a joke of what he had said: 'Sir,' she answered, 'even the puppy dogs under the table eat the children's crumbs.' Pleased with her faith, Jesus told her to go home, where she found her daughter lying on the bed, completely healed.

A light to the Gentiles

The disciples remembered this event, because Isaiah had said that the Messiah would be 'a light to lighten the Gentiles'. Although it couldn't be his priority in his lifetime, Jesus had shown compassion to one socially excluded Gentile family, thus proving himself to be the Messiah. The mission to the whole world would have to be carried out by his disciples, after they had been given the Holy Spirit. You and I are Christians, even though we're Gentiles, because the disciples carried on where Jesus left off. We remember this woman, every time we say in the Holy Communion the prayer of humble approach, 'we are not worthy even to gather up the crumbs under the table'. Let's try and share her humility, and her faith in Jesus's

226

willingness to accept anybody, even the socially excluded, at his table.

All-age worship

Find out about children with disabilities in your area. What could you do to help?

Suggested hymns

At even, when the sun was set; Give thanks with a grateful heart; Peter and John went to pray; They shall come from the east.

Fourteenth Sunday after Trinity (Proper 18)
9 September
Second Service   **Pray It Like Jesus**
Ps. 119.41–56 Delight in God's commandments; Ex. 14.5–31 Crossing the Red Sea; Matt. 6.1–18 Almsgiving, prayer and fasting

> *'[Jesus said,] "Pray then in this way: Our Father in heaven, hallowed be your name."' Matthew 6.9*

Pray it like Jesus

The film *Bend it Like Beckham* was about a girl who wanted to be able to play football like her hero, David Beckham. Jesus is *our* hero, so perhaps we should invent a similar phrase for imitating Jesus in the things he was good at. Jesus was every bit as much an expert on prayer as Beckham is at football – perhaps we should describe our aim in life as to be able to 'Pray it like Jesus'. Thanks be, Jesus taught us to be nearly as good at praying as he was, when he taught his disciples the 'Our Father', the Lord's Prayer.

The prairie tortoise

But first, do you know what a prairie tortoise is? A little girl reported that her Sunday school teacher had told them about Jesus, and about the prairie tortoise. It took her parents a little while to work out that she'd misheard the phrase, 'the prayer he taught us'!

Children are taught the Lord's Prayer at an early age, before they're familiar with the old-fashioned language in which it is usually couched. Here's just a small selection of the hundreds of mishearings and misunderstandings that children have come out with:

'Our Father Richard in Heaven, Harold be thy name.
Thy Kingston come, thy Willoughby done, on earth as it isn't heaven.
Give us this day Miss Brailey dead.
And forgive us our trash baskets as we forgive those who put trash in our baskets.
And lead us not into Thames station, but deliver us some e-mail. Ah . . . men!'

All you need

Yet although we smile at the way children misunderstand the prayer that Jesus taught us, it's easy to use it as one of the 'vain repetitions' that Jesus warned us against, without thinking about what the words mean. There's everything in the Lord's Prayer that you could possibly need when talking to your Heavenly Father. If you think about it as you speak it, you've done all that's necessary for a healthy prayer life.

First you establish a relation with your Maker, and address God as Father (or Mother if you prefer), showing that you trust him to love you as the best of parents love their children. Yet he's not an earthly parent, he's in heaven, so you remind yourself that God hears your prayers and can answer your deepest needs.

Then you remember that God's name and nature are 'hallowed', or holy, and you promise to treat him with respect, and pray that other people, also, through your witness, may come to know that God loves them, and come to worship him too.

You pray that God's kingdom may come; God's kingdom is wherever God is obeyed as king, and his will, what he wants people to do for him, is done. Starting, of course, with you. Then, if you and everybody else did what God wants them to, earth would become like a colony or outpost of heaven.

Give us our daily bread, you ask. You remind yourself that you are entirely dependent on God's love, for all the necessities of life. You thank God for all he's given you, and ask that, as well as the bread, you may have an occasional slice of cake! Then you

228

pray for the millions around the world who haven't even enough bread, or rice, to keep them alive, and ask God to show you what you can do to help them.

Next comes the prayer for forgiveness. Nobody's perfect, and if we look back over our lives, or even over the course of the day that's just past, we can all find things we're ashamed of. Anyone who can't must be somewhat lacking in humility! But you don't need to dwell on them; just admit them to God, who is only waiting for you to say you are sorry, so that he can forgive your sins and forget all about them. There are only two conditions: you must be willing to forgive yourself, and extend to others the same generous forgiveness that God has shown to you.

Finally you ask God to help you to avoid situations in the future where you would be tempted to do wrong; and deliver you from the grip of evil habits.

You conclude with praise, 'for thine is the kingdom, the power and the glory, for ever and ever. Amen'.

Conclusion

If you pray like that, if you 'pray it like Jesus', you've done all that's necessary to put your relationship with God on a sound footing. Or if you're too tired, just repeat the words, and let the Holy Spirit within you pray for you; God knows what's in your heart, and that's OK.

Suggested hymns

Be still, for the presence of the Lord; Behold us, Lord, a little space; Father, hear the prayer we offer; Great Shepherd of thy people, hear.

Fifteenth Sunday after Trinity (Proper 19)
16 September
Principal Service   Made-to-Measure
(*Continuous*): Prov. 1.20–33 Wisdom's call; Ps. 19 Law and nature, *or Canticle*: Wisd. 7.26—8.1 Wisdom; *or (Related)*: Isa. 50.4–9a Suffering; Ps. 116.1–8 Salvation from death; James 3.1–12 Controlling the tongue; Mark 8.27–38 Take up your cross

'[Jesus said,] "If any want to become my followers, let them deny themselves and take up their cross and follow me."' Mark 8.34

Yokes

Joseph and Sons, the carpenters' workshop in Nazareth, crafted many products out of wood. They probably worked on the houses in the new town of Sepphoris which was being built only five miles away. They made doors, chairs and tables, ploughs, winnowing-forks, and yokes. These weren't mass produced; each piece was made-to-measure for the situation where it was needed. Each yoke was carefully crafted to fit the shoulders of the particular ox or ass who would wear it, so that there would be no rubbing or chafing. Of course the animal didn't like wearing a yoke, but the care with which Jesus of Nazareth carved it must have made it just about bearable. Jesus said to the crowds, 'Come to me, all you that are weary and are carrying heavy burdens, and I will give you rest. Take my yoke upon you, and learn from me; for I am gentle and humble in heart, and you will find rest for your souls. For my yoke is easy, and my burden is light.' Being a Christian doesn't mean not having any burdens to carry. But at least we know that each of us has our yoke especially shaped to our shoulders by the carpenter of Nazareth. His yoke is easy, and his burden is light.

Crosses

Jesus also said to the crowds, 'If any want to become my followers, let them deny themselves and take up their cross and follow me. For those who want to save their life will lose it, and those who lose their life for my sake, and for the sake of the gospel, will save it. For what will it profit them to gain the whole world and forfeit their life?' He warned them that following him wouldn't be easy. A few years previously, the roads around Nazareth had been lined with crosses on both sides, when the revolt of Judas the Galilean was cruelly crushed by the Roman army, and he and his followers were executed in the most painful manner that's ever been invented. So many crosses were made in those days that there was a shortage of timber for many years, and the ancient forests of Israel never recovered. Those who listened to Jesus knew exactly what carrying the cross meant. He wasn't offering them a life of easy comfort and popularity; there would be grief, pain and self-sacrifice; but the choice was between taking up the cross, then following Jesus into eternal life; or opting for an easy life in this world, but losing their self-respect, honour, and dignity – losing their very soul.

Tailored to fit

But Jesus doesn't ask us to carry any old cross. He doesn't order us to bear one that is too heavy for us. He asks you to pick up *your* cross – the one Jesus has made specially to fit you, designed so that only you can carry it. In the Bavarian village of Oberammergau, every ten years, they re-enact the last week of the life of Jesus of Nazareth. The villager who's chosen to act the part of Jesus hangs on a huge wooden cross high above the stage. He isn't actually nailed to the cross, it only looks like it, and he doesn't have to stay there for three hours, like Jesus did. In fact it's more like 20 minutes, but it's a colossal physical strain. In fact, they have two men acting the part of Jesus in alternate performances. Each man hangs on a cross that's tailor-made to fit him. Now there's a thought.

Your personal cross

We grumble about what's wrong in our life. We wish we didn't have so much grief and pain. But maybe this is your own personal cross, tailor-made to fit you by the carpenter of Nazareth. You wish you never needed to suffer; so did Jesus, and complained about it in the Garden of Gethsemane. But then he yielded: 'Father, not my will, but yours be done.' Will you offer up your particular cross as your personal sacrifice, remembering that it's made-to-measure, and you are the only one who can bear it? Jesus told each us to take up our personal cross. But he also said, 'my yoke is easy, and my burden is light'.

All-age worship

Borrow a rucksack, and make a label for it reading 'My burden is light, says Jesus.' Children take turns to put it on, and see how much you can put in it before it is too heavy to carry.

Suggested hymns

I danced in the morning; Take up your cross, the Saviour said; When I survey the wondrous cross; Will you come and follow me?

Fifteenth Sunday after Trinity (Proper 19)

16 September

Second Service   **Measure for Measure**

Ps. 119.73–88 Give me understanding; Ex. 18.13–26
Administration of justice; Matt. 7.1–14 Judging others

> '[Jesus said,] "With the judgment you make you will be judged,
> and the measure you give will be the measure you get."' Matthew
> 7.2

Shakespeare

Measure for Measure is a comedy by Shakespeare with a hard
satirical edge. Cruel Angelo is the deputy to the Duke of Vienna,
and has been left in charge. His first act is to imprison Claudio
for the crime of getting his fiancée pregnant, and condemn him to
death. Claudio's sister Isabella, a postulant nun, comes to plead
with Angelo for her brother's life; Angelo replies that he will
spare Claudio only if Isabella yields to his sexual advances. But
Angelo has previously spurned his lover, 'Mariana of the moated
grange', ruining her life, so she cunningly takes the place of the
chaste Isabella in Angelo's bed. At first, when Angelo's hypocrisy is
revealed, he's condemned to death, in the place of Claudio whom
he'd judged so harshly:

> An Angelo for a Claudio, death for death!
> Haste still pays haste, and leisure answers leisure,
> Like doth quit like, and Measure still for Measure.

Mercy

This sounds like an invocation of the Old Testament law of 'an
eye for an eye and a tooth for a tooth'. Cruel Angelo had wanted
to 'make the punishment fit the crime', judging that the size of the
crime should be met with a punishment equally harsh, measure
for measure. So shouldn't he be treated in the same way himself?
But Angelo is pardoned, provided that he marries Mariana whom
he had ruined. Shakespeare and his audience knew full well that
'measure for measure' is a loose quotation from Jesus, who in the
Sermon on the Mount appealed for mercy to override justice: 'With
the judgment you make you will be judged, and the measure you
give will be the measure you get.' Jesus wittily turned the Old Testa-

232

ment law on its head, making it apply to the judge, not the offender: if the judge is lacking in mercy, says Jesus, how can he expect God to be merciful to him when he dies? 'Measure for measure' is a true slogan, but only if you see it as a call to be generous in your assessment of other people, so that they will judge us leniently in our turn.

Non-judgemental

The phrase 'a non-judgemental approach' has become the slogan of psychotherapists and counsellors. They are in the business of helping people to change, and they know they can never achieve this by condemning them. If you ask them, 'What do you think about what I did?' wise counsellors will toss the question back at you: 'Well, what do *you* think?' It's a lesson we could all learn, in conversation with our friends. If they catch the suspicion of a frown on our brow, they'll clam up, and the conversation will be at an end. If we can learn to be patient, sympathetic, non-judgemental listeners, however, we may help our friends to work out their own solution to their problems. Then they'll thank us for our wise advice, when all we've done is to sit and listen to them!

The disagreeable man

The opposite of this is parodied in Gilbert and Sullivan's operetta *Patience*. King Gama is always criticizing other people, and can't understand why they don't like him. He sings:

If you give me your attention, I will tell you what I am:
I'm a genuine philanthropist – all other kinds are sham.
Each little fault of temper and each social defect
In my erring fellow-creatures, I endeavour to correct.
To all their little weaknesses I open people's eyes;
And little plans to snub the self-sufficient I devise;
I love my fellow creatures – I do all the good I can,
Yet ev'rybody says I'm such a disagreeable man!
And I can't think why!

To compliments inflated I've a withering reply;
And vanity I always do my best to mortify;
A charitable action I can skilfully dissect;
And interested motives I'm delighted to detect;
I know ev'rybody's income and what ev'rybody earns;

And I carefully compare it with the income-tax returns;
But to benefit humanity however much I plan,
Yet ev'rybody says I'm such a disagreeable man!
And I can't think why!

I'm sure I'm no ascetic; I'm as pleasant as can be;
You'll always find me ready with a crushing repartee,
I've an irritating chuckle, I've a celebrated sneer,
I've an entertaining snigger, I've a fascinating leer.
To ev'rybody's prejudice I know a thing or two;
I can tell a woman's age in half a minute – and I do.
But although I try to make myself as pleasant as I can,
Yet ev'rybody says I'm such a disagreeable man!
And I can't think why!

The answer

The answer to his question is obvious: measure for measure, judge
not that ye be not judged!

Suggested hymns

*Father of heaven, whose love profound; 'Forgive our sins as we
forgive'; Just as I am; When I needed a neighbour.*

Sixteenth Sunday after Trinity (Proper 20)
23 September
Principal Service   **Welcome Everybody**
(*Continuous*): Prov. 31.10–31 A good wife; Ps. 1 A good
person; *or* (*Related*): Wisd. 1.16—2.1, 12–22 Conflict, *or* Jer.
11.18–20 Conflict; Ps. 54 Conflict; James 3.13—4.3, 7–8a
Wisdom and works; Mark 9.30–37 Be like children

> '[Jesus said,] "Whoever welcomes one such child in my name wel-
> comes me, and whoever welcomes me welcomes not me but the
> one who sent me."' Mark 9.37

Welcome, everybody

Welcome, everybody! I greet you in the name of Jesus Christ. Jesus is very pleased to see you here. So, incidentally, am I. I want each one of you, individually, to feel that you're welcomed here by the whole Church, the Body of Christ. Each of you is important to Jesus. Whether you've been coming here for years, or whether this is your first time, we want you to feel that there was a welcome for you today.

Welcome everybody!

But when I say, 'Welcome, everybody', those words aren't only a greeting. They are also an instruction. With no comma, Jesus gives you a commandment; he wants you to welcome everybody. According to the Bible, Jesus said, 'I give you a new commandment, that you love one another. Just as I have loved you, you also should love one another.' So just as Jesus welcomes you to this church, he commands you to welcome other people. He makes no distinction between rich and poor, young and old, winners and also-rans; you must welcome them all in the name of Jesus Christ. That doesn't mean you've got to clap them on the shoulders and hug them – some people seem allergic to being clapped on the shoulder! Be sensitive, and read the signs; smile at each person when they come in, or when they come to sit near you. A few will refuse to smile back – if they are surly, ignore them. But if you get an answering smile, you can say, 'Nice to see you', and leave it at that. But if they look as though they would like to talk, you can ask them if they've had a good week, tell them your name, that sort of thing. Then they'll think, 'What a friendly lot they are at that church!' But to one or two people, you may be the first person to show any interest them all week, and they'll have something they want to get off their chest. Don't walk away or shut them up; whatever else you were going to do is less important than lending friend or stranger a listening ear. So I say again: welcome, everybody; and welcome everybody!

No second-class citizens

There are no second-class citizens in Christ's Church – everybody's equally important. In the Letter of James, he writes:

If a person with gold rings and in fine clothes comes into your assembly, and if a poor person in dirty clothes also comes in, and if you take notice of the one wearing the fine clothes and say, 'Have a seat here, please', while to the one who is poor you say, 'Stand there', or, 'Sit at my feet', have you not made distinctions among yourselves? . . . you have dishonoured the poor.

Welcome children

Jesus was always taking the side of those whom others tried to make feel unwelcome. He went to parties with dishonest tax-collectors, disreputable prostitutes, and other despised sinners. He healed the hated foreigners. He welcomed women, giving them positions of responsibility among his followers. He took a child in his arms, saying, 'Whoever welcomes one such child in my name welcomes me, and whoever welcomes me welcomes not me but the one who sent me.' There are some churches, I'm afraid, where children are told they should be seen and not heard. That attitude could stop the children from ever coming to know Jesus as their friend.

Welcoming Jesus

'Whoever welcomes one such child in my name,' says Jesus, 'welcomes me and welcomes God who sent me.' When a child, or anyone else whom you regard as less important than you, comes into church, look on them as though they were Jesus himself sitting next to you. Don't laugh – that probably sounds even funnier to them than it does to you, but it's what Jesus said. Make them feel welcome. A little poem was found in the Methodist Church, in the lovely Lakeland village of Grasmere. Take it to heart:

If, after church, you wait awhile,
someone may greet you with a smile.
But if you quickly rise and flee,
we'll all seem cold and stiff. Maybe
the one beside you in the pew
is, perhaps, a stranger too.
All here, like you, have fears and cares;
all of us need each other's prayers.
In fellowship we bid you meet
with us, around God's mercy-seat.

Make as many cards as you can, reading 'Jesus welcomes you.' Give them to everyone you meet.

Suggested hymns

A new commandment I give unto you; And now, O Father, mindful of thy love; From heaven you came, helpless babe; Teach me, my God and King.

Sixteenth Sunday after Trinity (Proper 20)

23 September

Second Service   **Consecrating the People**

Ps. 119.137–152 God's righteous judgements; Ex. 19.10–25 Consecrating the people; Matt. 8.23–34 Demons into pigs

> *'The Lord said to Moses: "Go to the people and consecrate them today and tomorrow. Have them wash their clothes."' Exodus 19.10*

Consecrate

To consecrate something means to make it sacred or holy. In the olden days, people were greatly in awe of God. God's so powerful, they thought, that nothing unworthy can possible come into his presence and survive. If the animals they sacrificed, and the robes the priests wore, weren't spotlessly clean and the best type on the market, they would be just burnt up by the awful power of God's holiness, when they were brought into the Temple. The first thing to do, before they came into the sanctuary, was to consecrate them, making them holy and fit for purpose. From there, they got the idea that the priests, too, and all the worshippers, needed to be holy, if they were to come into the presence of God. When God called Moses to Mount Sinai to give him the Ten Commandments, the people felt they were unworthy even to come near the foot of the mountain. So 'The LORD said to Moses: "Go to the people and consecrate them today and tomorrow. Have them wash their clothes."'

Holiness

Now, God can only talk to people in the words and concepts they understand. In those days the Jews had got hold of some very fundamental truths. But they hadn't yet realized that far from burning us up if we come near, God wants to speak to each of us 'face to face, as one speaks to a friend', like he did to Moses on the top of the mountain. Far from troubling about whether we've washed our clothes, God's idea of holiness is a purely moral one. We're fit for the presence of God if our hearts are full of love; whereas, if we come into his presence with hatred for others in our hearts, we may find the intensity of God's love more than we can stand.

Personal holiness

So we all need to be consecrated before we can talk to God. But that means we must have holy hearts and live holy lives. As The Book of Common Prayer puts it, 'Ye that do truly and earnestly repent you of your sins, and are in love and charity with your neighbours, and intend to lead a new life, following the commandments of God, and walking from henceforth in his holy ways . . .' Then and only then are we worthy to 'draw near with faith' into God's presence. That's what personal holiness means.

The Last Supper

At the Last Supper, Jesus began a long prayer, which fills chapter 17 of St John's Gospel, sanctifying, consecrating his disciples. 'Sanctify them in the truth; your word is truth. As you have sent me into the world, so I have sent them into the world. And for their sakes I sanctify myself, so that they also may be sanctified in truth.' What truth is Jesus referring to? Surely he means the truth that God is a God of love. When we know that Jesus loves us, and requires of us that we should love our neighbours in the same self-sacrificing way as he has shown by yielding up his own life on the cross for our sakes, then we shall be fit for purpose. Then, and only then, shall we be ready to come into God's presence in our private prayer and public worship. Then, and only then, shall we be ready for Jesus to send us out into the world, to tell others of how much God loves them.

238

The consecration prayer

One of the reasons we come to church, then, is to be consecrated, or made holy. In the Holy Communion service, the central prayer is called the Great Thanksgiving, but the old name for it was the Consecration Prayer. It's true that the priest makes the bread and wine holy, consecrating them so that they may be, for us, the body and blood of Christ. But far more important is the fact that the priest is consecrating the people. By reading the Scriptures with us, explaining them in the sermon, praying for us, and pronouncing God's absolution when we confess, the priest makes us holy, fit for purpose. *God's purpose* for us is that we should pray to him for the world, and spread God's love wherever we go. We're made fit for this by our worship.

Consecrating ourselves

When God came close to his chosen people on Mount Sinai, he told Moses, 'Go to the people and consecrate them today and tomorrow.' God tells us, today, to consecrate ourselves, make ourselves holy, not by washing our clothes, but by living a life filled with love.

Suggested hymns

Be still, for the presence of the Lord; Blest are the pure in heart; I, the Lord of sea and sky; O for a closer walk with God.

Seventeenth Sunday after Trinity (Proper 21)
30 September
Principal Service   **Harming Children**
(*Continuous*): Esther 7.1–6, 9–10; 9.20–22 Esther's victory; Ps. 124 Salvation; *or* (*Related*): Num. 11.4–6, 10–16, 24–29 The Spirit given to leaders; Ps. 19.7–14 Law, guidance, forgiveness; James 5.13–20 Prayer, healing, repentance and conversion; Mark 9.38–50 Causes of offence

> '[Jesus said,] "If any of you put a stumbling block before one of these little ones who believe in me, it would be better for you if a great millstone were hung around your neck and you were thrown into the sea."' Mark 9.42

Mothers' Union

A few years ago the Mothers' Union ran a campaign against the commercialization of childhood. This focused on the pressure put on children by advertising campaigns aimed at them. They were worried that the pressure of consumerism can make children depressed. If an advertiser says that a particular product is 'cool', children may feel that unless they buy it, their classmates won't consider them 'cool', and will reject them. In school playgrounds, children's friendships can be made or broken by what they own. If children don't have the food in their lunchbox which has been featured in the latest advertising campaign, or aren't wearing a designer tee-shirt, they can be excluded, made fun of, or bullied, and so quickly become depressed.

Advertising

Advertisers try to persuade us that children are growing older younger. Children who want to be thought of as grown-up are pressured into begging their parents for miniaturized adult clothing; in the case of little girls, this can lead to an obscene desire to be thought 'sexy', with the consequent loss of childhood innocence. But if an item of clothing is advertised as a 'must have', how's a child supposed to feel if their parents won't buy it for them? Children are losing the use of their imagination in inventing their own games, and instead they're persuaded to buy ready-made kits or computer games. Thus the advertisers teach them that possessions are essential for happiness, and lifestyle is confused with quality of life.

Millstones

Jesus warned us, 'If any of you put a stumbling block before one of these little ones who believe in me, it would be better for you if a great millstone were hung around your neck and you were thrown into the sea.' I'd guess he was absolutely furious with adults who harm children in any way. The millstone he was talking about was the great lower millstone, which was too heavy to turn, but sat on the earth while the grain was ground into flour by turning the upper millstone above it. Can you imagine how terrible it would be to drown, while unable to reach the air because of this heavy weight tied to a rope round your neck? Jesus says, what will happen to you if you harm children in any way will be much, much worse than that.

Punishment

This may not mean that those guilty of hurting children must be punished by the state particularly harshly – far less that they must me set upon by a lynch mob. All that's necessary is for the guilty person to realize the horror of what they have done in destroying a child's future happiness, and the thought of that will be worse than death by drowning. Of course they need to be punished, and prevented from doing it again, so that others who are tempted to do the same realize what remorse would follow.

Abuse

But when we talk about harming children, we jump to the conclusion that sexual abuse is the only thing that matters. Yet harsh punishment of children for minor misdemeanours is abuse. So is child-directed advertising which robs them of their childhood. So is making children feel unloved and unloveable. All these can make a child depressed, and rob them of the chance of growing into a happy adult. Once you realize this, the remorse you feel is much worse than drowning with a millstone tied to you.

Heaven

So Jesus warns us in the strongest terms of the wrongness of any form of hurt done to children. Does he mean that this results in eternal punishment for the offender? It's hard to know. He certainly promises forgiveness to all those who repent, even on their death-bed. Yet it's difficult for us to imagine the hardened paedophile being let off absolutely. Perhaps if they don't repent, God in his mercy allows them eternal death; we must leave that to him. But even for the lesser sin of being a bad parent, a stern wake-up call is in order. Any harm we do to a child or vulnerable person, even if it's only verbal, is horrific in God's eyes. We need to repent, apologize, and resolve never to do anything of the sort ever again.

All-age worship

Advise children how to resist advertising and other forms of bullying. Make posters advertising ChildLine 0800 1111.

Suggested hymns

Father of heaven, whose love profound; For the beauty of the earth; I heard the voice of Jesus say; Loving Shepherd of thy sheep.

Seventeenth Sunday after Trinity (Proper 21)
30 September
Second Service **Treating People, Not Diseases**
Ps. 120 Lying lips, 121 I lift my eyes; Ex. 24 Blood of the
Covenant; Matt. 9.1–8 Forgiveness and healing

> *'"So that you may know that the Son of Man has authority on earth to forgive sins" – [Jesus] then said to the paralytic – "Stand up, take your bed and go to your home."' Matthew 9.6*

How doctors work

When you go to the doctor, first he or she will listen to your complaints and symptoms and then make an examination, to seek objective evidence to interpret them. Next, the symptoms are compared to those of common illnesses, to check which is most likely to explain what's wrong with you. Finally, the doctor will give you an opinion, and probably prescribe a course of treatment that has been effective in curing that type of sickness. Usually, this gives some relief straight away. When you return for a check-up, if the treatment is not working, the doctor will change it and try another. If that doesn't work, the doctor will reconsider the diagnosis, to see if there's an alternative explanation. This process is usually effective in healing what they call organic illnesses, which have an obvious physical basis.

Functional illnesses

But many illnesses have no clearly discernable physical cause, and respond less well to treatment. These are often described as functional illnesses; bodily functions are disturbed, but these disturbances are not easily explained in conventional medical terms. Patients often blame the doctor for not being able to cure them, and resent any suggestion that their illness may not have a physical cause. But this doesn't mean that the patient is imagining their symptoms. Inventing illness is almost unknown outside deliberate manipulation to get time off work. There are millions of people suffering from a wide variety of symptoms which are rarely properly explained in medical scientific terms – these include such symptoms as back pain, diarrhoea and tummy cramps, ringing in the ears, headaches and inability to sleep. Sometimes they are just too sick and tired to cope. These are the illnesses that doctors can't cure.

Feelings

That's no excuse for not going to the medical professionals and following the treatment prescribed. But in addition, the sick person should examine themselves, to see if the cause is either partially or entirely of their own making. A psychotherapist may uncover feelings of anger, guilt, inadequacy and low self-esteem which put us under great stress. Refusing to admit to these feelings may prolong the stress and the illness, whereas acknowledging to ourselves that we have these emotions helps us deal with them. That's where religion comes in. Jesus tells us that all sins can be forgiven if confessed to God; those who hate each other can be reconciled; and everyone is of value to God. Sick people can be helped to face up to their feelings, and then feel forgiven and loved. This relieves the stress and begins the healing process. Knowing they are being prayed for gives them back their self-esteem. Again, accept all the doctors can do for you, but add to this the healing power of faith – mind and body affect each other. We're treating people, not diseases.

A paralysed man

In the light of all this, let's look again at the story of the paralysed man in the Gospels. His friends had enough faith to put him on a stretcher and carry him to Jesus. Seeing this, Jesus said to the paralysed man, 'Take heart, son; your sins are forgiven.' The religious experts objected that only God has the power to forgive sins; who was Jesus claiming to be? So Jesus asked them, 'Which of these two things is easier: to forgive the paralysed man his sins, or to heal him?' They couldn't answer: human beings can heal some diseases, so obviously some human beings, who talk with God, can tell people they are forgiven. Jesus was a human being, but especially close to God our Father. He told the objectors, 'The "Son of Man" has authority on earth to forgive sins.' Then he said to the paralysed man, 'Stand up, pick up the stretcher and go home.' Then the man, who had been unable to walk, stood up, and went home. The astonished crowd praised God, who gives such authority to human beings. The paralysis had been a way for the man to escape from the world and deny his feelings of guilt; once he faced up to them and accepted God's love and forgiveness, he could deal with both his guilt and the demands of the world.

Conclusion

In conclusion, go to your doctor, and follow the treatment prescribed. Then acknowledge your feelings, pray, confess, and believe that God loves you. If God's still got work for you to do on earth, he'll probably gradually remove your symptoms. If not, he'll give you the patience to endure them, until he gives you the joys of heaven. God bless you.

Suggested hymns

At even ere the sun was set; God forgave my sin in Jesus' name; Thine arm, O Lord, in days of old; When I needed a neighbour.

Eighteenth Sunday after Trinity (Proper 22)
7 October
(Alternatively the Dedication Festival)
Principal Service **The Book of Job**
(*Continuous*): Job 1.1; 2.1–10 Job tested by suffering; Ps. 26 Righteousness; *or* (*Related*): Gen. 2.18–24 Creation of Eve; Ps. 8 Stewardship of nature; Heb. 1.1–4; 2.5–12 Creation of humankind; Mark 10.2–16 Family and children

> *'The Lord said to Satan, "Have you considered my servant Job? There is no one like him on the earth, a blameless and upright man who fears God and turns away from evil."' Job 1.8*

The little-known book

Most people know very little about the book of Job. It's one of the finest verse-dramas in the ancient world, grappling with the problem of innocent suffering. We've the choice of reading from Job this Sunday and the next three Sundays. Better still, go home and read it right through: less than an hour. You'll find it just before the Psalms. Use a modern translation for comprehensibility; though the King James Version is a high point of English literature, full of famous quotations, like 'I know that my Redeemer liveth'.

Summary

The story of Job was already an old one when Ezekiel mentioned him alongside Noah and Daniel. Chapters 1–2 and 42 are a prose introduction and conclusion; originally, that's all there was. Job, an Edomite, is prosperous and religious; one of the heavenly beings, called the Satan – which means, the accuser – tells God that Job's only religious because he's rich; so God gives him permission to take away Job's health and wealth. As one disaster follows another, Job is left sitting among the ashes scraping his sores; but he refuses to 'curse God and die'. 'The LORD gave, and the LORD has taken away; blessed be the name of the LORD.' At the end he's rewarded for his patience, or endurance, with more sons and daughters, houses and wealth.

Poem

Sandwiched between the prose are 39 chapters of the most glorious poetry. Four 'friends' come to reason with him, telling him that the innocent never suffer, so, because he's suffering, he must be guilty. We refer to them as 'Job's comforters' because they were no comfort at all. In the poetic parts Job is not patient: Job's quite clear that he's innocent, and complains that God is unjust. Job longs for someone who will defend him against God: a 'Redeemer' is the next-of-kin who comes to rescue you. That's why this is a book everyone should read, because who is there among us who hasn't cried out at some time, 'If God's a god of love, why does God allow it?' When you read of people killed or orphaned in road accidents, or if a child you love is sick; if you have a spark of humanity in you, you demand to know 'Why does God let wicked people go unpunished, yet allows such terrible things to happen to people who are quite innocent?'

Comforters

Job's four friends sound eminently reasonable and persuasive. 'God has laid down certain rules,' they say. 'If you keep the rules, obey the laws, like we do, you'll be all right. If you break the rules and God punishes you, you've only yourself to blame.' All that poor old Job can answer is, 'It ain't necessarily so.' He wishes that God would appear and defend himself, answering Job's questions.

God speaks

Then God does appear; but he doesn't answer any questions. Instead, God gives Job a quick tour of creation, and asks him if he could have done as well. God's not a nice sugar daddy giving you everything you ask him for. God has plans that are far greater than you can understand. Look at the hippopotamus and the crocodile, the horse and the ostrich, would a sugar daddy have created those? You see, the intellectual answer to the problem of innocent suffering is very simple: God wanted someone to love, who could love God in return. Love can't be forced, so it would have been no use making obedient machines – machines can't love – so God had to make humans, free to love him or not, to obey him or not, just as they chose. If we're free to disobey, we're free to smoke, eat or drink ourselves to death, fight, kill and drive too fast. If we suffer because of that, we've only ourselves to blame.

Head and heart

That's the intellectual answer to Job's questions, but it doesn't satisfy us, because we're heart as well as brain. What Job needed was a vision of the greatness of God, who is in control and will make everything all right in the end. Then he was prepared to live with questions he couldn't answer. But the real answer lies in the cross of Jesus: a God who comes down to earth and shares our suffering. Only a crucified God can satisfy a crucified people.

All-age worship

Together, draw a strip-cartoon telling the story of Job.

God moves in a mysterious way; I know that my Redeemer lives; In heavenly love abiding; O for a heart to praise my God.

Eighteenth Sunday after Trinity (Proper 22)
7 October
Second Service   **Crossing the Jordan**
Ps. 125 Firm as Mount Zion, 126 Like those who dream; Joshua 3.7–17 Crossing the Jordan; Matt. 10.1–22 Mission of the Twelve

> *'While all Israel were crossing over on dry ground, the priests who bore the ark of the covenant of the Lord stood on dry ground in the middle of the Jordan, until the entire nation finished crossing over the Jordan.' Joshua 3.17*

Joshua

The book of Joshua tells how the Israelites, having crossed the Red Sea on dry land, which was to the west of the Promised Land, went all round their future nation, and approached it from the east, over the River Jordan. Miraculously, the river stopped flowing, and they were able to pass this water-barrier, too, dry-shod. The parallels between Joshua and Moses were obvious. If this really happened, it may have had a natural explanation – up river the banks of the river were steep, and a landslide may have blocked the flow of water for a few hours until it broke through again. Whether or not that's true, deep in the Israelite consciousness was the certainty that they had taken control of the land that God had promised them through God's mercy, not by their own efforts.

Heaven

Much later, Christians thought of the Promised Land as a symbol of heaven. But this reinterpretation didn't happen all at once. In Jesus's time most Jews thought of a bodily resurrection, with the righteous dead standing on earth once again. Jesus spoke about the kingdom of God, but most people thought he meant an earthly kingdom. Heaven was where God lived with the angels; when people died, so they believed, they would go down to the underworld to wait for the Messiah to call them back to earth. Then Jesus was raised from the dead and ascended into heaven, and that changed the way everybody thought about death. Now heaven became the Promised Land, the supernatural kingdom to which we can all be admitted. Significantly, the way into the kingdom of heaven was also through water – the water of baptism. John the Baptist had baptized Jesus in the River Jordan. So a parallel was drawn between the font and the River Jordan, and before that to the divided waters of the Red Sea.

Slaves

The next stage on this journey of reinterpretation came with the black slaves in America. Mostly, they were treated with appalling violence, and only longed to get away from their bondage. More-over, they had no patch of soil to call their own, and they longed for their own land. Ultimately, they dreamt that they might one day return to Africa, the other side of the Atlantic Ocean. In fact, this was impractical, but they didn't know that. Then a few freed slaves, with the help of some Quakers, set up what was known as 'the Underground Railroad'. Slaves who escaped from their owners were secretly passed from house to house until they reached Canada, or one of the states where slavery was forbidden. So the spirituals sung by the slaves, about crossing the waters of the Jordan into heaven, took on a second, secret meaning. Innocent as they sounded to the whites who heard them, they were also a symbol to the slaves of their escape across the water to an imagined land of freedom. What a wealth of deeply felt melodies that reminds us of:

> One more river, and that's the river of Jordan, One more river, there's one more river to cross.
> Swing low, sweet chariot . . . I looked over Jordan, and what did I see? A band of angels, coming after me.
> Deep river, my home is over Jordan; Deep river, I want to cross over into camp-ground.
> Michael, row the boat ashore, alleluia . . . River Jordan is deep and cold, alleluia – Chills the body but not the soul, alleluia!
> . . . and many more in the same vein.

Bread of heaven

So this imagery passed into well-loved hymns all round the world:

There is a land of pure delight . . . Could we stand where Moses stood, and view the landscape o'er, Not Jordan's stream nor death's cold flood. should fright us from the shore.

And 'Guide me, O thou great Redeemer,' with the last verse: 'When I tread the verge of Jordan, bid my anxious fears subside; death of death and hell's destruction, land me safe on Canaan's side.'

By grace alone

Yet amid all this watery imagery, the underlying message is the same as Joshua discovered. We can't reach the Promised Land, whether of Canaan or of heaven, through our own efforts. It takes the miracle of God's grace and mercy before we can overcome the obstacle of our own sin. But then, because he loves us, Jesus is standing on the further shore to welcome us into our eternal dwelling place.

Suggested hymns

Guide me, O thou great Redeemer; Let saints on earth in concert sing; Shall we gather at the river?; There is a land of pure delight.

Nineteenth Sunday after Trinity (Proper 23)
14 October
Principal Service   **Tempted As We Are**
(*Continuous*): Job 23.1–9, 16–17 God's greatness and justice; Ps. 22.1–15 Faith and assurance; *or* (*Related*): Amos 5.6–7, 10–15 Justice for the needy; Ps. 90.12–17 Salvation; Heb. 4.12–16 Tempted as we are; Mark 10.17–31 Possessions

'We do not have a high priest who is unable to sympathize with our weaknesses, but we have one who in every respect has been tempted as we are, yet without sin.' Hebrews 4.15 (margin)

Jesus

'Oh, it was easy for Jesus,' you hear people say. Maybe you've said it yourself, and it's quite understandable. We think that Jesus was different from us. After all, he was God's Son, he doesn't understand what I have to put up with, the frustrations, the thwarted desires. We think that, but we're quite wrong. Jesus, the Son of Man, was completely human. He suffered pain; he was hungry and thirsty just as we are. The Letter to the Hebrews, in the Bible, compares him to the High Priests sacrificing in the Jerusalem Temple. But, it adds, 'We do not have a high priest who is unable to sympathize with our weaknesses, but we have one who in every respect has been tempted as we are, yet without sin.'

Like us

Listen to that carefully. Jesus was exactly like us; he had the same needs and desires as we have; and he found it just as hard as we do to resist. The temptation to sin was just as strong for Jesus as it is for us. The only difference was that he always won the struggle, and resisted the temptation. Whereas although we, most times, say no to temptation; yet more times than we care to remember, we give in. But Jesus *never* gave in – he never sinned.

Sin

What do we mean by sin? Most people think sin means sex. So did Jesus have sexual desires? He was human, so he must have. Many people find that shocking. But there's nothing wrong in having desires; it's what we do with our desires that matters. Jesus must have channelled his natural feelings into deep, deep love for everybody he met. Yet sex isn't the only form of sin. What sin means is 'disobedience to God', and its essence is selfishness. Whenever you do anything selfish, without considering its effect on others, that's sin. Selfishness ignores what God wants us to do, and that's disobedience.

Temptation

A schoolboy was asked what 'temptation' means. He answered, 'Temptation's when I do something wrong, but it wasn't my fault, because the devil made me do it.' Ah, if only! Temptation is want-

250

ing to do something when you know it's wrong. And Jesus actually *wanted* to do wrong things. There were three moments in his life when that became particularly clear.

Desert

First, after his baptism, he withdrew to the desert, and pondered as to what he was going to do with his life. He wanted to draw people to follow him, and he could have done it in four different ways: he could feed them, force them, or fascinate them. Or he could die for them.

> He could turn stones into bread. In other words, he could become popular by feeding the poor and solving their economic difficulties.
> Or he could lead an army and force out the Roman soldiers. But you can't use the devil's methods to do God's work.
> Or he could do miracles like throwing himself from the pinnacle of the Temple, and landing unhurt on the ground. Provided he didn't challenge their way of life, people would have followed him if he'd been a healer; but that sort of fascination doesn't last long before people come bored.

So Jesus resisted those three temptations, taking instead the only way that endures – to win people's love, by dying for them to prove that you love them. He chose the way of the cross.

Gethsemane

Yet it wasn't easy. In the Garden of Gethsemane he sweated blood as he asked his Father to find another way. But he resisted the desire to disobey, and at the cost of his own life, he prayed, 'not what I want, but what you want'.

Forsaken

Even on the cross, however, Jesus was tempted to lose his faith. 'My God, my God, why have you abandoned me?' That's when we find it hardest, when our faith's worn thin, and we're tempted to give up on religion. But even then, we can conquer temptation, through the grace of God, by remembering that our Saviour triumphed in a battle just as hard as ours. 'In every respect [he was] tempted as we

251

are, yet without sin.' We're all tempted, but if we pray, Jesus will help us to resist.

All-age worship

List the naughty things you sometimes want to do. Make up a prayer asking Jesus to help you say no.

Suggested hymns

God of mercy, God of grace; Jesus, lover of my soul; Lead, kindly light; O Jesus, I have promised.

Nineteenth Sunday after Trinity (Proper 23)
14 October
Second Service   **Divine Compassion**
Ps. 127 Unless the Lord builds [128 Family life]; Joshua 5.13—6.20 Walls of Jericho; Matt. 11.20–30 Come to me

> *'[Jesus said,] "Come to me, all you that are weary and are carrying heavy burdens, and I will give you rest. Take my yoke upon you, and learn from me; for I am gentle and humble in heart, and you will find rest for your souls."' Matthew 11.28–29*

Friars

After Henry VIII abolished the monasteries, there were no monks or nuns in the Church of England for several centuries. The nineteenth century, however, showed new interest in the history of the early Church, and several monastic communities were set up. The first to be modelled on the friars of St Francis was founded in Plaistow, then one of the most deprived slums in East London. When they drew up their Rule of Life in 1899, they called themselves the Society of the Divine Compassion. 'The Society', they wrote, 'seeks to revive the spirit of St Francis of Assisi by living a poor life, sharing the privations and discomforts of ordinary poor people.' Most of them had been brought up in quite comfortable circumstances, so this was heroic self-sacrifice. When the periodic outbreaks of cholera came, they nursed their parishioners through the worst of it. Thus they identified not only with St Francis, but with Jesus himself, who, in his divine compassion, shared with the poor and outcast.

Jesus

Jesus revealed his compassion when he said, 'Come to me, all you that are weary and are carrying heavy burdens, and I will give you rest. Take my yoke upon you, and learn from me; for I am gentle and humble in heart, and you will find rest for your souls.' He understands that many people are exhausted by the sheer struggle to stay alive. 'Don't give up,' he says. 'Let me share it with you.' The carpenter of Nazareth knew all about making wooden yokes, fitted exactly to the shoulders of two animals, so that they could share the effort of pulling along a heavy plough. 'Let me share your burden,' he says to all of us, 'and then you can help me carry my burden, of love for all your neighbours.' Caring for the needy is only a light task when you share it with Jesus, for he has a gentle and humble heart, full of divine compassion.

The Sacred Heart

We know now that the heart is simply an organ for pumping blood. Formerly it was considered to be the seat of the emotions, and we still use the word poetically and metaphorically when we speak romantically about a heart full of love. So it's not surprising that in the Middle Ages, devotion to the Sacred Heart of Jesus should grow up in the Roman Catholic Church. It probably started in the writings of a Franciscan called St Bonaventure in the thirteenth century. The Jesuits and St Francis de Sales promoted it, and in the eighteenth century it received the official approval of the Pope. You may not like the devotional statues of Jesus with a big red heart in the middle of his chest, but forget the aesthetics, and remember that this is a symbol of the divine compassion at the heart of his love.

Wounds of Christ

Similarly puzzling is the devotion to the Sacred Wounds of Christ, with its concentration on the physical body, when many people would rather emphasize the spiritual nature of Christ's sacrifice. Yet it does us no harm to be reminded that Jesus couldn't retreat into the spiritual and ignore the physical pain of life, if he was to redeem us as whole people, body and soul together.

Horatius Bonar

From the opposite end of the spectrum of denominations comes a very similar devotion to the loving heart of Jesus. Horatius Bonar was a minister in the Free Presbyterian Church of Scotland. In 1846 he published a hymn based on the same text from St Matthew's Gospel. 'I heard the voice of Jesus say,' begins the first verse, 'come unto me and rest. Lay down, thou weary one, lay down thy head upon my breast.' The second and third verses are based on words of Jesus in St John's Gospel, 'I will give you living water', and 'I am the light of the world'. These words are sung, either to a folk tune adapted by Ralph Vaughan Williams called 'Kingsfold', or a tune by John Bacchus Dykes, representing the apex of High Victorian Romanticism. In both tunes, the major key symbolizes the joy of those who take up Christ's offer. Have you found the rest that Jesus offers yet? Do you know his joy in your heart? If not, tell him today that you are willing to share his yoke if he will share yours.

Suggested hymns

Glorious things of thee are spoken; I heard the voice of Jesus say; Lord, the light of your love is shining; O love that will not let me go.

Twentieth Sunday after Trinity (Proper 24)
21 October
Principal Service   **Service to Others**
(*Continuous*): Job 38.1–7, [34–41] Creation; Ps. 104.1–10, 26, 35c Creation; *or* (*Related*): Isa. 53.4–12 The suffering servant; Ps. 91.9–16 Providence, salvation; Heb. 5.1–10 Christ a priest for ever; Mark 10.35–45 Humility and service

> 'The Son of Man came not to be served but to serve, and to give his life a ransom for many.' Mark 10.45

How do you know?

A boy of 11 was discussing with his vicar what he believed, to help him understand the promises he was going to make in his confirmation. This is quite an old story, so I'll use masculine pronouns, though today it could equally well have been a girl and a female vicar. The first question the vicar asked the boy was,

'Do you think God loves you?'

'Oh, yes,' replied the boy.

'Why?' asked the priest, in that irritating way that some grown-ups have. The boy thought about it for a while, then said, 'Because I have a happy home.'

'But some youngsters don't have a happy home,' continued the clergyman. 'Do you think God doesn't love *them?*'

That needed puzzling about; after a pause, the boy suggested, 'Well, because my mother loves me.'

'But some unfortunate kids have a mother who's unkind to them,' continued the vicar. 'How can *they* know that God loves them?'

The boy realized that, although home, friends and nature gave him much happiness, there's also a lot of sadness and suffering in the world, from poverty, hatred, war and so on. A God who loves his children has to leave them free will to choose whether or not to obey him, knowing that they'll often use it to hurt each other. So you can't *prove* God's love by looking at the world around you.

'Let's think about your mother again,' continued the priest. 'How do you *know* that she loves you?'

'Because of the things she does for me,' the lad replied at once.

There was a crucifix hanging nearby, and the boy knew the story of how Jesus died to redeem us. The clergyman turned to look at it, and the boy's eyes followed his. There was a long silence, then the clergyman asked again, 'How do you know God loves you?'

Quietly, the boy answered him, 'Because of what he's done for me.'

Proving love by deeds

The only way to prove love is by loving actions. God knew that we should never work out for ourselves that our Creator made us out of love, so he came to earth and died on a cross to save us from our sins. But Jesus told us to love God and love our neighbours, not just in words but by practical action. Our neighbours often challenge us by saying, 'You don't have to go to church to be a Christian.' Of

255

course, they are right. But once you realize that God showed by his self-sacrifice that he loves us, how can you respond to it except by sacrificing an hour of your time in going to church to tell him you love him. We say that we love our families, but they would have every reason to doubt that we mean what we say if we never show it by being kind to them. And the only way to show your neighbours that your love for them is more than empty words, is by sacrificially serving their needs.

Service

So the Christian Church proclaims the message of God's love for us, shown in the cross of Jesus. It also provides opportunities of worship like this one, so that we can show God in the simplest way possible that we love him. And it has programmes of practical service to our neighbours – the needy in this country and around the world – so that we can show our love for them in deeds as well as words. We serve them, because they, too, are God's children, and in gratitude for God's love shown for us, we must love those whom he loves. Jesus said, 'I give you a new commandment, that you love one another, just as I have loved you.'

Sharing God's love

We serve our neighbours not only because God loves them, but because we want to share God's love with them. They may not realize that God loves them, until they see God's love reflected in the way we Christians serve our neighbours. Without service, evangelism is useless, because they won't start to believe what we say about a God of love until we prove it to them in our lives. Jesus said, 'The Son of Man came not to be served but to serve, and to give his life a ransom for many.'

All-age worship

Make four lists: 'Things my mother does for me'; 'Things I can do for Mother'; 'Things God has done for me'; 'Things I can do for God'.

Suggested hymns

Brother, sister, let me serve you; Come down, O Love divine; From heaven you came; God forgave my sin.

Twentieth Sunday after Trinity (Proper 24)
21 October
Second Service   **Sunday Observance**
Ps. 141 Prayer like incense; Joshua 14.6–14 Caleb; Matt. 12.1–21 God's servant

> *'[Jesus said,] "It is lawful to do good on the sabbath."' Matthew 12.12*

Chariots of Fire

The film *Chariots of Fire* concerns the great Scottish runner, Eric Liddell, known as 'The Flying Scotsman', and his rivalry with the Jewish athlete Harold Abrahams. Both were victims of prejudice in different ways, and both triumphed in the end. When Liddell went to compete in the 1924 Olympic Games, the 100-meter race was fixed for a Sunday. But Liddell, a devout Christian, refused to break the law of the Sabbath as he understood it, and wouldn't take part. He gave up his chance of winning a medal, but his religion was more important to him than his sporting achievements. The gold medal was won by Abrahams, whose Sabbath, of course, was on the Saturday. To everyone's surprise, however, on a later day Eric Liddell went on to win bronze in the 200 meters, then gold in the 400 meters, at which he was comparatively inexperienced, in the, then, record time of 47.6 seconds. The next year, he completed a degree in science and a degree in divinity, and, sacrificing his chances of a brilliant career in the UK, he went to China to work as a missionary.

Sabbath

But was the law of the Sabbath worth sacrificing a gold medal for? Liddell would have said yes. The Ten Commandments tell us that the seventh day of the week is holy to God; on it we must do no work. Jesus rose from the dead on a Sunday, so Christians transferred the Sabbath observance onto the first day of the week, called the Lord's Day. The Old Testament ruling that anyone who works on the Sabbath day should be put to death hasn't been applied for centuries. Yet in those countries where people still don't work on Sundays, there's an air of relaxation and calm on that day which is quite unknown among the rush and bustle of the seven-days-a-week nations. Workers who have no regular day off produce less in seven days than others do in six, and are less healthy.

Jesus

But Jesus came into conflict with the Pharisees over the Sabbath. Five times he healed people on the Sabbath, which was considered to be work. The Pharisees were willing to bend the rules to save an animal, said Jesus; but objected when he saved a human life. Once, Jesus gleaned ears of corn on the Sabbath. He quoted King David, who ate sacrificial bread in a temple, showing that human need overrides the letter of the law. 'The Sabbath was made for human beings,' he said, 'not human beings for the Sabbath.' Yet Jesus didn't abolish the Sabbath law for Jews, he only called for a common-sense approach.

Gentiles

A different situation arose when non-Jews became Christians. In the Roman Empire everybody worked on Sundays: employees would be fired and slaves whipped if they refused. So the Church decided that the whole Jewish law doesn't apply to Gentiles, only the laws against pagan sacrifices, murder and adultery. Yet the Sabbath law wasn't really about working hours, but about setting time aside to worship God. Without worship, life can turn 100 per cent materialistic. As a sign outside a church put it, 'Seven prayerless days make one weak'.

Sabbath observance

So where do we strike the balance? Jesus wouldn't want us to be like strict Sabbatarians who object to all forms of pleasure. Provided we devote at least an hour a week to worshipping the Almighty, our day of rest can be spent in recreation, or re-creation of our mind and body. 'The family that prays together stays together', so we should make time when the whole family can worship together at least once a week. But worship's a voluntary choice, and we can't insist that others should worship unless they want to. Yet by devoting Sundays to shopping and professional sport, we risk making worship impossible for some faithful Christians, whom we compel to work for us in catering, travel, retail and entertainment.

Sacrifice

So all praise to those like Eric Liddell, who are prepared to sacrifice their careers and their wealth for their principles. An old book quotes the singers Jenny Lind and Harry Lauder, both famous in their day, as examples of people who were willing to do just that. We should give everyone freedom to spend an hour with God if they want to. Would you be willing to risk opposition and mockery from your employer or your family by your insistence on coming to church on Sundays? And how do you feel about the number of people who are made to go in to work and prevented from worshipping on Sundays by your insistence on shopping and watching professionals performing on the Lord's Day?

Suggested hymns

Dear Lord and Saviour of mankind; I danced in the morning; Prayer is the soul's sincere desire; This is the day, this is the day which the Lord has made.

Last Sunday after Trinity (Proper 25)
SS Simon and Jude   28 October
(Alternatively Bible Sunday or the Dedication Festival)
Principal Service   Bartimaeus
(*Continuous*): Job 42.1–6, 10–17 Repentance and forgiveness; Ps. 34.1–8 [19–22] Salvation; *or* (*Related*): Jer. 31.7–9 Salvation; Ps. 126 Forgiveness, Salvation, and joy; Heb. 7.23–28 Christ our high priest; Mark 10.46–52 Healing of a blind man

> 'Jesus said to [Bartimaeus], "What do you want me to do for you?" The blind man said to him, "My teacher, let me see again."' Mark 10.51

Bartimaeus

At the roadside sat a blind beggar. Nobody knew his first name; he was just known by his surname, Bartimaeus, which means Timson. Some people beg because they like it, it's an easier way of getting a living than working for it. Timson had no choice: he begged because he couldn't work. But he dreamt of meeting a man who would cure his blindness. One day he was swamped by a crowd. People all round him were shoving and chattering; and he was confused. 'What's the fuss about?' he asked. Someone answered, 'Everyone wants to see this man Jesus.' 'Who's he? Who's Jesus?' asked Timson. 'A famous healer,' they told him. Timson knew at once his moment had come – this was the man he was looking for. 'Take me to him! Lead me to Jesus!' he yelled, grabbing the nearest person in the crowd by the arm. 'Where is he?' he shouted. He was becoming a real pest. 'Shut up,' they told him, but he wouldn't. Maybe Jesus was the long-awaited Messiah! 'Son of David,' cried the blind man, 'for pity's sake help me.' His voice was almost lost in the din of the crowd, but Jesus heard it, and to everyone's astonishment, he stopped still. Everyone fell silent. 'Tell that man to come here,' said Jesus. Timson leapt to his feet, throwing off his beggar's cloak so that he could move faster, feeling his way towards the first sympathetic voice he had heard for years. Being blind he knew he might not be able to find the cloak again, but somehow he'd a feeling he was never going to need it.

Persistence

The first thing we notice about blind Bartimaeus was his persistence. Some people have a vague curiosity about Jesus – but it only lasts for a moment, then they turn to what they think are more interesting enquiries. Bartimaeus wouldn't let anyone or anything get in his way. To find Jesus was now the most important thing in his life. He realized this was the one man who could help him, and he went for him like a bull at a gate, though he'd only his ears to lead him. Is getting to know Jesus your obsession, or is religion just a sort of hobby for you? It's those with desperate desires who get things done.

Immediate

Secondly, his response was immediate. No procrastination. 'Lead me to him,' he yelled. 'Now!' Many people read about Jesus, but decide to investigate further when they've time. They put off the search for meaning and purpose in their life until tomorrow. And tomorrow never comes. Some people are stuck in a rut, with bad habits they know they ought to break, but they're just too lazy to change. I don't know whether blind Mr Timson had heard the Latin proverb *carpe diem*, 'seize the day'; but that's what he did. Are you good at grasping your opportunities, or do you 'let [your] golden chances pass you by'?

Direct

Thirdly, Bartimaeus was direct – he went straight to the point. He knew what he needed most, and asked for it – his sight. When you go to the doctor or the dentist, it's no use saying you feel generally unwell; you've got to describe specific symptoms. You must examine yourself. Nobody likes doing that, knowing some things will have to change in their lifestyle. Yet it's the only way to be healed. When you turn to Jesus, you are wasting time if you say, 'I'd like to be a better person.' God can only help you if you say, 'I've looked carefully at my life; please help me change this and this and this.' Then you must be willing to work at it.

Insight

Blind people often have more insight than those with 20/20 vision. Bartimaeus saw in his mind's eye what he wanted, and his persistence, immediacy and directness got it for him. 'What do you want?' asked Jesus. 'To see again, boss,' he replied. 'Off you go,' said Jesus, laughing – 'your trust in me has made you well.' 'At once', the Gospel says, Bartimaeus could see, and then 'he followed Jesus in the way'. No one could stop him, now. We can learn a lesson from people like that.

All-age worship

Play blind-man's bluff, only everyone is blindfolded except one, who represents Jesus, and stands still calling people towards him or her. The first one to touch him or her swaps places.

Suggested hymns

Amazing grace; Immortal Love, for ever full; Jesu, lover of my soul; Make way, make way, for Christ the King.

SS Simon and Jude, Apostles 28 October
The Apostolic Church
Isa. 28.14–16 A foundation stone; Ps. 119.89–96 I am yours, save me; Eph. 2.19–22 The foundation of the apostles; John 15.17–27 You have been with me

> *'You are no longer strangers and aliens, but you are citizens with the saints and also members of the household of God, built upon the foundation of the apostles and prophets, with Christ Jesus himself as the cornerstone.' Ephesians 2.19–20*

Missionaries

Today we commemorate Saints Simon and Jude, who were apostles. Jesus had many followers, all Jews, known as his disciples. Twelve disciples, Simon and Jude among them, were put in a position of leadership. St Paul may have been the first to call them apostles; the word means people who are sent, or missionaries, and Paul wanted to show that all Christians are missionaries, whether or not they are members of the Twelve. At the crucifixion most of them deserted, and Jesus was left alone, except for a few women who attended to his burial. Then the risen Christ appeared in the upper room to 'the eleven and their companions' – probably the Twelve less Judas, together with the faithful women. On the basis of their missionary preaching, 3,000 were baptized as Christians on the Day of Pentecost. Then St Paul took the revolutionary step of preaching to the non-Jews – he was an apostle to the Gentiles. The Christian Church grew like wildfire, but it was never more than a minority religion in the Roman Empire. What made it different from all the other religions, however, was that it was a *missionary* religion. The others were national cults, people from one tribe worshipping their tribal gods who, they believed, would support them in their battles against rival tribes. Most religions were a divisive influence in the Empire, setting tribe against tribe, nation against nation. Only Christianity claimed to be a religion for everybody, with no distinctions: 'There is no longer Jew or Greek, there is no longer slave or free, there is no longer male and female; for all of you are one in Christ Jesus,' wrote the apostle Paul; 'in that renewal there is no longer Greek and Jew, circumcised and uncircumcised, barbarian, Scythian, slave and free; but Christ is all and in all!' Built on the foundations laid by the Jewish apostles, missionary Christianity became a force for interracial unity.

Constantine

In AD 312 Constantine fought his rival at the Battle of the Milvian Bridge, to settle who should become the Emperor of the Roman territories spread across the then known world. It's said that before the battle Constantine saw a flaming cross in the sky: a letter X, crossed with a letter P, the first two letters of the Greek word for Christ. He heard the words, 'In this sign you will conquer.' When he won, the new Emperor became a supporter of Christianity – people still argue whether his conversion was genuine, and like many others at that time, he postponed his baptism until his death-bed. But, a year after the battle, the Emperor Constantine passed the Edict of Milan, bringing an end to persecution and giving civil rights and tolerance to Christians throughout the Empire. There may, however, have been an element of shrewd calculation in his choice. The different religions in his far-flung Empire were dividing citizens against each other on racial grounds. Only missionary Christianity could bring the whole world together under one God.

Nicaea

At least, that would have been so, if Christians had been of one mind. But people love to row about religion; it's second only to politics in providing excuses for a good argie-bargie. So, although all Christians believed in God, and Jesus, and the Holy Spirit, there were many disputes about how the Three were related to each other. Constantine was appalled: the new unifying religion he'd chosen turned out to be itself divided. So he basically summoned all the Christian bishops from across the Empire to the town of Nicaea, now called Iznik in Turkey, and locked them into a church until they could come up with a statement of the one, single Christian faith. The result is what we call the Nicene Creed. It made a reconciling statement about the doctrine of the Trinity; if you disagree with that you can't really call yourself a Christian. And the Creed went on to say: 'we believe in One, Holy, Catholic and Apostolic

Church'. Christians must live together as one family in love, open to all people – that's what 'catholic' means – and based on the faith taught by the early apostles – including Simon and Jude.

Apostolic

When we talk about the Apostolic Church, then, we mean that we're continuous with the Church founded by the apostles, built on their teachings, and like theirs, a missionary church, eager to spread the message of Jesus, supporting love and opposed to prejudice, open to every race and tribe under heaven.

Suggested hymns

Captains of the saintly band; Disposer supreme; God, whose city's sure foundation; In Christ there is no east or west.

All Saints' Sunday   4 November
Who is Good Enough?

(These readings are used on the Sunday, or if this is not kept as All Saints' Sunday, on 1 November itself; see page 352.) Wisd. 3.1–9 The righteous in God's hand *or* Isa. 25.6–9 A refuge for the needy; Ps. 24.1–6 Open the temple gates for the Lord; Rev. 21.1–6a The new Jerusalem; John 11.32–44 The resurrection of Lazarus

> *'Who shall ascend the hill of the Lord? And who shall stand in his holy place? Those who have clean hands and pure hearts.' Psalm 24.3–4 (NRSV)*

Churchgoing

St Paul wrote a letter 'To the church of God that is in Corinth, including all the saints in [that area]'. Then he gave them a right telling-off for some very un-saintly behaviour! In the language of the Bible, 'all saints' doesn't mean people who are perfect, but all Christians, everyone who goes to church. For some people, going to church is a duty, a grudging obligation. All praise to them if they keep on attending – particularly if you don't like the style of worship or the choice of music, but you keep coming because your family want to, or to support your local community. In that case, what the Bible calls 'the sacrifice of praise' may be a real sacrifice for you, but one that God accepts because it's a way of showing that he is important. We're in church to worship God, not just to enjoy ourselves. But if you *are* enjoying yourself it helps a lot! For many people, coming to church is the high point of the week. Many people like meeting their friends, or enjoy the beauty of the building and music, or like singing, or mental stimulation, or being told that God loves them, or even in some cases all of the above. If circumstances prevent them being in church one Sunday, the week seems to get off on the wrong foot, and they feel something important is missing from their lives. If you haven't reached that point yet, examine your attitude when you come to church, make up your mind to enjoy the service and the socializing and to ignore the minor irritations, and the pleasure of churchgoing will grow on you.

Pottering

It's not only during Sunday services that this pleasure is to be found. Many people go into church at other times, arranging the flowers, dusting the pews, practising the organ, or visiting old churches while they are on holiday, and find an atmosphere of indescribable peace. There's a real satisfaction to be found in pottering about in church. Logic tells us that if God exists, he must be everywhere. But it's easy to forget that. In church, the beauty and the calm, and the inspiring worship, remind you of the presence of God. It's above all in church that you can *feel* the presence of God close to you. When you step through the church door, say, silently or aloud, 'Hello, Jesus!'

God's presence

Then, when you have been in church, you can take God with you when you leave. Something jogs your memory later in the week, reminding you that, even if we forget God, he never forgets us and never leaves us. Gradually you become increasingly aware that every moment of every day you are living in the presence of God. This isn't anything solemn; God likes to watch you enjoying yourself in many different ways. Knowing that God is with you and loves you increases the enjoyment. Going to church once a week or more can transform your whole life.

Saints

Also, the saints are with us in church. When somebody dies we say they have gone to be with Jesus. Where's Jesus? In heaven, certainly, but he's everywhere. He's very specially present in God's house, the church. So when you feel the presence of Jesus in church, you are also especially close to those you love who've died. That's why churchgoing is such a comfort to the bereaved. The long list of famous Christians that you've read about are also with Jesus; so they, too, are close to us when we're in church. We call this 'the communion of saints'. Eastern Orthodox Christians fill their churches with icons because they are not only visual aids, but 'windows to eternity', reminding us of the great crowd of saints always present with us.

Family

For the Church is God's family. The communion of all the saints, in heaven and on earth, is our family life. Yet any family needs to meet regularly. I hope God never has cause to say to you, 'I love you, my child, and nothing will stop me loving you, because I'm your Father; but it's not much of a relationship, because you're hardly ever in my house with the rest of my family.'

All-age worship

Make a cardboard model of the screen in an Orthodox church, with pictures of famous Christians – www.kosovo.net/news/ archive/2005/November_10/1.html

Suggested hymns

O what their joy and their glory must be; Give us the wings of faith to rise; Let saints on earth in concert sing; Who are these like stars appearing?

266

Fourth Sunday before Advent 4 November

(For use if the Feast of All Saints is celebrated on 1 November, see page 264.)

Love God, Love Your Neighbour

Deut. 6.1–9 Love God, teach the law to your children; Ps. 119.1–8 Joy in the commandments; Heb. 9.11–14 Salvation through the sacrifice of Christ; Mark 12.28–34 Love God, love your neighbour

> '[Jesus said,] "You shall love the Lord your God with all your heart, and with all your soul, and with all your mind, and with all your strength.' The second is this, 'You shall love your neighbour as yourself.' There is no other commandment greater than these."'
> Mark 12.30–31

Laws

A London barrister was showing some visitors around his chambers. They commented on the number of law books on his bookshelves. 'Yes,' he replied, 'they contain every law a British parliament's ever passed. The first volume contains those passed in the twelfth, thirteenth and fourteenth centuries. The next three centuries are in seven volumes. There are over fifty volumes in all, with a new volume issued every year. Most of the laws that the present parliament has passed have never been tested in court!' The visitors soon realized that the more laws you have, the less effective they become.

Old Testament

The Bible contains hundreds of laws, beginning with the Ten Commandments. They were followed by many more telling the Israelites what to do when every imaginable misdemeanour was brought to trial. These were the written law; but there was also a long tradition of spoken law, explaining how to interpret these texts in more and more detailed circumstances. The scribes were those who made it their profession to record all these rules and regulations, discussing how to apply them to particular cases. It became more and more unwieldy, until some Jews gave up and decided to ignore God's law altogether, it was too complicated. They weren't bad people, just too busy, but the scribes lumped them together as 'the sinners'. Jesus said the 'sinners' would enter the kingdom of God ahead of the scribes and Pharisees, because they instinctively went to the heart of what the law was about, and were kinder and more loving people.

Simplifying

Some at least of the rabbis realized that a simplification of the law was necessary. Some believed there were lighter and weightier requirements of the law; the lighter ones could be broken occasionally, but the heavier ones never. The prophets pointed people away from ritual towards the moral heart of the law: Hosea speaks for God when he says, 'I desire steadfast love and not sacrifice, the knowledge of God rather than burnt offerings.' Rabbi Hillel was challenged to recite the whole law while standing on one leg. He replied, 'What you hate when it's done to you, don't do it to your neighbour. This is the whole law, the rest is commentary.'

Jesus

A scribe, who had obviously been puzzling about all this, came to Jesus and asked him, 'Which commandment is the first of all?' Jesus answered, 'The first is, "Hear, O Israel: the Lord our God, the Lord is one; you shall love the Lord your God with all your heart, and with all your soul, and with all your mind, and with all your strength." The second is this, "You shall love your neighbour as yourself." There is no other commandment greater than these.' The commandment to love God is quoted from Deuteronomy; it begins every synagogue service, and is contained in those little *mezuzah* cylinders which Jews nail to their doorposts. The commandment to love your neighbour is from Leviticus. Originally it only applied to people who live near your home, or perhaps to all your fellow Jews. But Jesus tells us to love everybody, of every race, without exception.

God and neighbour

Jesus was the first to put the commandments to love God and your neighbour together. A life full of love is more pleasing to God than a struggle to observe every detail of the written law. But the two commandments of Jesus have to go together. You can't claim to love God, and then ignore your neighbour, whom God loves at least as much as he loves you. You'll fail to love your neighbour if you do it in your own strength; you must love God first, then let him pour his love into your heart, so that it's really God who loves your neighbour, using you as his instrument. The scribe who challenged Jesus could see the connection between loving God and loving your neighbour, and Jesus said he was 'not far from the kingdom of God'. There are too many laws, of state and religion. Do you try to cut through the undergrowth to follow the two loves, of God and neighbour? Of course we fail over and again. But if the intention to love is there, Jesus smiles at us, saying, 'You, too, are close to God's kingdom.'

Suggested hymns

Brother, sister, let me serve you; Gracious Spirit, Holy Ghost; My God, I love thee – not because; When I needed a neighbour.

Third Sunday before Advent   11 November
Parishes
(For a service that is not a Service of Remembrance.)
Jonah 3.1–5, 10 God's forgiveness of Nineveh; Ps. 62.5–12 God's greatness and love; Heb. 9.24–28 Salvation through Christ; Mark 1.14–20 Fish for people

> *'Jesus said to them, "Follow me and I will make you fish for people."' Mark 1.17*

St Martin

Today is not only Armistice Day, it's also Martinmas, the feast day of St Martin of Tours. St Martin was a soldier and was born around AD 316, in a non-Christian family. He joined the Roman army, but was fascinated by the story of Jesus of Nazareth. But in those days, you couldn't be a soldier if you were a Christian. One cold day, as Martin was riding his horse, he saw a half-naked beggar shivering by the roadside. On a sudden impulse, he drew his sword and cut his warm military cloak in two, giving half to the beggar. The beggar revealed himself as Jesus Christ, calling Martin to resign from the army and be baptized.

Monks

Martin became a monk, living in a cave in the banks of the River Loire. Other monks settled nearby, his cell grew into a monastery, and Martin was appointed Bishop of Tours. Christianity spread along the Roman roads in those days, and the only Christians were in the larger towns. Monks were free to travel out from their monasteries, or minsters, to preach and minister to the people in the country villages. Many villagers were converted and baptized, but when the monks moved on, there was nobody to teach the new converts the faith. Martin had a brilliant idea, which changed the social history of Europe throughout the Middle Ages, and is still a powerful influence today.

Parishes

The Roman Empire had been divided into areas by the government, each administered by a governor. These areas were called dioceses, and when Christianity became the religion of the Empire, it was natural that bishops should be appointed to each diocese to administer the church there. Martin's idea was to divide the ecclesiastical dioceses into parishes. Everyone in the diocese lived in one parish or another; and parish priests were appointed to be responsible for each parish, care for the people and evangelize the pagans there. At first there were no church buildings, but soon the local landowners gave land and resources to build a parish church, often very beautiful but very cold and plain. Later, more land was given to the church as glebe, which was often farmed by the priest, who could now afford to live in the parish, and who received a tenth of the income of all the other farmers to maintain the church building, and care for the poor and sick.

Today

So St Martin's brainwave meant that the church was responsible for every person living in the parish, whatever their faith. Of course, if a group of Nonconformists wanted a church and a minister, they had to raise the costs among themselves, but Anglicans in the British Isles, like Roman Catholics and Lutherans in other parts of Europe, grew up thinking that someone else would always pay the bills for them. These days the tithes have been abolished; health and welfare workers are paid by the government, and landowners

270

don't feel responsible for the physical and spiritual needs of those who live on their lands. Many other forms of meeting place and entertainment are available, and fewer people see any need to go to church, or to support the parish where they live. The old sense of local community has been lost. Higher expectations in the upkeep and heating of buildings, support of the minister's family and provision of pensions, with costly administration in the diocese, all mean that the parish system, Martin's brainwave, is breaking down all over the country.

The future

Nonconformists, independent churches and Roman Catholics each have their own problems, but all are asking what the future holds for the Church. Everybody here loves *their* church, and would do anything in their power to keep it open, but nationally, many people say we may have to go back to the minster system. That means small numbers of paid clergy going out from a central base. Local churches would be cared for by ministers who earn their living in other ways, and each congregation would care for and evangelize the residents in their area. Some buildings may have to be handed to the local authority for social centres, and let out to different groups at different times. I don't know the answer to all this, but it's something we should all be thinking and praying about, especially at Martinmas.

All-age worship

Find out about the finances of your church, and draw up a rough budget. What could you do to increase church income?

Suggested hymns

An army of ordinary people; Soldiers of Christ arise; Through the night of doubt and sorrow; Will you come and follow me?

Remembrance Sunday   11 November
Patriots and Pacifists

(The readings of the day, or those for 'In Time of Trouble', may be used. These readings are for 'The Peace of the World'.)

Isa. 57.15–19 Peace for all; Ps. 72.1–7 May peace abound; 1 Tim. 2.1–6 Pray; John 14.23–29 Peace I leave with you

> *'"Peace I leave with you," [Jesus said]; "my peace I give to you. I do not give to you as the world gives. Do not let your hearts be troubled, and do not let them be afraid."' John 14.27*

Memoirs

I read this true story in the reminiscences of an elderly Englishman, who was a schoolboy, in an all-boys school, during the Second World War. The class all loved and admired the history teacher, who was giving a lesson about the Battle of Waterloo. He described how Wellington had given the famous order, 'Up, guards, and at 'em', and the British troops, having spent all day on the defensive, advanced on the French, driving them into the hands of the Prussians, who'd arrived on the battle-field just at that moment. 'Hurrah,' shouted one of the excited schoolboys. 'Who was that?' asked the teacher. It was the first time they had ever seen him angry. The culprit owned up, but the teacher waved to him to sit down, with an apology.

The teacher's opinion

When he had recovered his composure, the teacher explained. War, he said, is the end of civilization and a return to barbarism. War, in his opinion, is filth, created by self-serving, ruthless, power-crazed politicians. The armed services are the sanitary people sent in to clear up the mess. To say that 'it is a sweet and fitting thing to die for your country' is mere propaganda, intended to produce willing cannon-fodder. The teacher hoped that the current war, which he called 'this lunacy', would be over before his pupils became involved. If not, he hoped they would never be corrupted into murderous maniacs and brainless butchers.

Death cutting short promise

Doubtless some of you will disagree with what the teacher said, and everyone's entitled to their own opinion. But listen to how the teacher had arrived at that position. He pointed to a desk in the second row. 'Today we were told of the death in action of the lad who used to sit in that desk,' he said. 'He was a lad of great promise, and now he's been obliterated.' The teacher pointed to an empty place, reminding them it had belonged to one of this year's boy-scouts, and a brilliant athlete, who had been killed by shrapnel from a bomb while running messages for the ARP. What a waste! The children were astonished to see tears trickling down their teacher's face.

Two extremes, and in between

So that's the extreme anti-war position to which that teacher had been driven. As I say, you may not agree with him, but at least you'll sympathize with how he was driven to it. The opposite is those who hunger for battle. They probably call themselves patriots, yet those who oppose them are not unpatriotic. Probably most of us would claim to be somewhere in between.

Never hate

The man who described this, in his memoirs, continued that he had never forgotten that lesson. His teachers never taught him to hate, because hatred destroys reason. He would never hate the nations who had been their enemies, because no nation is innocent – 'Let those that are without sin cast the first stone.' He said he weeps whenever he hears the Remembrance Sunday words, 'They shall grow not old . . .' He wonders what the slain might have achieved if they had been spared to live productive lives? What might the handicapped have accomplished? In his opinion, nationalism kills; xenophobia murders; bigotry slaughters; racialism massacres; chauvinism destroys. 'Blessed are the peacemakers,' he quoted.

Reconciliation

That's all I want to quote from this elderly writer. But my hope is that on Remembrance Sunday, those who agree with him, and those who disagree, can meet and weep together at the terrible side-effects of war. Whether you are a patriotic pacifist or a patriotic war-monger or somewhere in between, there's no point in hating those who take the opposite opinion, because that merely perpetuates the tensions that create wars. Jesus calls us to reconciliation. Today, let's *all* honour those who died as a result of war; pray for the wounded and the bereaved; and support those who sincerely struggle to bring peace and justice on the earth.

All-age worship

Make a list of what the children would like to be when they grow up. Make up a prayer asking God to help them achieve their ambitions, and remembering those who died before they could do so.

Suggested hymns

God of our fathers, known of old; Judge eternal, throned in splendour; Make me a channel of your peace; O God of earth and altar.

Second Sunday before Advent   18 November
Principal Service   **Do You See These Buildings?**
Dan. 12.1–3 Conflict and resurrection; Ps. 16 Resurrection, life and death; Heb. 10.11–14 [15–18] 19–25 Assurance and faith; Mark 13.1–8 Conflict

> *'As [Jesus] came out of the temple, one of his disciples said to him, "Look, Teacher, what large stones and what large buildings!" Then Jesus asked him, "Do you see these great buildings? Not one stone will be left here upon another; all will be thrown down."' Mark 13.1–2*

Impressive

Jesus and his disciples were leaving the Temple in Jerusalem, recently rebuilt and enlarged, which rose white and huge on the hilltop. One of the disciples drew his attention to the large size of the stones and the impressive buildings. Jesus predicted that it would all be thrown down – not one stone left on top of another. When was this going to happen, they wondered – when the Messiah came, or was Jesus predicting the end of the world? In fact, a mere 40 years later, in AD 70, the Romans got fed up with the rebellious Jews, and set fire to their capital city. All that was left was some smoke-blackened ruins almost covered in rubble. For almost 2,000 years a handful of Jews, returning to the, now, mostly Arab city, gathered at the small section of the Temple wall that was left uncovered. Lamenting that this was all that remained of their impressive Temple, they called it 'the Wailing Wall'.

Revealed

If you make a pilgrimage to Jerusalem now, you will find that in the 1980s a lot of excavation was carried out in Jerusalem. The rubble has been removed from Cheesemakers' Valley, revealing the wall of the Temple to its full height for more than half its length, together with the impressive flight of steps, up which Jesus will have walked to the main entrance. The stones from which it's built really are enormous. So what does this reveal about the words of Jesus – 'not one stone upon another'? Why hasn't it come true? Was Jesus wrong?

Poetic

Fundamentalists will answer that Jesus wasn't talking about AD 70; he was predicting the end of the world, which will happen in a few years from now. The problem with this view is that Jesus said, 'This generation will not pass away until all these things have taken place.' And taking a literal, futuristic interpretation of his words misses their value as poetry. A widespread style of Jewish poetic writing in those days was called apocalyptic. Under the guise of predicting the future, it actually gives God's critique of the way people were living at the time it was written. Jesus could see that if the Jews went on fighting for an earthly kingdom, Rome would stamp on them. His poem is about life under siege, as it had been and always would be: enemy images desecrating their holy place; destruction of buildings; the misery of pregnant women running for their lives in wintertime; the danger of going back to fetch your possessions – 'twas ever thus. The details are painted with a broad brush; the only thing that was certain was that the Romans would react in just a few years. But even when it's over, there will still be wars and rumours of wars. The final solution won't be on earth, but in the timeless life of heaven, where we see the Son of Man coming on the clouds to God, to rule over everyone who's died.

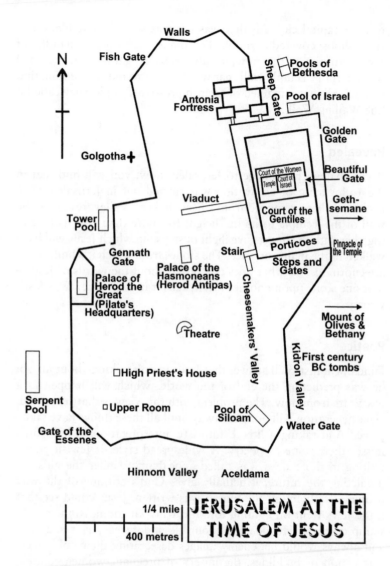

Walls

N

Fish Gate

Sheep Gate

Pools of Bethesda

Pool of Israel

Antonia Fortress

Golden Gate

Golgotha +

Court of the Women

Temple | Court of Israel

Beautiful Gate

Viaduct

Geth-semane

Court of the Gentiles

Tower Pool

Gennath Gate

Stair

Porticoes

Pinnacle of the Temple

Palace of the Hasmoneans (Herod Antipas)

Steps and Gates

Palace of Herod the Great (Pilate's Headquarters)

Cheesemakers' Valley

Theatre

Mount of Olives & Bethany

Kidron Valley

First century BC tombs

High Priest's House

Serpent Pool

Upper Room

Pool of Siloam

Gate of the Essenes

Water Gate

Hinnom Valley   **Aceldama**

1/4 mile

400 metres

JERUSALEM AT THE TIME OF JESUS

See these buildings

In a poem like that, there's no need to specify how many layers of stone are left standing. The fact that Jesus was vague about the stones, and never mentions the fire, shows that these words weren't made up after the event. A visit to the Holy Land helps you put the words of Jesus into context. It's always a struggle to interpret them; we easily get it wrong; but if you see where they were spoken, it helps you to get them into context. A famous preacher taught that 'a text without a context is a pretext'. Jesus asked: 'Do you see these great buildings?' Seeing the places in the Holy Land helps you to imagine what it looked like then, how the people lived, their figures of speech. If you can't go there on pilgrimage, imagine the places in your mind's eye: how close Bethlehem is to Jerusalem; how people fish in Lake Galilee; the five porticoes of the Pool of Bethesda; the Mount of Olives and the Garden of Gethsemane. See if these sacred places can help you choose the most likely interpretation of Jesus's teaching. You may find you come to a closer knowledge of Jesus as your friend. And that's why we're here.

All-age worship

On a map of Jerusalem in New Testament times, identify the places where Jesus walked and taught (see page 276).

Suggested hymns

A man there lived in Galilee; I want to talk with Jesus Christ; Jerusalem the golden; Through all the changing scenes of life.

Second Sunday before Advent   18 November
Second Service   Seeds and Weeds
Ps. 95 Let us sing; Dan. 3 (*or* 3.13–30) The fiery furnace; Matt. 13.24–30, 36–43 Seeds and weeds

> '[Jesus said,] "In gathering the weeds you would uproot the wheat along with them. Let both of them grow together until the harvest; and at harvest time I will tell the reapers, Collect the weeds first and bind them in bundles to be burned, but gather the wheat into my barn."' Matthew 13.29–30

Seed packets

On a seed packet you'll probably find words printed something like this: 'For good germination, sow in a well-raked seed bed, ensuring that the soil is fine and crumbly. Scatter the seed, rake lightly and firm down well. Keep well watered and weeded in the early stages.' Jesus must have been thinking in those terms when he told the parable of the weeds growing up among the wheat. Even the most careful gardener, or farmer, can't prevent some weeds springing up among the good plants. The trouble is, when they are both small, you can't tell them apart – all seedlings look the same. Yet by the time they've grown big enough to distinguish them, it's too late. All will have grown roots, and the roots on the weeds will be entangled with those of the good plants. If you try to pull up the weeds now, the roots of the good plants will come up with them, and you'll destroy your crop. The only time to separate them is at the final harvest.

Why does God allow it?

Jesus told this story to answer a very common question: why does a loving God allow innocent people to suffer? Sometimes the question is asked triumphantly by an atheist, as though asking it proved that there is no God. More often, it's asked agonizingly by people who are suffering, or whose loved ones are in pain. Jesus told us that God is like a father who loves all his children. How then can God stand by and watch us suffer, without doing anything about it? It sounds unanswerable. There is an answer, but it will take us several steps to get to it.

Creator

The first step is to look at how God created the universe. As St Augustine realized sixteen hundred years ago, reading Genesis as history misses the point. The Bible's story, or rather stories, of creation are about God's relation to his creatures, and us with him. That simply fitted into the timescale that most people believed at the time. Nowadays, we have observed that the distant galaxies are shooting away from us at a speed that proves they must all have started at a single point, billions of years ago, in what we call the Big Bang. The strata of the rocks show that, in turn, water-born sediment, wind-blown sand, and volcanic lava, must have been laid down over the course of millions of years, with footprints of different animals in the mud at several different layers, and fossils of primitive life forms lower down in the sequence, and more complex ones at higher levels. God must have created matter that was itself creative, and could develop by trial and error over many generations under God's guidance until intelligent, sentient humans could evolve. Why did God take so long? Surely it was because he wanted creatures that could respond consciously to his love, and love must be freely chosen, it can't be forced. So God had to step back from his creation and give it freedom to go wrong. The gift of free will is the essential first step towards love; robots can't love. But if we're free to choose, we shall sometimes choose wrongly, and depart from the course our Creator planned for us. And that will involve pain.

Pain

Pain isn't necessarily a bad thing. It's pain that teaches us to take our hand out of the fire when we're burnt. Pain is an essential part of evolution, so that only the least vulnerable are fit to survive. But dumb animals can't ask the question 'why?' It's only intelligent creatures that complain, and then pain becomes suffering. Here we come back to the parable of the weeds. If God weeded out all the humans who are capable of causing pain to others, or themselves, by their misuse of free will, he'd have to wait to see how they developed, and then it would be too late. Because, you see, good and evil are all mixed up together in the soul of every human being, and God couldn't pull up the evil without tearing out the good. The only time to sort it out is at death, the last harvest, when God forgives and removes the evil from our souls, taking any good that remains to live with him in heaven. Just like removing the weeds and taking the wheat into his barn. Jesus shared our suffering to show that God understands.

Suggested hymns

Come, ye thankful people, come; God forgave my sin in Jesus' name; Happy are they, they that love God; Lord, it belongs not to my care.

Christil the King 25 November
Principal Service **True Kingship**

Dan. 7.9–10, 13–14 The kingship of Christ; Ps. 93 The Lord is
King; Rev. 1.4b–8 The greatness of Christ; John 18.33–37 Are
you the King?

> *'Jesus answered, "My kingdom is not from this world. If my king-
> dom were from this world, my followers would be fighting to
> keep me from being handed over to the Jews. But as it is, my
> kingdom is not from here." Pilate asked him, "So you are a king?"
> Jesus answered, "You say that I am a king. For this I was born, and
> for this I came into the world, to testify to the truth. Everyone who
> belongs to the truth listens to my voice."' John 18.36–37*

Pilate

Jesus was on trial before Pontius Pilate, the local representative of
the Roman Emperor. Rome had been ruled by kings, and then for
500 years it was a Republic, designed to prevent any tyrant taking
charge ever again. Following the assassination of Julius Caesar,
Augustus Caesar declared himself Emperor in 31 BC. Pilate was
afraid that the 'Christ' or 'Messiah', the 'anointed one', was claiming to be Caesar's rival. So he asked Jesus, 'Are you the King of the
Jews?' Jesus wouldn't give a direct answer. It all depends, he said,
what you mean by kingship. There have been many types of king,
from absolute monarchs to those who saw their role as to serve the
people and establish justice. Jesus wasn't a tyrant. But he was a
king, if by that you mean the source of ultimate authority. He was
King of kings and Lord of lords. But he couldn't tell Pilate that,
because the Governor would have misunderstood him.

Telling truth

'To tell you the truth,' Jesus replied, 'I am a sort of king.' Or perhaps he put the sentence round the other way: 'I was born a king
to tell you the truth.' It wasn't just a word-game; he was arguing to
save his own life. It certainly got Pilate confused, so that he went
off on a tangent discussing the nature of truth, instead of examining
the nature of kingship. He forgot what question he'd just asked,
but he had to admit that there was no case against Jesus. Pilate
tried to acquit him of the charges, but the prosecution – the priests

and Pharisees – warned Pilate that if he released Jesus he couldn't call himself 'Caesar's Friend'. Pilate said to the Jews, 'Here is your King!' The priests answered, 'We have no king but Caesar,' persuading the crowd to demand capital punishment. We all know what happened next.

What sort of king?

So what sort of king *was* Jesus? He told us himself: he's the sort of king who tells the truth. Always and in all circumstances. The truth, the whole truth, and nothing but the truth. Many people today would say that truth-telling would spell the end of any politician's career. So those in authority are 'economical with the truth', or express it in such a way that nobody will ask them to account for what they are doing with their authority. An absolute monarch can't tolerate too much truth. Neither can those who wish to cling to power despite all their mistakes. Jesus was the sort of ruler who justified his commands by drawing his subjects' attention to 'Inconvenient Truths'. Jesus doesn't just issue 'diktats'; he explains that if we go on behaving as we are, we shall bring disaster on our own heads. He warns us against sin, not to be difficult, but because he knows how much harm sin can do, to us sinners and to our neighbours.

Responsible

In the so-called 'United Kingdom', it used to be called a constitutional monarchy. The monarch was supposed to defend the people's liberty, by preventing any section of the state from gaining power over another: the Lords and the Commons, the Cabinet and the ordinary MPs, the judges and the lawmakers, the Government and the Church. Now we've stripped the monarch of all power, in the interests of democratic rule – but I'm not sure that we have any more freedom. There are similar difficulties at every level of authority, from Brussels and Washington down to the authority parents have over their children. Respect has to be earned; nobody's above the law, and all must be answerable to those under them for the way they use their power. Jesus was no tyrant; neither was he the puppet of those who appointed him. He was a king who told the truth, with no fear of the consequences. Whatever position of authority you are given in your life, you too are responsible to God for the way you use or misuse your power.

All-age worship

Make paper crowns. Write on them, 'A True King'. Wear them during the service, then cast them down before the altar.

Suggested hymns

Jesus is Lord – creation's voice proclaims it; Lord, enthroned in heavenly splendour; Rejoice, the Lord is King; Thy kingdom come, O God.

Christ the King   25 November
Second Service   Babylon

Morning Ps. 29 Enthroned, 110 The king at your right hand; Evening Ps. 72 An ideal king; Dan. 5 Belshazzar's feast; John 6.1–15 Feeding the crowd

> *'[King Belshazzar] said to the wise men of Babylon, "Whoever can read this writing and tell me its interpretation shall be clothed in purple, have a chain of gold around his neck, and rank third in the kingdom."' Daniel 5.7*

Belshazzar's feast

We have no way of telling how much historical truth there is in the story of Belshazzar's feast, but it makes very clear the truth that those in authority are responsible to God for how they use their power, and will suffer for it if they are vainglorious and proud.

Babel

Babylon was one of the greatest cities of the ancient world, the centre of one the most powerful empires ever known. Akkadian was the language spoken there, and many inscriptions in the cuneiform, or wedge-shaped, script have been preserved. Its Hebrew name was Babel, that means 'Gate of God', and several of the city's beautifully tiled gateways have been preserved in the world's museums. It began as one of the minor cities in Mesopotamia. In around 2000 BC, the story of a great flood was described in the Babylonian *Gilgamesh Epic*, and shortly afterwards King Hammurabi wrote a code of laws in Babylon. The *Enuma Elish* was a creation story, and all of these influenced the writers of the Old Testament, though the Jewish stories are more profound than those from Babylon. Babylon also left a legacy of astronomy, astrology and mathematics. Babylon defeated the kings of Assyria; in the sixth century BC a king whom the Bible calls Nebuchadnezzar captured Jerusalem, and many of its leading citizens were taken into exile in Babylon, a turning-point in their understanding of God's judgement on his people. Babylon at that time became one of the world's biggest cities, famous for its multi-storey temples called ziggurats, which may be the origin of the stories about the Tower of Babel, and for the Hanging Gardens, one of the Seven Wonders of the World.

Bible references

Stories about Nebuchadnezzar's successors in Babylon are found in the book of Daniel. Then Cyrus the Persian conquered Babylon, and allowed the Jews to return. Alexander the Great captured Babylon and gave it to Seleucus, one of his generals. St Peter pretends to be writing from Babylon, though in his time the city was already abandoned. The explanation is found in Revelation, which describes the destruction of Babylon 'seated on seven hills'. Now Rome was built on seven hills, so the Babylonian Empire is being used as a code name for that of Rome – that just shows the dangers of interpreting the Bible literally!

Archaeology

The remains of ancient Babylon were excavated by German archaeologists in the early twentieth century. When Iraq became independent, Saddam Hussein started to rebuild Babylon, 56 miles south of Baghdad, to show that he was King Nebuchadnezzar's true successor as the ruler of Mesopotamia, the country between the Tigris and the Euphrates. During the Iraq wars, untold damage was done to the ruins of Babylon by military vehicles. Restoration has started, and in 2009 the remains were reopened to visitors.

A movie

In 2006 a hauntingly brilliant film was produced with the tantalizing title of *Babel*. Four different stories were told side by side, taking place in four different countries. Gradually the viewer realizes that they are interconnected, and misguided actions by ordinary people in one place can cause untold suffering to an unrelated family on another continent. The error in each case arose from lack of communication. The fact that the four families spoke different languages reminds us of the story of the Tower of Babel, when humankind's vaulting ambition led to splits into different language groups. But even when people speak the same language they often don't listen to each other – one of the characters, significantly, was a profoundly deaf Japanese girl. We are all too immersed in our own worries to pay attention to other people, and even if we understand their language, we don't make the effort to put ourselves into their shoes and imagine what our actions look like to somebody from a different culture.

Imagination

This lack of imagination in dealing with others lies behind all the stories told of Babylon in the Bible. The exile of the Jews; the statue with the feet of clay; the young men thrown into the fiery furnace; Nebuchadnezzar's madness; Belshazzar's feast; Daniel in the lions' den; the visions of the great beasts symbolizing warring empires; all are about human selfishness and failure to communicate. That's still true today, and from world empires to ordinary families, we all need to learn the lessons from the destruction of Babylon. 'By the waters of Babylon we sat down and wept' – for the harm done by the sins of others and by our own sins.

Suggested hymns

Judge eternal, throned in splendour; O God of earth and altar; O what their joy and their glory must be; Ten thousand times ten thousand.

Sermons for Saints' Days and Special Occasions

St Stephen, Deacon, First Martyr

26 December 2011

Jews and Gentiles

2 Chron. 24.20–22 The stoning of Zechariah; *or* Acts 7.51–60
The death of Stephen; Ps. 119.161–168 Persecuted without a
cause (*if the Acts reading is used instead of the Old Testament
reading, the New Testament reading is* Gal. 2.16b–20 Crucified
with Christ); Matt. 10.17–22 Persecution

> *'You are the ones that received the law as ordained by angels, and
> yet you have not kept it.' Acts 7.53*

Greek

Stephen was a Jew, but he had a Greek name: *stephanos* is the
Greek word for a crown. Quite a lot of Jews adopted Greek names
during the time when their country was part of the Roman Empire
– Greek, not Latin, was the language understood all across the civilized world. Many Jews had settled outside the Holy Land, and only
used Hebrew in the synagogues; their children grew up with Greek
as their first language. Most of the Jewish residents of the area that
the Bible calls 'Galilee of the Gentiles' were bilingual – they had to
use Greek to do business with the Romans. The apostles Philip and
Andrew had Greek names. Quite a few of the earliest Christians
in Jerusalem preferred Greek; the others called them 'Hellenists',
and began to argue with them, saying that by assimilating with the
surrounding culture, they were no longer worthy to be called Jews.
As usual, the argument came down to money in the long run: how
much should each language group receive in the charitable distribution to poor widows? The apostles nipped this potential split
in the bud, by appointing seven assistants, or deacons, of whom
Stephen was one, to take charge of the distribution. These seven
all had Greek names: Stephen, Philip, Prochorus, Nicanor, Timon,
Parmenas, and lastly Nicolaus, who wasn't even born Jewish: he'd
been converted to the Jewish faith in Antioch.

Stephen's speech

Stephen didn't only distribute charity; he spread the good news of
Jesus among other Hellenistic Jews. The Hebrew speakers didn't
like this; they thought they were losing control over their own

religion, with all these new-fangled ideas. So they set up false witnesses who accused Stephen of attacking the Temple and the Law,
and preaching that Jesus would change the traditional customs
handed down from Moses. Stephen replied very cleverly, initially
praising the Jews, chosen by God as the first to hear the good news
of his love. But then Stephen pointed out that the Israelites had
rejected each of God's messengers and prophets, one after another.
'You are the ones', he said, 'that received the law as ordained by
angels, and yet you have not kept it.' Reading between the lines,
you can see the implication: if the Jews wouldn't spread the good
news to other nations, God would choose non-Jews, or Gentiles as
they called them, to do it instead. This made the Jewish authorities
furious, and before Stephen could say another word they stoned
him to death.

Jews and Gentiles

The new Christian movement had come to a crossroads. Up until
now, almost all the Christians had been Jewish, no matter what language they spoke. Stephen, though he was a Jew, had proclaimed
that God's strategy of spreading the Christian message exclusively
through Jews wasn't working. If that was true, the Jewish church
would have to start admitting non-Jews. This was a great shock to
their national pride. Jesus had praised the Roman centurion and
the woman from Tyre, but hadn't actually asked Jews to sit down
at table with foreigners; now their shared meals would never be
kosher again.

Paul

Fortunately, the Christian Church rose to the multi-racial challenge. One of the people present at the stoning of Stephen, who
held the coats of the men who threw the stones, was a Jew from
Tarsus called Saul; he changed his name to Paul and spent the rest
of his life travelling across the Empire, trying to reconcile Jewish
Christians with Gentile Christians. Thank God he did, or you and
I, Gentiles by birth, might never have been allowed to become
Christians. The effects of St Stephen's speech have spread across
the world and down the ages, and we have all benefited.

Unprejudiced

Because of that, however, we must be ready to have our prejudices overturned, as the national pride of the Jews was. On St Stephen's day, we are challenged to welcome people of every race and culture to share with us at the Lord's Table, and at meals in our own homes, as the opportunity arises. We are here, thank God, because Paul and his followers rose to that challenge. The least we can do is to show a similar hospitality to others, whatever their origins.

Suggested hymns

For all thy saints, O Lord; Good King Wenceslas looked out; In Christ there is no east or west; Joy to the world.

St John, Apostle and Evangelist   27 December
The Word of Life

Ex. 33.7–11a The tent of meeting; Ps. 117 Praise God, all nations; 1 John 1 The word of life; John 21.19b–25 The Beloved Disciple

> 'We declare to you what was from the beginning, what we have heard, what we have seen with our eyes, what we have looked at and touched with our hands, concerning the word of life.' 1 John 1.1

Hansel and Gretel

In Humperdink's opera *Hansel and Gretel*, the witch puts a spell on Hansel, so that he can't move. Then she removes it by reciting the magic words, 'Hocus-pocus, elderbush! Loosen, rigid muscles, whoosh!' At the end of the opera, Gretel says the same words to the children whom the witch has turned into gingerbread, and brings them back to life. Those nonsense words in the story are life-giving – they are words of life. In the first chapter of Genesis, God uses equally powerful words to bring inanimate nature to life: 'And God said, "Let the earth bring forth living creatures of every kind . . ." And it was so.' This isn't meant to be a scientific account of the origins of life, any more than *Hansel and Gretel* is. But it conveys an image of the power of the Creator, and the magical effectiveness of the right word at the right moment.

St John

At the beginning his Gospel, St John describes Jesus as the Word of God: 'All things came into being through him, and without him not one thing came into being. What has come into being in him was life, and the life was the light of all people.' Jesus is the magic word; God's way of saying 'I love you.' As soon as those syllables were uttered, life started to evolve; when God speaks them today, people whose vitality seems to have vanished suddenly spring to vigorous and joyful life. At the end of the Gospel, someone else – who may also have been called John, it was a very common name – says that the Beloved Disciple is a witness to the words of Jesus, and wrote the first draft of the Gospel: 'This is the disciple who is testifying to these things and has written them, and we know that his testimony is true.' And in the First Letter of John, whatever John it is writes, 'We declare to you what was from the beginning, what we have heard, what we have seen with our eyes, what we have looked at and touched with our hands, concerning the word of life.' The compilation of the Gospel began with an eye-witness, whose words bear witness to the words of Jesus, the Word of God.

Celebration

So on this day, close to Christmas, we have two things to celebrate: the birth of Jesus, the Word of God, and the work of the Gospel-writer who set out the words of Jesus so that we might hear their message. How should we know that God loves us, unless the Son of God had himself come down and been born as a baby in Bethlehem? God spoke his words of love through the mouth of his Son; but how should we know that, unless the Gospel-writers had translated them, putting pen to paper to convey this message to our hearts?

The gift of life

The effect of these words on us is as startling as was that of the words of Hansel on the gingerbread children. When we imagine that nobody loves us, we eke out our living, bored, depressed, and with no purpose to our existence. Discovering that another human being loves you is a transforming experience. Whether or not we have that privilege, we all have the chance, through the words of the Gospel-writers, to hear God say, 'I love you.' Then 'Love changes everything.' I realize that I'm not a nobody, I'm a VIP, someone worth loving. The whole aim of my life becomes hearing God speak those words over and over, and responding to them by loving God with all my heart. Now my life has meaning and purpose and I come fully alive, filled with joy. To hear God say, 'I love you', truly is the word of life.

Eternal life

It doesn't stop there. The words 'eternal life' occur 22 times in the writings of St John, slightly more than in the whole of the rest of the Bible. He brings us the message that life doesn't end with death, but continues into eternity, for those who return God's love with love. In some other dimension, impossible to describe, we shall continue to know each other and love each other, to know God and dwell with him in mutual love. Then life on earth, glorious as it is, becomes merely the prelude to an unending symphony of love in the next world. That, surely, is the Word of Life – something worth celebrating on this day.

Suggested hymns

Fill now our life, O Lord our God; Jesus, name above all names; Lord, for the years; Lord of all being, throned afar.

Holy Innocents   28 December
Herod, You're a Loser!
Jer. 31.15–17 Rachel weeping for her children; Ps. 124 When our enemies attacked us; 1 Cor. 1.26–29 God chose what is weak; Matt. 2.13–18 The Massacre

> *'When Herod saw that he had been tricked by the wise men, he was infuriated, and he sent and killed all the children in and around Bethlehem who were two years old or under, according to the time that he had learned from the wise men.' Matthew 2.16*

A winner

King Herod achieved much. Not even a Jew, he was an Edomite, from an Arab tribe forcibly converted to Judaism. He was put in charge of the Galilee area, and was notorious for oppressing the rebellious peasants. The Roman Empire then made him the client-king of Judah in 40 BC. Herod the Great, as he came to be called, clung to power, grew rich, and embarked on a vast building programme. The climax was his reconstruction and enlargement of the Jerusalem Temple, one of the largest religious buildings of its day, rising white and magnificent on its hilltop site. He extended the courtyards to cover 144,000 square meters, including for the first time a courtyard for women and another for non-Jews. He built himself palaces in Jericho, Masada, Caesarea, and one near Bethlehem where he was eventually buried, called the Herodium. He and his family spent much of their time in Rome, and Herod's troops accompanied the Roman army on several campaigns. On his travels he won many privileges for Jews living abroad, and several extensions to his kingdom. He was named president of the Olympic Games. Herod lived in luxury, and must have thought he had it made. He really considered himself a winner.

Insecure

But underneath it all, King Herod was deeply insecure. He divorced his first wife, and married Mariamne because she came from a high-priestly family. Yet he was deeply suspicious throughout their ten-year marriage, and had her killed under suspicion of adultery. He married ten times in all, and his many sons all tried to inherit his empire. So he had several of them murdered, as possible rivals for his throne, giving rise to the Emperor Augustus's witticism that he'd rather be Herod's pig than his son – converts to Judaism, of course, don't kill pigs!

Bethlehem

According to St Matthew, wise men or Magi came from the East, and stayed a while in Jerusalem. Yet the question they asked, perhaps naively, was deeply threatening to Herod: 'Where is the child who has been born King of the Jews?' Poor Herod! He thought he'd got rid of all his rivals, and now another child had been born, claiming his throne. Desperately he sent for his advisers – did they have any idea where new kings were born? They consulted the book of the prophet Micah, and came up with the answer that Bethlehem, the birthplace of King David, the greatest Jewish King, was predicted to be the birthplace of David's descendant, the promised Messiah.

A descendant of David would have solid Jewish ancestry, whereas hardly any of Herod's ancestors were born Jews. This would give the upstart a stronger claim to the throne than its present occupant. What was Herod to do? He couldn't challenge the magi to tell him who his rival was; once they knew that he intended assassination, they'd clam up and tell him nothing. So Herod *pretended* to be on their side, and promised to come and worship the new king when they'd identified him.

Massacre

Warned in a dream, the magi frustrated Herod's plans by going home by a different route, avoiding Jerusalem. Aaargh! What could Herod the Great but Insecure do now? The only thing was to kill all the babies of Bethlehem under two years old. And by this desperate measure, Herod 'the Winner' showed that he'd lost. If he'd worshipped the baby, Jesus wouldn't have dethroned him, because his kingdom is not of this world. By ordering the massacre, Herod missed Jesus, whose parents had already flitted, but he created a whole town full of new enemies. Herod, you poor sap! Unrestrained by the love of the weeping mothers and mourning fathers, or even the sobs of the children, you destroyed the weak and made them the first martyrs. By venting your rage on these innocents, King Herod, you're paying them the highest compliment. Even little children can triumph over your impotent rage, because moral purity outlasts cruel tyranny. You sought to prolong your life by assassinating the child who was Life himself – in a few short months you'll be lying on your deathbed, writhing in agony from a loathsome internal disease. Your personal power will be dispersed, and your rivals will fight over your legacy. Baby Jesus will become the king of all the earth. Poor Herod, you thought you were the great winner, and look what's happening. Herod, you're a loser! Ha!

Suggested hymns

How bright these glorious spirits shine; In vain the cruel Herod's fear; Lully, lulla, thou little tiny child; Unto us a boy is born.

Naming and Circumcision of Jesus   1 January 2012

(*See page 33.*)

Epiphany 6 January
Journeying into God

Isa. 60.1–6 Bringing gold and incense; Ps. 72.[1–9] 10–15 Kings will bow before him; Eph. 3.1–12 Preaching to Gentiles; Matt. 2.1–12 Visit of the Magi

'In the time of King Herod, after Jesus was born in Bethlehem of Judea, wise men from the East came to Jerusalem.' Matthew 2.1

A long journey

In the Second World War, with the aim of conserving fuel supplies, there were posters at the stations reading, 'Is your journey really necessary?' T. S. Eliot, in his poem *The Journey of the Magi*, emphasizes the problems of the journey the wise men had to take – 'A cold coming' he calls it, with the innkeepers charging high prices. In the days before motorcars and aeroplanes, any journey was exhausting. The Magi probably came from Persia, what we now call Iran – a journey of anything between 600 and 1,600 miles. But I'm sure they felt it was worth the discomfort. Many people travelled in camel trains across the desert, but this was a special journey. They were searching to find out more about God, and they believed the new King of the Jews could teach them. The new king was unlikely to come to them, so they must travel to meet him. Studying the stars, they had already journeyed a long road in their minds, trying to find out about God, and God's influence on history. Now the stars had told them of a new revelation, and they followed their star just as far as was necessary, until they found what they were looking for. Were they surprised when the answer turned out to be a child in a manger, or had the stars led them to expect something like this? We don't know, but they offered their gifts to the baby: gold, frankincense and myrrh. Then they went home, satisfied that their journey had been not only necessary, but very worthwhile.

Other faiths

The wise men weren't Jews. When they set out, they weren't Christians, though they came to be among the first to worship Jesus. They were probably followers of some astrological religion taught in Babylon. The story stands there in the Gospels as a witness that all faiths can lead us to God, if we search hard enough. The whole of life is a journey of discovery, as we learn more about the world around us, and about ourselves. Those who sit still and wait for knowledge to come to them never learn anything. You have to go out and look for wisdom. This means keeping an open mind; expecting the unexpected; being willing to learn from your mistakes, and learn from other people. Persians then probably felt about Jews what the leaders of Iran say about Israelis today. Yet the Magi were willing to learn about God, even from those they hated or despised. It's been wisely said that God is like a high mountain. Viewing the peak from various angles, it may appear completely different to different observers. But if we make the demanding effort to climb up, starting from where we are, and keeping our eyes fixed on our destination, people from different cultures may well find they will meet at the summit.

Journey into God

If we're to follow the example of the wise men from the East, we must each make our own journey into God. God wants to reveal his loving nature to us. We can't discover him by our own efforts, but he can't reveal himself unless we make some effort to understand him. So reading the Bible and other books, prayer, and discussion with other seekers, become part of our pilgrimage, and as precious to us as their trek was to the Magi. God promised the Israelites, as they set off for the Promised Land, 'from there you will seek the LORD your God, and you will find him if you search after him with all your heart and soul'. St Paul told the people of Athens – who like the Magi were followers of pagan religions – that God 'made all nations to inhabit the whole earth . . . so that they would search for God and perhaps grope for him and find him'. The search for meaning in life is common to all human beings. We may give that meaning different names – that doesn't matter; the Muslims say that Allah has a hundred names – but in fact it's a deeper understanding of God that we're searching for. Thank God he doesn't leave us to search on our own, but like the father of the Prodigal Son, he comes out to greet us. But our journey of discovery is as necessary to us as theirs was to the wise men. If we're as open-minded as they were, we may find the meaning of life and the secret of the universe in the love of a mother, and the smile in the eyes of a child.

Brightest and best of the sons of the morning; From the Eastern mountains; Hail to the Lord's anointed; We three kings of orient are.

Week of Prayer for Christian Unity 18–25 January
Membership or Relationships?

Ezek. 36.23–28 Back to your own land; Col. 3.9–17 No longer Jew and Greek; Ps. 122 A city at unity; John 11.45–52 Gather the dispersed;

> *'Being high priest that year he prophesied that Jesus was about to die for the nation, and not for the nation only, but to gather into one the dispersed children of God.' John 11.51–52*

Caiaphas

The priests were worried about Jesus. 'If we let him go on like this', they moaned, 'everyone will believe in him, and the Romans will come and destroy both our holy place and our nation.' Caiaphas, the High Priest, warned them, 'You know nothing at all! You do not understand that it is better for you to have one man die for the people than to have the whole nation destroyed.' Caiaphas had unwittingly proclaimed a profound truth: that Jesus was about to die for the nation; 'and not for the nation only, but to gather into one the dispersed children of God'. What Caiaphas didn't realize, however, was that Jesus's self-sacrifice would reveal God's love for us; draw people back to God; and enable us to receive God's freely offered forgiveness of our sins. Not only the Jewish people, either, but all the nations of the world will be drawn into unity, when they see the love of Jesus placarded on the cross.

Divisions

The way that God had planned for this to happen was through the family of Christians, living together in love, proclaiming the love of Jesus and showing it in their own lives. But very soon Christians began to argue with each other, and cracks appeared in the unity of the Church of Christ. How were people to believe in the love of God, if believers in God can't even love each other? So the divisions in the Church hinder the spread of the gospel – disunity in the Church prevents unity coming to the world.

The Ecumenical Movement

It was Christian missionaries who first realized how serious disunity is. They were trying to spread the gospel. But they were hindered because new converts would have to decide to affiliate to a particular denomination, and thus cut themselves off from fellow members of their race or tribe who joined a different church. The first World Missionary Conference, held at Edinburgh in 1910, led to the formation of the International Missionary Council, which welcomed members of all denominations. Missionaries who translated the Bible into different languages formed the United Bible Societies. From 1925 onwards the 'Life and Work' Movement was an opportunity for Christians from different backgrounds to work together in serving others. The 'Faith and Order' Movement provided a forum for discussing, and seeking to resolve, issues of doctrine and church government, in the hope of growing towards unity. It was the Greek Orthodox who urged the churches in 1920 to form a fellowship modelled on the League of Nations; and in 1948 the World Council of Churches was born in Amsterdam.

Councils of Churches

When the WCC was founded it had 144 member churches; now it has over 340 in more than 100 countries, including most of the Eastern Orthodox Churches and the larger Protestant denominations. Yet few on the Evangelical wing have joined, and not the Roman Catholic Church, who claimed that there is only one true Church. However, the Second Vatican Council reaffirmed the 'irrevocable commitment of the Roman Catholic Church to ecumenism as an organic part of her life and work'. Local Councils of Churches were formed in many towns and suburbs, with the same limitations on membership. More recently these mostly changed their name to 'Churches Together in such-and-such a place', and Roman Catholics were happy to join.

What sort of unity?

In the early days of the movement, many keen 'ecu-maniacs' dreamt of an organic union of denominations into a single organization.

As a first step, United Churches were formed out of two or more denominations in England and Wales (The United Reformed Church), the USA (The United Church of Christ), and in Canada, Australia, South India, North India, Pakistan and Sri Lanka. 'Inter-church Aid and Refugee service' evolved into Christian Aid, which works closely with CAFOD, its RC equivalent. But as so little progress has been made towards widespread reunion, people began to ask what sort of unity it is that Jesus wants in his Church. Is it a question of all being members in one denomination, or a matter of establishing a warm relationship of co-operation between local congregations, even with those that are not in the Churches Together groups? Do we need a common strategy, so that we don't tread on each other's toes and duplicate our efforts? In this week, we should surely be praying for answers to these questions about membership or relationships.

Suggested hymns

Bind us together, Lord; I the Lord of sea and sky; In Christ there is no East or West; Thy hand, O God, has guided.

Conversion of St Paul   25 January
Paul in Context

Jer. 1.4–10 The call of a prophet; Ps. 67 Let all the peoples praise you; Acts 9.1–22 Saul's conversion (*if the Acts reading is used instead of the Old Testament reading, the New Testament reading is* Gal. 1.11–16a Called me through his grace); Matt. 19.27–30 The reward of eternal life

> *'[Saul] is an instrument whom I have chosen to bring my name before Gentiles and kings and before the people of Israel.' Acts 9.15*

What was St Paul getting at?

In many churches, 25 January is a day for remembering the Conversion of St Paul. It's also the last day of the Week of Prayer for Christian Unity. St Paul wrote many letters, which are in the New Testament. If I asked you what he was getting at in those letters, what answer would you give? The most honest answer, probably, is 'Don't know!' He uses lots of long words in long, long sentences, and seems to write about abstract theological arguments which are of no concern to us at all. Even the Second Letter of Peter says:

> So also our beloved brother Paul wrote to you according to the wisdom given him . . . as he does in all his letters. There are some things in them hard to understand.

Dictated

Part of the problem is that Paul dictated his letters when he was feeling passionate about something: 'You stupid Galatians – who's cast a spell on you?' When you are in a towering rage like that, you don't stop to tell your secretary where to put the full stops. A simple, modern translation helps enormously. So what was Paul angry about? The main snag is that we don't understand the context in which the letters were written, and context is everything.

Context

Paul was brought up to believe that the most important thing in life is obeying every one of the Old Testament regulations. When every Jew does that, he thought, the Messiah will come, kill all the non-Jews and raise all the dead Jews to life again on earth. The Christians, who said that the Messiah had already come, were a threat to everything he held dear. Yet on his way to Damascus to root out the Christians there, he saw the risen Christ, and realized that the resurrection had already begun. So he was baptized. But for the rest of his life he was persecuted by Jews who were loyal to the Law of Moses.

Travels

Paul was fluent in both Hebrew and Greek. The city of Antioch sent for Paul to preach to the Greek-speaking Jews about Jesus. He visited Cyprus, where the Roman Governor became a Christian even though he wasn't a Jew. This opened up the astonishing possibility that the whole Roman Empire might come to Christ. From then on, Paul's life was dedicated to the attempt to get Jews and non-Jews to accept each other as equals. That's where you and I come in. He travelled through Galatia, where many non-Jews became Christians. No way could they keep the Jewish Sabbath laws when all their work-mates worked seven days a week, or demand kosher food at parties. Paul wrote, angrily demanding that Jewish Christians stop trying to make the non-Jews follow Jewish culture.

Corinth and Rome

In Corinth some people believed that speaking in tongues was the test, and anyone who couldn't do this wasn't really a Christian. Paul wrote that everybody has different gifts, but the most important thing was loving each other despite our differences. The church in Rome was bitterly divided between Jewish Christians, who said you could only get right with God by keeping all the Old Testament laws, and non-Jews, who found that impossible. Unfortunately, the word they used for getting right with God translates awkwardly into English as 'justification'. Paul wrote that Jews and non-Jews alike are justified by trusting in Jesus, not by obeying the Jewish Law. So when he talks about justification by faith, not works, Paul's not preaching complicated theology; it's an appeal for unity between different types of quarrelling Christians. His vision was of the whole world united in love, with Christ as the head, which can only be brought about through a Church that is united in love. Everything St Paul wrote was a desperate plea for church unity. Trust Jesus, and love all your fellow Christians, treating them as brothers and sisters despite your differences.

Unity

The Week of Prayer for Christian Unity is the most important week in the year. But we still have to work out what we mean by unity. Maybe the Baptist Union has something to teach other churches, as a model for co-operation without any one congregation dominating the others. Jesus didn't pray that his disciples might always be right, but that they might be one. Let's pray with him for church unity, in whatever way he chooses. Then let's work together in every way we can.

Suggested hymns

A heavenly splendour from on high; In Christ there is no East or West; Thy hand, O God, has guided; We sing the glorious conquest.

Presentation of Christ in the Temple (Candlemas)

2 February (*or may be observed on Sunday 29 January*)
Mary's Tragedy

Mal. 3.1–5 The Lord shall come to his Temple; Ps. 24.[1–6] 7–10
Open the gates for the Lord; Heb. 2.14–18 Jesus became like
the descendants of Abraham; Luke 2.22–40 The presentation of
Christ in the Temple

> '*Then Simeon blessed them and said to his mother Mary . . . "A
> sword will pierce your own soul too."*' Luke 2.34–35

A little job for God

I wonder what it was like to be the Virgin Mary. She's living a hum-
drum life, when the Angel Gabriel turns up and says, 'Hey Mary,
God's got a little job for you. Nothing much. Just give birth to his
son and bring him up. Is that all right with you, love? Oh good.
That's settled then.' What an honour! But when she brought her son
to the Temple, to present him to God, the old priest Simeon warned
her it might not be that simple: 'It will feel like a sword stabbing
right through your heart, dear,' he said. What did he mean? Might
she have to watch her baby suffer, one day?

Mary's tragedy

The feelings of any mother are the same, as she gazes lovingly into
her baby's eyes. Your baby is the whole world to you, and to see
your child in pain would be worse than suffering yourself. All you
want is to build a new life from scratch – feeding, caring for them
and training them to be an adult. Your hopes well up for your
child's future happiness and fulfilment. It seems so unfair that a
child should have to endure pain. But there's no rule that says only
adults suffer. There's no way that parents can suffer in their children's place. How Mary must have suffered, then, later on, when
it became clear that Jesus was to be betrayed by his friends, tried,
and sentenced to a horrible and barbaric death? However unfair it
seemed, she'd no choice but to accept God's plan for her son.

Lessons to learn

There must be many parents who have to go through times like that, watching their children suffer, in childhood or in later life. Can we learn any lessons from Mary's experience? Can we find any positive value in such negative experiences? It would be insensitive to try to 'cheer them up' in such a terrible time, but I believe that God can bring good out of the most terrible experiences, even as he brought good out of Mary's suffering, the 'sword stabbing into her own heart' as she stood by the cross where her son was hanging. Maybe some new medical discovery will come out of the doctors' care for the sick child. Maybe the loving devotion of the child's parents will bring about a healing that medical science would never have expected. Maybe the experience will draw the whole family together in a new unity of love that they could never have discovered in any other way. Whatever happens, we believe, God will bring some lasting good out of it.

Prayer

Then, as a wave of prayer spreads around the world, for the sick child or the sick adult, and for the agonizing parents, everyone who knows them will learn something of the power of prayer, and the power of love. There may be a new sense of the closeness of God, and of God's love for everyone. God cares for us all, and can uplift us and support us through our times of trial.

If it comes to the worst

This sermon's based on the words of a mother as she sat by the bedside of her sick son in Great Ormond Street Children's Hospital. She described the experience of being prayed for as like being 'swathed in the finest pashmina of love'. I had to read that sentence twice before I understood what it meant. A pashmina is a shawl made from soft goats' wool. Being prayed for, she wrote, is like being 'swathed in the finest pashmina of love. That's the good that's come out of all this,' she went on. 'Once you can recognize the good, it's possible to keep strong . . . to stay positive and to recover. Above all, when you have such love, there is no fear. And a difficult journey becomes easier.' While that child continues to have a serious condition, the mother's faith enables her to accept this without bitterness or anger and to keep striving to support her son. Did Mary manage to keep her faith in a loving God after what happened to her son? Yet Jesus rose again, and teaches us that there is life beyond death for us all. If it comes to the worst, we must cling to the example of Mary, and the witness of other grieving parents. God's love *will* support us, and bring good out of the most terrible evil, if we remain faithful.

Suggested hymns

For Mary, Mother of the Lord; Gentle Jesus, meek and mild; In a world where people walk in darkness; There's a song for all the children.

St David, Bishop of Menevia, Patron of Wales
c. 601 1 March
Christianity in Wales

Ecclus. 15.1–6 Whoever holds to the law will obtain wisdom; Ps. 16.1–7 I have a goodly heritage; 1 Thess. 2.2–12 Entrusted with the gospel; Matt. 16.24–27 Take up your cross

> 'All my delight is upon the godly that are in the land, upon those who are noble in heart.' Psalm 16.2

Origins

How much do you know about how Christians lived in Wales centuries ago? Even historians admit that the early centuries are a bit hazy, because few archaeological remains have survived, and even fewer books. A sixth-century monk called Gildas wrote a history, suggesting that the first Christians in Britain were Roman soldiers and settlers, and when the Roman legions left, Christianity survived as a weak and scattered minority. In south-east Wales, Cadoc, Dubricius and Illtyd were teachers and preachers, and among their followers were Teilo, Padarn and David. These early leaders were later called saints, though there was no official system of canonization. In north Wales, Deiniol and others founded churches. These early missionaries travelled by sea between Scotland, Ireland, Wales and Brittany, and tombstones, scattered all over the area, bear this out. Monasteries were founded, and as many of the Welsh clergy in those days were married, these communities of Christian families grew into small towns. Some, like that in Bangor, were quite large, forming the religious capitals of large areas. Those near the coast had to defend themselves against the attacks of the marauding Norsemen. In larger monasteries the abbot-bishops became territorial bishops governing a large diocese, such as those in Llandaff, St Asaph, St David's and Bangor.

Anglo-Saxons

Anglo-Saxons began to settle in East Anglia, and the pagan culture they brought slowly spread across Britain, restricting the Christians to the west. The Pope sent St Augustine, an Italian, to Canterbury to convert the heathen English, and he was very successful. Hearing that there were already British Christians in Wales, he called them to a meeting. He was so discourteous that they showed no interest in coming under his leadership. In AD 664, a Synod was called at Whitby to discuss relations between the Celtic and Roman Christians, and they agreed at least to celebrate Easter on the date that had been calculated in Rome. Apart from that, little progress was made towards uniting the two churches.

Normans

When the Normans invaded England, Archbishop Anselm of Canterbury was more successful in bringing the four Welsh dioceses under the control of Canterbury, despite local opposition. Diocesan boundaries were defined, parishes organized, tithes collected, and monasteries became centres of international learning. The Welsh princes admired the Cistercian monks at Tintern Abbey, and welcomed them to set up monasteries at Strata Florida and elsewhere.

Kings

Llewelyn ap Gruffydd, the last of the native Welsh princes, persuaded the bishops to support King Edward I in his conquest of Wales. Later, many of the clergy supported Owain Glyn Dwr in his revolt, but when it failed, the power of the English was increased. The church in Wales was lazy, and many monasteries had few monks. But when the Tudor King Henry VIII, descended from a Welsh family, came to the throne, he was supported by the Welsh church. They raised little objection to the break with Rome and the dissolution of the monasteries. The clergy were mostly educated at Jesus College in Oxford. Yet the Bible and Prayer Book were printed in Welsh, and a split developed between the Anglicized clergy and their Welsh-speaking parishioners. Not until 1822 was a college founded at Lampeter for the education of the Welsh clergy.

Nonconformists

Nonconformists began to emerge, but they were few in number and many of them emigrated to America. Methodism spread in Wales in the early nineteenth century, aided by the hymns of William Williams of Pantycelyn. Yet it remained within the Established Church until the Calvinistic Methodists, believers in predestination, broke away in 1811. Nonconformists were influential in radical politics, and encouraged temperance and the Sunday closing of shops and public houses. In 1914 the Church in Wales was disestablished.

Lessons

What lessons can we learn from this long history? First: even when Wales was outwardly Christian, the survival of the faith depended on the deep devotion of the few, who spread the gospel to their family, their friends and their neighbours. Second, we must find a way in which different cultures, even different languages, can coexist in the same community, if ever the Christian Church is to be that source of unity that Jesus and St Paul called us to be. And third, people of every nation can be proud of their history and the example of heroes of bygone days, while at the same time admitting that there have been many mistakes. Differences with our neighbours needn't lead us to fight them, for the Christian religion is one of universal love.

Suggested hymns

God, that madest earth and heaven; God, whose city's sure foundation; Guide me, O thou great Redeemer; Rejoice in God's saints, today and all days!

St Patrick, Bishop, Missionary, Patron of Ireland
c. 460   17 March
Showers of Blessing

Deut. 32.1–9 Let my teaching drop like rain, *or* Tob. 13.1b–7 In the land of my exile; Ps. 145.12–13 Make known to all peoples; 2 Cor. 4.1–12 This ministry; Matt. 10.16–23 Warnings for missionaries, *or* John 4.31–38 Ripe for harvest

> *'May my teaching drop like the rain, my speech condense like the dew; like gentle rain on grass, like showers on new growth.'*
> *Deuteronomy 32.2*

Soft weather

If you go motoring or on a coach tour down the West Coast of Ireland, fine weather will show you the magnificent views of Galway bay and the River Shannon. But it's also possible that you will have a light drizzle, or even a torrential downpour. In which case your friends who live in that area will say to you, 'Sure, 'tis lovely soft weather we're having.' There are always two ways of looking at anything. The sunny days, which show you the Aran Islands in the distance, may be disaster to the farmer whose crops are crying out for moisture. Whereas the rain that seems to spoil your holiday may be just what the farmer needed. Thank God for both of them, remembering that nobody can please all of the people all of the time, not even God!

Soft speaking

Irish people have wonderful ways of speaking. 'Soft weather', indeed! There's something liquid about the way words are pronounced in Ireland, which fall from the lips like the sweetest of raindrops from heaven. The book of Deuteronomy, the fifth book of Moses in the Old Testament, contains this beautiful prayer: 'May my teaching drop like the rain, my speech condense like the dew; like gentle rain on grass, like showers on new growth.' These words introduce what's called the 'Song of Moses', in which he addresses the people of Israel, who had travelled for 40 years with him from Egypt, past Mount Sinai, to the very borders of the Promised Land. He charges them to remember the Lord God who had been their guide through the wilderness; to obey God and never to forget what they owed to him. It was a difficult message to get across. There's a promise that God will give his children a fertile land to live in. But there are also rebukes for past disobedience, and warnings of possible punishment – 'Vengeance is mine, I will repay,' says the Lord. Moses prayed for the oratorical gifts necessary to bring this message home to the hearts of his hearers, without losing their sympathy. If he came too hot and strong, they would close their ears.

St Patrick

So it must have been for St Patrick. When he began to preach to the pagan people he found in Ireland, he shared the good news of the love of Jesus. But Patrick also had to warn them about the disastrous effects of inter-tribal fighting. He needed all the skills of oratory that God could give him, if he was to win the people over. As he read through the Holy Scriptures, he must often have said for himself the prayer of Moses: 'May my teaching drop like the rain, my speech condense like the dew; like gentle rain on grass, like showers on new growth.'

Leadership

There's another famous Old Testament passage, which also compares the effect of a God-called leader to the reinvigorating effect of sun and rain. I'm going to quote it in the King James Version:

The God of Israel said, the Rock of Israel spake to me, He that ruleth over men must be just, ruling in the fear of God. And he shall be as the light of the morning, when the sun riseth, even a morning without clouds; as the tender grass springing out of the earth by clear shining after rain.

Showers of blessing

As we thank God for his gifts of speaking and leading on blessed Patrick, let's also pray for these gifts for ourselves, and for all in positions of leadership. 'May my teaching drop like the rain, my speech condense like the dew; like gentle rain on grass, like showers on new growth.' 'He that ruleth over men must be just, ruling in the fear of God. And he shall be as the light of the morning, when the sun riseth, even a morning without clouds; as the tender grass springing out of the earth by clear shining after rain.' Then in the words of the old hymn,

'There shall be showers of blessing':
this is the promise of love;
there shall be seasons refreshing,
sent from the Saviour above.
Showers of blessing,
showers of blessing we need;
mercy drops round us are falling,
but for the showers we plead.

Suggested hymns

As the deer pants for the water; As water to the thirsty; Sometimes a light surprises; There shall be showers of blessing.

St Joseph of Nazareth   19 March
Chosen to Teach
2 Sam. 7.4–16 Descendants of David; Ps. 89.26–36 David's line; Rom. 4.13–18 Abraham's descendants; Matt. 1.18–25 Joseph's dream

'When Joseph awoke from sleep, he did as the angel of the Lord commanded him; he took [Mary] as his wife.' Matthew 1.24

Joseph the Chosen

In the years before Jesus was born, there must have been thousands of people who could prove they were descendants of King David. Why did God choose Joseph, the carpenter of Nazareth, to be the father – or perhaps we should say stepfather – of Jesus the son of David? Joseph was chosen to teach the child Jesus the things he would need to know when he became a man. Not just carpentry; Joseph had to teach the child honour, manliness and moral fibre. Joseph was in charge of Jesus at least until the lad was 12, when his parents took him to Jerusalem for his bar mitzvah. By that time he would have learnt the fundamentals of the Jewish religion, and it was the father's task to begin a boy's religious education. Joseph will have taught his stepson to be proud he was a Jew, a child of

Abraham; and to wonder whether he might be the Messiah, the chosen descendant of King David.

Ancestry

Both St Matthew and St Luke in their Gospels trace the family tree of Jesus's ancestors through Joseph. This is perfectly correct, because when Joseph married Mary, he automatically adopted her child, and descent was always traced through the male line. Both Gospels trace the family tree back through King David to Abraham, the ancestor of the Jewish people – and St Luke continued the tree all the way back to Adam, the ancestor of everybody. Yet Jesus, like Joseph, was, in fact, a Jew, descended from Abraham, so that made him one of the Chosen People. When a non-Jew hears a Jew talking about the Chosen People, it sounds racist, as though they were claiming to be better than everybody else. To most Jews, it doesn't feel like that at all – being chosen seems to have brought them nothing but trouble! To decide this, we must ask, what were the Chosen People chosen *for?* I suggest that, like Joseph, they were chosen to teach.

Teaching the world about God

God didn't choose the Jews because they were better than anybody else, but because they had nothing. Slaves in Egypt, they had no homeland, no territorial deity, no king and no future. So they, alone of all the nations in the world, knew that they were totally dependent on God's mercy. Other nations believed there were different gods for different territories; the children of Israel were the first to conclude there was only one God for the whole world. The gods of the nations could be played off against each other, and bribed with sacrifices; at Mount Sinai the Israelites discovered that having one God means you have to obey that God, whether you like it or not. The Lord God made a covenant with his Chosen People – they would obey his laws and he would care for them. Theirs was the first religion to expect moral behaviour from its adherents. Being the Chosen People meant their faith was what we call ethical monotheism – that there is one God, who loves me and wants me to love him, and to love my neighbours as myself. But they weren't to sit complacently on this new and radical faith; they were to share it with others. The Chosen People were chosen to teach.

Teaching their children

This couldn't happen overnight – it would take generations. So to begin with, each generation had to pass down what they had learnt about God to the next generation. The great Jewish cultural tradition was, at its heart, a way of teaching your children that God loves us, wants us to love him, and to be loving to everybody we meet. Then to pass on this news to their children in turn, and to the other nations of the earth as quickly as they could, for God's sake. But the Jews in the time of Joseph and Jesus had hardly started on this second part of their call, the task of evangelism.

What Joseph taught Jesus

This is what Joseph was called to do; to teach his son to be a man, a descendant of Adam; a Jew, a descendant of Abraham; and to rule in love over the whole world as a Son of David. Jesus taught his disciples what his stepfather taught him: ethical monotheism, a religion of universal love; and to spread it to all the other nations on earth. That's what the early missionaries taught our ancestors in this country. That's what you and I were chosen by God for, as Joseph was: to love God and teach God's love to our children and to every other nation on the earth.

Suggested hymns

As Joseph was a-walking, he heard an angel sing; Good Joseph had a garden; Joseph dearest, Joseph mine; Joseph was an old man.

Annunciation of our Lord to the Blessed Virgin Mary 26 March (transferred)

Miracles Isa. 7.10–14 The sign of Immanuel; Ps. 40.5–11 I love to do your will; Heb. 10.4–10 I have come to do your will; Luke 1.26–38 The angel's message

> *'Mary said to the angel, "How can this be, since I am a virgin?"'* Luke 1.34

Virgin birth

The angel appeared to Mary and told her she was going to have a baby. 'How can this be,' asked Mary, 'since I am a virgin?' A very proper and sensible question. Even before the development of modern science, everyone knew that a woman had never conceived a child in her womb until after she'd made love with a man. So if Mary did so, it must be a miracle.

Miracles

But what is a miracle? Most people today would answer that it's when something happens that breaks the laws of nature. But in New Testament times they knew nothing about the laws of nature. It's a mistake to imagine that people living in a different age thought in the same terms as we do today. Miracle simply means something that makes you marvel, or 'admire' – it's a related word – the person who does it. In this sense we say today that a computer is 'a miracle of modern science'. There's nothing unscientific about it, but it amazes us to see how wonderfully it works.

Laws

So a better question, when we say that a miracle is an event that breaks the laws of nature, would be to ask, what do you mean by the laws of nature? Science grew out of a belief that the universe is rational and orderly. In other words, events follow upon each other's heels as cause and effect. But we can't be sure of that. All we can say is that I've observed this particular combination of circumstances many times, and the outcome's always been like this. Yet all our laws are open to modification, and most of them have been altered from time to time, in very particular circumstances. Sir Isaac Newton, when the apple fell out of the tree onto his head, made the inspired suggestion that there's a force of attraction between any two bodies proportional to the product of their masses and inversely proportional to the square of their distance apart. Yet Einstein showed that in the case of large bodies travelling at high speed, this isn't quite true, and Newton's Law of Gravity had to be modified. There may be exceptions to other laws, too, in certain circumstances which we haven't yet observed. The law that every child has two parents is generally true, but we have only once observed the case in which that child is the Son of God, so how can we be sure that the same rules apply in those exceptional circumstances?

Probability

All our scientific laws should really be expressed in terms of probability. 'When A and B happen, the chances are 999 to 1 that the result will be C.' That sort of thing. In his presidential address to the British Association for the Advancement of Science in 1960, Sir George Thomson, the Nobel Prize-winning physicist, said,

> We have been forced, some of us very unwillingly, to believe that, at bottom, the laws of physics are not statements of what *must* happen, but of the relative chances of a variety of alternatives.

God's laws

There's nothing unscientific, then, in holding that the laws of science are a description of how God normally behaves, and miracles, like that of the Virgin Birth, are descriptions of how God behaves in exceptional circumstances. Metropolitan Anthony of Sourozh wrote: 'A miracle is not the breaking of the laws of the fallen world. It is the re-establishment of the laws of the kingdom.' Science is very useful for predicting what will probably happen, but no use at all at telling us what can't possibly happen in any circumstances.

Praying for a miracle

When the angel foretold that Mary would have a baby, she replied, 'How can this be?' Gabriel's response was that nothing is impossible for God. In which case, we're right to pray for miracles in our own lives. The answer may not be anything unscientific; simply something happening that's statistically improbable, but still possible. Or the coincidence of two relatively unlikely events happening at the same time. God's very reluctant to bend the laws of nature, because that would leave us feeling insecure in an unpredictable world. Neither can we have miracles on demand, because to give us what we ask for might prevent God giving somebody else what they need, when their need is greater. Nevertheless, we should pray in faith, as Mary did, and then be open to the probability that something very unexpected will happen, for with God, all things are possible.

Suggested hymns

God moves in a mysterious way; Her virgin eyes saw God incarnate born; Tell out, my soul, the greatness of the Lord; The angel Gabriel from heaven came.

St George, Martyr, Patron of England c. 304
23 April
Shakespeare
1 Macc. 2.59–64 Be courageous, *or* Rev. 12.7–12 Michael fights the dragon; Ps. 126 Restore our fortunes; 2 Tim. 2.3–13 A soldier of Christ; John 15.18–21 They will persecute you

> *'Share in suffering like a good soldier of Christ Jesus.'* 2 Timothy 2.3

George the soldier

St George is the patron saint of England. He is an odd choice to make; he wasn't English, but then St Andrew wasn't Scottish and St Patrick wasn't Irish. Yet the Crusaders brought the legend of St George, who rescued the maiden from the evil dragon, back from the Middle East as a model of manly virtue, and he's been held up as a symbol of Englishness ever since. Though in these days when we're trying to live at peace with our Muslim neighbours, we mustn't lay too much stress on the Crusaders. And we get embarrassed when rowdy football supporters wrap themselves in the flag of St George, or paint their faces with his cross. We feel this is dishonouring to our patron saint and to the nation.

Shakespeare

Yet there's another reason for celebrating Englishness on the 23rd of April, and that is that it's Shakespeare's birthday. William Shakespeare, the English playwright, who in the reign of Queen Elizabeth I contributed more to the growth and beauty of the English language than anyone else until in King James's reign it reached its flowering in the Authorized Version of the Bible.

Was it he?

Now I know that for centuries there have been disputes as to whether the plays of Shakespeare could possibly have been written by the William Shakespeare who was born in Stratford-upon-Avon on the 23rd April in 1564. Some say that he can't possibly have had the education that it required to write the plays, or the experience of travel, or the experience of life. As a comedian of a past generation remarked, who cares whether the plays were written by William Shakespeare or by another man of the same name? He was a hard-working actor, at the heart of a company of actors, who discussed, revised and changed the texts as they went along. There was no long tradition of professional drama at that time, yet together they created a series of plots and structures which have influenced theatre worldwide ever since. To see them performed in the round at Stratford, or at Shakespeare's Globe in London, is to understand how perfectly crafted they were for their environment. Actors can recognize Shakespeare's genius; Sir Laurence Olivier said 'Shakespeare – the nearest thing in incarnation to the eye of God.'

Language

There are 46 pages of quotations from Shakespeare in my *Dictionary of Quotations*, more than any other writer, more even than the Bible, such is his influence on our language. He also invented a whole new way of writing, in apparently effortless poetry, by catching his subject sideways on, with words that allude to the truth without actually coming straight out with it. This has influenced writers ever since, even many for whom English was not their first language and who only met Shakespeare in translation. Schiller founded the tradition of literature in German on the plays of Shakespeare. The composer Berlioz fell in love with the plays of Shakespeare and with a Shakespearean actress at the same time. Some of Verdi's greatest operas are adaptations of Shakespeare: Othello, Macbeth and Falstaff. Shakespeare is England's greatest contribution to world culture.

Religion

What was Shakespeare's attitude to religion? We can't be sure. Like many when English Protestantism had just begun he was divided in his loyalties between the new faith and the old religion of his parents' generation. He made Hamlet recognize God's providence, when he says,

> There's a divinity that shapes our ends,
> Rough-hew them how we will.

But like all good writers, Shakespeare subsumed his own views in those of the characters he was writing for, so that some sound devout and others sceptical. Yet his respect for greatness, his sympathy with weakness, and his scorn of pomposity, achieved a truly religious purpose in moulding the moral attitudes of all who take the trouble to go and see one of his plays. Othello gives us a profound insight into the nature of jealousy; Hamlet wrestles with despair; Romeo and Juliet show what happens when we allow family rivalries to override human love; and many of the characters wrestle with their consciences, pitting their duty against their desires. Shakespeare's birthday and St George's Day fall on the same day, so thank God we don't have to choose between them, to be our ideal of Englishness and our patron saint.

Suggested hymns

God, whose city's sure foundation; How bright these glorious spirits shine; Rejoice in God's saints, today and all days; When a knight won his spurs.

St Mark the Evangelist   25 April
Evangelists All

Prov. 15.28–33 Good news, *or* Acts 15.35–41 Paul rejects Mark; Ps. 119.9–16 How can young people keep their way pure?; Eph. 4.7–16 The gift of an evangelist; Mark 13.5–13 Staying power

> *'The gifts [God] gave were that some would be apostles, some prophets, some evangelists, some pastors and teachers, to equip the saints for the work of ministry, for building up the body of Christ.' Ephesians 4.11–12*

Messengers

The word 'angel' was the normal Greek word for 'a messenger'. If an army on campaign had won a notable victory, they sent a messenger to report back to headquarters – a 'carrier of good news' – literally an ev–angel–ist, or evangelist. This soon became the standard word for someone who brought to his hearers the good news about Jesus.

Strategy

St Paul's Letter to the Ephesians contains a carefully worked-out strategy for making new converts, or 'church-planting' as we should call it today. A city with a flourishing church chose a neighbouring town where few people had heard of Jesus, then sent Christians, one after another, each with a different task to do. The first to arrive were the 'apostles' – the word simply means 'people who are sent'. They would work for a while in the target area, finding out who was eager to hear more about Jesus. Then the apostle would move on elsewhere, having first sent for a prophet, a proclaimer, who could speak boldly to groups or even crowds, warning them of what was wrong with their society, and God's judgement on their sins. But the prophets were quickly followed by the evangelists, who brought the news about Jesus. The townsfolk weren't left to feel guilty for long, because the evangelist brought them the good news of forgiveness, offered by Jesus to all who'd repent. People were so relieved by the good news the evangelists brought that all wanted to become followers of Jesus the Christ, or Christians. The evangelists baptized them, but they needed others, pastors and teachers, who would stay there to build up the new converts in the faith, and explain to them what they should believe, while the apostles, prophets and evangelists travelled on to plant churches in new cities. The task of the pastors and teachers was 'to equip the saints for the work of ministry, for building up the body of Christ'. In other words, it was the ordinary church members who were responsible for making new converts and building up the Church. So the Church grew by leaps and bounds, as it does in parts of Africa, China and America today.

Mark

Today is St Mark's day. I wonder where he fitted into all this. It's just a guess, but he might have been one of the travelling evangelists, following in the steps of the apostle Paul to bring the good news of God's love to those who were feeling thoroughly depressed. Yet Mark soon realized that all these different tasks were too difficult for recent converts, and even experienced Christians need a manual of instruction. So he set about writing one, and he gave it a unique title. Mark's book is named in the very first verse as 'The beginning of the good news of Jesus Christ, the Son of God'. And the Old English word for Good News is 'Gospel'. We call Mark an evangelist because he wrote a Gospel, and invented the name for the book. My suggestion, however, which nobody can possibly prove, is that he was an evangelist before he ever started writing, because he spoke the Good News about the life of Jesus to the people who had been stirred up by St Paul's preaching, on their way towards becoming Christians.

Evangelists all

That's something we can all do. Anyone can tell people who are interested about the life of Jesus. I can. You can. We'll need to refer regularly to the written crib which St Mark so helpfully prepared. But we can tell the story of Jesus and his love in our own words, and though our tongues may stumble, it will be all the more convincing because it comes from the heart. We are evangelists all. Not everyone can write a book about Jesus, but anyone can talk about him, with a little bit of help from our friend the Holy Spirit. Not that everyone is given the gift of evangelism, as Mark was, because we may be called to something else; but everyone's got some part to play in the process. Preachers don't make converts, they just start the process, and God calls others to take over from them. Listen again: 'The gifts [God] gave were that some would be apostles, some prophets, some evangelists, some pastors and teachers, to equip the saints for the work of ministry, for building up the body of Christ.' Everyone's got a job to do – where do you fit in?

Suggested hymns

Break thou the bread of life; Disposer supreme, and Judge of the earth; Lord, thy word abideth; We have a Gospel to proclaim.

SS Philip and James, Apostles 1 May
Followers of the Way

Isa. 30.15–21 This is the way; Ps. 119.1–8 The way of the Lord;
Eph. 1.3–10 The mystery of forgiveness; John 14.1–14 I am the
way

> *'Happy are those whose way is blameless . . . who also do no*
> *wrong, but walk in his ways . . . O that my ways may be steadfast*
> *in keeping your statutes!' Psalm 119.1–5*

The new religion

What was the first name for Christianity? It wasn't called a religion,
or a belief system. It wasn't a denomination, or a new philosophy. When Jesus was alive, his friends could be called followers,
or disciples of Jesus. Disciple's a Latin word for somebody who is
taught by Jesus, or 'disciplined'. It applied to all his followers, not
just those closest to him, who were called, at first, the Twelve, and
later were called apostles or missionaries. In Antioch the majority
of believers spoke Greek as their common language, so they came
to be called by the Greek word 'Christians'. But long before that,
when Saul of Tarsus went to persecute the disciples in Damascus,
they were called *'followers of the Way'*. He asked the High Priest
for letters to the synagogues at Damascus, 'so that if he found any
who belonged to the Way, men or women, he might bring them
bound to Jerusalem'.

Followers of the Way

'Followers of the Way'. I like that. It implies that Christians are
exploring and developing their faith as they go along. Jesus said,
'I am the way, and the truth, and the life. No one comes to the
Father except through me . . . Philip said to him, "Lord, show us
the Father, and we will be satisfied." Jesus replied, "Whoever has
seen me has seen the Father."' Jesus is the way leading to God,
and if we're followers of Jesus, we shall end up meeting our loving
heavenly Father. Jesus is the starting point, our guide in life, and he
will meet us there at our destination.

Apollos

Apollos was a Greek-speaking Jew, educated at the famous library in Alexandria, who had learnt a little about Jesus – 'He had been instructed in the Way of the Lord; and he spoke with burning enthusiasm and taught accurately the things concerning Jesus, though he knew only the baptism of John ... when Priscilla and Aquila heard him, they took him aside and explained the Way of God to him more accurately.' In the synagogue at Corinth some Jews 'stubbornly refused to believe and spoke evil of the Way before the congregation', so Paul left the synagogue and gave lunchtime lectures in 'the lecture hall of Tyrannus'. The riot in Ephesus, when Paul nearly died, is modestly described as 'no little disturbance ... concerning the Way'. Paul explained to a Tribune who'd arrested him: 'I persecuted this Way up to the point of death by binding both men and women and putting them in prison' ... and to the Governor Felix: 'I admit to you, that according to the Way, which they call a sect, I worship the God of our ancestors.' But Felix, who was rather well informed about the Way, adjourned the hearing. So throughout the Acts of the Apostles, Christianity is known as 'the Way', and Christians are 'followers of the Way'. And that includes you and me.

Daoism

When the first westerners arrived in China, they found three great philosophies, Buddhism, Confucianism and Daoism. Often pronounced Tay-oh-ism, but properly Dow-ism, this last takes its name from the Chinese word Dao, meaning 'the way'. Christians thought at first that this might be a link with Christianity, 'The Way of God'. Gautama Buddha had nothing to say about God, and taught detachment, overcoming desire. Yet Chinese Buddhism absorbed the worship of all the old Chinese gods. Confucius was only concerned with right relationships in the family and in the nation, though his teachings were organized rigidly by the Mandarins. Daoism, too, was an atheistic philosophy, teaching the way to a good life through harmony between the individual and the natural world. But it acquired a system of shamanistic beliefs. Each of these philosophies could have been harmonized with Christianity, but they became so associated with pagan gods that the attempt was abandoned.

The Way

For Christianity is the true 'Way of Life' – the way to live, the way that leads to eternal life. Self-denial, abandonment of selfish desire, leads to union with God. In the family we learn how to tolerate and forgive, which leads to right governance in the state. Meditation on the world of nature leads to mystical union with the Creator. St Philip learnt that Jesus is the way, the truth and the life. Jesus is the Way for philosophers and activists, for East and West, for yesterday, today and for ever.

Suggested hymns

In Christ there is no East or West; Let me have my way among you, do not strive; They shall come from the East, they shall come from the West; Thou art the way – by thee alone.

St Matthias the Apostle   14 May
Promotion

Isa. 22.15–25 Eliakim replaces Shebna; Ps. 15 Who shall dwell in your house?; Acts 1.15–26 Mathias replaces Judas (*if the Acts reading is used instead of the Old Testament reading, the New Testament reading is* 1 Cor. 4.1–7 Stewards of God's mysteries); John 15.9–17 I have appointed you

> *'[Jesus said,] "You did not choose me but I chose you. And I appointed you to go and bear fruit, fruit that will last."' John 15.16*

Ambition

It's good to be ambitious, wanting to climb to the top of the tree. It's good to be confident in your God-given abilities, and to put them to good use. It's good to want to give your family a comfortable standard of living. Promotion in your job is the right thing to aim for. But overweening ambition is the very devil. Jesus's Board of Directors had seen enough of that. The Twelve knew they would never be top-dog in the kingdom of God, that job was obviously reserved for the boss himself. But there was plenty of scrabbling for position among the various posts of Deputy Director, Assistant Director, Deputy-Assistant, Assistant-Deputy, and Deputy-Assistant to the Deputy-Assistant Director, and each of them was determined to get a foot on the ladder somewhere! 'Let my brother and me sit, one on your right and the other on your left in your kingdom.' So Jesus washed their feet, an acted parable to show them that anyone holding a senior position has to become the slave of all. They weren't too keen on that job description.

Vacancy

Then there was a vacancy on the Board. Never mind that it came about by the unfortunate suicide of the deluded Judas Iscariot. It meant that a whole lot of new people could start competing for the upper echelons of kingdom leadership. That would certainly bring a new set of rivalries and cut-throat competition. The ambitious could either fawn on Simon Peter, who seemed to be top-dog now that Jesus had died. Or they could call for an election, and then try their hand at rabble-rousing so that they got more votes than anybody else. With a little bit of cash slipped into the right pockets.

Peter's dilemma

What was poor Peter to do? He could cut through the squabbling and make an appointment himself. But whoever he chose, their rivals would be furious, and he'd find himself presiding over a house divided against itself. Or he could call an election, with all the arguing that that would bring, the arrogance of whoever won, and the wrath of whoever was passed over. So he did neither of these. He came up with a much more cunning plan. First he listed the qualifications that any applicant would need on their curriculum vitae. 'One of the men who have accompanied us during all the time that the Lord Jesus went in and out among us, beginning from the baptism of John until the day when he was taken up from us – one of these must become a witness with us to his resurrection.' That would winkle out the upstarts and the Johnny-come-latelys, together with the cowards who had ducked out of the limelight after the crucifixion. In fact it narrowed the shortlist down to two, Joseph Barsabbas and Matthias. Then they held a most unusual form of election, in which there was only one voter – God!

Casting lots

They called it 'casting lots' – what you and I know as a lottery – pure chance. They took a small, flat stick, and wrote the name of one candidate on one side and the name of the other on the other side. Then they prayed, and asked God to control which way up it should land when they tossed it into the air, like spinning a coin. You see, for the Christian, there's no such thing as chance, because God's in control all the time. Matthias's name came out on top, and he won the coveted post among the Twelve. Thereby, he probably signed his own death-warrant – like most of the apostles, he was martyred, the tradition says, perhaps in Ethiopia.

The loser

What about the loser in this one-vote election? We never hear another cheep out of Joseph Barsabbas. It's not surprising. As St Peter had worked out, if your rival's appointed by God himself, there's nobody you can complain to that the vote was rigged. Before he died, Jesus said to his apostles, 'You did not choose me but I chose you. And I appointed you to go and bear fruit, fruit that will last . . .' Remember that, if ever you're hungry for promotion. If you don't get the job, it may be because God didn't want you to. It may even be because God's got another job for you up his sleeve, for which God knows you have all the talents it needs. There are no coincidences when you give God the vote.

Suggested hymns

Jesus, take me as I am; O thou who camest from above; Strengthen for service, Lord, the hands; Thy way, not mine, O Lord.

Visit of the Blessed Virgin Mary to Elizabeth
31 May
Three Wise Women
Zeph. 3.14–18 Sing, daughter Zion; Ps. 113 Making her a joyous mother; Rom. 12.9–16 Hospitality; Luke 1.39–49 [50–56] Magnificat

'*Mary set out and went with haste to a Judean town in the hill country, where she entered the house of Zechariah and greeted Elizabeth.' Luke 1.39–40*

Can women be saved?

Osbert Lancaster wrote about a Vicar of St John's Church, Notting Hill, who announced to his predominantly female congregation in the early 1900s that it had been revealed to him that there were no women in heaven! 'Women', he said, 'are incapable of salvation.' Probably the congregation took as little notice of what he said then as they did of any of his other sermons! After all, misogyny was common among Christians for centuries. Yet Jesus treated Mary Magdalene and the other women who shared in his ministry with respect as equal to the men. St Paul said that in Christ there's neither male nor female, and he had a female colleague, Junia, whom he described as 'prominent among the apostles'. But after that, church leaders mainly used women as useful servants or enclosed nuns.

Three wise women

But that's not how it is in the Bible. The Old Testament's full of powerful women like Sarah, Rebecca and Rachel, not to mention Jael and Esther. Yet at Christmastime, we hear a lot about the Three Wise Men. What about the Three Wise Women in the Christmas story? As well as honouring the Magi, why shouldn't we reserve a bit of respect for Mary, Elizabeth and Anna? Anna the Prophetess, an elderly widow, came into the Temple when baby Jesus was being presented by his parents to God. Then she 'began to praise God and to speak about the child to all who were looking for the redemption of Jerusalem'. We commemorate Anna at the Feast of the Presentation of Christ in the Temple, or Candlemas. Yet she's almost ignored in the Gospels, and totally absent from the Candlemas hymns. Today we think about the other two wise women, Mary and Elizabeth.

Elizabeth

Elizabeth was the mother of John the Baptist. Matthew and Mark give John a prominent place at the beginning of Jesus's ministry; St Luke begins his Gospel not with the birth of Jesus, but with the story of how John the Baptist came to be born to Zechariah and Elizabeth. When the angel Gabriel told Mary she was going to have a baby, he added: 'Your relative Elizabeth in her old age has also conceived a son; and this is the sixth month for her who was said to be barren. For nothing will be impossible with God.'

Elizabeth's shame

Elizabeth knew what it was like when people laugh at you behind your back. In those days before social security, every couple needed children to support them when they grew too old to earn their own living. A wife's prime duty was to produce a son, who would take over as the principal wage-earner in the family and care for his aged parents. Elizabeth was barren. So she'd failed in the one thing that was expected of her. The disgrace of it! Then, discovering she was pregnant, she cried out, 'This is what the Lord has done for me when he looked favourably on me and took away the disgrace I have endured among my people.' Yet she was an old woman. So the neighbours still covered their mouths as they giggled and pointed. Whatever could she have been up to? Her relations would be ashamed to have anything to do with her after this. That was until her cousin Mary honoured her with a visit.

Mary's shame

Yet Mary knew shame, too. The child in her womb had been conceived out of wedlock – indeed she wasn't married until after the baby was born. Being an unmarried mother, which is now hardly noticed, was then a deep disgrace. So it was to give her own morale a boost, as much as to encourage Elizabeth, that Mary trekked in the early months of her pregnancy all the way to the Judean hill-village where Elizabeth lived. Together, by praising the God who exalts the humble and meek, they could gather the courage to face their neighbours, and face down those who sneered at them.

Women's shame

They say the English are good at being dignified in defeat because they have so much experience of being defeated at cricket! Perhaps women are specially qualified to ignore the taunts of their neighbours because they have so much experience of being ignored by men? Yes, I'm being deliberately controversial. But we can all learn from the Three Wise Women of the nativity story that it's possible to keep your dignity, even when all the other things you take pride in are denied to you.

Suggested hymns

Her virgin eyes saw God incarnate born; Tell out, my soul, the greatness of the Lord; The great forerunner of the morn; Virgin-born, we bow before thee.

Day of Thanksgiving for the Institution of Holy Communion (Corpus Christi) 7 June
Mysterious Meals

Gen. 14.18–20 Melchizedek brought bread and wine; Ps. 116.10–17 The cup of salvation; 1 Cor. 11.23–26 The Last Supper; John 6.51–58 Living bread

> *'When many of his disciples heard it, they said, "This teaching is difficult; who can accept it?"' John 6.60*

Incomprehensible

Jesus said, 'Those who eat my flesh and drink my blood have eternal life, and I will raise them up on the last day; for my flesh is true food and my blood is true drink.' Many of his disciples exclaimed, 'This is a difficult teaching; who can take it in?' It's hard enough for us, with hindsight, to understand what Jesus meant; what must it have been like to hear his words for the first time? They must have found them quite incomprehensible.

Sacrifices

Yet in one way it was easier for them, because Jesus was using metaphors from events they had shared in, which are quite outside our experience today. One of these was the use of animal sacrifices in worship. People of all religions, when they wanted to thank God for something, or celebrate something, or ask God for a favour, instinctively rounded up an animal from their flock, tied it up and brought it to their temple. There they'd hand it to the priest, who would deftly cut its throat, collect the blood in a bowl, and pour it over the altar as God's portion. They would keep back some of the meat for the priests to eat or sell, as their 'perk'. The rest of the flesh would be dealt with in one of two ways. Either they would burn all of it on the altar-fire, so that their god could enjoy the smell. Or, in most cases, they'd burn a little, and hand the rest back to the worshippers, who would cook it and eat it then and there in the temple.

Meaning

What did they think they meant by this? Sacrifice wasn't a bribe – all the god got was the blood and the smell, a pretty inadequate back-hander. The first thing to remember is that the blood represented the life of the animal – indeed, it *was* the life, for without blood the animal was dead. To sacrifice was to offer a life to God. Part of the ritual was when the worshippers laid their hands on the head of the animal, to identify themselves with it, so that they could say that they were offering their own lives as a sacrifice to God. So Jesus meant us to understand that when we eat bread and drink wine in memory of him, we're identifying the sacrifice of our own lives in union with his sacrifice on the cross. Then we're taking his life into us as we eat and drink.

Internalizing

This was a thought already familiar to the temple worshippers of old. As they offered the animal to the god and then shared it with him, their god was considered to be their guest at the feast. Moreover, the god was considered to have entered into the food, so that when they ate it the god entered into them. This, surely, is what Jesus meant, when he said, 'Those who eat my flesh and drink my blood abide in me, and I in them.' When we take Communion, we 'internalize' the life of Jesus, and Jesus becomes a part of us, in our thinking and doing. Then Jesus loves other people *through us*, using us as his instruments or tools.

Mysteries

This thinking was demonstrated graphically in what were called the mystery religions. The 'dying' of the plants in winter, and the return of new life in the spring, were symbolized in the death of their god, and his descent into Hades, followed by his rising to new life. These mythical events were acted out in the rituals of these cults. The worshippers in the temples of the mystery religions might not *understand* what they were doing, but they *felt* in their hearts that they'd been caught up in something tremendous, and filled with the new life that their god died to bring to them. Many Christians had worshipped in the temples of Hermes, Isis, Osiris or Mithras, where these ceremonies were held, before they converted. So they'll easily have understood that every Holy Communion is a re-enactment of the death and rising of Jesus, a Passion play, in which the life and power of the Saviour became a part of them when they ate and drank. The ideas were sufficiently widespread in those days that Jesus may have meant us to understand this mysterious meal in those terms when he said, 'Just as the living Father sent me, and I live because of the Father, so whoever eats me will live because of me.' What a depth of different meanings!

Suggested hymns

All for Jesus; Bread of heaven, on thee we feed; Broken for me; Thee we adore, O hidden Saviour, thee.

St Barnabas the Apostle   11 June
David Livingstone
Job 29.11–16 Like one who comforts; Ps. 112 Generous; Acts 11.19–30 Barnabas encourages Saul (*if the Acts reading is used instead of the Old Testament reading, the New Testament reading is* Gal. 2.1–10 Barnabas and me); John 15.12–17 Love one another

> *'Now those who were scattered because of the persecution . . . spoke the word to no one except Jews. But among them were some men . . . who, on coming to Antioch, spoke to the Hellenists also, proclaiming the Lord Jesus. The hand of the Lord was with them, and a great number became believers and turned to the Lord . . . and they sent Barnabas to Antioch.' Acts 11.19–22*

Livingstone

David Livingstone was born in 1813 in Scotland, and educated himself while working in a cotton factory. He decided to dedicate his life to the relief of human suffering, and trained to be a doctor. He went to what's now called Botswana with the London Missionary Society, gaining the respect of the African people by his medical work and by opening schools. There were advanced civilizations in parts of Africa, but there's nothing racist in facing the fact that over great swathes of the continent most people were subject to hunger and fear. Livingstone cared passionately about their suffering, and decided that the only solution was to persuade people from other

326

nations to invest in improving their conditions. Human nature being the same all over the world, the only reason they were likely to do this on a big scale was if they could earn themselves a living by doing so – it was essential, he said, to open the continent to commerce. He explored dangerous terrain, trying to find safe routes for the merchants to travel, but reported that there were many warring tribes, who would think nothing of killing anyone who came to help them. The chiefs sold their captured enemies to Arab slave-dealers, who marched them to the coast in irons – Livingstone's report on this trade made a major contribution to the abolition of slavery. So the Europeans sold trade-goods which enabled the Africans to rise out of their poverty, in return for labour and raw materials. They built roads and railways to carry this trade in and out, and appealed to their governments at home to send soldiers to defend their goods from marauders. So colonial expansion began – not what Livingstone had wanted, but the inevitable result of his appeal to open Africa to commerce. There was much cruelty on both sides, so David Livingstone made a famous speech in Cambridge, calling for missionaries to travel to Africa, bringing healing, education, and an understanding of right and wrong.

Horizons

Most people in every country have their horizons bounded by their nation's boundaries. Today television brings us images of people suffering in other parts of the world, but few viewers identify with them enough to go and help them. In Livingstone's day none of the European newspapers reported the pain of Africa. Only the missionaries knew about it and tried to do something to alleviate it. They weren't all saints, and some of them shared the patronizing attitude towards foreigners of the people at home. Yet their hearts were in the right place; they wanted to help, and in most respects they brought many blessings. The unfortunate connection between mission and colonialism, however, distorted the reputation of the missionary societies, so that today you hardly dare to mention the word missionary. Yet through their labours the gospel has taken root in many lands, and the people of those countries are now acting as missionaries to their neighbours.

Barnabas

All of this forms an interesting parallel with the career of Barnabas the apostle. Barnabas wasn't one of the so-called 'Twelve apostles'. The word 'apostle' is Greek for 'missionary'. Barnabas was a Jew, and was proud of his nation and the moral standards revealed to them by God. For most Jews, this went with a contempt for non-Jews, 'the lesser breeds without the law', and a determination to have nothing to do with them. Except, of course, in the way of business, to make money out of them. Barnabas was different. In Antioch, Christians met Greek-speaking non-Jews, and, if that's what the word 'Hellenists' means, some of them had become Christians. So they sent for Barnabas – that rare bird, a Jew who understood foreigners and could talk to them. So the Jewish foreign missions began, and eventually Barnabas handed over the leadership to his friend Paul. But if he hadn't enlarged his horizons, realizing that suffering and ignorance are the same wherever they are found, you and I would still be suffering from violence and ignorance, which isn't pleasant, in whatever continent you live. Caring for your neighbours at home must go hand in hand with sharing the gospel with those overseas. Let's pray for more people with the wide horizons that fired Barnabas to begin his mission.

Suggested hymns

Captains of the saintly band; God is working his purpose out; God, whose city's sure foundation; One shall tell another.

The Birth of St John the Baptist   24 June
(See page 174.)

SS Peter and Paul, Apostles   29 June
Foot-and-mouth Disease
Zech. 4.1–6a, 10b–14 Two anointed ones; Ps. 125 Stand fast for ever; Acts 12.1–11 Peter released from prison (*if the Acts reading is used instead of the Old Testament reading, the New Testament reading is* 2 Tim. 4.6–8, 17–18 Poured out); Matt. 16.13–19 Peter recognizes the Messiah

or for Peter alone: Ezek. 3.22–27 Preaching to his own; Ps. 125; Acts 12.1–11 (*if the Acts reading is used instead of the Old Testament reading, the New Testament reading is* 1 Peter 2.19–25 Suffering for God); Matt. 16.13–19

> '[Jesus] turned and said to Peter, "Get behind me, Satan!"' Matthew 16.23

Foot-and-mouth disease

Simon Peter was a blunderer. In the words of the old joke, 'He had foot-and-mouth disease: whenever he opened his mouth, he put his foot in it.' Or as an American humorist put it, 'He only opened his mouth to change feet.' Peter was always saying the wrong thing.

The transfiguration

For instance, one day Jesus took Peter and James and John up a high mountain. The Gospels tell us that Jesus 'was transfigured before them, and his face shone like the sun, and his clothes became dazzling white. Suddenly there appeared to them Moses and Elijah, talking with him.' What would you have expected the privileged three to say? Something like, 'What's happening to you, Master? Why do you look like that? Who are those men, and why are they here?' That's what intelligent people would have said. But what did Peter say? 'Lord, it is good for us to be here; if you wish, I will make three dwellings here, one for you, one for Moses, and one for Elijah.' Clang! If he meant solidly built houses, where was he going to get the building materials on top of a mountain, and however long would it take him? The word he used, however, usually means a tent, or the sort of lean-to shelter of branches that farm workers make for themselves in the fields when they've no time to go home at harvest time. Obviously, Peter's mind was wandering far, far away from the business in hand. Poor old Peter; when you should have been thinking about the glory of Jesus, that was not a clever thing to say.

Caesarea Philippi

On another day, Jesus was walking with his disciples among the villages around Caesarea Philippi, a Roman city in the extreme north of Israel. As they walked, Jesus asked his disciples, 'Who do people say that I am?' They answered, 'Some say you are John the Baptist come back to life; others say you're Elijah come back to earth; and yet others say one of the prophets of old has returned.' Jesus then asked them the crunch question, 'But who do *you* say I am?' Peter got it right, this time – to begin with. 'I think you're the Messiah,' he said. Probably Peter meant that Jesus would raise an army to drive every Roman off the Jewish land. But Jesus began to teach them that he would have to suffer greatly, and be killed. Peter was deeply shocked, and pulling Jesus to one side, out of earshot of the others, he began to give him a right telling off. A suffering Messiah? What a shocking idea! Yet Jesus said that Peter was tempting him to evade his destiny, and take the easy way out. The Hebrew word for 'tempter' is 'the Satan', and Peter was behaving like a real devil. Clang again!

The servant girl

Finally, at the Last Supper, Peter promised that he would always be faithful to Jesus. Then, when Jesus was on trial, a chit of a girl teased Peter that he was a friend of Jesus. Peter was so scared that he, too, would be arrested, that he told the girl that he had never met the man. In fact he denied Jesus three times. Triple clang! It seemed like a real case of foot-and-mouth – Peter could never get it right.

The apostle

And yet Jesus forgave Peter, and told him to 'feed my sheep'. He became an apostle, or missionary, and carried the faith all the way to Rome, the most important city in the world at the time. And who do you think reported on Peter's early failures? There are details in the account that only Jesus and Peter could have known; so Peter must have told these stories against himself. He had become humble enough to admit his inadequacy. It was entirely by God's mercy, he must have told people, that he'd become a church leader; the credit was God's, not his. So you see, there's hope for us too. There have been times when I too felt as though every time I opened my mouth I put my foot in it. Maybe you have. But it's through unpromising bunglers like Peter and us, who admit our mistakes, that God's mercy becomes known.

Disposer supreme and judge of the earth; The Church's one foundation; Thou art the Christ, O Lord; 'Tis good, Lord, to be here.

St Thomas the Apostle   3 July
Sharing Doubts?

Hab. 2.1–4 The righteous live by faith; Ps. 31.1–6 I trust in
the Lord; Eph. 2.19–22 The foundation of the apostles; John
20.24–29 Doubting Thomas is convinced

> *'Unless I see the mark of the nails in his hands, and put my finger
> in the mark of the nails and my hand in his side, I will not believe.'*
> *John 20.25*

Ticking Boxes

A well-known musician was being interviewed. He said that he
enjoyed music with Christian words, but he called himself an
agnostic, because, he said, 'I can't tick all the boxes to say that I'm
a believer.' Now that was very sad, because it's a misunderstanding
of what agnosticism is, and what faith really means.

Agnosticism

'Agnostic' means 'not knowable'. The word was coined by T. H.
Huxley in 1869 to describe his belief that all knowledge of a Divine
Being is in principle and in practice totally impossible. In other
words, there may be a God or there may not be, but even if there
is, we can never find out anything about him. This is opposed to
religion, but it's also opposed to atheism – the atheist is absolutely
certain that God doesn't exist. Yet many people – like, I suspect,
the musician I've mentioned – aren't prepared to be so extreme.
They think there might be a God, but his existence hasn't yet been
proved to their satisfaction. In the public opinion poll, they don't
answer yes and they don't answer no; they haven't made up their
minds yet, and they think calling themselves agnostics counts as a
don't know vote.

Faith

Now there are many things in life that we can't prove. On some of them you can keep an open mind, but on others you need to come to a decision quickly. You can't prove that your partner loves you; you can't prove that honesty is the best policy; but on the evidence you have, the probability is that these things are true. So you weigh up the probability, plump for the most likely alternative, and act on it. This is called 'the leap of faith' – it's something every lover does when they decide on marriage. Faith doesn't mean certainty; faith is the courage to live with uncertainty. It's not a question of ticking boxes; it's a relationship of trust in the unseen.

Thomas

Doubting Thomas started as an agnostic. He thought it was impossible that Jesus, who had died, was now alive, so he kept apart from the other apostles. Yet when he agreed to experiment, he was overwhelmingly convinced by the evidence of his senses, and hailed Jesus as 'My Lord and my God'. That's the position taken by every believing Christian. We don't swallow a package of unlikely propositions, we don't tick boxes and say, 'I believe the whole of theology.' Instead we say, I trust Jesus, and I'm content to remain agnostic on the rest.

Creeds

The Christian Creeds, which we recite in church, proclaim the outline of what Christians have believed down the centuries. If you have problems with one of the doctrines, that doesn't mean you can't be a Christian. You simply express solidarity with your fellow Christians, pray to Jesus, and make sure the centre holds. On the edges of the faith, however, every Christian is entitled to say, I haven't had time yet to think that through. Or even, I understand why our ancestors put it in that way, but to explain it to people today, you have to use an entirely different set of words. You can be a convinced Christian, and agnostic on many of the details, at the same time.

332

Agnostic clergy

But you might be well advised to keep your doubts to yourself. Jesus said that the punishment for disturbing the faith of the little ones who believe in him is worse than drowning with a millstone tied to your neck. So should preachers share their doubts from the pulpit? I think the answer is 'definitely not'. But that doesn't mean we don't have any. Maybe that's a disappointment to you. You look up to us as an example of faith. Many people regard us as proxies: 'I'm not a believer myself,' they say, 'but it's nice to know that there's somebody up there in the clergy house who can do the believing for me.' Now that's not fair. Moreover, a minister who is not human would be no use as an example. It's only if we are having the same struggle with our doubts as you are, that you can be sure we sympathize with where you're at. Whether your minister's name is Thomas or Thomasina, we're not saints yet. We hold on to our relationship with Jesus for dear life, but we should be honoured if you tell us what beliefs you have problems with, and we'll try to work out the answers together. None of us can tick *all* the boxes.

Suggested hymns

Firmly I believe and truly; Lead, kindly light, amid th'encircling gloom; Thine be the glory; Through the night of doubt and sorrow.

St Mary Magdalene   22 July
(see Seventh Sunday after Trinity, p. 193.)

St James the Apostle   25 July
Jewish Christianity
Jer. 45.1–5 Seeking greatness; Ps. 126 Sow in tears, harvest in joy; Acts 11.27—12.2 Herod kills James (*if the Acts reading is used instead of the Old Testament reading, the New Testament reading is* 2 Cor. 4.7–15 Treasure in clay pots); Matt. 20.20–28 Seeking greatness

> *'And you, do you seek great things for yourself? Do not seek them; for I am going to bring disaster upon all flesh, says the Lord.' Jeremiah 45.5*

Sons of Zebedee

James and his brother John, the sons of Zebedee, were Galilean fishermen who left their boat to follow Jesus. But later, they and their mother – Mrs Zebedee – started pressurizing Jesus to give James and John positions of honour in his kingdom. They were still expecting the Messiah to drive out the Romans and establish an earthly kingdom in the land of Israel, with the Twelve apostles as his honoured assistants. They asked him to appoint them two thrones, one on his right hand and one on his left, in his glory. Those who would be honoured in the sort of kingdom he was going to establish, replied Jesus, would be those who could 'drink the cup that I drink, [and] be baptized with the baptism that I am baptized with'. Puzzled, the brothers said they'd do whatever was necessary to gain the honour they craved. But Jesus meant the cup of suffering, and, as we say, 'a baptism of fire'. His followers, he said, might suffer as painful a death as his. Some 14 years later, James the brother of John was beheaded by King Herod Agrippa I, as recounted in the Acts of the Apostles and by the Jewish historian Josephus. Their friends must have remembered how ambitious the brothers had been, and probably thought of the words of Jeremiah to Baruch, his ambitious secretary: 'And you, do you seek great things for yourself? Do not seek them; for I am going to bring disaster upon every living person, says the LORD.' James and John remind us that it's good to be ambitious to serve, but selfish ambition for glory is the very devil.

Church leader in Jerusalem

Both James and John were very common names in those days. So we needn't be surprised that a man called James was a leader of the church in Jerusalem, four years after James the son of Zebedee had been martyred. There was a heated argument over whether non-Jews who were converted to Christianity needed to keep the full traditional Jewish laws and customs. The church leaders met in Jerusalem to thrash it out, and when they came to a decision, this James acted as the spokesman for the whole Church. St Paul describes him as 'a pillar of the church' and 'the Lord's brother'; he could have been one of brothers of Jesus mentioned in the Gospels, although some Christians claim those were only half-brothers, sons of Joseph by a previous marriage. In either case, they opposed Jesus in his lifetime. Yet the risen Christ told Mary Magdalene to go and tell his brothers, and Paul says Christ appeared first to James, and then to the other apostles. If they became followers after the resurrection, it must have been tempting to form a dynasty of Jesus's relations to carry on his authority. And it may be this James, James the Less, whom we celebrate on the 1st of May together with St Philip.

Letter of James

There's also in the New Testament a letter from someone describing himself as 'James, a servant of God and of the Lord Jesus Christ', writing to expatriate Jews. It seems very likely that this was the leader in Jerusalem whom we have already mentioned, for it's a very Jewish letter. It praises 'the perfect law of liberty', which may mean the Law of Moses, and says we mustn't set ourselves up in judgement on the Law. James writes that 'a person is justified by works and not by faith alone', which sounds like an attack on St Paul.

Jewish Christianity

So how different *were* Jewish Christians from the rest of the Church? Later generations called them Ebionites, meaning 'the poor', and suggested that they didn't really believe that Jesus was the Son of God. The Letter of James doesn't mention Jesus, and it's possible that his fellow countrymen thought of him more as an important Jew than as the Saviour of the World. It's true that Jesus taught in a Jewish context, and observed Jewish laws and customs unless they conflicted with the law of love; it was only after his death that the universal implications of his teachings became clear. So if we learn from the first James to shun earthly ambition, then from this other James we learn that the Christian faith can be expressed through many different cultures. We must learn to respect and tolerate those with a different interpretation from our own.

Suggested hymns

For all thy saints, O Lord; O for a closer walk with God; The God of Abraham praise; Who are these, like stars appearing?

Transfiguration of our Lord   6 August
Visions and Hallucinations

Dan. 7.9–10, 13–14 The Son of Man; Ps. 97 Clouds are around him; 2 Peter 1.16–19 We saw; Luke 9.28–36 The transfiguration

'For we did not follow cleverly devised myths when we made known to you the power and coming of our Lord Jesus Christ, but we had been eyewitnesses of his majesty.' 2 Peter 1.16

Second Peter

In the New Testament there's a short letter called the Second Letter of Peter, which includes these words: 'We did not follow cleverly devised myths when we made known to you the power and coming of our Lord Jesus Christ, but we had been eyewitnesses of his majesty. For he received honour and glory from God the Father when that voice was conveyed to him by the Majestic Glory, saying, "This is my Son, my Beloved, with whom I am well pleased." We ourselves heard this voice come from heaven, while we were with him on the holy mountain.' After long debate, the early Church decided to accept the claim of this letter that it was written by St Peter, and include it in the list of books in the Bible. But it doesn't really matter who wrote it; what matters is what he says about Jesus.

Eyewitness

The disciples of Jesus certainly did see a real man walking the dusty roads of Galilee. Gradually they came to realize that he was different from other men. They called him the Messiah, the Christ, but the Messiah was expected to drive out the Roman army of occupation, and Jesus didn't do that. By his teaching, life and death, Jesus revealed the character of the God whom he referred to as 'Father', a character of love and self-sacrifice. Then on the Mount of Transfiguration they heard God's voice saying, 'This is my Son.' So they realized that the human Jesus was also the Son of God. They were 'eyewitnesses of his majesty'. How are we to interpret this?

Visions and hallucinations

I think it's perfectly legitimate to regard what happened to the disciples on the mountain as a vision. This isn't a 'private interpretation', because many great Christians down the centuries have regarded the Transfiguration in this way. It was something that happened in the minds of the disciples, as God made them aware of the inner meaning of who Jesus was. Many people have visions, and are deeply affected by them. But just as Jesus warned against 'false prophets', so we have to distinguish between true visions and hallucinations. Generally speaking, hallucinations are caused by the workings of a deranged mind, but visions are caused by some other person, living or dead, who wishes to 'appear', or make themselves seen, so as to convey an important message.

Telling the difference

It's not always easy to tell the difference. For the most part, the Church accepts visions as genuine when they fit into the character of the God of love, described by Jesus in the Gospels. Visions frequently use symbols, because there are many truths that can't be described in ordinary words. Often these will be symbols that are common in the imagery of the time, though they may seem strange to another generation. Yet it's not the symbols that are 'true' or 'untrue', but the message that they convey which we must interpret and act upon. Many visions in the Middle Ages involved appearances of the Virgin Mary or other popular saints; and even in our own day people have visions of angels. Then there are humble Christians who see, in a dream, perhaps, someone they love who has died, who wants to reassure them that their loved ones are happy in heaven. This is very different from the spiritualist medium who accepts payment for conjuring up magical messages from the dead, a procedure that is strongly condemned in the Scriptures.

Transfiguration

The transfiguration of Jesus has nothing to do with witchcraft or hallucinations. God, Moses and Elijah wanted to appear to the disciples, to tell them that Jesus was God's Son, and the fulfilment of the law and the prophets. Jesus wanted to appear to his friends in a way that would convince them that the human being they knew, and who was shortly going to die, was in fact the mighty conqueror

337

of sin and death. This is a truth that the disciples urgently needed to understand. We, too, need to know that Jesus is both human and divine. God was prepared to use any symbols that were familiar to them, to get this message across through their eyewitness account.

Suggested hymns

A Man there lived in Galilee; Lord, the light of your love is shining; The Son of God proclaim; 'Tis good, Lord, to be here.

The Blessed Virgin Mary 15 August
Greece

Isa. 61.10–11 As a bride, *or* Rev. 11.19—12.6, 10 A woman in heaven; Ps. 45.10–17 You shall have sons; Gal. 4.4–7 Born of a woman; Luke 1.46–55 Magnificat

> *'A great portent appeared in heaven: a woman clothed with the sun, with the moon under her feet, and on her head a crown of twelve stars. She was pregnant and was crying out in birthpangs, in the agony of giving birth.' Revelation 12.1–2*

Greek Festival

Imagine you are in Greece on the 15th of August. For the Greeks, this is one of the greatest celebrations of the year, second only to Easter. They call it the Feast of the Falling Asleep of the God-bearer; it's a public holiday, and many people try to return to their home town or village. On the evening before, there's a procession, probably starting in one church and walking to another, and almost everyone who isn't actually in the procession will be lining the streets. It's led by a banner with a picture of the Virgin Mary, with robed men carrying the banner, and two huge candles on either side. Then come the clergy; in a town this may be a bishop or bishops, with a double column of priests, all with full beards and wearing stove-pipe hats and a long flowing silk cloak embroidered in many colours. Then there will be musicians: maybe a choir and one or more brass bands. Then in the centre of the procession there's an icon, a painted image of the Virgin Mary, possibly carried by sailors in uniform. Above the icon there's a rack, and whenever the procession stops, young and old alike rush forward to toss ribbons across it. A canopy is carried over the icon on four poles. Next come the mayor and other civic dignitaries, and as the procession passes them, everybody else joins in behind them.

Party

The procession over, the partying begins. Most families roast a whole sheep on a spit outside their homes, and everyone joins in the festal fare. When the music starts, everyone dances. It's amazing to see a bent old woman, dressed entirely in black, leaping and pirouetting to the traditional folk tunes as though she was a girl again. On that evening, everybody joins in the celebrations and the prayers, in honour of the Virgin Mary, whom they call the *Panaghia*, or the All-holy Woman. Though it sometimes seems that what they're celebrating is, in fact, being Greek!

Community

For the Greeks have a sense of community that many other nations seem to have lost. You know where your family comes from, and you all meet once or twice a year. You belong to a Christian nation, so the faith of the community, joining in the Christian festivals, is more important than what an individual personally believes. Understandably, the Orthodox Church sees itself as the original Christian Church, founded by the apostles when they came to Greece, from which all other Christians have broken away – to them, the Pope was the first protestant! The majority of the world's Christians spoke Greek to begin with, and Greek Christians have honoured the Virgin Mary, at least since she was declared to be the God-bearer, or Mother of God, at the Council of Ephesus in 375. The Church proclaims that Mary's body was carried up to heaven after she died – or rather 'fell asleep' – so Greeks accept that as part of their identity, no matter what individuals may believe. In the West we call it the Assumption of the BVM.

Assumption

There's no doubt that many Greeks, old and young, believe that's literally true. But those with a modern education know that heaven isn't a place above the clouds – the astronauts have been up there and proved it. So those who haven't lost their faith completely accept that heaven isn't so much a place, as the spiritual state of

339

being with God in eternity. *Jesus* entered heaven on Ascension Day, and his disciples saw a vision of him being enveloped by the clouds, which symbolize the presence of God. But the doctrine of the bodily Assumption of Mary is just that, an assumption! Yet the spiritual truth is unchanged by these modern discoveries. Mary, by her obedience to God's command, and the purity of her love for her Son, was counted worthy to be in the eternal presence of the Trinity. And we, in our humble way, must strive to be worthy of it too. We belong to a Christian community, and the community as a whole believes in God and serves him. By our communal faith, we shall all, in God's mercy, be taken into that higher existence which we call heaven. The fact that different individuals use different words to express the details of what they believe can't alter that. So we, too, say 'Hail, Mary', or as the modern translations put it, 'Greetings, favoured one! The Lord is with you.' And because of your obedience, God is with *us*, too.

Suggested hymns

Her Virgin eyes saw God incarnate born; Lord of the home, your only Son; The Angel Gabriel from heaven came; The God whom earth and sea and sky.

St Bartholomew the Apostle   24 August
Where Did Bartholomew Go?

Isa. 43.8–13 My witnesses; Ps. 145.1–7 Speak of your wondrous acts; Acts 5.12–16 The apostles heal (*if the Acts reading is used instead of the Old Testament reading, the New Testament reading is* 1 Cor. 4.9–15 The shame of the apostles); Luke 22.24–30 Judging the twelve tribes

> '[Jesus said,] "I confer on you, just as my Father has conferred on me, a kingdom, so that you may eat and drink at my table in my kingdom, and you will sit on thrones judging the twelve tribes of Israel."' Luke 22.29–30

Bartholomew the Apostle

Recently an American clergyman, the Reverend Christopher Webber, set himself the task of writing a series of hymns, one for each of the so-called 'red-letter saints' days' in his prayer book. But when he reached St Bartholomew, he found there was a lack of background information. So in despair he simply wrote one verse of sardonic humour – it goes like this:

Give thanks for St Bartholomew,
Of whom we don't know much.
They say he went to India,
but didn't keep in touch!

In India

In fact all we do know is that his name appears in the list of the Twelve apostles in Mathew, Mark, Luke and Acts. The great historian of the early Church was called Eusebius. He was Bishop of Caesarea, in Palestine, in the early fourth century. He wrote the biography of the Emperor Constantine, and an invaluable *Ecclesiastical History*, which is almost our only evidence for what went on in the first three centuries after Christ. According to Eusebius, a certain head-teacher from Alexandria in Egypt travelled in India between AD 150 and 200, he found there a book in Hebrew called 'The Gospel according to Matthew', claimed to be the original from which St Matthew's Gospel in the New Testament was translated. This book was said to have been left behind by 'Bartholomew, one of the Apostles'. This story is repeated by St Jerome at the end of the fourth century. St Bartholomew is traditionally supposed to have been a missionary in the area around Bombay, now called Mumbai. So there is some evidence that he went to India, but how reliable that is, I couldn't say.

St Thomas

Certainly Christianity came to India many centuries before it came to Britain. St Thomas is supposed to have done missionary work in the Kerala area. Indian Christians are convinced that their church was founded by the apostle Thomas. An Indian scholar said recently that there's just as much evidence for Thomas being in India as there is for St Peter going to Rome. The ancient Syrian Church seems to have looked east for its mission field since the very first, and one section is called the Mar Thoma Church, which is Syrian for St Thomas. Confined for many centuries to a small area in south-west India, the 'Syrian' community has in recent years spread widely in the East, and developed a strong missionary activity. Perhaps Thomas and Bartholomew divided India between them, and St Bartholomew was so busy doing mission in Bombay he had no time to 'keep in touch' with the other apostles!

Armenia

There is also a tradition that St Bartholomew went to Armenia. He became a martyr there, it's claimed, when all the skin was flayed off his back, while he was still alive. He was then crucified. There's a prominent thirteenth-century Armenian monastery on the supposed site of his martyrdom, in an area that used to be called Armenia, but is now in south-eastern Turkey. Some of his relics were taken from there to Iraq, then to an island off Sicily, then to an island in the Tiber at Rome which was a great healing centre. This led to Bartholomew becoming the patron saint of medicine. There is even said to be one of Bartholomew's arm bones in Canterbury Cathedral.

Does it matter?

Does it matter whether any of these contradictory stories is true or not? Frankly, no it doesn't. The Twelve apostles were sent out by Jesus to be his 'witnesses in Jerusalem, in all Judea and Samaria, and to the ends of the earth'. We can be sure that most of them tried to do this as best they could. India and Armenia were important parts of the civilized world at that time. We can't look down on the people of these ancient nations as benighted heathen, when they have had believers in Jesus longer than we have. And we can learn from the apostles that nobody is beyond the reach of the Christian mission, that the love of Jesus extends to every race and nation and colour on the earth.

Suggested hymns

Captains of the saintly band; God is working his purpose out; Seek ye first the kingdom of God; The Church of God a kingdom is.

Holy Cross Day   14 September
O Love That Wilt Not Let Me Go

Num. 21.4–9 The bronze serpent; Ps. 22.23–28 All the earth shall turn to the Lord; Phil. 2.6–11 Obedient to death on the cross; John 3.13–17 God so loved the world

> 'For God so loved the world that he gave his only Son, so that everyone who believes in him may not perish but may have eternal life.' John 3.16

The cross

How can God allow it? How can a God of love permit so many of his followers to suffer the most appalling pain and loss? Good people, faithful Christians, yet they seem to bear more than their fair share of the world's agony. You can't give an answer to those queries in words – you simply have to point the questioners to the cross of Calvary.

Matheson

George Matheson was studying for the ministry of the Church of Scotland, in the 1860s. He was a brilliant student, and engaged to be married to a lovely young woman. Then the doctors told him that he was going blind, and there was no possibility of a cure. His fiancée broke off their engagement, saying that she couldn't face life looking after a blind man. From that point on, his beloved sister looked after him, and he resigned himself to the life of a blind bachelor theologian. He was ordained, and pursued an academic career, publishing several books. But the reviewers of one of his books criticized him for some serious mistakes, which they said couldn't have been made by anyone who'd read the other books on the subject. Then Matheson realized that academia, too, was denied to him by his blindness.

Agony

He withdrew to a quiet pastoral ministry. Then, when he was 40, his beloved sister was married. The whole family went to Glasgow for the wedding, leaving him alone. Not only was George Matheson now without a carer, but his sister had achieved the married state which he had longed for yet never gained. His situation, he wrote later, 'caused me the most severe mental suffering'.

Hymn

Then he had a sudden flash of inspiration, giving him new hope. He snatched up a pen and paper, and in five minutes only, he'd written what subsequently became for many people one of the best-loved hymns in the hymnal. You probably know it, beginning,

> O Love that wilt not let me go,
> I rest my weary soul in thee;
> I give thee back the life I owe,
> That in thine ocean depths its flow
> May richer, fuller be.

Faith

Matheson had rediscovered his faith in the love of God. The Bible tells us, 'God so loved the world that he gave his only Son, so that everyone who believes in him may not perish but may have eternal life.' Whatever our disappointment and weariness, if we offer it back to the God who gave it to us, God gives life new significance and meaning. For a blind man, the light of God was an obvious symbol:

> O Light that followest all my way,
> I yield my flickering torch to thee;
> My heart restores its borrowed ray,
> That in thy sunshine's blaze its day
> May brighter, fairer be.

Rainbow

In 1856 the Pre-Raphaelite artist John Millais painted a child trying to describe a rainbow to her blind sister. George Matheson had admired rainbows in his sighted years, and now he missed them. Yet in the story of Noah, God describes the rainbow as his battle-bow, which he has hung up in the clouds to show that he would never again go to war with the human race. The rainbow is a symbol of hope, and of the promise that out of the most terrible suffering God can always bring something good if we trust him. Many, many Christians in the depth of despair have been cheered by these words:

344

O Joy that seekest me through pain,
I cannot close my heart to thee;
I trace the rainbow through the rain,
And feel the promise is not vain,
That morn shall tearless be.

The cross

God gives us hope even in the darkest hours. Today is Holy Cross Day, reminding us that Jesus didn't leave us alone in our suffering, but came down to share it with us. His cross is the promise that, if we'll let him bear our griefs for us, he will bring us to the tear-free morning of eternal life:

O Cross that liftest up my head,
I dare not ask to fly from thee;
I lay in dust life's glory dead,
And from the ground there blossoms red
Life that shall endless be.

Triumphant living

Later, George Matheson looked back, describing his as 'an obstructed life, a circumscribed life ... but a life of quenchless hopefulness, a life which has beaten persistently against the cage of circumstance, and which even at the time of abandoned work has said not "Good night" but "Good morning".'

Suggested hymns

From heaven you came; O love that wilt not let me go; On a hill far away; When I behold the wondrous cross.

St Matthew, Apostle and Evangelist 21 September
A Banquet in His Heart

Prov. 3.13–18 Wisdom more precious than jewels; Ps. 119.65–72 Better than gold; 2 Cor. 4.1–6 The open statement of the truth; Matt. 9.9–13 The call of Matthew

'As Jesus was walking along, he saw a man called Matthew sitting at the tax booth; and he said to him, "Follow me." And he got

345

up and followed him. And as he sat at dinner in the house, many tax collectors and sinners came and were sitting with him and his disciples.' Matthew 9.9–10

Friendless

Matthew the tax-collector had no friends among respectable folk. Hardly surprising, when he cheated most of them with his excessive tax demands, and collected money to pay the brutal army of occupation. He had hung around on the edge of the crowd when Jesus was speaking, and he liked what he'd heard. Wistfully he'd thought, wouldn't it be wonderful if I could live as Jesus is describing, a life of kindness to others and acceptance by God? But there was no chance of a tax-collector being accepted into that sort of society. So he was caught off guard when Jesus turned to him and said, 'Follow me!' Like a young woman who has received an unexpected proposal of marriage, he was lost for words. 'What can I say?' he stammered. Jesus smiled. 'One word will do,' he said. 'Yes,' answered Matthew. 'Oh yes, yes, yes, yes, *yes!* I will, I will. I'll follow you wherever you want me to!' Then, what should he do next? he wondered. What he really wanted to do was throw a party. But Jesus would surely never come to a party where the only guests were the outcasts and despised like Matthew. So Matthew went off into a daydream, preparing for Jesus a banquet in his heart. Jesus startled him again, asking, 'What are you thinking about, friend?' 'W-w-well, I dreamt I was giving you a banquet. Oh, not a real banquet, you understand – it was a banquet in my heart.' This time, Jesus laughed out loud. 'I've never been to one of those,' he chuckled. 'I'll accept your invitation. But you'll have to be a big-hearted man if there's to be room for me and all your tax-collector friends!'

Friend of sinners

All right, I know it doesn't say all that in the Bible, but a vivid imagination helps to make the Bible stories come alive. And the Bible does say that when Jesus 'sat at dinner in the house, many tax collectors and sinners came and were sitting with him and his disciples'. So the location had moved from Matthew's heart to Matthew's house, but people were astonished at the company Jesus kept. It took them a long time to understand that the Saviour of the world loves the outcast and those with a shady reputation, just as much as he loves the celebrities and the VIPs. He enjoys parties, and he's happy to go to a party with anyone who invites him, in their home or in their heart. Jesus is the friend of sinners.

Invite Jesus in

Have you ever invited Jesus to a banquet in your heart? No, really, it's a serious question. Where does Jesus come in your life? Do you leave him behind in church when you go home? Do you only think about him when you're being po-faced and respectable? That isn't good enough. Jesus wants to be with you in the whole of your life. He wants you to open your heart, and share all your hopes and fears with him, your anger and your joy. So why not give Jesus a party? A banquet in your heart is quite good enough for starters. Jesus wants to be your close friend, your bosom pal. He wants you to consult him over all your decisions, and thank him for all your successes. That's a cause for celebration, isn't it?

Big-hearted

But like Matthew, you've got to be big-hearted. Jesus loves to have a cosy one-to-one with you, but soon you have to invite all your friends into your heart, too. Jesus likes going to parties with cheating tax-collectors and similar sinners, so include them on the guest list, too. Then, who knows, one day you may feel ready to give a party in your house, just like Matthew did, where the presence of Jesus is openly rejoiced in, and where everyone is equally welcome. What would you do if Jesus turned, looked you in the eyes, and said, 'Follow me'? Perhaps you've already answered that with, 'Yes! Yes Lord, I will, gladly, I'll follow you wherever you want me to!' If you haven't already done that, say it now, in the silence of your heart. Then you'll be ready to throw a banquet in your heart, for Jesus and all of your friends and acquaintances. I hope you enjoy it.

Suggested hymns

He sat to watch o'er customs paid; They shall come from the east; Welcome, all ye noble saints of old; What a wonderful change in my life has been wrought.

347

St Michael and All Angels 29 September
Raphael's Cherubs

Gen. 28.10–17 Jacob's ladder; Ps. 103.19–22 Bless the Lord, you angels; Rev. 12.7–12 Michael fought the dragon (*if the Revelation reading is used instead of the Old Testament reading, the New Testament reading is* Heb. 1.5–14 Higher than the angels); John 1.47–51 Angels descending on the Son of Man

> '*Do not neglect to show hospitality to strangers, for by doing that some have entertained angels without knowing it.*' Hebrews 13.2

What do angels look like?

What do angels look like? In the famous painting of the Virgin Mary by Raphael, known as the Sistine Madonna, at the bottom, you can see two cherubs, or *putti* as they are called in Italy. They have wings, so very obviously they're meant to be angels, but they look more like two very bored urchins! Are we allowed to make jokes about angels? Obviously Raphael thought so. The tradition that identifies angels as women with wings is quite a modern one. In the Bible, the cherubim and seraphim that guard the throne of God in the Temple, according to Exodus and Isaiah, have four or six wings, but they are not human figures – more like the winged lions with human heads that you find in the ancient temples of Persia. God flies on a throne supported by winged creatures in Ezekiel and Revelation, but they are described as being like a lion, an ox, an eagle and a man. All the other angels in the Scriptures are described as men, and early medieval carvings show angels with beards. Of course, you may say that's only how the artist depicts them, but as spiritual creatures they have no body and therefore no gender. When they were called to appear to human beings the angels took human form, but the Letter to the Hebrews warns us, 'Do not neglect to show hospitality to strangers, for by doing that some have entertained angels without knowing it.' So it would seem that the angels chose to appear as perfectly ordinary human beings, with no obvious distinguishing features to identify them as angels.

Tobit

The writer to the Hebrews was probably referring to the book of Tobit, in the Apocrypha. This is a story about a family of Jews living lives of piety and charity in Jerusalem while most of the Jews are exiles in Babylon. Tobit was then exiled to Nineveh, and became blind, praying to God for help. He had previously left some money with a businessman in the kingdom of the Medes, and sent his son Tobias to fetch it back. Tobias searched for a man who could guide him to his destination, and 'found the angel Raphael standing in front of him; but he did not perceive that he was an angel of God'. From then on Raphael is referred to as 'the young man', and he guides Tobias and his pet dog along the road – even the dog doesn't recognize the angel. They stop at the house of Tobias's relative Raguel and his wife Edna, and a marriage is arranged for Tobias with their daughter Sara. Sara had previously had seven husbands, each of whom had been killed by a demon on their wedding night, but the angel Raphael has given Tobias some medicine with which he was able to kill the demon when it appeared. Raphael went to fetch the money, and then they all return to blind Tobit in Nineveh. Raphael prescribes some medicine that heals Tobit of his blindness, and eventually reveals that he is an angel, who had carried Tobit's prayers before God. It's a good story, and the anonymity of the angel adds to the suspense. Obviously the artist Raphael, who painted the bored urchins, was named after him. But if people like Tobit and his son Tobias can 'entertain angels unawares', it brings us no nearer to an answer to the question we started with: what do angels look like?

No answer

So perhaps there is no answer to this question. Angels are spiritual beings, they dwell in another dimension and can travel faster than light. When God sends them to help a human being, they can appear in any form they choose, whichever will be most helpful. If you like to think of your guardian angel as a woman with wings, there's no harm in that. You probably won't see him or her until you die, and then our physical form will be unimportant. We are not allowed to worship the angels, for they are much lower than God, though a little higher than human beings. So, in the famous words of Hamlet, we have to accept that there are more things in heaven and earth than are dreamt of in our philosophy, and thank God that he has more ways of helping us than we shall ever understand.

Suggested hymns

Angel voices, ever singing; Hark! hark, my soul, angelic songs are swelling; Stars of the morning, so gloriously bright; Ye watchers and ye holy ones.

St Luke the Evangelist   18 October
Blind, Deaf, Lame, and Dumb

Isa. 35.3–6 Healing in the new age *or* Acts 16.6–12a The Macedonian call; Ps. 147.1–7 God heals the broken hearted; 2 Tim. 4.5–17 Only Luke is with me; Luke 10.1–9 Sending out the seventy

'Then the eyes of the blind shall be opened, and the ears of the deaf unstopped; then the lame shall leap like a deer, and the tongue of the speechless sing for joy.' Isaiah 35.5–6

Political correctness

We laugh at 'political correctness gone mad'. Taken to extremes it can certainly be comical. But the reason for it is deadly serious. We speak in a PC way because many folk, who struggle with problems in their lives, feel marginalized and robbed of their dignity when treated as a category, rather than as individuals. So we've learnt to speak of handicapped people as 'people with disabilities', so that each one should be treated as unique, not just defined by their disabilities.

Isaiah

St Luke, whom we commemorate today, and whom St Paul describes as 'the beloved physician', usually describes ill people as those 'who were sick with various kinds of diseases'. As a doctor, he knew that not even Jesus could heal sufferers by pigeon-holing them. The prophet Isaiah would have got into hot water if he'd written today that 'the eyes of the blind shall be opened, and the ears of the deaf unstopped; then the lame shall leap like a deer, and the tongue of the dumb sing for joy'. Yet Isaiah was writing poetry, and poets must be allowed to take liberties with the language in order to make a point. Christians have interpreted this passage as a prediction of the coming of the Messiah. When Jesus healed people who were blind, and so forth, this was seen to fulfil that prophecy. But as well as their surface, literal meaning, those words also have a deeper, symbolic significance. St Luke knew that any doctor who heals a physical illness has to consider the patient's emotional and spiritual needs as well. Jesus pointed out that, as a result of his ministry, 'the blind receive their sight, the lame walk, the lepers are cleansed, the deaf hear, the dead are raised, and the poor have good news brought to them'. Yet he wasn't only talking about the physically disadvantaged – he was helping us to see that we're all spiritually blind to the love of God and the needs of others, and we all need Christ's healing.

Blind

So let's draw out the spiritual symbolism of each of the disabilities Isaiah mentions. He wrote, 'Then the eyes of the blind shall be opened.' People who have what we should really call visual impairment used to be put in a corner as a nuisance. Now, if they're partially sighted, they can read large-print books and enlarged text on the computer screens. Those with little or no sight can use a guide dog, and even become members of the Cabinet. But when it comes to spiritual blindness, as the proverb says, 'There's none so blind as those that will not see.' We are so wrapped up in our own desires, we don't even notice what God is doing for us, and what he wants us to do for others.

Deaf

Isaiah wrote, 'the ears of the deaf [shall be] unstopped'. Those with a hearing impediment can now be helped with hearing aids and sign language. It's harder to help the spiritually deaf. Don't you wish that God would speak to you? Have you considered that maybe he's talking to you all the time, through nature, the Bible and the sermons, and you don't hear him because you're too busy with your own affairs?

Lame

Next, said Isaiah, when Messiah comes, 'the lame shall leap like a deer'. Saints Peter and John healed a lame man in the Temple, who went 'walking, and leaping, and praising God'. If you feel insignificant and ineffectual, perhaps you need Jesus to heal your spiritual lameness?

Dumb

Finally, Isaiah mentions the dumb, though in the USA that word means 'stupid'. So the NRSV translates it as 'the tongue of the *speechless* [shall] sing for joy'. Maybe you don't have an impediment in your speech, can speak persuasively or chatter for hours on most subjects. But when it comes to talking to your friends about Jesus and what he means to you, you're completely tongue-tied. Then you need Jesus to remove the impediment of shyness and heal you.

Healing

You hadn't realized how spiritually sick you are, had you? Luke the physician knew that physical and spiritual healing go together. Jesus heals you, so that you may enjoy life more, but also to make you more useful to God. God wants you to see his love for everybody, hear his guidance, then walk the walk and talk the talk for Jesus.

Suggested hymns

Give thanks with a grateful heart; Lord, I was blind, I could not see; Make way, make way; O for a thousand tongues to sing.

SS Simon and Jude, Apostles   28 October
(*See Last Sunday after Trinity, p. 262.*)

All Saints' Day   1 November
Embracing Poverty
(*If 4 November is not kept as All Saints' Sunday, the readings on page 264 are used on 1 November. If those are used on the Sunday, the following are the readings on 1 November*)
Isa. 56.3–8 My house for all people, *or* 2 Esd. 2.42–48 Crowned by the Son of God; Ps. 33.1–5 Rejoice, you righteous; Heb. 12.18–24 Come to Zion; Matt. 5.1–12 The Beatitudes

'[Jesus said], "Blessed are the poor in spirit, for theirs is the king-dom of heaven."' Matthew 5.3

Egypt

Most people haven't time to celebrate a different saint every day, so on All Saints' Day we think of the ones we have ignored. One important but little-known saint was St Antony, who lived in Egypt, in the third century AD. Many people in the Roman Empire at that time had become immensely rich through trade and commerce. Most of the rest were thoroughly materialistic, eager to become rich also. The poor were very poor, and the rich were corrupt. Most people were nominally Christian, but there was little interest in spiritual things. Yet many good Christians agonized over the state of the world, then as now. A few, of whom Antony was one, decided that the only way to avoid the temptations of materialism was to give up everything and escape. In the desert they could meditate alone in silence. These hermits were known as the Desert Fathers, though there were some women among them also.

Embracing poverty

One day, Antony heard the Gospel read in church, and was struck by the words of Jesus to the rich young man, 'If you wish to be perfect, go, sell your possessions, and give the money to the poor, and you will have treasure in heaven; then come, follow me.' So Antony gave away all his possessions and went to live alone in the desert. In the stunning silence of the desert, Antony found he could pray as never before. He was free from the distractions of having money and wondering how to spend it. He found that poverty, when it's not imposed on you but is willingly chosen, is a great blessing, and he embraced poverty gladly. Jesus said, 'Blessed are the poor in spirit, for theirs is the kingdom of heaven.'

Attracting followers

The discipline of Antony's life of self-denial was in contrast to the luxury of the world around. The news of what he had done began to spread, and other Christians travelled out into the desert to ask him questions and learn from him. Some of them stayed and built their hermit cells nearby so that they could pray and discuss with him daily. Soon, so many followers flocked out to learn from them that it was said 'the desert was made a city'. It seemed as though the whole purpose of his flight into the desert had been destroyed, but Antony knew where his duty lay. He came out of his self-imposed isolation for a while, to form them into a loose-knit community with a common rule of life. This was something never seen before. Before that there had been hermits living alone; now there were communities of monks living together.

Work and prayer

Once Antony was filled with despair. His loneliness brought many sinful thoughts. He said to God, 'Lord, I want to be saved, but these thoughts won't leave me alone. How can I be saved?' Soon afterwards, he noticed a man sitting at his work, plaiting a rope, then getting up from his work to pray. He went on like this all day long. Antony realized God was telling him that prayer needs to be combined with physical exercise and work. In this way, Antony lived to over 100. Once he asked God, 'Lord, why do some people die young, while others drag on to extreme old age? Why are some people poor and others rich? Why do wicked people prosper while good people are needy?' He heard a voice saying to him, 'Antony, concentrate on yourself; God decides these things; it won't do you any good to know the reasons.'

Today

So what about us today? What must *we* do to be saved? Antony clearly saw that poverty is not a good thing when people are forced to be poor. But it does have its advantages when it's willingly chosen. So we should work and pray to lift other people out of their poverty. That will mainly consist in creating fairer patterns of trade. It will cost us, by removing the protection enjoyed by our own industries and agriculture. But after making adequate provision for our families, we should give away our surplus wealth, and enjoy the blessings that come with a simpler lifestyle. We can 'live simply, so that others may simply live'. As Antony discovered, it's much easier to pray when your life isn't cluttered with a lot of possessions.

Suggested hymns

All for Jesus, all for Jesus; Blest are the poor in heart; Take my life, and let it be; Teach me, my God and king.

Commemoration of the Faithful Departed
(All Souls' Day)   2 November
Requiems

Lam. 3.17–26, 31–33 New every morning, *or* Wisd. 3.1–9 Souls of the righteous; Ps. 23 The Lord my shepherd, *or* 27.1–6, 16–17 He shall hide me; Rom. 5.5–11 Christ died for us, *or* 1 Peter 1.3–9 Salvation ready to be revealed; John 5.19–25 The dead will hear his voice, *or* John 6.37–40 I will raise them up

> *'In the day of trouble he shall hide me in his shelter;*
> *in the secret place of his dwelling shall he hide me.'*
> *Psalm 27.6 (Common Worship)*

Prayers for the dead

When someone died, the Old Testament described them as 'sleeping with their fathers'. Jesus said that his dead friend Lazarus was sleeping, and St Paul wrote to the Corinthians about those who 'die in Christ'. So it's natural that Christians should think of death as a rest, waiting for the resurrection. When Polycarp, the elderly Bishop of Smyrna, was martyred in AD 155, his friends wrote that they celebrated the Lord's Supper in his memory. So when Missal books were written to guide Roman Catholic priests, they usually contained a Mass for the Dead to be said on the day of a funeral, on important anniversaries, and on All Souls' Day, the 2nd of November. There were many variations, until in 1570 Pope Pius V established the present form of what we call the Requiem Mass. There have been many glorious musical settings of the traditional words.

Outline

The Requiem takes its name from the opening words of the Introit, in Latin, *Requiem aeternam* . . . 'Rest eternal grant to them O Lord . . .', which are sung as the priests enter the church, followed by the words *Te decet hymnus* . . . meaning 'A hymn is due to you, Lord in Sion . . .' from Psalm 65.

This is followed by the only words in the Latin Mass to be retained in the original Greek: *Kyrie eleison* . . . meaning 'Lord, have mercy.'

Next come chants referred to as the Gradual and the Tract, followed by the great Sequence, the *Dies irae,* from the thirteenth century. This is taken from the words of the prophet Zephaniah in the Old Testament, warning that the day when God judges the earth will be a day of wrath. Its truly terrifying imagery is taken from the Bible and from Greek mythology, with references to the Sybil, a prophetess in Delphi, and punishment in Tartarus, a place in the underworld. The Roman Catholic Church dropped the *Dies Irae* from the Requiem Mass when they reformed the liturgy in 1969.

The prayer said while the bread and wine are being offered comes next.

During the great Prayer of thanksgiving, the traditional *Sanctus* and *Benedictus* are sung.

But the *Agnus Dei* . . . meaning 'Lamb of God . . .' is quite different from the words said at other services.

During the communion, a prayer is sung asking that 'Eternal light' may shine on the souls in paradise, and sometimes a prayer beginning *In paradisum* . . . is added, asking that angels may lead the souls of the dead into paradise, as Jesus on the cross promised to the penitent thief.

Another addition is the beautiful motet, *Pie Jesu* . . . 'O sweet Lord Jesus, grant them rest.'

Musical settings

Most people today think it strange that the Latin language is used in referring to the movements in this service, but that's because so many great musicians have been inspired by this text to set the words to beautiful music. At first they were set to Gregorian chant, which was followed by early polyphonic choral writing. Between about 1600 and 1900, marvellous Mass settings were written by Monteverdi, Alessandro Scarlatti and Pergolesi among others. Mozart's Requiem was left incomplete when he died in mysterious circumstances, and finished by others. Berlioz and Verdi wrote Requiem Masses which are like Grand Operas. Brahms wrote *A German Requiem,* replacing the Latin texts with words from

Luther's German Bible. After 1900, much less pessimistic adaptations of the Requiem were made by Fauré, Duruflé, and many others. Benjamin Britten's *War Requiem* married the traditional Latin words with the anti-war poems of Wilfred Owen, providing a musical resolution to the contradictions of faith and doubt when they can't be resolved logically.

Comfort

It's a comfort to the dying to know that their friends are praying for them, and will go on doing so. It's a comfort to the bereaved to be able to remember their loved ones who have passed on. Whether it's in a great concert hall or a small church, on All Soul's Day or any other occasion, the Requiem Mass brings consolation to all.

Suggested hymns

Be still, my soul; Give rest, O Christ (Russian Kontakion); In our day of thanksgiving; Jesu, Son of Mary.

Saints and Martyrs of (our own Nation)
8 November
Eulogies and Epitaphs
Isa. 61.4–9 Build up the ancient ruins, *or* Ecclus. 44.1–15 Let us now praise famous men; Ps. 15 Who may dwell in your tabernacle?; Rev. 19.5–10 A great multitude invited; John 17.18–23 To be with me to see my glory

> *'Let us now sing the praises of famous men, our ancestors in their generations.' Ecclesiasticus 44.1*

Ecclesiasticus

In between the Old Testament and the New Testament, some Bibles print a selection of other books. Mostly they were written by Jews, but in Greek, during the time between the Old and New Testaments. St Jerome included them in his Latin translation of the Bible; Martin Luther separated them out in his German version, calling them 'The Apocrypha'. One of these is headed 'The Wisdom of Jesus son of Sirach'. It became known as The Church Book, or in

357

Latin, Ecclesiasticus. Don't confuse it with another book, which *is* in the Old Testament, called Ecclesiastes. Sirach, or Ecclesiasticus, is all poetry, most of it very beautiful, and many people believe that it's truly inspired.

Vaughan Williams

One of the most moving passages, often used at funerals and memorial services, has been set by the composer Ralph Vaughan Williams as an anthem, once heard, never forgotten. So I'll quote it in the King James Version, as Vaughan Williams did. It's appropriate today, the commemoration of the saints and martyrs of our own nation:

Let us now praise famous men, and our fathers that begat us.
The Lord hath wrought great glory by them
through his great power from the beginning.
Such as did bear rule in their kingdoms,
men renowned for their power,
giving counsel by their understanding, and declaring prophecies:
Leaders of the people by their counsels,
and by their knowledge of learning meet for the people,
wise and eloquent are their instructions:
Such as found out musical tunes, and recited verses in writing:
Rich men furnished with ability,
living peaceably in their habitations:
All these were honoured in their generations,
and were the glory of their times.
There be of them, that have left a name behind them,
that their praises might be reported.
And some there be, which have no memorial;
who are perished, as though they had never been;
and are become as though they had never been born;
and their children after them.
But these were merciful men,
whose righteousness hath not been forgotten.
With their seed shall continually remain a good inheritance, and their children are within the covenant.
Their seed standeth fast, and their children for their sakes.
Their seed shall remain for ever,
and their glory shall not be blotted out.
Their bodies are buried in peace;

but their name liveth for evermore.
The people will tell of their wisdom,
and the congregation will shew forth their praise.

Eulogies

The author of that poem was thinking of famous men among his ancestors, the Jews. But every race can boast some heroes and heroines of the past. We shouldn't idolize them – nobody is perfect, and they wouldn't thank us for pretending that they were. But to describe their virtues encourages us to follow their example, in serving God and our neighbours. Concentrating on our fellow country-men and women doesn't imply that we're better than anyone else; but we naturally want to serve our own nation, in gratitude for all that earlier generations have left for us. Such a speech, in praise of somebody who has died, is called a 'eulogy'. Sometimes eulogies are carved into a tombstone, when they're called 'epitaphs'.

Funerals

Some day you may be called to deliver a eulogy at a funeral. A newspaper once gave guidance on how to do this, suggesting you ask yourself the following questions:

To whom am I speaking?
How would the person like to be remembered?
What made the person special? What were their favourite pas-times and interests, likes and dislikes?
When was the person happiest?
Who was really close to him or her?
What did I like about the person? What did other people like about him or her?
What are the highlights of the person's life story?
If I could only say three things about him or her, what would they be?
Do I want someone else to give the eulogy on my behalf on the day?
Is anyone else speaking about the person at the funeral? Should we avoid saying the same things?

Olden days

Whether you have to speak at a funeral, or write an obituary, ask yourself those questions. Yet while there are still people living who loved them, you shouldn't speak ill of the dead. However, when you're considering people from the olden days, famous or obscure, you can balance the lessons to be learnt from their good points with warnings to avoid their mistakes.

Suggested hymns

God, whose city's sure foundation; Let saints on earth in concert sing; Rejoice in God's saints, today and all days; We sing for all the unsung saints.

St Andrew the Apostle   30 November
Christianity in Scotland

Isa. 52.7–10 The messenger who announces peace; Ps. 19.1–6 The heavens declare God's glory; Rom. 10.12–18 God's messengers reconcile Jew and Greek; Matt. 4.18–22 The call of the fishermen

> *'As [Jesus] walked by the Sea of Galilee, he saw two brothers, Simon, who is called Peter, and Andrew his brother, casting a net into the sea – for they were fishermen. And he said to them, "Follow me, and I will make you fish for people."' Matthew 4.18–19*

Patron Saint

St Andrew is said to have been crucified at Patras, in Greece, but the wood of his cross was arranged diagonally. St Andrew is Scotland's patron saint, and his saltire cross, white on blue, is part of the union flag. The reason for this is one of those stories which can neither be proved nor disproved. Probably his remains were buried in Patras. About 300 years after Andrew died, the Emperor Constantine decided to move the saint's bones to his new capital of Constantinople. A legend tells us that a monk in Patras was warned of this in a dream by an angel, who told him to remove the saint's bones to the 'ends of the Earth' to keep them safe. Scotland was as near to the ends of the ancient Greek world as you could get, and the monk brought them ashore at what is now the city of St

Andrews. Why that should have been thought to be a safer resting place than Constantinople has never been explained. These bones have since disappeared; but some of St Andrew's bones had been taken to Amalfi in Italy. The church there sent some fragments in 1879 to Scotland as a gesture of friendship.

Picts and Celts

The first recorded mission to Scotland was by St Ninian, the son of a converted chieftain in Cumbria, who travelled to Rome and was there consecrated a bishop and sent to convert the Pictish people of Scotland. He based his mission at Whithorn in Wigtownshire, at a church known as *Candida Casa* or the White House. Next, St Columba came from Ireland to the island of Iona, and from there his missionaries spread among the Celtic people of northern England; St Aidan settled on Lindisfarne and converted the pagans of Northumberland. The Celtic Church was based on monastic communities, sometimes mixed, living a common life in a small village and closely in touch with the natural world. Its leaders were presbyter-abbots, not bishops. They were independent of Rome, wearing a different tonsure and celebrating Easter on a different date from the Roman Church. Under the influence of St Hilda of Whitby, the two churches agreed to adopt the Roman customs for convenience; but reconciliation was only completed in the reigns of Queen Margaret and her son King David I in the eleventh and twelfth centuries.

Reformation

The Church in Scotland resisted claims by the Archbishops of Canterbury and York to rule over them, and supported the Scottish wars against the English. They founded universities in St Andrews, Glasgow and Aberdeen. When the Reformation came to Scotland, however, first Lutheran, then Swiss, there were martyrs. After George Wishart was killed in 1546, his mantle fell on John Knox, a strong Calvinist. The reformed Church of Scotland was established under the rule of presbyters, not bishops, and so was called Presbyterian.

361

Enemies

The Stuart Kings were determined to make the Kirk episcopal, like the Church of England, and this was fiercely resisted by the Scots. In 1674 the Scottish Covenanters signed an alliance with the English Puritans who had executed King Charles I. When Charles II returned to England, episcopacy was re-established in Scotland, and a long and bloody struggle ensued. In 1690 the Church of Scotland became Presbyterian again, and has remained so ever since, though the Scottish Episcopal Church remains a strong minority. The Scottish Church is governed by General Assembly, with worship based on *The Book of Common Order,* and faith defined by the Westminster Catechism. Between the unpopular Patronage Act of 1712 and the Disruption of 1843 nearly a third of the Presbyterian ministers left to join the Free Church, commonly known as the Wee Frees. Gradually most of them were reunited to the Presbyterians, where the influence of the Iona Community, in retreats and worship, has been wonderful.

Reconciliation

The rivalries between Presbyterians and Episcopalians have been largely reconciled now, though attempts at reunion have not so far been successful. Relations between Catholics and Protestants have also calmed down – except when Celtic are playing Rangers! The history of Christianity in Scotland contains some glorious moments, and some very sad ones. The best that can be said is that there were martyrs on all sides, and while we rejoice in the memory of their courage, we should also resolve that the terrible bloodshed must never return, for Christ's sake.

Suggested hymns

Amazing grace (Scottish melody); Lord of life, we come to you (Eriskay Love Lilt); Spirit of God, unseen as the wind (Skye Boat Song); The Lord's my shepherd (Brother James's Air).

Sermon for Harvest Festival
Creationism

Joel 2.21–27 Eat and be satisfied; Ps. 126 Sow in tears, reap in joy; 1 Tim. 2.1–7 Thanksgiving for everyone, *or* 1 Tim. 6.6–10 Money the root of all evil; Matt. 6.25–33 Lilies of the field

> *'[Jesus said,] "If God so clothes the grass of the field, which is alive today and tomorrow is thrown into the oven, will he not much more clothe you – you of little faith?"' Matthew 6.30*

Harvest and creation

At harvest time, we give thanks to God, in the words of one of the harvest hymns, 'For the fruits of his creation'. But 'creation' is a very emotive word, and different people use it in different ways, as a weapon to attack each other with. Some Christians, basing their beliefs on a literal reading of Genesis chapters 1 and 2, claim that there's only one way to think of creation: as the production of a mature, fully functional universe, much as we observe it today, during the course of seven 24-hour periods somewhere between six and ten thousand years ago. If you don't believe that, they say, you can't be a believer in God. These extremist Christians are known as 'young-earth creationists'. Reacting against this, some scientists claim that as there is clear evidence that earth is much older than that, it can't have been created by God, and this proves that God doesn't exist. In which case, we in this church are wasting our time today, thanking a God who doesn't exist for a harvest that came about as a result of a series of random accidents!

Evolution

But both these groups, the Creationists and the Evolutionists, are using the word 'creation' in the wrong way. When Charles Darwin published *On the Origin of Species by Means of Natural Selection* in 1859, his readers didn't immediately divide into two camps. Many scientists didn't at first accept his theory. That was because the Austrian monk Gregor Mendel hadn't yet published his theory of genetics. Many religious people, however, enthusiastically welcomed Darwin's theory, as explaining how God had created a world of such astonishing diversity. The novelist and clergyman Charles Kingsley said that God could easily have created a ready-made world, but instead had done something much cleverer, in creating a world so endowed with potential that creatures 'could make themselves', through the shuffling explorations of natural selection. The Creator had made a universe that was itself creative.

Interpretation

The folly of the Creationists was to interpret the poetry of the Bible in a flat-footed literal way. Genesis 1 and 2 are not a divinely dictated scientific text, intended to save us the trouble of actually doing science. Thus the Creationists miss the deeper teaching of the biblical poem. Mistaking poetry for prose leads to false conclusions. When Robert Burns tells us his 'love is like a red, red rose', he doesn't mean his girlfriend has green leaves and prickles! When the Bible tells us, over and over, that 'God said, "Let there be . . ."', it's giving us the reason why anything exists: because God wants it to. Darwin told us how he did it. Genesis said that on the seventh 'day', 'God rested from all his work that God had *created to do*'. Jewish commentators understood this to mean that God had actually implanted creativity into nature.

Jesus

It's significant, then, that in our gospel reading today from the Sermon on the Mount, Jesus says that 'If God so clothes the grass of the field, which is alive today and tomorrow is thrown into the oven, will he not much more clothe you – you of little faith?' He says 'clothes' in the present tense, as if to teach us that God is still at work in the growth and evolving of the natural world. Thank God for that!

Tolerance

There are many people who believe in God, and believe also in evolution. While respecting those who believe in 'young-earth creationism', we think that, by taking a merely literal interpretation of the Bible, they're missing the vital message which God is giving us in the poetry. Their extremism makes it harder for people who have had a scientific education to accept the good news of Christ and become believers. Therefore I think we should discuss with them, and try to persuade them to accept a more mature and reasonable understanding of the faith. But to attack them as atheists do, trying to destroy their faith in God, is a very cruel thing to do. We need not just to be tolerant, but to respect varying opinions and discuss them calmly. It was, after all, through encouraging diversity in nature that God evolved the harvest that we're thanking him for today!

Suggested hymns

Above the moon earth rises; Every star shall sing a carol; For the fruits of his creation; O Lord of every shining constellation.

Sermon for a Wedding
I Love You
1 John 4.7–11

> *'Beloved, let us love one another, because love is from God.'*
> *1 John 4.7*

I love you

One of the reasons why couples get married is usually, 'Because we love each other!' I hope each has said to the other, 'I love you', and that you'll go on saying it often for the whole of your lives. Marriage is built on love as its foundation. But the words 'I love you' can mean a whole range of things.

To begin with

The first time we say those words is to our parents: 'I love you, Mummy.' Then it means, 'Give me a cuddle. I need you to give me food, warmth and protection – don't ever leave me.' Later, when you say 'I love you' to someone of the opposite sex, it means that and more. The first time, you whisper those words very nervously, watching for the reaction. In that case, it means, 'I've enjoyed being your friend, and I just wonder if, perhaps, you might possibly . . . be interested in our relationship going deeper than that?' Then, if the other one says, 'I love you too', that means, 'I'd been hoping you'd say that, because my feelings towards you are changing.' Or perhaps it means, 'I want to love you, but I'm not sure yet.' Or else, 'Say that again, it makes me feel good about myself.' Later, it means, 'Being with you gives me warm feelings inside, and I hope we might soon pluck up courage to kiss.' And so on. Wonderful, isn't it?

Marriage

Later comes the nerve-racking day of the proposal. Then 'I love you' means 'You're wonderful, and I'd like to live with you all my life, but I'm scared to ask you. What do you feel about that?' If the answer is yes, from then on saying 'I love you' may include, 'let's live under the same roof, let's commit ourselves to each other, let's have sex, let's make babies. Let's do it soon!' On the wedding day it means, 'I meant those promises seriously, and I want to care for you and cherish you till death us do part.' Newly-weds use those words to say what they said to their parents, 'Give me a cuddle. I need you to give me food, warmth and protection – don't ever leave me.' They mean, 'You're so beautiful (stroke) handsome, I get excited every time I look at you; I can't wait till you get home; I never had all these feelings for anyone before; isn't marriage wonderful?' The meanings tumble over each other in your brain, and you can't say 'I love you' often enough.

Later

Later, as your relationship matures, so does your understanding of what love means. When a married couple say those three words, they can mean, 'Say you love me.' Or 'Let's go to bed.' Or 'I'm too tired now, but don't ever doubt that I still love you.' Or 'You've been behaving badly recently, why don't we have a talk?' Or 'I'm sorry about what I said and did just now, but I don't know how to say it. Please forgive me.' Or 'Shush, stop talking and hold me tight.' Or 'Indulge me, and do what *I* want this time.' Or 'Stop shouting.' Or 'I'm addicted to you, and I'd be devastated if you ever stop loving me.'

God's love

If 'I love you' can have so many meanings, why do we get married in church? Surely it's because the ideas of love and God are very closely connected. In the Bible, St Paul writes about what 'I love you' should mean: 'Love is patient; love is kind; love is not envious or boastful or arrogant or rude. It doesn't insist on its own way; it's not irritable or resentful.' Could you use those words to describe your love for each other? But it's not only married couples who love like that; we should love all our neighbours in the same way. The Bible tells us that Jesus loves us like that, and was willing to sacrifice his life for us, and in this way he revealed that God is love. The Bible is God's love-letter to tell us he loves us. If you told your partner that you loved them, and they never spoke to you, you would be pretty disappointed. So God wants us to talk to him in prayer, and tell him we love him. Then he'll plant his love in your heart, which helps you to go on loving your spouse, even when you don't feel like it. Then you'll all live happily ever after, deeply in love with each other: you, and your spouse, and God, for ever and ever. As the Bible says:

> Beloved, let us love one another, because love is from God . . . for God is love. God's love was revealed among us in this way: God sent his only Son into the world . . . to be the atoning sacrifice for our sins. Beloved, since God loved us so much, we also ought to love one another.

Sermon for a Baptism or Christening
Giving Back to God
Matt. 22.15–22

'Jesus said, "Give back to the government what you've received from the government, and give back to God what God has given to you."' Matthew 22.21 (my translation)

Howler

In the old translations of the Bible, when Jesus was asked about paying income tax, he called for a penny and asked, 'Whose *image and superscription* are these?' meaning, 'Whose name and picture are stamped on the coin?' A child sitting a Scripture exam had mis-heard these words, and wrote down, 'They showed Jesus a penny, and he asked, "Whose is this *mingy subscription*?"' A penny in those days was a day's wage for a labourer. The correct answer was given in the Bible: it was the Roman Emperor's name and face on the coinage. Now, you put your name in your books or on your clothes, to show that they belong to you. The Emperor's name was on the coin that Jesus was holding, showing that our prosperity comes from the things the Government does for us. The nation has lent us its wealth; it has the right to ask for some of it back again in taxes.

Baptism

What's this got to do with today's christening service? Well, when a baby's born, we often say 'it's the image of its father'. Actually each child inherits the genes – I don't mean the trousers, I mean the genetic characteristics – of both sides of the family. But we give the child a surname, to show which family the infant belongs to. The people listening to Jesus knew that in the Bible human beings are said to be made 'in the image of God'. That doesn't mean that we look like God, because God's a spiritual being who doesn't have a body. We resemble God in that he has given us the power to create, to choose, and to love. So Jesus hinted that, just as the coin belonged to the Emperor, because it was made in his image, so each child belongs to God – the baby is God's child, as well as yours. God loves your baby as much as you do, and more. God will take as much trouble looking after your child as any parent could.

Christian names

In Christian countries, a child's first name is called the 'Christian name', because it's given to the child at the christening, or 'Christian-ing', when the child is made a Christian. And then God signs it with his name, to show that the child belongs to God. Now I don't mean that God gets a marker-pen and writes 'Property of God Almighty' on the baby's forehead. Of course not – God can't write! So he does what everyone else who can't write does – God signs himself with a cross! That's appropriate, because the cross is the symbol of Jesus, the Son of God. On his behalf, the minister makes a cross with water on the baby's forehead. Then, for the rest of their lives, people who have been baptized carry an invisible cross on their foreheads, meaning, however far they stray from God, God owns that person. God will always recognize them as one of his children.

Lent to you

The baby is your child, and belongs to your family, so you have the task of looking after them. But you don't *own* this child. Your children are *lent* to you by God. Parenthood is a colossal responsibility, because you've been entrusted with the care of God's child. You need all the help in this task that you can get, so in this service the whole congregation promise to welcome you and your baby every time you come to church, and share in teaching your child what it means to be a Christian. The godparents join with the parents in promising to pass on to the children, by word and example, the stories and teaching of Jesus; how to pray; and how to be good and loving. These are the best christening presents you can possibly give them.

Dangers

The schoolchild thought Jesus wouldn't be satisfied with a 'mingy subscription'. That's true – he said, 'Give back to God what belongs to God.' Your child belongs to God, so you can't claim sole owner-ship. You have the privilege of having them to live in your house with you. But there's nothing worse than parents who think they can form their children in their own image. Some children are made to dress like their parents, share the same hobbies, and even follow the same line of business, whether they like it or not. You can't make children in your own image; they are in the image of God, with the power to choose for themselves. If you love them, you can hope they'll follow your example. But once you've done your bit, you have to 'Give back to God what belongs to God' – includ-ing your children. Meanwhile, God will help you look after them, because they're God's children, as well as yours.

Suggested hymns

A little child the Saviour came; All things bright and beautiful; Child of blessing, child of promise; God forgave my sin in Jesus' name.

Sermon for a Funeral or Memorial Service
Love is Stronger than Death
Song of Solomon 8.6–7

'Love is strong as death, passion fierce as the grave.' S. of Sol. 8.6

When I die

When I die, some people may remember me for my gifts and achievements. A few will remember the laughter we shared. But, most of all, I hope I'm remembered for my love. What the bereaved miss most, usually, are the kind words, the hugs and cuddles, and all the other expressions of their love which the departed gave them in life. So one of the questions we want to ask at a funeral is, does love die when the person we love dies?

Does love die?

Most people feel deeply that this isn't so. We have the happy memories to cling to, and we shall never forget them. The ones we loved live on in our hearts, for sure. But by thinking about the nature of love, can we come up with any answers to the deeper question as to whether our beloved is still alive somewhere, in another dimension perhaps?

Song of Songs

The Old Testament contains one of the oldest, and most beautiful, love poems in the world. It's called the Song of Songs, or sometimes the Song of Solomon. It takes the form of a drama, with different speakers taking turns: the lover, the beloved, and the women of Jerusalem who form a sort of chorus. In the final chapter are two beautiful verses, which point towards an answer to our questions about death. They go like this:

> Set me as a seal upon your heart, as a seal upon your arm; for love is strong as death, passion fierce as the grave. Its flashes are flashes of fire, a raging flame. Many waters cannot quench love, neither can floods drown it. If one offered for love all the wealth of his house, it would be utterly scorned.

Love as strong as death

'Love is as strong as death', it says. Love is a feeling in our hearts, a belief in our minds, and a giving of our whole lives to the other. Even when the one we love dies, we don't stop loving them. Some people also have a strong feeling that they are still being loved from somewhere beyond the grave. Death is serious, but it isn't so important that we're going to allow it to interrupt our relationship.

The God of love

Jesus assured us that God loves us, each one of us. In fact the very reason why God caused the world to come into being, with the possibility of human life in it, was so that God could have people to love, and who would love God in return. God loves absolutely everybody, whether they realize it or not. Now ask yourselves, would God go to all that trouble just so that he and his children could have a few decades of mutual love? Hardly. God isn't going to allow the death of the body to bring his love for us to an end, for God is love. So God must have arranged that there is more to us than just a body, an inner core of our personality which, for lack of a better word, we call the soul – and it must be immortal. God's love for the person we're remembering today still goes on, outside of time and space, somewhere in eternity, for God is eternal. Love is stronger than death.

They are still with us

So, if the love between God and his children continues after the person has died, because that's the nature of love, then surely the love between two human beings also continues. Bereaved people sometimes find themselves talking to the person they love as though he or she was still in the room, and then pull themselves up short, feeling a bit silly. There's nothing to be ashamed of; because, in the nicest possible way, the deceased are still with us. Jesus rose again and appeared to his disciples to convince us that love really is stronger than death, and we shall all meet again in heaven, where all is love.

Suggested hymns

Gracious Spirit, Holy Ghost; God is love, his the care; Hark, my soul, it is the Lord; The God of love my shepherd is.

Scripture Index to Sermon Texts

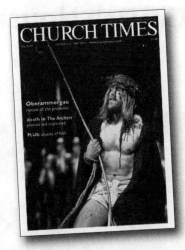

Subject Index

Entries in *italics* are sermon titles

NEED HELP WITH YOUR CHURCH'S FINANCES?

The UK Church Fundraising Handbook

BY MAGGIE DURRAN

This comprehensive and information-packed manual is a must for every church treasurer seeking to maximise their church's income in the face of rising costs, while remaining generous to others in need.

It offers clear, step-by-step guidance on all aspects of fundraising for a church, from growing existing resources, to applying for grants and funding, drawing up a business plan, creating publicity, and finally celebrating hard-earned success!

978 1 84825 002 4 · 216x135mm · 288pp · £19.99

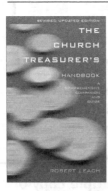

The Church Treasurer's Handbook

BY ROBERT LEACH

This clear, user-friendly guide to the duties and responsibilities of the church or charity treasurer is essential reading for anyone in this important position.

This new edition includes all the latest updates on the many issues affecting churches and charities, including accounting, banking, expenses, tax, insurance, charity law, employment and fundraising. It assumes no specialist knowledge and will help treasurers meet the requirements of current legislation.

978 1 84825 019 2 · 234x172mm · 288pp · £16.99

To order: tel: 01603 785925, fax: 01603 785915, write to: Norwich Books and Music, 13a Hellesdon Park Road, Norwich, Norfolk NR6 5DR, email: orders@norwichbooksandmusic.co.uk, or visit: www.canterburypress.co.uk
UK orders: To cover p&p, please add £2.50 for orders under £25 or £3.50 for orders under £75. Orders over £75 dispatched postage free. For details of overseas carriage, please contact our Norwich office or email: admin@norwichbooksandmusic.co.uk
Please quote code CPCTR11

CANTERBURY PRESS
Norwich

Canterbury Press is an imprint of Hymns Ancient & Modern Ltd. Regd. Charity No. 270060.
Regd. in England No. 1220696. Regd. Office: 13a Hellesdon Park Road, Norwich, Norfolk NR6 5DR.
VAT Reg. No. GB 283 2968 24.

378

Author Index

Notes

Notes

Notes

Notes

Notes

Advance order for the 2013 editions *(available May 2012)*

Order the 2013 editions now, to avoid disappointment! *(All to be published in May 2012)* quantity
Prices are subject to confirmation and may be changed without notice

CANTERBURY CHURCH BOOK & DESK DIARY 2013 *Hardback*   **£17.99** + p&p* ....

CANTERBURY CHURCH BOOK & DESK DIARY 2013 *Personal Organiser (loose-leaf)* **£17.99** + p&p* ....

CANTERBURY CHURCH BOOK & DESK DIARY 2013 *Personal Organiser (A5)*   **£17.99** + p&p* ....

CANTERBURY PREACHER'S COMPANION 2013 *Paperback*   **£17.99** + p&p* ....

For details of special discounted prices for purchasing the above in any combinations
or in bulk, please contact the publisher's Norwich office as shown below.

Order additional copies of the 2012 editions
Subject to stock availability

Hardback Diary **£17.99*** ....   Organiser **£17.99*** ....

Preacher's Companion **£17.99*** ....   A5 Personal Organiser **£17.99*** ....

Ask for details of discounted prices for bulk orders of 6+ copies of any individual title when ordered direct from the Publisher.

Sub-total £ ....

*Plus **£2.50** per order to cover post and packing (UK only): £ ....

All orders over £50 are sent POST FREE to any UK address.
Contact the Publishers office for details of overseas carriage.

TOTAL AMOUNT TO PAY: £ ....

I wish to pay by ...

... **CHEQUE** for £ .... made payable to **Hymns Ancient and Modern Ltd**

... **CREDIT CARD** All leading credit and debit cards accepted *(not American Express or Diners Club)*
Your credit card will not be debited until the books are despatched.

Card number: ....   Expiry: ____ / ____

Issue No: ____ Valid from: ____ / ____
Switch or Maestro only

Signature of
cardholder: ....   Security code: _____

Last three digits on signature panel

Please PRINT all details below.

Title: ....   Name: ....

Delivery address: ....

....

....

.... Post Code: ....

Telephone or e-mail: .... Date: ....

Please ensure you have ordered the edition you require for the correct year. No liability will be accepted for incorrect orders

Return this order form or a photocopy – with details of payment – to

Norwich Books and Music, 13A Hellesdon Park Road, Norwich NR6 5DR

Telephone: 01603 785900   Fax: 01603 785915   Website: www.scm-canterburypress.co.uk